Development Economics, International Economics and Statistics

Development Economics, International Economics and Statistics

Debes Mukherjee

Former Teacher-in-charge
St. Paul's C.M. College, Kolkata

Dr. Debkumar Bhattacharjee

Associate Professor
Santipur College, Nadia

New Central Book Agency (P) Ltd

LONDON

HYDERABAD ERNAKULAM BHUBANESWAR

NEW DELHI KOLKATA PUNE GUWAHATI

NCBA

REGD OFFICE
8/1 Chintamoni Das Lane, Kolkata 700 009, India
email: ncbapvtltd@eth.net

OVERSEAS
NCBA (UK) Ltd, 149 Park Avenue North, Northampton, NN3 2HY, UK
email: ncbauk@yahoo.com

EXPORT
NCBA Exports Pvt. Ltd, 212 Shahpur Jat, New Delhi 110 049
email: ncbaexports@ncbapvtltd.com

BRANCHES

212 Shahpur Jat
New Delhi 110 049
email: ncbadel@ncbapvtltd.com

Shop Nos. 3 & 4, Vinayak Towers
681/B Budhwar Peth, Appa Balwant Chowk
Pune 411 002
email: ncbapune@ncbapvtltd.com

Shop No. 15, Bharati Towers, Ground Floor
Forest Park, **Bhubaneswar** 751 001
email: ncbabub@ncbapvtltd.com

House No. 3-1-315, 1st Floor
Nimboliadda, Kachiguda, **Hyderabad** 500 027
email: ncbahydb@ncbapvtltd.com

GSS Shopping Complex, 1st Floor
Opposite College Post Office, Convent Road
Ernakulam 682 035
email: ncbaernk@ncbapvtltd.com

Radhamayee Complex (Second Floor)
Opp. SBI, Panbazar, Jaswanta Road
Guwahati 781 001
email: ncbaguwahati@ncbapvtltd.com

Development Economics, International Economics and Statistics • D. Mukherjee and D. Bhattacharjee

First Published: July 2013

PUBLISHER AND TYPESETTER
New Central Book Agency (P) Ltd
8/1 Chintamoni Das Lane, Kolkata 700 009

PRINTER
New Central Book Agency (P) Ltd
Web-Offset Division, Dhulagarh, Sankrail, Howrah

COVER DESIGNER
Soumen Paul

COVER PRINTER
Techno Process, Kolkata

PROOF CHECKING
Subas Maitra, Sarab Chatterjee, and Rina Basak

PROJECT TEAM
Pradip Biswas, Prodip Baidya, Pradyot Majumdar, and Prabhat Jas

ISBN 978 81 7381 854 7

Price: ₹ 165.00

CONTENTS

Preface xi-xii

DEVELOPMENT ECONOMICS

1. Growth, Development and Human Development 3-23

1.1 Introduction 3
1.2 Growth vs Development 4
1.2.1 Economic Growth—a Narrower Concept 5
1.3 Meaning of Underdevelopment 7
1.4 General Factors in Economic Development 8
1.5 Net National Income and Per Capita Income as Growth Indicators 11
1.6 What is Human Development? 14
1.6.1 Essential Components of Human Development 15
1.6.2 Human Development Index 16
1.6.3 Classification of Countries according to Human Development Index 19
1.6.4 Classification of Indian States according to HDI 20
1.6.5 Limitations of HDI 21
1.6.6 A Summary of HDI Reforms 22
Questions with Answer-Hints **23**

2. Development Planning and the Strategy of Growth 24-44

2.1 Introduction 24
2.2 A Brief History of Economic Planning 24
2.3 What is Economic Planning? 25
2.3.1 Nature and Scope of Planning 26
2.3.2 Rationale of Planning 26
2.4 The Strategy of Growth 28
2.5 The Strategy of Growth—(A) Balanced vs Unbalanced Growth 29
2.5.1 The BG Doctrine 29
2.5.2 The UG Doctrine 31
2.6 The Strategy of Growth—(B) Agriculture vs Industry 34
2.6.1 Role of Agriculture 34
2.6.2 Role of Industry 36
2.6.3 Interdependence between Agriculture and Industry 37
2.7 Role of Technology in Agriculture and Industry 38
2.7.1 Role of Technology in Agriculture 38
2.8 Choice of Techniques in Industry 39
Questions with Answer-Hints **43**

3. Population Growth and Problems of Capital Formation 45-65

3.1 Introduction 45
3.2 Different Views on the Role of Population Growth 46
3.3 Relationship between Population Growth and Economic Development 46
3.4 Effects of Economic Development on Population Growth 49
3.5 A Note on Malthusian Trap/Low Level Equilibrium Trap 50
3.6 The Vicious Circle of Poverty and the Scarcity of Capital 51
3.7 Capital Formation 54
3.7.1 Importance of Capital Formation 55
3.7.2 The Processes or the Stages of Capital Formation 56
3.7.3 Sources of Capital Formation 57
3.8 Problems of Capital Formation in LDCs 60
3.9 Incentives for Savings 61
3.10 Incentives for Investment 63
Questions with Answer-Hints 64

4. Foreign Investment and International Institutions— The IMF and The World Bank 66-90

4.1 Introduction 66
4.2 Types of International Capital Flows 66
4.3 What is Foreign Aid? 67
4.3.1 Types of Foreign Aid 68
4.4 Private Foreign Investment : Benefits and Costs of Development 69
4.4.1 Meaning and Size of MNC 72
4.5 Foreign Aid—The Debate 74
4.6 Global Governance and International Institutions 76
4.6.1 Background to the Establishment of the Bretton Woods System 76
4.6.2 Creation of the IMF : Objectives and Functions 77
4.6.3 Organisation and Management of the IMF 78
4.6.4 Financial Structure of the IMF 79
4.6.5 Special Drawing Rights (SDRs) 79
4.6.6 Essentials of the Bretton Woods System 79
4.6.7 Instruments of IMF Lending and Loan Conditionality 80
4.6.8 Working of the IMF 82
4.6.9 Role of the IMF in Economic Development of LDCs 84
4.6.10 IMF vis-a-vis India 86
4.7 The World Bank 87
4.7.1 The IMF and the World Bank—Similarities and Differences 88
4.7.2 A Critical Evaluation of the World Bank Activities 88
Questions with Answer-Hints 89

5. Gender and Economic Development 91-106

5.1 Introduction 91
5.2 Multiple Roles of Women 92
5.2.1 Different Forms of Gender Inequality 92
5.2.2 Desirability of Gender Equality 98
5.3 Policies to Reduce Gender Gap 99
5.4 Gender-related Development Index (or GDI) and its Indicators 100
5.4.1 How is GDI Constructed? 102
5.4.2 Gender Empowerment Measure (GEM) 103
5.4.3 A Note on Gender Inequality Index (GII) 105
Questions with Answer-Hints 106

INTERNATIONAL ECONOMICS

6. International Trade : Theory, Policy, and Balance of Payments 109-139

6.1 Introduction 109
6.2 Why Do We Need a Separate International Trade Theory? 109
6.3 Need for International Trade or, Relationship between Trade and Development 110
6.4 Why Nations Trade : The Classical Trade Theory 112
6.4.1 Adam Smith's Absolute Advantage Doctrine 112
6.4.2 David Ricardo's Comparative Advantage Doctrine 113
6.4.3 Extending Ricardo's Doctrine : (i) Many Commodities but Two Countries 116
6.4.4 Extending Ricardo's Doctrine : (ii) Many Countries but Two Commodities 116
6.4.5 Extending Ricardo's Doctrine : (iii) Multi-countries, Multi-Commodities 117
6.5 The Concept of Terms of Trade and Reciprocal Demand 117
6.6 Gains from Trade 118
6.7 Trade Policy : Free Trade and Protection 119
6.7.1 Trade under Free Trade 119
6.7.2 Free Trade : Arguments and Counter-arguments 120
6.8 Protection : Arguments and Counter-arguments 121
6.8.1 Tariff vs Quotas 124
6.8.2 Effects of Quotas 125
6.8.3 Advantages of Quotas 125
6.8.4 Disadvantages of Quotas 125
6.9 What is Balance of Payments? 126
6.9.1 Components of BOP Accounts 126

6.9.2 Distinction between BOP and BOT 128
6.9.3 BOP always Balances 128
6.10 Foreign Exchange Rate 129
6.10.1 Determination of Exchange Rate 130
6.11 Exchange Rate Management Policy 132
6.11.1 Advantages and Disadvantages of Fixed Exchange Rate System 134
6.11.2 Advantages and Disadvantages of Flexible Exchange Rate System 136
Questions with Answer-Hints **137**

STATISTICS

7. Basic Concepts **143-159**
7.1 Introduction : Origin and Development of Statistics 143
7.2 Meaning of Statistics 143
7.3 Statistics and Economics 144
7.4 Data—Its Classification 144
7.4.1 Examples of Primary and Secondary Data Sources 146
7.4.2 Methods of Collecting Primary Data 146
7.5 Classification of Data and Its Various Types 148
7.6 Variable and Attribute 149
7.7 Presentation of Data 149
7.7.1 Types of Tabulation 150
(a) Simple Tabulation 150
(b) Complex Tabulation 151
7.8 Population, Sampling, and Complete Enumeration 151
7.8.1 Advantages of Sampling over Complete Enumeration 153
7.9 Points to be Remembered while Preparing a Statistical Table 153
7.10 Graphical or Diagrammatic Representation of Statistical Data 153
7.10.1 Line Diagrams 154
7.10.2 Bar Diagrams 155
(a) Simple Vertical Bar Diagram 155
(b) Horizontal Bar Diagram 155
(c) Multiple or Component Bar Diagram 156
7.10.3 Pie Diagram 156
7.10.4 Ogive or Cumulative Frequency Polygon 157
Questions with Answer-Hints **158**
8. Measures of Central Tendency **160-175**
8.1 Introduction 160
8.2 Meaning and Concept of the Term Central Tendency 160
8.2.1 Classification of the Measures of Central Tendency of a Variable within a Particular Range of Variations 161

8.3 Mean 161
8.3.1 Simple AM 161
8.3.2 Weighted AM 162
8.3.3 Composite Mean from Two Separate Groups 163
8.3.4 Important Properties of AM 163
8.3.5 Advantages and Disadvantages of AM 164
8.4 Geometric Mean (GM) 164
8.4.1 Advantages and Disadvantages of GM 164
8.4.2 Computation of GM 165
8.4.3 Important Properties of the GM 165
8.5 Harmonic Mean 166
8.5.1 Important Properties of the HM 166
8.5.2 Computation of the HM 166
8.5.3 Merits and Demerits of the HM 167
8.6 Interrelationship among AM, GM, and HM 167
8.7 Median 167
8.7.1 Advantages and Disadvantages of Median 170
8.8 Mode 171
8.8.1 Advantages and Disadvantages of Mode 172
8.9 Essential Characteristics of a Good Statistical Average 172
8.10 Relation among Mean, Median, and Mode 172
Questions with Answer-Hints 173

9. Measures of Dispersion 176-189

9.1 Dispersion—Meaning and Classification 176
9.2 The Usual Measures of Dispersion 176
9.2.1 Absolute Measures of Dispersion 177
9.2.2 Relative Measures of Dispersion 182
9.3 A Comparative Analysis among the Usual Measures of Dispersion (Range, Quartile Deviation, Mean Deviation, and Standard Deviation) 185
9.4 Lorenz Curve—The Curve of Concentration 186
9.5 Measurement of Economic Inequality among the Weavers of Nadia, W.B. 186
Questions with Answer-Hints 188

Index 191-197

PREFACE

After getting an exposure to Microeconomics and Macroeconomics at the previous level of study, the present book is an introduction to Development Economics, International Economics, and elementary Statistics for students of undergraduate courses in economics in almost all universities. This book is accessible to them whose knowledge of economics is limited to the introductory course.

However, the book focuses largely on the economics of development of poor developing countries. As readers have gathered some rudimentary knowledge and basic training in economics at the previous level of study, such training will be highly relevent for understanding various developmental problems—such as poverty, inequality, population growth, problems of capital formation, poor level of HDI—that are faced by the countries of Asia, Africa, Latin America. In addition, gender inequality needs to be eradicated as it is strongly believed that gender equality highly matters in development. The first five chapters concentrate on Development Economics.

The study of economics is rather incomplete bereft of knowledge of International Economics. Chapter Six addresses multifarious facets of International Economics.

The last three chapters form the core of statistical methods that are being used increasingly in almost every branch of study. No longer the influence of statistics is confined to people who have special training of mathematics and statistics. It has spread to economics, education, biological sciences, science, business, engineering and umpteen other fields. Basic statistics has been presented in such a way that the students of economics can apply the statistical techniques (e.g., frequency distribution and associated measures of central tendency, dispersion, Lorenz curve as a measure of economic inequality) in their research problems. However, undergraduate students of other disciplines can also beneficially use this book as a profitable supplementary reading.

The three-part current book comprising *Development Economics, International Economics and Statistics* has been written considering the principle of 'comparative advantage' of the two authors into account. Thus our individual gains from specialisation are expected to stimulate in the knowledge-hungry students further interest in both economics and statistics.

We have tried our best to make the book simple so as to make it a student-friendly one. Even then we are cent-percent sure that there is ample room for improvement of the book. Constructive feedback and suggestions from any and many quarters are solicited. While shaping this book, we—the authors—owe a debt of gratitude to many friends and colleagues of different colleges and universities.

Our special thanks go to Sri Amitabha Sen, Director of New Central Book Agency (P) Ltd, without whose ardent help the book would not have seen the light of day. We also appreciatively put on record the sincerity and commitment of the entire team of the publishing house.

1 May 2013 **Debes Mukherjee**
Kolkata **Debkumar Bhattacharjee**

Contact Numbers

DM : 09 8308 59152
DB : 09 4331 45039

DEVELOPMENT ECONOMICS

CHAPTER 1

Growth, Development and Human Development

1.1 Introduction

Here people live in abject poverty. Quite a large number of population do not have any shelter and spend their entire life on footpaths. Medical care is not meant for these people. That is to say, the basis of life—adequate food, clothing and shelter—are not available to the vast majority of the population. In contrast, people in the developed countrerparts enjoy decent living. These parts of the world are called affluent societies. We reproduce here two quotès to describe the glaring contrasts between the developing and developed countries :

"Most of the people of the world are poor, so if we knew the economies of being poor we would know how much of the economics that really matters."—Theodore W. Schultz

"More than three-fourths of the world's people live in developing countries, but they enjoy only 16 per cent of the world's income—while the richest 20 per cent have 85 per cent of global income."—*Human Development Report*, 1995.

The *2011 Human Development Report* says that income inequality in most countries has deteriorated. The gap between the rich and the poor has widened over the last two decades in more than three-quarters of Organisation for Economic Cooperation and Development (OECD) countries and in many emerging market economies. Exceptions in Latin America and Sub-Saharan Africa are, however, not able as far as income inequality is concerned. Anyway, such increasing income disparities have offset large improvement in health and education inequality. The *HDR 2011* claims that 'the aggregate loss in human development due to inequality sums to 24 per cent' since 1990 for as many as 66 countries.

The said Report has shown its concern and anxiety on sustainability of human development. Lack of environmental sustainability impedes the progress of human development. Amartya Sen adds that "a fouled environment in which future generations are denied the presence of fresh air ... will remain foul even if future generations are so very rich." In recent years, despite income growth and inprovement in *Human Development Index* (HDI), the issue of environment unsustainability has been posing a great global threat to our earth's resources. And, in the name of higher growth, every country—both developed and developing—is sailing on the same boat. Future progress is under a threat.

Even in the 21st century (2008) people die from starvation and 907 million people of the global South (i.e., LDCs) are malnourished out of the total malnourished population of 963 million in the world. Hunger causes more than 91 million deaths per year worldwide : more than 25,000 a day. 65 p.c. of the word's hungry live in only seven countries : India, China, Bangladesh, Pakistan, Ethiopia, the Democratic Republic of

Congo, and Indonesia (Data source : FAO). These people are unable to secure minimum nutritional requirements of food. Thus, these countries suffer from the problems of food insecurity, inaccessibility of basic education and primary health facilities, and so on.

Thus, the study of the '*poverty of nations*', is more important than the study of the '*wealth of nations*', since poverty anywhere is a threat to poverty everywhere. Western economists often exhibit their anxiety over the huge gap between the North and South. They pose questions like this "Why isn't the whole world developed?" "Why are we so rich and they so poor?" These questions are thus linked to the development records of two types of countries—developed countries and less developed countries (LDCs). The present chapter is deveoted to the economic problems of developing or underdeveloped countries. But the process of economic development in any country is an ongoing process. These less developed countries are making sincere effort in raising their standards so as to catch the developed world. Some of these poor countries have moved to the ranks of middle income countries or newly industrialising countries, like South Korea, Taiwan, Singapore, and Hong Kong.

In this chapter, we will trace out the causes of underdevelopment in these countries. Solutions to the problems of backwardness will be discussed here. Before this, we must define economic growth and economic development.

1.2 Growth vs Development

Development economics emerged as a distinct field of study during the post-World War II. Growth and development were thought to be synonymous.Development economics then appeared to be'a bastard child of growth economics' (J. Dreze and A. Sen). Though development econo-mics in its infancy has had a strong relation to growth economics, it began to emerge as a separate field of study during the post-War II. As develop-ment economics is also preoccupied with income growth, it can be thought of as a 'genuine son of growth economics'.

In ordinary discussion, people use these two words interchangeably. But economists argue that economic development is not identical with growth. These are two slightly different concepts.

The concept of economic development is broader than the concept of economic growth. Economic growth simply means an increase in per capita income of a country.

In the words of Simon Kuznets : "Economic growth may be defined as a sustained increase in its population and product per capita." But economic development is not the same thing as economic growth. Economic development implies progressive changes in the socio-economic structure of a country. Economic growth implies not only more output, but also more inputs and more effieiency, i.e., an increase in output per unit of input, or, in other words, an increasing productive capacity of the economy. Development, however, is something more than that. It is 'growth plus change'. Development implies changes in the structure of output and in the allocation of inputs by sectors.

It follows from this definition that economic development encompasses social, political and cultural development of a country. Clearly, it is a value-based concept or a normative concept. It includes not only sustained rise in gross (or net) per capita national product but also includes welfare of masses, reduction in income inequality, increase in employment opportunities, and so on. Thus, economic growth is a quantitative concept while economic development is a qualitative concept. Economic development may be defined "as the process of increasing the degree of utilisation and improving the productivity of available resources of a country which leads to an increase of the economic welfare of the community by stimulating the growth of national income." Economic growth, indeed, is not concerned with the poverty-inequality reduction, unemployment situation and, above all, better quality of living. Thus, economic development is more than economic growth.

Economic growth = increase in per capita income—a quantitative expression.

Economic Development = increase in per capita output + welfare of the masses—a qualitative expression.

"Growth involves focussing on height or weight while development draws attention to the change in functional capacity", says C. P. Kindleberger.

1.2.1 Economic Growth—a Narrower Concept

Economic growth and economic development are, thus, not synonymous. Economic growth may be a necessary condition for economic development of countries, but it is not a sufficient condition. In fact, economic growth does not give us correct assessment of an economy for the following reasons :

Per capita income growth does not measure welfare : *Firstly*, economic growth is associated with an increase in GNP/GDP per capita. It measures wrongly—per head GNP does not, by itself, constitute or measure of welfare or success in development. GDP assumes that people have money or assets and thus operate in the market without any hitch. It is observed that a vast number of people fail to operate in the market as they don't have enough money or assets and are subject to torture and exploitation by the people who have money or assets. This then suggests that per capita income does not give any information about income distribution. It is observed that, despite high rate of growth, some of the countries experience high incidence of poverty and unemployment.

Secondly, economic growth does not talk about the quality of life. Undernutrition, diseases, and the associated problems of lower life expectancy at birth and higher infant mortality rates, literacy rates, and many other indicators of health and education of different populations comprise human development. In poor developing countries (i.e., global South), people end themselves at low level of literacy, low standards of health and nutrition, etc. Miseries arising from lack of food and shelter do not get reflected in the concept of economic growth.

Rising per capita income gives us the impression that the economy is growing, wealthier. But it does not take into account the above-noted aspects of life. India's GDP is rising but she is down in terms of other indicators. It has been revealed that 42.3 p.c. of under- 5 Indian children are severely and moderately underweight. This kind of undernutrition is a 'national shame'. There is more to the 'quality of life' than having more income.

Growth ignores environmental issues : *Thirdly*, economic growth does not deal with environmental issues. In the process of achieving higher economic growth, environmental considerations like depletion of renewable natural resources, air pollution, etc., are given little weightage. These aspects have an important bearing on the economic development of a country in the long run. Desire for higher and higher economic growth is associated with environmental damages. It is economic development that cares for environmental issues.

Economic development—'a multidimensional process' : It is, thus, obvious that economic development involves something more than economic growth. In fact, there are certain qualitative dimensions in the process of development that are conspicuous by their absence in the growth or expansion of an economy. Economic development implies both more output and changes in the technical, institutional arrangements by which it is produced, and a change in attitudes and values. "Development concerns not only man's material needs but also improvement of the social conditions of his life. Development is, therefore, not only economic growth but growth plus change—social, cultural and institutional as well as economic. Development is, thus, not purely an economic phenomenon; it has to be conceived of as a multi-dimensional process." Naturally, economic development is a value-based concept. It should include not only the acceleration of economic growth but also the reduction of inequality and eradication of poverty, increase in employment opportunities and welfare of the masses, etc.

Growth is silent about the quality of life and broad human development : However, economic development may mean more. Economic development must encompass human development. Amartya Sen defines economic development in terms of '*entitlement*' and '*capability*'.

Entitlement refers to be set of alternative commodity bundles that an individual can command through the totality of rights and obligations that he or she faces. Thus, '*entitlements*' of people generate 'capabilities'. Entitlements of people do not only depend on their incomes but also on a host of power relations in a society, the spatial distribution of resources in a society (like facilities of health care and schooling) and what individuals can accumulate from such supplied by the state. Capability represents a person's freedom to achieve various functioning combinations. Thus, the notion of capability is essentially one of freedom—the range of options a person has in deciding what kind of life he or she wants to pursue.

Poverty, according to Amartya Sen, is a kind of '*capability deprivation*'. Sen says that economic development should be interpreted as a process of expansion of the freedoms that people enjoy. Important areas of unfreedom that people face are famine and undernourishment, mass illiteracy, poor state of health of people, lack of shelter and other basic needs, economic insecurity, denial of basic civil and political liberty, etc.

Through the policies of expansion of human capabilities, development processes can be initiated. That is why it is said that the basic objective of development is the process of expansion of entitlements and human capabilities. That is to say, how GNP growth is used to improve human capabilities and, in turn, how people utilise their capabilities is economic development.

Amartya Sen, thus, emphasises that, instead of concentrating on GNP or GDP, development economics should take into account both entitlements and capability expansion. He argues that income does not necessarily address the nature of entitlement. Taking a cue from the Chinese famine (1958-1961) as well as the Bengal famine (1943), he emphatically demonstrated that famines, in general, were to be attributed to the *entitlement failure* rather than the shortage of food. Despite abundant supplies in food, people had to suffer miserably from hunger and famine in Bengal due to the entitlement failure in collecting food from the market. Famine is one source of unfreedom.

Sen Says: "Development requires the removal of major sources of unfreedom." The basic condition for economic development are the freedoms from hunger and famine, malnutrition, deficient schooling, poverty, poor health, economic insecurity, denial of civil and political rights, social inequalities, etc. These human goals of economic development as emphasised by Amartya Sen have brought about a radical change in development thinking—at least since the 1970s.

Amartya Sen, carrying on his value-loaded development economics, talks on social justice. He says that undernourishment of children, absence of opportunities of basic schooling, lack of entitlement of basic medical attention, particularly to the underprivileged of our society, etc., are nothing but social injustices. Since most of these facilities—meant for all Indians—crowd out the underdogs through the dominant class or partners of the society, injustices pile upon the vulnerable sections of the population. This kind of gross injustice is nothing but denial of development or 'exclusive development'. Thus, in the development discourse, social justice—a more normative concept—needs to be provided to all. And that is economic developement.

How economic growth and economic development are interrelated can be known from the Fig. 1.1.

Growth says nothing about Gross National Happiness (GNH): With the change in development thinking 'new' measures of success have been unveiled—social well-being is an important component of development. In other words, well-being has emerged as a substitute for 'wealth'. Overall public happiness or satisfaction with life describes well-being. The GNH aims to ensure that prosperity or well-being is shared across society and it is balanced against preserving cultural identities and traditions, protecting the ecology, preserving democracy with social equality.

We have seen that 'growth is not necessarily good' as it ignores some very crucial issues. Growth does not increase human well-being. Growth may improve standard of living but undermines 'quality of life'. That is why, today, we see 'de-growth' movement—a movement that attempts to shift emphasis from material goods to non-material factors, or human well-being or, more specifically, 'happiness'.

Economic progress of a country is to be measured not only in terms of GNP/GDP or poverty-unemployment-inequality but also in terms of 'pursuit of happiness'. Economic progress must be such that happiness levels of people across society without damaging environment need to be included. Happiness of people is measured through surveys when people are asked to assess how happy they are. This 'happiness index' is used in Bhutan—the Buddhist economy—and is called 'Gross National Happiness' (GNH). National happiness score is attained when basic needs of the people are met. These are : housing, health, employment, environment protection, peaceful atmosphere, morality, basic healthcare, preservation of cultural traditions, love and respect, democracy, etc.

These aspects of life are missing both from the concepts of growth and even from economic development. Anyway, the economy does not grow in a conventional sense. GNH uses more complex hybrid indicators. Some of these elements are invisible things but essential to our happiness or well-being.

As per 2007 GNH criterion, Bhutan was ranked the second fastest developing country in 2007. To keep the level of happiness of Bhutanese people, a decree had been issued for afforestation of the country to the extent of 60 p.c. But, since tourism has the potentiality of damaging environment, it has also been decided that it needs to be controlled and regulated. Otherwise, tourism will pull down the level of GNH. Thus the end of happiness depends on how environmental damages are minimised.

Till the other day, we had been concentrating more on the wrong indicator—the GNP/GDP—for too long. However, measurement of 'GNH' is a difficult task. Anyway, the concept of GNH is gaining ground—Canada, France, Costa Rica, U. K. and many other countries have been contemplating on measuring GNH. The basic objective is to measure 'social welfare'.

1.3 Meaning of Underdevelopment

Immediately after the industrial revolution (1750 onwards) some of the countries experienced a dramatic increase in their national outputs. Most of these countries are capitalist countries, like the U.K., the USA, etc., or the global North. As these countries enjoy high income as well as one of the best living standards they are called the *First World* countries or the developed countries. Countries that experienced large economic growth in-between the two World Wars (1914-18 and 1939-1945) are called the *Second World* countries or the socialist countries, like the erstwhile USSR. Newly independent but poor countries of Asia and Africa are making serious efforts to raise ther living standards since the termination of the Second World War. These are called *Third World* countries (or the Global South). These countries, in

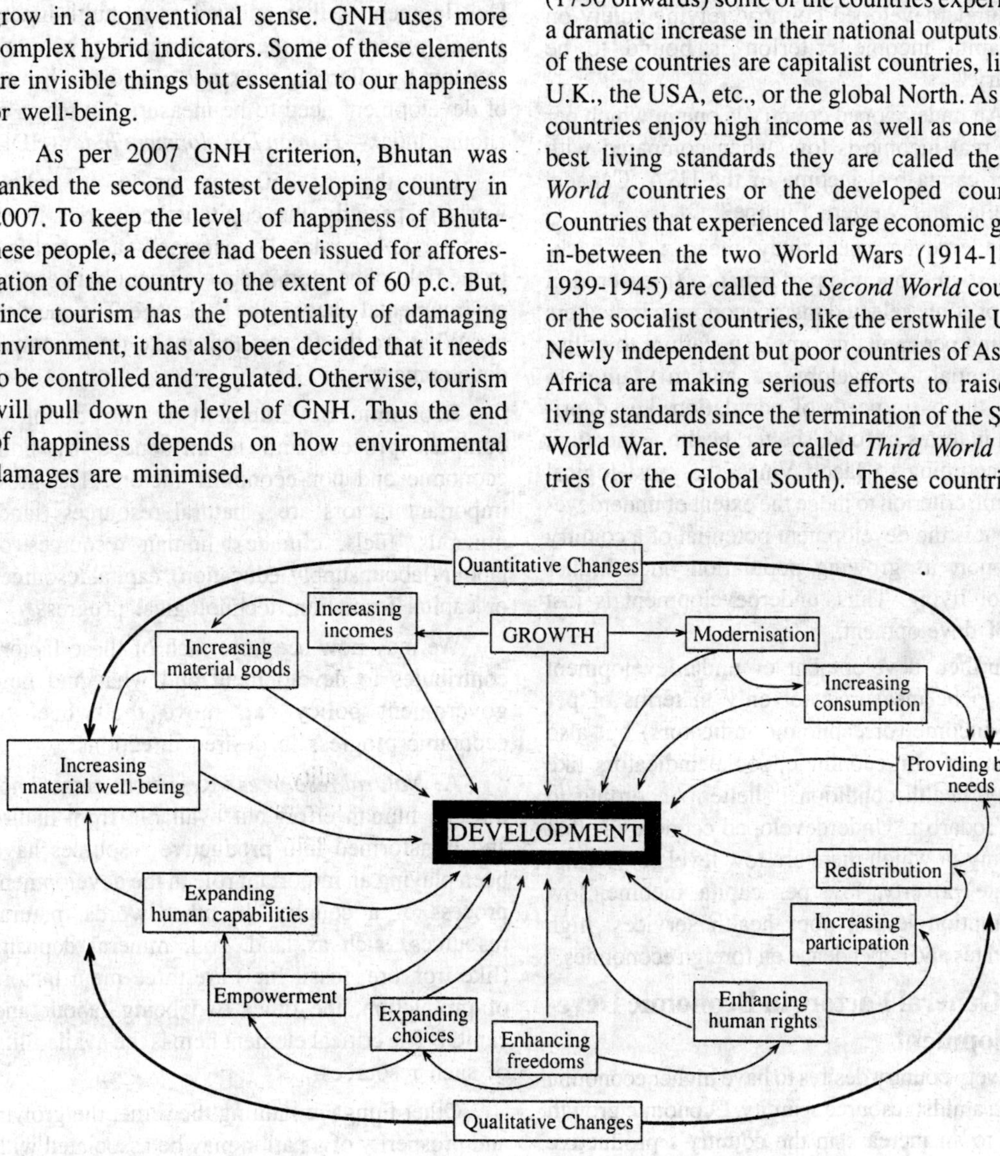

Fig. 1.1 : Concepts of Growth and Development

economic literature, have earned various names. Other names are : 'backward', 'underdeveloped', 'developing', 'low income', 'less developed countries (LDC's) etc.

A country may be regarded as a developed one or an undeveloped one if per capita income of a nation crosses a limit. The Word Bank classifies economies into four categories in accordance with the per capita gross national income measured in terms of US dollar. It will not be irrelevant here to reproduce Hla Myint's observation : "Definition of an underdeveloped country, relying solely on per capita income criterion is bound to be arbitrary."

"An undeveloped country is one in which per capita real income is low, when compared with the per capita real income of the USA, Canada, Australia, and Western Europe."

Underdevelopment may mean : (i) backwardness in economic performance (measured in terms of some selected macroeconomic indicators including per capita income), (ii) failure to utilise the potential for development, and (iii) failure to satisfy the basic needs of population, i.e., deprivation in terms of food, shelter, health, education, etc. According to Jacob Viner, the most logical scientific criterion to judge the extent of underdevelopment is the development potential of a country to support its growing population on a higher level of living. Thus, underdevelopment is just lack of development.

Further, development or underdevelopment needs to be measured not only in terms of per capita income (or economic indicators) but also in terms of non-economic, social indicators like literacy, health conditions, shelter. According to M. P. Todaro : "Underdeveloped economy is that economy in which there are low levels of living, absolute poverty, low per capita income, low consumption levels, poor health services, high dcath rates and dependence on foreign economies."

1.4 General Factors in Economic Development

Every country desires to have higher economic growth amidst resource scarcity. Economic growth refers to an increase in the country's productive capacity over time. Economic growth generally concerns long-term trends in the economy. Traditionally, economic growth of a country is measured in terms of GNP/GDP. An alternative to this index of growth and prosperity is per capita GNP/GDP. Though a defective measuring stick, GNP per capita measure of economic growth throws light on the 'size gaps' in income between nations. Economic development, being a broader concept, takes into account the levels of living of masses of people. Economic development is then defined as 'growth plus change'. The challenge of development is to improve the 'quality of life'. Development is then viewed as a multi-dimensional process. It means increasing people's freedom by enlarging the range of choices. Levels of development need to be measured in terms of another index—*Human Development Index* (HDI).

Over the last 250 years or so, the whole world, especially the capitalist countries, have witnessed phenomenal expansion— a central fact to the field of economic development but keeping environmental issues at the backstage. The question is : What are the factors that make for economic development?

Economic development is, no doubt, a complex process and is influenced by both economic and non-economic factors. The most important factors are : natural resources (land, minerals, fuels, climate), human resources or labour (labour supply, education), capital resources or capital formation, technological progress.

We may now see how each of these factors contributes to development and what and how government policy can move the wheel of economic progress in desired directions.

A. *Natural resources* : Resources created not through human effort but available from nature and transformed into productive resources have been playing an important role in the development process of a country. In other words, natural resources, such as land, soil, mineral deposits (like iron ore, fossil fuel) are three main factors of production, the other two being labour and capital. The critical element here is the availability of such resources.

Other things remaining the same, the growth and prosperity of a nation may be associated with the kind and size of the resources possessed by it. There is a presumption that natural resources are 'finite'. In fact, no one should ignore the possibility of adding more resources through discovery. Through discovery, opening up and by utilising new resources, many countries in the past had made a higher contribution in output. However, that does not mean natural resources are 'infinite'. Economic processes •impact on the environment. For instance, perils of resource depletion— both renewable and non-renewable— through uses generate insunmountable problems on growth and development of a nation. This then suggests conservation of resources so as to have a sustainable development.

Anyway, an abundant supply of natural resources conduces to both agricultural and industrial development. Just as availability of fertile land and abundant supply of water for irrigation purposes are the two essential prerequisites for achieving faster agricultural growth, minerals like coal, bauxite, iron ore, crude oil, copper, tin, etc., if available in plenty, can help the process of industrialisation. Shortage of natural resources often acts as a constraint on output expansion and is often considered as an obstacle to economic development. For example, some poor countries of Asia and Africa have limited natural resources such as land and minerals. And whatever little is available is to be shared by the large population.

However, one also sees an inverse association between natural resource abundance and economic growth. There is enough evidence to support that many resource-poor economies have outperformed many resource-rich economies in terms of economic growth! In other words, such an adverse association between resource abundance and growth at least demonstrates that the possession of natural resource is just a nece-ssary condition— but not a sufficient condition—for economic development.

Above all, resources that we have may be fixed and exhaustible. Growing exploitation of such natural resources to fulfil man's insatiable demands has now raised the issue of environmental damage that adversely affects economic development. The poor people of poor countries are dependent on their natural environment. Thus the greatest victims to the damage of natural environment are, obviously, the poor people. Herein lies the importance of protecting natural environment so as to have a sustainable development.

B. *Human resources* : Labour is a basic input for virtually all production. It is not possible to make the best possible utilisation of existing natural resources unless there is sufficient manpower. If a country is able to utilise its manpower properly, it will certainly prove to be an important factor in development. The supply of manpower—called human resources—depends, among other things, on population growth. Thus the size of the population is an important factor of economic development. More labour should, therefore, mean greater potential output. In an under-populated (relative to resources) country, population increases do indeed mean economic growth—as more land can be cultivated or more workers may be employed in industry and services.

It is to be remembered that not only the size of population but also the quality of laboure force is also an important determinant of an economy's capacity. There is a feeling among some economists that the quality of labour input—human capital— is the single-most important factor of economic development. Modern economists consider resources devoted to education and training as investment in human capital. The effective use of capital and the application of modern technology depend on the availability of skilled manpower. Educated, skilled workers are generally more productive than uneducated, unskilled workers. At the same time workers are also consumers. So, with population growth, there is an expansion in the size of the market and there is greater scope for division of labour and specialisation. Healthy people can work harder and longer than sick people.

Anyway, the stock of educated and healthy labour force in any economy contributes to growth and development by (a) creating a more productive and healthy labour force endowed with skills and knowledge, (b) opening up employment opportunities in various sectors of the economy. (c) Indeed, an educated and skilled labour force is a necessary condition for sustained economic growth. Further, there is ample evidence that health and nutrition of a nation affects employment, productivity, and wages favourably. A healthy population is a pre-requisite for economic development.

However, the relationship between population growth and economic development is a complex one. Experiences of many countries suggest that 'rapid' rates of population growth acts as constraint on development. It reduces per capita income of a nation. It creates environemental problems and overcrowded cities and towns. It reduces savings and capital formation. Thus economic growth is hampered. This means that we have landed in a two-way problem because of two-way relation between population growth and economic development. Even then, the quality of human capital is an important element in the progress of a nation.

C. *Capital resources* : Increases in labour and land productivity, in their turn, depend greatly upon new technology and increased capital resources. The amount of output that workers can produce depends largely on the availability of complementary resources like capital. It is argued that lack of capital is the principal obstacle to growth and no plan for economic development will succeed unless adequate capital is forthcoming. No country can achieve higher growth if certain minimum rate of capital formation is not realised.

Capital accumulation or investment refers to the creation of additional capital like plant, equipement, machinery, structures, etc. (physical capital), and social and economic structures like roads, electricity, water, sanitation, etc.,—to augment output and income. An increasing amount of capital per worker—a rising capital/labour ratio—is clearly a major source of productivity or output per man-hour. In other words, by increasing the amount of capital per worker, it is possible to increase labour productivity. Capital formation enables a country to enjoy the advantages of large scale production and specialisation. It is indispensable not only for augmenting output but also for providing employment to the people. Further, capital accumulation provides a growing labour force with an increased supply of tools and machinery per worker. This then raises efficiency of the workers.

Often, poor countries are handicapped by low volume of capital accumulation because of low income and low savings. If domestic capital is not sufficient to meet the investment needs, a poor country may be required to import capital from abroad. However, there is a question mark on the use of foreign capital in the poor developing countries.

Modern economists like T. W. Schultz, Jan Tinbergen, Gary S. Becker, etc., have pointed out that human capital formation (investment in training and investment) is as important as physical capital formation, if not more. They have emphasised the contribution of investment in human beings for economic development.

D. *Technology* : Technological progress is considered as the most important source of development by many economists. It is said that technology has been revolutionising our lives since the dawn of human history. Modern day technological progress that is going on is something unique as far as its depth and rapidity are concerned. Technology refers to our knowledge of how to convert resources into goods and services. Technical progress refers to an improvement in the art of production. Technological progress leads to an improvement in productivity of existing resources. It is the result of research, invention, development, and innovation. With the advancement of scientific and technological knowledge, people discover more and more sophisticated techniques of production which steadily raise the productivity levels.

It is thus dear that technological progress in a country depends on both pure and applied science. And science depends on the resources allocated towards research and development. Thus education is of crucial importance in any economy in furthering technological improvement. Besides education, entrepreneurial ability is another important determinant of technical progress. Joseph A. Schumpeter assigned a very important role to the entrepreneur in the economic development of a country. In his view, one of the most important functions of the entrepreneur is innovation—getting new methods adopted in effective ways. Thus, through new techniques and methods of production, a country can increase its productive capacity. To an economist, this implies that new technology is a sufficient condition for economic growth. However, technological progress is also a necessary condition for sustained growth.

Without it, there would not be enough new capital formation to allow continued increases in labour productivity.

It may be noted that a continued increase in labour productivity requires both increased capital and new or modern technology. Continual capital formation will occur only if there is a continual flow of new technology. Thus there is a close relation between technological change and capital and capital formation. These two not only complement but also depend upon each other. New methods may require new machinery. Or, when a firm decides to build a new factory, this may lead to discovery of new and better methods of production.

E. *Institutional environment* : Further progress of present day market economies is now largely influenced by the institutional environment. In other words, market economies can flourish provided an appropriate institutional environement prevails. Development requires effective state participation. In today's changing world, state should complement market. However, benefits of development must be widespread and inclusive so that poor people can harvest benefit from the market-oriented growth. It is observed that the state, because of poor governance and ineffective institutional framework, fail to protect property rights, law and order, freedom of individuals, human rights, and so on. Even it fails to protect the poor, vulnerable people. An effective economic institution can ensure public services to the poor and give economic incentives through opening better opportunities and empowering the excluded and vulnerables.

Often it is found that institutional environment gets vitiated by the rich powerful of the sociey and ultimately institutions serve their purposes. Under the circumstance, market, as an institution, marginalises poor people, Protecting poor people from insecurity requires participation and empowerment of these people so that public action is designed by them according to their priorities.

Institutional failure results in bad and poor governance and corruption. And corruption definitely hampers progress of majority of the countries. If the institutional environment is made effective the prospect for good investment is likely to brighten. It is the experience of the people that poor governance and corruption has been choking off and disturbing investment at the cost of the poor people. It is said that good institutions encourage people to invest, accumulate, and develop new technologies. All these are elements of economic progress of a nation.

The role of the government as the builder and provider of effective institutions is undeniable. It has to bring institutional reform 'in the fields of land tenure, taxation, asset ownership and distributions, educational and health delivery systems; credit allocation; labour relations; pricing policies; ..., and the machinery of government itself.' (M.P. Todaro and S.C. Smith).

Conclusion : Now a basic question : Which factors in economic development mentioned above are to be assigned greater weights? Truly speaking, economists have made several studies to give quantitative weights to these various growth factors. These studies are rather inconclusive and support that "modern growth is not simply a question of increases in the society's factors of production, but involves significant changes in the way these factors of production are utilised." Thus, no one has discovered a single driving force behind economic development of a nation. Partha Dasgupta elaborates : "All would appear to agree that the accumulation of manufactured capital, human capital, and the production, diffusion, and the use of new scientific and technological ideas go together, each contributing positively to the contributions of the others."

Above all, today's focus centres around the role of institutions in development. Poor economic performance is often attributed to institutional failure. Bad institutions put constraints on economic growth."

1.5 Net National Income and Per Capita Income as Growth Indicators

When we say 'Growth in What'?, we answer such growth in terms of GNP/GDP per capita. In other words, success and failure of an economy need to be measured. One such important measuring rod is GDP per capita. The World Bank ranks different countries in terms of per capita income. Countries ranked by the World Bank are labelled : *low-income economies, lower-middle income economies, upper-middle income economies, and high-income economies*. These classifications of countries are based on GNP per capita measured in US dollars.

[In this connection, a distinction between GDP and GNP requires to be spelt out. GDP measures the aggregate money value of outputs of goods and services produced in an economy by both residents and non-residents over a year. GNP equals GDP plus factor incomes accruing to nationals from abroad less the factor incomes earned by foreign nationals. It may be noted that GDP per capita is easier to estimate while GNP per capita is the 'correct' measure of per head income.]

Whether we use GNP or GDP per capita to measure the extent of economic growth of a country, the word 'gross' is used. The word 'gross' means no deduction for depreciation is allowed. When depreciation is deducted from GDP/GNP, one obtains 'net' domestic product/ 'net' national product. Anyway, such net national income speaks little about the extent of benefit of growth accruing to majority of the people. This figure speaks nothing about health, education, nutrition of people. Although over the years many low- and lower-middle income economies have seen rapid growth, but benefits of 'net national income' have flown massively to a small minority of population. This r. sure of development speaks little about income inequality and poverty, 'entitlements' and 'capabilities' of persons, etc. Above all, nothing about 'human development' can be read from net national income figures.

Net national income, thus, is a crude index of measuring development on the ground that it does not consider population growth of a country. A faster growth of net national income in a year may be eaten away by a much faster growth rate of population, thereby nothing is left for saving and capital accumulation. Further, this index of net national income does not say anything of the standard of living of the people. In spite of economic growth, the standard of livng may be eroded because of high growth of population, income inequality, etc.

Another limitation of this index of development is that it does not say anything about the composition of goods and services produced. If 'public bads' (e.g., pollution) are produced more, society's welfare will decline. In this sense, how much national income figure impinges 'cost' on the society following environmental pollution remains unaccounted. Any economic activity— say, use of natural resources for extracting our needs— damages environment. Since such is not deducted from the net national income figures, a good measure of human welfare is denied.

Per Capita Income as a Growth Indicator : Dividing GDP/GNP by the total population one gets per capita GDP/GNP. Conventionally, per capita income is used as an index of development. Economic development involves something more than economic growth. Economic development emphasises on the qualitaive aspects of economic expansion processes.

Anyway, this view says that increases in per capita income over a long period of time are suggestive of economic development. Greater the income, higher the standard of living of people, and lower the incidence of poverty and inequality. The only thing that has to be taken into account is that the growth rate of per capita income should exceeed the country's population growth—to have more growth and development.

However, the reality is not so simple as it has been painted here. Although there may be a positive association between high income and higher level of development and between low income and a state of undevelopment, there are many reasons that suggest per capita income is not an acceptable criterion of development.

In the first place, per capita income is a 'crude' index of measuring economic performance of a nation as it throws no light on income distribution within countries. In other words, per capita income does not necessarily indicate equity and justice. If there is inequality in income distribution, then, in spite of a rise in per capita income, the income gaps between the rich and the poor would be larger—rich would become richer and the poor poorer. There are some countries in the world whose per capita incomes are comparable with the high-income economies; but the majority of population live in abject poverty. In view of this, per capita income criterion speaks very little about economic development. To measure the living standard of population, what one should know is the nature of distribution of income in tandem with national per capita income—that is, how much of it is shared between the rich and the poor.

Secondly, economic well-being is measured by income—higher the income, greater is the living standard. However, per capita income figure does not give an idea about the composition of goods and services produced in an economy. This means that whether society produces more of consumer goods or capital goods or public goods like health, education, etc., is not known from this conventional criterion of development. Futher, many human needs like security against crime and violence, political and cultural freedoms, democracy, grassroots participation in decision-making process extend far beyond economic well-being. In this sence, per capita income is an inadequate index of development. However, consumption of these commodities increases human well-being. That is why modern development economists describe the state of development/underdevelopment in terms of accessibility of people to these goods that do not get reflected in per capita income. The basic purpose of development is to enlarge people's choices. Per capita income cannot 'buy' all pleasures of life (e.g., law and order, good governance, democracy, etc.).

Thirdly, per capita income does not reveal, naturally, a country's economic and social environment under which goods and services are produced in an economy. Whether such goods and services that are marketed in an economy are the result of market economy, or a planned economy, or the military economy, cannot be known from income figures. In fact, the influence of the entire environment upon which per capita income is dependent remains totally obscure. On the contrary, standard of living or the quality of life largely depends on such environment.

Fourthly, growth measured by. per capita income is good since such is equated with progress, advancement, higher consumption, and a better quality of life. Thus, growth in that sense is desirable. But can economies grow indefinitely? Answer is : There are *'Limits to Growth'* since economic growth is not compatible with environmental quality. As per capita income grows, the ecomomy's productive base shrinks. Such depletion of resources involves huge social cost —future generations get less resources to meet their needs than the present generation. Attempt to have more economic growth through the use of more resources and energy of an economy ultimately leads to environmental degradation. Growth will then suffer—cost of damage to the environment is not deducted from the per capita income. Growth in per capita income is not compatible with the concept of sustainable development.

It is now clear that this traditional notion of per capita income as the criterion of development reflects nothing but the differences in potentialities for development between countries, distribution of income, poverty, state of unemployment, and qualitative indicators of living standards. Above all, this conventional measure is conspicuously silent on economic, social and political freedoms/ unfreedoms that a country's citizens experience. Thus, the per capita income figure does not throw light on the holistic approach to development. One may then conclude that this index is a 'crude' one; it may be a necessary condition for nation's economic and social uplift but not a sufficient condition. This is because increase in income involves both costs and benefits. Costs arising out of economic activities (e.g., pollution) do not get reflected in the per capita income figures.

In spite of these limitations of per capita income as an index of development, it is used widely as a measure of growth. Per capita income figures of different nations are 'used as a starting point for classifying levels of development, and can certainly be used to identify the need for development.' The World Bank classifies different countries in accordance with per capita income data. It ranks countries in four categories on the basis of per capita income measured in U.S. dollars. Further, such data has the merit of devising policies to close the gaps betweeen different economies as far as practicable within a period of time.

Finally, since per capita income figure alone fails to capture the living standards, the United Nations Development Programme (UNDP) has devised an index to measure the standards of living. This index is most popularly known as *Human Development Index* (HDI) that takes into account (i) per capita GDP, (ii) life expectancy at birth, and (iii) access to knowledge. Since people-centred HDI is a "summary measure" of key human development outcomes, the distinction between growth and development becomes clear. However, HDI supplements per capita GDP (*goods-centred*) notion. Even then, 'One does not have to "rubbish" economic growth.'

1.6 What is Human Development?

Why are Norway, Japan, the USA well ahead of India, China, Vietnam, etc.? Answer is simple : the former produces more than the latter—so per capita incomes of these countries are much higher than India or China. This index of per capita income measures the average standard of living of a country measured by access to a wide range of economic choices. But this figure does not reflect real situations. For instance, a person's income does not throw light on his expectation of life. Many human choices like health, education, pollution-free environment, various freedoms, etc., are not dependent on income. These indicators of quality of life that people cherish answer the question : How are people of different countries of the world faring? It should be noted that an expansion of income is important but it serves as a 'means' and not 'ends' or to achieve education, health, nutrition, and many others including 'freedoms'. That is why development economists focus on human lives as the goal of development. In other words, development puts 'people at the centre'. Human development approach is 'people-centred approach', while per capita GDP approach is known as 'goods-centred approach' that captures very little about several kinds of human choices.

Before we define human development, it is important to remove confusion associated with this term. To some people, human development needs to be linked with social development and thus investments in health, education, and nutrition are associated with human development. This, however, is a wrong perception. Some others mistakenly equate human development with human resource development. Truly speaking, human capital formation differs from human capability expansion, that is, the ability of human being to decide what kind of life one wants to pursue.

The term 'human development' may be defined as an expansion of human capabilities, a widening of choices, an enhancement of freedom, and a fulfilment of human rights. At the beginning, the notion of human development incorporates the need for income expansion. However, income growth should consider expansion of human capabilities. Hence development cannot be equated solely to income expansion. Income is not the sum-total of human life. As income growth is essential, so are health, education, physical environment, and freedom. Human development should embrace human rights, socio-eco-politico freedoms. Based on the notion of human development, *Human Development Index* (HDI) is constructed. It serves as a more humane measure of development than a strictly income-based benchmark of per capita GNP.

The first UNDP *Human Development Report* published in 1990 stated that : "The basic objective of development is to create an enabling environment for people to enjoy long, healthy and creative lives." It also defined human development as "a process of enlarging people's choices", "and strengthing human capabilities" in a way which enables them to lead longer, healthier and fuller lives.

From this broad definition of human development, one gets an idea of three critical issues involved in human development interpretation. These are : to lead a long and healthy life, to be educated, and to enjoy a decent standard of living. Barring these three crucial parameters of human development as a process enlarging people's choices, there are additional choices that include political freedoms, other guaranteed human rights, and various ingredients of self-respect. One may conclude unhesistantly that the absence of these essential choices debars or blocks many other opportunities that people should have in widening their choices. Human development is thus a process of widening people's choices as well as raising the level of well-being achieved.

What emerges from the above discussion is that economic growth measured in terms of per capita GNP focuses only on one choice, that is income. On the other hand, the notion of human development embraces the widening of all human choices—whether economic, social, cultural or political. One may, however, contest GDP/GNP as a useful measure of development since income growth enables persons in expanding their range of choices. This argument is, however, faulty. Most importantly, human choices go far beyond income expansion. There are so many choices that are not dependent on income. Thus, human development covers all aspects of development. Hence, it is a holistic concept. "Economic growth, as such, becomes only a subset of human development paradigm." (Mahbub ul Haq, 2003) *Readings in Human Development*, Sakiko Fukuda-Parr and A. K. Shivkumar, OUP).

1.6.1 Essential Components of Human Development

In the traditional development economics, development meant growth of per capita real income. Later on, a wider definition of development came to be assigned that focused on distributional objectives. Economic development, in other words, came to be redefined in terms of reduction or elimination of poverty and inequality. These are, after all, 'a goods-oriented' view of development. True development has to be 'people-centred'. When development is defined in terms of human welfare it means that people are put first. This 'people-oriented' view of development is to be called human development.

It is thus clear that per capita income does not stand as a true index of development of any country. To overcome this problem and to understand the dynamics of development, the United Nations Development Programme (UNDP) developed the concept of *Human Development Index* (HDI) in the 1990s. This index brought in revolutionary changes not only in development, but also in the policy environment in which the government was assigned a major role instead of market forces.

Economic development now refers to expanding capabilities. According to Amartya Sen, the basic objective of development is 'the expansion of human capabilities'. The capability of a person reflects the various combinations of 'doings and beings' that one can achieve. It then reflects that the people are capable of doing or being. Capability thus describes a person's freedom to choose between different ways of living. For example : Can people read and write? Are foodstuffs distributed among people in a universal manner? Do poor students get midday meal in schools? Do the poor children get adequately nourishing diets at home? No one would doubt that an illiterate poor person cannot have the same capabilities that a rich literate one gets. Thus capability failure leads to poverty and deprivation. This perspective of development, as enunciated by A. Sen, suggests why development economists put greater emphasis on education and health.

There are many countries in the world which —despite high levels of per capita GDP growth/ real income—experience high mortality rate, undernourishment rate, poor literacy, and so on. This is a case called 'growth without development'. M. P. Todaro and S. C. Smith assert : "Real income is essential, but to convert the characteristics of commodities into functions. ... surely requires health and education as well as income." In other words, income does not define peoples' 'well-being' adequately. Well-being, although a diverse notion, should consider health and education, in addition to income. Sen's intellectual insights and fundamental ideas induced UNDP to formulate *HDI* as a comprehensive measure of development. It may be reiterated that the *HDI* as used in the *Human Development Reports* to compare different countries in the world has been designed as alternative to per capita GDP/GNP. Today, it is the most single commonly used measure to evaluate development outcomes.

Components of Human Development : The noted Pakistani economist Mahbub ul Haq considered four essential pillars of human development. These are : equality, sustainability, productivity, and empowerment.

Equality : If development is viewed in terms of enhancing people's basic capabilities, people must enjoy equitable access to opportunities. Such may be called equality-related capabilities. To ensure equality-related capabilities or access to opportunities what is essential is that the societal institutional structure needs to be more favourable or progressive. In other words, the unfavourable initial asset distribution, like land, can be made more farmer-friendly through land reform and other redistributive measures. In addition, uneven income distribution may be addressed through various tax-expenditure policies. Economic or legislative measures that interferes with market exchange may enable people to enlarge their capabilities and, hence, well-being.

Further, to ensure basic equality, political opportunities need to be more equal. In the absence of effective political organisation, disadvantaged groups are exploited by the 'rich' to further their own interests rather than social goals. However, participatory politics gets a beating by the inequality in opportunities in having basic education. It is to be added here that basic education serves as a catalyst of social change. Once the access to such opportunity is opened up in an equitable way, women or religious minorities or ethnic minorities would be able to remove socio-economic obstacles of development. This then surely brings about a change in power relations and make society more equitable.

Sustainability : Another important facet of human development is that development should 'keep going', should 'last long'. The concept of sustainable development focuses on the need to maintain the long term protective capacity of the biosphere. This then suggests that growth cannot go on indefinitily; there are, of course, '*limits to growth.*'

Here we assume that environment is an essential factor of production. In 1987, the Bruhtland Commission Report (named after the then Prime Minister Go Harlem Bruntland of Norway) defined sustainable development as '... development that meets the needs of the present without compromising the ability of future generations to meet their basic needs.' This means that the term sustainability focuses on the desired balance between future economic growth and environ-mental quality. To attain the goal of sustainable development, what is of great importance is the attainment of the goal of both intra-generation and inter-generation equality. This kind of inequality includes the term 'social well-being' not only for the present generation but also for the people who will be on the earth in the future. Any kind of environmental decline is tantamount to violation of distributive justice of the disadvantaged peoples. Social well-being thus, then, depends on environ-mental equality.

Productivity : Another component of human development is productivity which requires investment in people. This is commonly called investment in human capital. Investment in human capital—in addition to physical capital—can add more productivity. The improvement in the quality of human resources raises the productivity of existing resources. Theodore W. Schultz—the Nobel Prize-winning economist—articulated its importance : "The decisive factors of production in improving the welfare of poor people are not space, energy, and crop land; the decisive factor is the improvement in population quality." Empirical evidence from many East Asian countries corroborate this view.

Empowerment : The empowerment of people—particularly women—is another component of human development. In other words, genuine human development requires empowerment in all aspects of life. Empowerment implies a political democracy in which people themselves make the decisions about their lives. Under it, people enjoy greater political and civil liberties and remain free from excessive controls and regulations. Empowerment refers to decentralisation of power so that the benefits of governance are reaped by all peoples. It focuses on grassroots participation which promotes democracy by enfranchising the disadvantaged groups. Unfortunately, benefits are cornered by the elites because of lack of empowerment of people. Participation as a goal is a feature of 'bottom-up' development strategy rather than 'top-down'. Further, development policies and strategies are male-dominated. But the benefits of development are to be made 'gender-sensitive'.

Discrimination against women in health and education is very costly from the viewpoint of achieving development goals. Education of women can lead to a virtuous circle of lower fertility, better care of children, more educational opportunity, and higher productivity. Above all, as women's education rises, women's independence in making their own choices also increase. Anyway, decentralization and participation empower people, specially the women and the poor. It then breaks the 'deprivation trap'. Mahbub ul Haq asserts : "If people can exercise their choices in the political, social and economic spheres, there is a good prospect that growth will be strong, democratic, participatory and durable."

1.6.2 Human Development Index

When countries' per capita GDP ranking rise from one year to the next, governments find satisfaction and they boast over the achievements. But since per capita GDP ranking hides a lot of things, a new indicator has been evolved to understand the dynamics in achievements in the quality of life. This index, popularly called—*Human Development Index*—was first launched in the *1990 Human Development Report*. This index provides an assessment of a nation's achievement and helps ranking of different countries. The HDI is calculated to emphasise that people and their capabilities should be the ultimate criteria for assesing the development of a country, not growth alone. It is a single statistic that serves as a benchmark for both social and economic development.

Since 1990, a family of human development indices has been constructed over the years. The most important among them introduced in 1995 are '*Gender-related Development Index*' (GDI) and '*Gender Empowerment Measure*' (GEM). In addition, '*Gender Equality Index' (GEI), 'Human Poverty Index*' (HPI), etc., have been introduced. In 2010, the UNDP devised a new index, called '*Multi-dimensional Poverty Index*' (*MPI*) that captures various dimensions of human poverty.

Calculating the *Human Development Index*

In 1990, the UNDP introduced *HDI* as a policy tool for comparing development achievements between countries and between groups/states/regions within countries over time. The *HDI* ranks all countries on a scale of 0 (lowest human development) to 1 (highest human development). Such ranking is based on three basic dimensions/indicators of human development. These are : a long and healthy life, access to knowledge, and a decent standard of living.

Longevity—a long and healthy life—is measured by life expectancy at birth. Access to knowledge is measured by combination of mean years of schooling and the expected years of schooling. *Thirdly*, a decent standard of living is measured by 'real' GNP per capita at purchasing power parity, PPP, in US dollars. It is, thus, evident from these indicators that the *HDI* is a multi-dimensional concept that takes into account not only health and education but also per capita income.

To construct *HDI*, an index—fixed minimum and maximum values—is created for each of the three indicators. To calculate these dimension indices, the maximum and minimum values, called goalposts, are chosen for each of the three dimensions.

Table 1.1 : Goalposts for Calculating HDI

Dimension	*Observed Maximum value*	*Minimum value*
Life expectancy at birth (years)	83.5	20.0
Mean years of schooling	13.1	0
Expected years of schooling	18.0	0
Per capita income (PPP US $)	1,07,721	100

Now for any component of HDI, performance in each indicator is computed according to the following general formula :

$$\text{Dimension index} = \frac{\text{actual value} - \text{minimum value}}{\text{maximum value} - \text{minimum value}}$$

Each index is expressed as a value between 0 and 1. If the actual value of an index coincides with the minimum value, the index becomes zero, or if the actual value of an index becomes equal with the maximum value, the index becomes one.

Calculating the life expectancy index (L) : The life expectancy index measures the relative achievement of a country in life expectancy at birth. For instance, India's life expectancy at birth as per 2011 census is 75.2 years. Now the life expectancy index is 0.870.

Life expectancy index

$$(L) = \frac{65 \cdot 3 - 25}{85 - 25} = \frac{75 \cdot 2 - 20}{83 \cdot 4 - 20} = 0.870$$

Calculating the education index (E) : The education index is composed of two parts : mean years of schooling index and expected years of schooling index. This index, thus, measures a country's achievements in these two sub-indices. First, we calculate an index for mean years of schooling index and then another one—expected years of schooling index. Then these two indices are combined so as to calculate education index.

To calculate education index (E), let us apply the dimension index of each of the two sub-indices: mean years of schooling index and expected years of schooling index. Then geometric mean of these two sub-indices using 0 as the minimum value and the highest geometric mean (GM) of the resulting indices as the maximum. In other words, E is the geometric mean of the two indices.

For India, let us assume the maximum mean years of schooling is 5.5 years while the observed maximum mean years of schooling is 13.1 years in 2011. Thus, the mean years of schooling index

$$= \frac{5 \cdot 5 - 0}{13 \cdot 1 - 0} = 0.478$$

The maximum expected years of schooling in India is 10.4 years and the observed maximum expected years of schooling is 18 years. Thus the expected years of schooling index

$$= \frac{10 \cdot 4 - 0}{18 - 0} = 0.576$$

Combining these two sub-components, one obtains the education index

$$\text{Education index (E)} = \frac{\sqrt{0 \cdot 478 \times 0 \cdot 576} - 0}{0 \cdot 978 - 0}$$

$$= 0.503$$

Calculating the real GNP index (PC) : The construction of real GNP index is somewhat complex. It may be noted that the above two indices—life expectancy index and education index—are primarily dependent on the income level, although such income level does not get reflected straight forward in these two indices. Accordingly, income is adjusted simply by taking the logarithm of current income. To enable cross-country comparisons, per capita income is adjusted for PPP reflecting the relative purchasing power of the currency. Indeed, this is expressed in US dollars. If India's per capita real GDP in 2010 is $ 2,248, internationally adjusted real GNP per capita becomes :

Income index (PC)

$$= \frac{In(2,805) - In(100)}{In(1,07,721) - In(100)} = 0.478$$

This says that the natural logarithm of the actual and maximum values is used to get income index (PC).

Calculating the HDI : Now we are in a position to calculate HDI as a geometric mean of the three dimension indices :

$$\left(I_L{}^{1/3} \times I_E{}^{1/3} \times I_{PC}{}^{1/3}\right)$$

$$\text{Now, HDI} = \sqrt[3]{0 \cdot 870 \times 0 \cdot 503 \times 0 \cdot 478}$$

$$= 0.593$$

Thus the HDI reflects the average achievements of a country along the above three dimensions. Its value lies between 0 (zero) (the lowest level of human development) and 1 (the highest level of human development) and countries are then ranked according to the HDI. In the *Human Development Reports* published annually by the UNDP, countries with an HDI value of 0.800 and above are considered 'high human development countries, and those below 0.500 are considered 'low' human development countries. It may be added here that there is a close relationship between economic growth and *HDI*. More economic growth enables a country to have more resources so as to permit 'sustained improvements in human developments'. On the other hand, improvement in the quality of human capital triggers growth further.

Changes in HDI Methodology : How the HDI is constructed can be simplified with the aid of the diagram on the next page :

New Definitions : (a) *Mean years of schooling* : Average number of years of education received by people aged 25 and olders, converted from education attainment levels using official durations of each level.

(b) *Expected years of schooling* : Number of years of schooling that a child of school entrance age can expect to receive if prevailing patterns of age-specific enrolments persist throughout child's life.

Gross NI per capita : Aggregate income of an economy is generated by its production and ownership of factors of production, the incomes paid for the use of factors of production owned by the rest of the world, converted to international dollars using PPP rates, divided by the mid-year population.

The HDI methodology was revised in 2010. *HDI* is a composite index in 3 basic dimensions—health, knowledge, and income. From 2010 *HDI*, health is still measured by life expectancy at birth. However, the *2010 HDI* measures achievement in knowledge by combining the expected years of schooling for school-age children entering school today with the mean years of prior schooling for

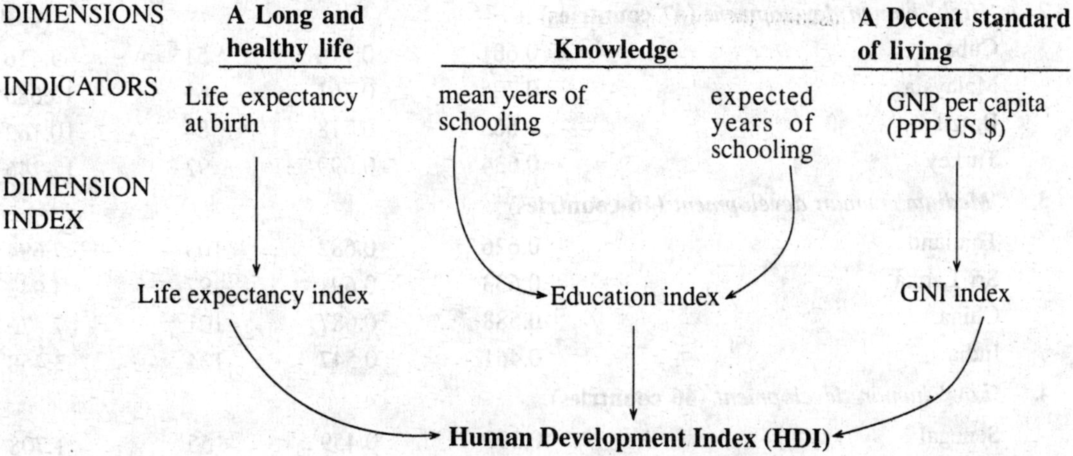

Fig. 1.2 : Graphical Construction of HDI

adults aged 25 and older. Further, the income measurement has been changed from PPP-adjusted per capita GDP to PPP-adjusted per capita GNI that includes remittances.

These changes are of importance for many reasons. *First*, adult literacy rate used in the old HDI (which is simply a binary variable—literate or illiterate, with no gradations) is inadequate in measuring the attainment of knowledge. By including average years of schooling and expected years of schooling one can better capture the level of education. *Secondly,* GDP is the monetary measure of goods and services produced in a country, irrespective of how much is retained in the country. On the other hand, GNI measures the income accrued to residents of a country, including some international flows, and excluding income generated in the country and repatriated abroad. Thus, GNI is a more accurate measure of a country's economic welfare. *Thirdly,* prior to 2010, the HDI report used the arithmetic mean (AM) From 2010, it uses geometric mean (GM) of dimension indices.

1.6.3 Classification of Countries according to Human Development Index

Countries are grouped and ranked by their HDI value. The UNDP earlier classified countries in three groups : high, medium, and low HDI. The UNDP, in its 2010 Report, classified it into four groups : *very high, high, medium,* and *low*. In this Report as many as 187 countries have been considered. The *very high, high,* and *medium* HDI groups have 47 countries each, and the *low* HDI group has 46 countries.

The number of *very high* human development countries now (2012) stands at 47 out of 187 countries. 47 countries fall in the category of high human development. Again, 47 countries have been placed in the state of *medium* human development and that of *low* human development falls in the range of < 0.500. In this category, there are as many as 46 countries, as per the *Human Development Report*, 2012. This splitting of *very high* and *high* HDI value clasification, however, was made in 2009 *Human Development Report.*

Table 1.2 : HDI for Selected Countries, 2000 and 2011

Country	*HDI 2000*	*HDI 2011*	*HDI Ranking 2011*	*Real GNI per capita ($ PPP) 2011*
1. '*Very high*' *human development* **(47 countries)**				
Norway	0.913	0.943	1	47,557
United States	0.897	0.910	4	43,017
Canada	0.879	0.908	6	35,166
Japan	0.868	0.901	12	32,295

2. *'High' human development* **(47 countries)**				
Cuba	0.681	0.776	51	5,416
Malaysia	0.705	0.761	61	13,685
Brazil	0.665	0.718	84	10,162
Turkey	0.634	0.699	92	12,246
3. *'Medium' human development* **(46 countries)**				
Thailand	0.626	0.682	103	7,694
Sri Lanka	0.633	0.691	97	4,943
China	0.588	0.687	101	7,476
India	0.461	0.547	134	3,468
4. *'Low' human development* **(46 countries)**				
Senegal	0.399	0.459	155	1,708
Zimbabwe	0.372	0.376	173	376
Burundi	0.245	0.316	185	368
Congo Democratic Republic	—	0.286	187	280

Source : *UNDP, Human Development Report,* 2012

1.6.4 Classification of Indian States according to HDI

We can also present HDI value for the Indian states, as per 2011 *State Human Development Report.* According to this report, Kerala stands first in HDI among the states of India. However, Chandigarh stands first in HDI among the Union Territories of India (Table 1.3).

Table 1.3 : HDI for Selected Indian States and Union Territories

State/Union Territory	HDI 2005	HDI Ranking
1. *'High' human development*		
Kerala	0.814	2
Chandigarh	0.860	1
Delhi	0.789	3
2. *'Medium' human development*		
Lakshadweep	0.796	4
Goa	0.779	6
Pudducherry	0.748	10
Manipur	0.707	11
Maharashtra	0.689	12
Punjab	0.679	15
Tamil Nadu	0.675	16
West Bengal	0.625	19
All India	**0.575**	
3. *'Low' human development*		
Jharkhand	0.513	31
Uttar Pradesh	0.490	32
Odisha	0.452	34
Bihar	0.449	35

Source : *State Human Development Report, 2011*

The Indian Planning Commission has been constructing the HDI for the Indian states. Such attempt was made first in 2001. The methodology used for the construction of HDI is similar to that of the UNDP in terms of the 'dimensions' used. However, in terms of process 'indicators', the methodology is slightly different from that of the UNDP's.

In recent years, many states have also prepared state-level HDRs in which district-level HDI is computed. Despite limitations of HDI—both at the all-India level and the state-level—it is used as a useful tool for policy analysis. The HDI data enables one to evaluate inter-country, intra-country among the different regions or states, and inter-district disparities within a state. This, then, spurs competition among different countries, states, and districts to improve their HDI rankings.

1.6.5 Limitations of HDI

As soon as human development was brought into the domain of development economics, attention was shifted from GNP. It then broadened the concept of human measure of development.

Since 1990-91 we have seen the most extensive use of HDI to understand the state of differences across countries in their levels of development. As is clear from the above discussion, the HDI is simple to compute. In view of this, its appeal as a measure of well-being or the quality of life—rather than only per capita income—is rather strong and universal. But that does not mean that this index is fault-free. Because of certain limitations of HDI, several attempts have been made to remove some inaccuracies. Even then, inaccuracies in the index persist. Most important among them are noted :

A mixture of stock and flow variables : The HDI takes both stock variables (e.g., adult literacy index, life expectancy at birth index) and flow variables (real per capita GDP, gross enrolment rates, etc.,) into account to construct the HDI value. It is because of mixing of these two types of variables that one sees erratic movements in HDI. For instance, India's ranking across countries was 119th in 2010 *Human Development Report*. Despite an improvement in HDI value in 2010, India slipped to 134th. And for China, the ranking fell from 89th in 2010 to 101 in 2011. Again, comparison of GDP and HDI ranking becomes complicated since the former is a flow variable while the latter is the combination of both stock and flow variables.

Neglect of distributional issue : The HDI is criticised for its neglect on issues of distribution relating to gender, religion, ethnicity, income, caste, occupation, etc. In other words, the HDI is 'a summary measure of average human development', but ignores distributional aspects of human development.

However, to overcome this problem, some supplementary indices such as *Gender-related Development Index (GDI), Gender-equality Index (GEI), Human Poverty Index (HPI), Multi-dimensional Poverty Index (MPI)*, etc., have been introduced to measure empowerment and deprivations. Further, in India, state-wise HDI ranking is being carried out so as to measure developmental gaps and benefits accruing to each state/union territory.

New dimensions need inclusion : Besides these conceptual limitations, the HDI has a limited use. Indeed, it is true that the concept of human development is a broader one than the traditional concept of development. But it is silent on many integral parts of human development, like political freedom, civil and political rights, environmental quality, food and nutrition security, job security, health security, energy security, crime and violence, etc. It is known to all that despite high GDP and high HDI values, countries like the United States, Canada are troubled heavily by social divisions and conflicts, as also rising criminal activities. These surely lower the level of 'real happiness'. Further, illegal drug businesses result in a variety of social problems in these countries : rape of women, rising number of jail-birds, killing of human beings and suicides, divorce, pre-marriage birth, etc. Had these issues been incorporated in HDI, these countries could have been ranked at lower level. Of course, these dimensions are of great importance to measure a good quality of life.

Problems associated with the choice of indicators : Based on three indicators—educational attainment index measured by adult literacy and gross enrolment ratios, longevity index, and income per head—HDI is constructed. Critics argue that it is difficult to define literacy, particularly due to language differences. It is difficult to grasp Spanish and Chinese languages. It is also said that the literacy measure speaks very little about the quality of literacy. A man, however, is said to be literate if he can read and sign his name. Human Development Report considers this definition of literacy. An example will suffice our purpose : Despite an adult literacy rate of 99 p.c. in Canada, it had been found in 2000 that 20 p.c. of Canadians were not functionally literate as they could not read and understand a simple set of instructions.[1] In other words, literacy index as used is not thought to be an ideal one. This functional literacy can also be called *lasting literacy*.

Questionable data quality : Data quality is subject to serious scrutiny. Most of the data—particularly on adult literacy and life expectancy—are not updated regularly. Often, old data are used to construct HDI. Possibly, because of these limitations, *literacy index* has been replaced by *access to knowledge* in 2010.

Conclusion : In spite of these limitations, the concept of HDI as a summary measure of human development serves as a better guide to the policy-makers. Some of the above limitations have already been addressed. HDI remains a very widely used tool today than the normally income-based indicator—GNP. The success of the HDI is remarkable.

1.6.6 A Summary of HDI Reforms

It may be noted that the HDI construction method used since the early 1990s revealed some deficiencies. To overcome such, the HDI construction method has been marginally changed by assigning new maximum and minimum values of each three indicators. The two indicators of 'knowledge' dimension—the adult literacy rate and the combined gross enrolment ratio—of the earlier HDI reports has been modified in 2010 HDR by taking into account expected years of schooling and mean years of schooling. Further, instead of GDP per capita (PPP US $) indicator to assess the standard of living, the *2010 HDR* considers GNI (gross national income) per capita. The meanings of these 'three' new indicators have been discussed earlier. Let us have a look at the HDI construction methods used before 2010 and 2010 onwards in the following form (Table 1.4).

Table 1.4 : Pre-2010 and Post-2010 HDI Construction Methodology

Dimensions	*Previous (Aggregation : AM)* *Indicators*	*Transformation* Minimum	Maximum	*2010 (Aggregation : GM)* *Indicators*	*Transformation* Minimum	Maximum
Health	Life expectancy at birth (years)	25	85	Life expectancy at birth (years)	20	83.2
Know-ledge	Adult literacy rate (%)	0	100	Expected years of schooling	0	18.0
	Combined gross enrolment ratio (%)	0	100	Mean years of schooling	0	13.1
Standard of living	GDP per capita (PPP US $)	100	40,000	GNI per capita (PPP US $)	100	107,721

1. Sakkio Fukudda-par and A. K. Shiva Kumar (eds) (2006), *Readings in Human Development*, p. 170

QUESTIONS WITH ANSWER-HINTS

Long-Answer Questions

1. It is said that economic growth is a narrower concept than economic development. Why?
   Ans. 1.2 and 1.2.1
2. Why do economists talk about economic development instead of GDP growth?
   Ans. 1.2 and 1.2.1
3. Per capita GDP measures wrong thing. Discuss.
   Ans. 1.2 and 1.2.1
4. Discuss, in brief, the general factors that contribute to the process of economic development.
   Ans. 1.4
5. Is per capita income an index of development?
   Ans. 1.5
6. What is meant by human development? What are its essential components?
   Ans. 1.6 and 1.6.1
7. What is meant by Human Development Index? How is it constructed?
   Ans. 1.6.2
8. How are different countries classified in the Human Development Index?
   Ans. 1.6.3
9. Human Development Index also fails to capture the various developmental issues. Explain.
   Ans. 1.6 and 1.6.4

Short-Answer Questions

1. Economic development is a multi-dimensional process—Explain.
   Ans. 1.2
2. GDP growth does not say anything about the quality of life. Explain.
   Ans. 1.2
3. What is Gross National Happiness? What are its basic elements?
   Ans. 1.2
4. Define Underdevelopment.
   Ans. 1.3
5. How do productive natural resources help economic development?
   Ans. 1.4(A)
6. Human resource is an important factor of development. Justify your answer.
   Ans. 1.4(B)
7. Modern growth is largely explained in terms of institutional environment. Explain.
   Ans. 1.4(E)
8. Per capita income growth is silent about equity and justice. Explain.
   Ans. 1.5
9. What is human development index?
   Ans. 1.6.2
10. What are the essential components of human development?
    Ans. 1.6.1
11. How is Human Development Index constructed?
    Ans. 1.6.2
12. What are the major limitations of HDI?
    Ans. 1.6.5

CHAPTER 2 Development Planning and the Strategy of Growth

2.1 Introduction

Underdevelopment economies has grown along two paths. *First* is the development planning. The basic issue facing all economies is how to allocate scarce investible resources among competing uses. Thus the central question in economic planning is : how much out of its income should a country invest? It is thus based on the premise of government intervention in the development process. Then different nations adopt various forms of planning for the allocation of resources. However, it may be noted that economic planning is not synonymous with any form of state intervention.

The *second* aspect is the 'strategy' of investment that a nation should adopt to achieve the desired goal of higher growth. As we have said that economic planning is a matter of resource allocation, poor underdeveloped economies are handicapped by its inability to invest more. An economy must strive how to maximise growth with the scarce available resources. Besides determining the quantum of investment, allocation decisions centre on (i) which sectors are required to be invested and in what quantity, and (ii) which technique of production to be chosen.

The first allocation decision concerns the 'balance' to be preserved between different sectors of the economy. Policymakers and economic planners need to settle the fact that whether growth should be 'balanced' over a number of sectors (e.g., agriculture-industry balance) or 'unbalanced' or concentration of investment in specfic sector(s) in a deliberate manner to obtain the greatest growth. In the development litereature one encounters differing opinions over these two rival growth strategies, popularly known as a debate between *balanced growth* or *big push* doctrine, and *unbalanced growth*. Closely allied to this policy choice, there is another issue of choice of techniques—whether techniques should be labour-intensive or capital-intensive—to have a higher growth.

All these issues have been discussed in this chapter.

2.2 A Brief History of Economic Planning

The concept and the idea of planning is indeed an old one used in different senses by different authors. In most, economic planning 'was essentially a war-time phenomenon'. For instance, Germany gave the concept of planning a concrete shape during the First World War and this concept was sent to the coldstorage once the war was over. However, the most notable capitalist countries—the United States and the United Kingdom—successfully applied the use of planning to achieve war priorities during the Second World War. Since planning involves a deliberate governmental effort for achieving some macroeconomic social objectives over the long run, intervention by the government in these economies is of 'indicative' variety. This means that in the fulfilment of macroeconomic goals, no command or dictates of the goverment or the planning authoity is entertained as is done in socialist countries. Planning in socialist countries is, by nature, 'authoritarian' or a 'directive' one where planning involves strict government regulation as opposed to the 'free play of market forces'.

However, the belief in the virtues of a 'free market economy' came under big assault in the inter-War years (1919-38) when the Soviet experiment of centralised economic planning for a 5-year period (1928-33) made her as 'second world power' next to the USA. Indeed, after the October Revolution (1917), the then Soviet Union seceded first from the market economy and undertook centralised economic planning for a 5-year period, 1928-33. After the World War II, Central and Eastern Europe and the Baltic states and subsequently China, North Korea and Vietnam undertook national planning. This vast experiment of economic planning in socialist states was a lesson for the *Third World* countries which attained independence from the colonial rule in the 1940s and 1950s. Seeing the success of the Russian experiment of planning, India launched her 'democratic planning' on 1 April 1951. In the 1960s, India became a 'model country' for the newly independent states that made efforts to centralize control of production and allocate resources through state planning. The basic philosophy at that time was : *government is good* and the *market is bad*.

Meanwhile, disillusionment with planning started gathering its force in the 1970s and 1980s as governments faulted in many directions. Euphoria over planning sanked because of corruption, governance failure, state capture by vested interests, etc. *Market is good* and *government is bad* argument started gathering storm in the 1980s. In Eastern Europe, government deficit rose to a great height resulting in a high inflation. There was virtually a total breakdown of distribution and transporation even of basic necessities. Grey and black markets flourished. Thus, to correct the inefficienies of economic planning, market solution was deemed to be an ideal solution. The experience of goverment failure in many developing countries and the emergence of *market economies* even in China, Central and Eastern Europe and the Commonwealth of Independent States (CISs) of the former Soviet Union served as policy lessons to the *Third World* countries of the South.

However, against this backdrop, one can only argue that planning has a great role to play in many areas in the developing economies. The following section starts with the meaning and rationale of economic planning.

2.3 What is Economic Planning?

Economic planning is often regarded as a technique of managing an economy. When the structure of an economy becomes complex and subject to rapid change and transformation (due to population growth, discovery of resources, industrialisation, etc.,) some sort of advance thinking becomes necessary to resolve that complexity and to prepare the economy for those changes. Such preparation is nothing but planning.

Economic planning, to most people, means state invervention in an economy, as opposed to the 'free' play of market forces. However, any form of state intervention must not be confused with planning. It may be noted that such governmental intervention can be thought of as concerted, deliberate attempt of alternative method of allocating economic resources to achieve some predetermined goals— either to replace or supplement the market mechanism. From this idea, one can argue that economists are divided over the concept of economic planning.

One author defined economic planning as collective control or suppression of private activities of production and exchange. To another economist, planning means the direction of productive activity by a central authority. It is evident then that the basis of authority is different. An economic plan is simply a specific set of quantitative targets (e.g., faster economic growth, higher consumption, lower unemployment, reduction in income-consumption inequality, etc.,) to be achieved within a scheduled time, with a strategy for attaining those targets. Economic planning is thus an exercise of organising and utilising scarce resources and allocating them in accordance with the pre-determined priorities so as to have maximum social welfare.

An economic plan is regarded as a programme of action; it is not a guarantee for action. It may also be taken to mean an instrument for regulating a free private enterprise economy. In short, a good plan is one which makes adequate provision for and ensures that its targets are properly fulfilled.

2.3.1 Nature and Scope of Planning

Economic planning is not peculiar to a socialist economy. Planning, as viewed in different countries, varies from one economic system to the other. In other words, the nature and scope of planning is largely governed by the types of economic systems. This means that the content of economic planning as seen in a capitalist economy is different from that of a socialist economy. For instance, *directive planning* as practised in a socialist economy differs from *indicative planning* as viewed in a capitalist economy.

Planning in socialist economy : Under socialism, as means of production are owned by the state, the government formulates and implements plans where only governmental control and regulation direct economic activities to achieve the societal goals. This kind of planning is known as *directive planning/centralized planning/imperative planning/planning from above*. This kind of planning replaces free market principles. With regard to this kind of planning, the national plan represents a binding directive. The targets of national plan and its financial provision represents orders to be carried out by the various ministries and the enterprises controlled by them. Planning by direction clearly reflects a bureaucratic and totalitarian outlook.

Planning in a capitalist economy : Truly speaking, plannning has no role to play in a capitalist economy. In spite of this, some sort of planning, call it *indicative planning*, is associated with capitalism. Arthur Lewis remarks : "The state can plan as much as it wants but it should plan not by direction, but by manipulating the market." In a capitalist country, planning is initiated at a decentralised level. The implementation of the plan is not by command or order of a central planning authority. Planning, here, is indicative in nature. Here the private sector works rather in an uncontrolled manner. The state acts as an agent of forecasting or consultation in the sense that superior economic information in the form of forecasts will be provided by the state to the private sector.

Planning in a mixed economy : Less developed countries are engaged in development planning. Further, these economies are known as mixed economies. In these economies, one finds private sector as well as government ownership and control over resources. In other words, mixed economies are characterised both by government activity, intervention and action of market forces. Certain areas are kept reserved for public sector so as to attain maximum growth. But, through various instruments of control, private businesses are made to fall in line with the objectives and targets of the national plan. Thus, planning under mixed economy reflects both market inducement and state control. Indian planning—a classic example of planning in a mixed economy—is a *democratic planning*. Being democratic planning, it is a decentralized one as opposed to socialist centralized planning. Further, it is called *planning from below*.

2.3.2 Rationale of Planning

The basic task of economic planning in developed countries is one of controlling the trade cycle flunctuations—the ups and downs of economic acctivity. But in less developed countries, planning is the way of securing higher growth by harnessing the available natural and human resources as far as possible. The task is one of securing economic development and, thus, this kind of planning is called *developmental planning*.

Generally, poor economies experience vicious cycle of poverty. For growth, these countries are required to break this vicious circle which by no means is easy to accomplish. Now, it is a historically testified truth that it is never accomplished under free enterprise market economy. Herein lies the rationale of planning in a less developed country.

Several economic and institutional arguments are advanced towards the rationale of planning. These are :

Limitations of free market : It is said that free market allocates resources efficiently through the Smithian so-called *invisible hand* or price mechanism. This mechanism determines an economy's decision of what, how, and for whom to produce.

It is argued that decentralized decision-making is more efficient. In other words, market works, market is efficient, and market is good.

But, in real life, markets do not work efficiently. As far as resource efficiency is concerned, markets fail. Hence the name *market failure*. It is an outcome that results in economic inefficiency. Market failure means any market performance that is judged to be less superior than the best attainable outcome. In the real world, markets fail to achieve allocational efficiency of society's scarce resources. Monopoly or any form of imperfect competition distorts market signals thereby adversely affecting people's interests. 'Public goods' is an example of market failure. Free market is shy of delivering public goods since these goods are non-exclusive and non-rivalrous in character. Since people are unwilling to share the costs of public goods, such must be subsidised or provided by the government if they are to be produced efficiently. 'Externalities' also cause market failure. With externalities, consumers or producers do not have to pay all the costs of their activities or are unable to get all the benefits. Thus, externalities cause allocational inefficiency of resources.

Further, in poor developing countries, goods market and inputs market are not well-organised. It then results in distorted prices that give wrong signals and incentives. Thus, the building up of an efficient organised market requires government to play an effective role so that resources are allocated efficiently.

This market failure argument is definitely an incentive to opt for economic planning both in developed and developing ecconomies. In view of this, planning has become an essential and integral part of development programmes as a universal strategy.

The equity argument : It was believed earlier that the market mechanism fosters efficiency. Further, the policymakers of the *Third World* countries in the 1950s and 1960s argued that higher economic growth would ensure equity and justice. However, our experiences tell us a different story : its trickle down effect does not occur. Thus, markets fail to achieve not only efficiency but also equity. The most important aim of the government of the so-called developing mixed economies is to promote equity. Market forces operate in such a manner that income and wealth get concentrated in the hands of a few. High economic growth then bypasses the under-previleged. In other words, growth becomes *exclusive*, instead of being an *inclusive* one. Again, private investors do not like to invest in physical infrastructures and social sectors like health, education, etc. Economic planning is assumed to help in these directions. Government can utilise its investible resources to provide the basics of life for a larger segment of population. Planning process can help to break the vicious circle of poverty. Planned adjustment can ensure fairness and justice.

The resource mobilisation argument : Resources are always limited, and for developing economies too. Under the circumstance, wastage or ill-direction of investible resources may be thought of as criminal offence. Resources are to be utilised judiciously. Private investors put their money in manufacturing quick return-yielding lipstick, face powder, and other elitist consumption goods than articles of primary necessity. Investment in such low-priority areas is governed by the motive of private profitability. But social benefits must be the benchmark for allocating investible resources in productive ventures. Government intervention is deemed necessary so as to channel scarce resources into the most productive projects with a view to optimising societal gains. The following quote from a 1965 report of a United Nations Conference on planning is worth presenting :

"It is an integral task of planning to achieve the best possible use of scarce resources for economic development .... The need for using appropriate criteria for selecting projects arose because of the failure of market mechanism to provide a proper guideline. In less developed economies, market prices of such factors of production as labour, capital, and foreign exchange deviated substantially from their social opportunity costs and were not, therefore, a correct measure of the relative scarcity or abundance of the factor in questions."

Learning by experience argument : It is strongly argued that economic planning can help poor *Third World* countries of Asia and Africa to come out from colonial domination. Such colonial relationship for the last few hundred years created a wide gap between the developed countries and less developed countries. After winning political independence most of these countries opted for economic planning so as to have higher growth and improved living standards of the masses. These economies must not rely on market mechnism and need to address their problems in the light of state intervention and planning. Planned intervention provides the necessary background to challenge the economic supremacy of the developed economies and in the process this can be seen as essential for self-reliant growth.

The attitudinal or psychological argument : There is a further element—enthusiasm of the people about the growth prospects—which can also be delivered by planning. A planned economy may encourage people to participate in various socio-economic programmes, such as illiteracy drive, elimination of killer diseases, removal of poverty, etc. The importance of participation in social change is undeniable. Indeed, actual participation and public action help in changing governmental influence and its priorities. Thus, by involving people in various planned programmes, the government can destroy religious taboos and old customs, casteism and many other conservative outlooks which act as drag on economic development. A congenial socio-psychological climate can better be established if governmental interference in market economies takes place. A progressive government, through its development planning, can best provide the needed incentives to overcome inhibiting and reactionary forces, like sectionalism, fundamentalism, casteism. This then brings about material and social advancement.

Conclusion : On the contrary, the prevailing neoliberal economic thought suggests that the market mechanism and competition can attain allocational efficiency better than a comprehensive macro-economic planning. The practice of planning pursued in different countries has failed to bring many of the benefits expected from it. One talks about implementational failure, institutional failure, etc. No longer, planning is considered a sacred cow; it cannot work well. But from a realistic frame of mind one can contest this market supremacy. Allocative decisions in developing countries cannot be left, however, to the market forces. It is the market imperfection that leads to wrong resource allocation. Further, its role in establishing distributive justice is subject to serious scrutiny.

Anyway, there are both *market failures* and *plan failures*. Plans and markets indeed are not thought to be as incompatible opposites. What is now recomended is rather a 'balanced growth' of both planning and market. Planning or government intervention in a market-oriented deregulated economy should :

(i) ensure that markets function in a manner desired by people;
(ii) plan action in areas where externalities emerge;
(iii) lobby for the poor so as to fulfil social objectives; and
(iv) maintain macroeconomic stability so that the interests of the poor, vulnerables are not compromised.

Thus, planning has a great role to play in a poor, developing deregulated liberal economy. The context of planning needs to be changed.

2.4 The Strategy of Growth

Development economics over the last 50 years or so has undergone a sea-change. Meanwhile, it has come to be known as the 'economics of developing countries'. The significance of these countries is that these are poor, underdeveloped countries. It requires then strategies of growth and development. In the 1950s and 1960s, development economists concentrated on broad strategical approaches to economic development. However, the 1980s onwards saw less emphasis on strategical approaches to growth and development.

It is said that LDCs are caught in a chain of interlocking vicious circles of poverty. In other words, these countries experience a variety of obstacles in their development paths. To overcome these numerous obstacles, the most important key issue that needs to be resolved centre around allocation of investible scarce resources among competing ends. This key issue or the starting point in the realm of resource allocation is the raising of the rate of capital formation to achieve economic progress. Being capital-poor, these countries attempt to raise investment via domestic and external sources.

As soon as investible resources are garnered, the policy decision, that is, the strategy of investment to promote growth needs to be mapped out. Should investment be concentrated on the industrial sector over agriculture? Or should agriculture be the prime target of investment instead of industry, or should a country strike a 'balance' in which all the sectors develop side by side? The issue of the choice between industry and agriculture has generated debates and disputes over time. The complementainty between the sectors is now a conventional wisdom. Anyway, the debate over industry vs agriculture is a part of the debate between *balanced growth* (BG) vs *unbalanced growth* (UG). Should a country go for BG or UG? Should we focus on certain key or leading sectors? Or should we put importance over a broad range of sectors to have higher economic prosperity?

The next two sections are concerned with the debates over the development strategy needed to be pursued in a poor LDC.

2.5 The Strategy of Growth—(A) Balanced vs Unbalanced Growth

In the 1950s and 60s, development economists showed their interest and enthusiam over the state of underdevelopment in many newly independent poor developing countries. These people talked extensively about the patterns of development to be chosen. And, in the process, two divergent views appeared in the development literature. These two views are popularly known as the debate between BG and UG. It is assumed that UDCs are caught by *low level equilibrium trap*. The way to escape from this trap is the *critical minimum effort thesis* as recommended by Harvey Lienbenstein. Development is not an automatic process. A critical minimum effort is required in poor countries for persistent growth. The actual size of the critical minimum effort, that is investment requirement, needs to be 'large' or 'big' to break the vicious circles. Libenstein's critical effort thesis leads us to another but closely related doctrine of a *big push* that says about a planned large-scale expansion of a wide range of economic activities.

P. N. Rosenstein-Rodan, first in 1934, and afterwards in 1961, pleaded for a concerted programme of large-scale industrialisation to escape from the trap or vicious cricle. The name given to this doctrine is BG doctrine—a closely similar view to *big push* theory. But the opponents think otherwise and recommend UG doctrine which recommend for the growth of certain key leading sectors, rather than large-scale expansion of all the sectors. Hence the debate.

2.5.1 The BG Doctrine

The BG—the synchronized application of capital to a wide range of industries—advocates such as, P. N. Rosenstein-Rodan, Ragnar Nurkse, Arthur Lewis recommend that the minimum size of investment programme must be made in various sectors of the economy to initiate the economic development. Or, it may refer to the path of development and the pattern of investment necessary to keep the different sectors of the economy in a balanced growth relationship with each other. An isolated effort is unlikely to fructify.

In other words, BG approach suggests that agriculture and industry should develop simultaneously as there exists a complementary relationship between the two sectors. In addition to this complementary role played by agriculture and industry, Nurkse recommends for the expansion of selected industries with a bias towards consumer goods or light industry. Most industries catering for mass consumption are complementary in the sense that they provide not only a market for each other but also support each other. To Nurkse, the case for BG rests on the need for a "balanced diet". This BG doctrine thus involves the Chinese strategy 'marching on two legs'—one being large industry and the other agriculture and light consumer goods industry; the best foot must be put forward first.

According to Ragnar Nurkse, the biggest bottleneck of development of LDCs is the small size of the market. It is because of low purchasing power underdeveloped countries suffer from limited size of the market. This then explains limited inducement to invest. What is required to break the vicious circle is the expansion of the size of the market. Through the application of investments in various industries, liberal trade policy, extension of infrastructural facilities, the general level of economic efficiency is raised and the size of the market is widened. A. W. Lewis suggests a strategy of balance between domestic and foreign trade also.

Before Nurkse, Rosenstein-Rodan also finds smallness of the market as an impediment to development and pleads for a scheme of planned concerted programme of industrialisation. Like Nurkse, the central idea here is the need to overcome the smallness of the size of the market created out of low per capita income and, hence, low purchasing power of people in LDCs. He argues that a single shoe factory may fail when established on its own because of the smallness of the market for its output or the low volume of societal demand. The proposed solution to this problem is to build a number of industries that derive benefit from the simultaneous development of other complementary industries. In the process, what is seen is the growth of income and therefore the growth of demand/purchasing power that provides a large market for each other.

The BG doctrine focuses on the indivisibility of supply of social overhead capital and indivisibility of demand. The BG doctrine refers to the scale of investment or big push to overcome indivisibilities on both the supply side and demand side of the development process. Indivisibilities on the supply side refer to the 'lumpiness' of capital (mainly social overhead capital like road, irrigation, electricity, a piped water supply, etc.) which is scarce. Once these are developed it can take advantages of external economies. It may be noted that since these forms of investment are indivisible and have long gestation periods there must be a simultaneous development of a variety of consumer goods and producer goods industries so that the supply bottlenecks are removed and excess capacity generated by these capital is utilised.

Indivisibilities on the demand side in LDCs arise from the small size of the market created by low per capita income and, thus, low purchasing power. Now, if enough projects or economic activities are started simultaneously, each would provide a market for the other. Therefore, a big push is essential to enlarge the size of the market.

In the light of these demand and supply considerations, the authors of the BG doctrine recommended a massive investment programme to initiate a 'big push'. 'Proceeding " bit by bit" will not add up in its effects to the sum total of the single bits. A minimum quantum of investment is a necessary—though not sufficient—condition of success. This, in a nutshell, is the contention of the *theory of big push.*

An obvious question was raised by the authors of the BG doctrine : Who will provide all the capital which the BG demands? According to Rosenstein-Rodan, BG would require a 'big push' in the form of government action. Neither the private sector is capable of making such massive investment programmes nor has it the incentive of attainning profitability. Profitability of immediate investment proposal is to be viewed in terms of 'social marginal net product', rather than 'private marginal net product'. In other words, market forces may not lead to optional investment decisions. Rosenstein-Rodan argues that the rate of growth would be slow in the absence of a planning board/central authority rather than innumerable private entrepreneurs. The BG doctrine thus makes a plea for large-scale state action.

Limitations of the BG Doctrine : The *major* criticism of the BG doctrine is that it fails to suggest measures that can be taken to overcome the fundamental obstacle to growth—the shortage of productive resources. In fact, development in most of the LDCs is constrained by the inadequacy of resources, especially capital and entrepreneurs. Under the circumstance, the BG approach may not provide a sufficient stimulus to the spontaneous mobilisation of productive resources or the inducement to invest.

Secondly, given the paucity of investible resources in LDCs, it seems improbable that any LDC would be likely to have enough resources to carry through such massive programme of BG. One of the leading critics of the BG doctrine is Hans Singer. Singer argues that the BG doctrine fails to come to grips with the true problem of LDCs—the scarcity of resources. 'Think Big' is a sound advice for any poor country but 'Act Big' is unwise counsel. Singer and Albert O. Hirschman candidly argued that if a country were ready to apply the BG doctrine amidst paucity of resources, then it would not, in fact, be underdeveloped in the first place! Thus, the BG concept is an unrealistic one for such countries.

Thirdly, the most damaging criticism of the BG theory seems to be the fact that it fails as a theory of development. By development we mean transition from one state of development to a higher one. But if BG doctrine were applied, it would usher in a dualistic pattern of development, as was elaborated by A. O. Hirschman—the main proponent of the UG doctrine. The BG doctrine advocates that an extremely new self-contained modern industrial economy must be superimposed on the stagnant self-contained traditional stage of an economy. This transition from one stage of development to the modern state of development cannot be called a higher stage of development; it is simply a dualistic pattern of development.

Fourthly, critics like Hirschman articulate that the BG doctrine combines a defeatist attitude towards the capabilities of LDCs with completely unrealistic expectations about their creative abilities. Initiation of development process involves the simultaneous start of multiple activities at one instance. Being an underdeveloped economy, it experiences shortage of critical inputs like capital, technical knowhow, entrepreneurship, managerial skills, inefficient and imperfect institutions, etc. Such deficiencies cannot be overcome overnight. After a long time gap these deficiencies can be met. Thus the BG theory appears to be a contradiction in itself.

Fifthly, the strategy of BG, according to H. Singer, lacks historical sense. It assumes that an LDC starts from the scratch. In reality, it is not so but reflects previous investment decisions coupled with positive outcomes, that is, development. Thus, at any point of time one finds that there are highly desirable investment programmes which are not in themselves balanced investment packages, but which represents unbalanced investment to complement existing imbalance. And once such investment is made, a new imbalance is likely to appear which will require still another 'balancing' investment and so on. Thus, historically speaking, "Growth does not take place in a balanced way but is unbalanced." In other words, unbalanced growth is a natural path to development.

Conclusion : Despite the above weaknesses and criticisms, the BG doctrine has certain role to play in the economic development of a nation. Recently, the doctrine has been modified in the light of an imperfectly competitive economy. It is argued that industries with large fixed costs generate pecuniary external economies. Once external economies accrue, an industrial firm can enlarge the market size of another firm through demand spillovers. Through a big push, the limitations of the small size of the market can be overcome.

However, we can conclude here in terms of Singer's comment : "The doctrine (theory) of balanced growth is premature rather than wrong in the sense that it is applicable to a subsequent stage of sustained growth rather than to the breaking of deadlock."

2.5.2 The UG Doctrine

Against this BG doctrine, a rival doctrine was suggested by A. O. Hirschman, Paul Streeten, H. Singer, etc., who pleaded for deliberate unbalancing of the economy in accordance with a predestined strategy to achieve economic growth.

Proponents of this doctrine of *unbalanced growth* argue that it is a state of unbalance or disequilibrium which sets in motion the forces which demand prompt action. If there is equilibrium or balance between demand and supply then decision-makers find no incentive to venture on new projects. Authors of this doctrine do not deny the need for a 'big push' as recommended by the BG advocates. Like Ragnar Nurkse, these authors emphasise complementarity among industries. UDCs are handicapped by not only shortage of capital resources, but also by the lack of skills and knowledge of human labour as well as entrepreneurial/ managerial skills. How then can a big push work? Hirschman argues for a big push in strategically selected industries or sectors of an economy through the creation of tensions and disequilibria.

Given the limited amount of investible resources, Hirschman emphasies on concentration of investment in important industries that provide stimuli for further development. Initial primary investment gives birth to induced investment. Such investment in leading sectors lead to disequilibrium and imbalance in other industries and so on *ad infinitum.* Development of key sectors will call for development of other sectors in the longrun. In Hirschman's words : "If such a chain of unbalanced growth sequences could be set up, the economic policymakers could just watch the proceeds from the sidelines."

Unequal development of leading sectors often generate conditions for rapid growth. Hirschman argues that there are two ways of creating imbalance in the economy. To this end, Hirschman divides initial investment into two related activities : *social overhead capital* (SOC) and *directly productive actvities* (DPA).

SOC is defined as those basic services without which primary, secondary and tertiary activities cannot function. It includes many forms of infrastructure like education, public health, public utilities like water, power, irrigation, transporation, communication, etc. These basic services are provided by the state agencies both for the promotion of social welfare and for the encouragement of DPA like setting up of industries (both heavy and light), commerce, trade, etc. SOC investments provide stimuli for trade, agriculture, industry, etc., and, hence, a great stimulus for investment in DPA. In other words, SOC is thought to be as a prerequisite of DPA.

However, imbalances in an economy may also be created by making investment in DPA at the first instance. Initial investment on DPA may reflect poor growth of the economy due to the shortage of SOC. However, faced with the inadequacy of SOC, the pressure on SOC starts building up. Thus, initial investment on DPA induces investment on SOC.

In Hirschman's scheme of things, we thus have two paths of development : The first path (from SOC to DPA) is designated as '*development via excess capacity*', while the second path (from DPA to SOC) is called as '*development via shortages*'. It may be noted that both these paths create inducements and pressures required for development. But which sequence should be adopted by the policymakers can be analysed in terms of Fig. 2.1 where we measure cost of SOC on the horizontal axis and cost of DPA on the vertical axis.

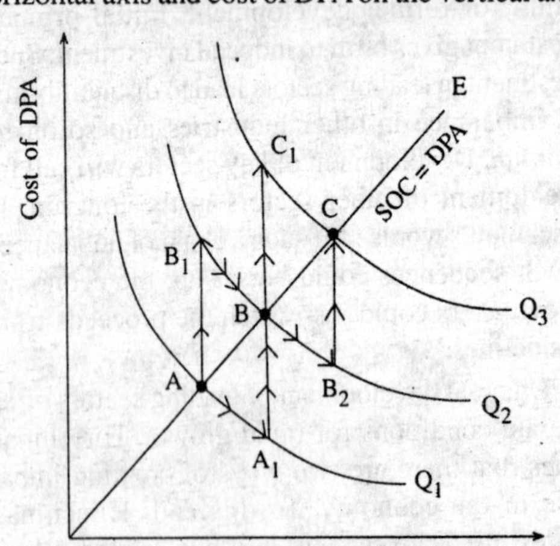

Fig. 2.1 : Two Alternative Paths of UG

The negatively sloped convex curves Q_1, Q_2, etc., are the isoquants representing different levels of DPA output from a successively higher investment in DPA. Higher curves represent higher levels of output. A line OE has been drawn in such a way that the optimal points fall on this line. This efficient expansion path A → B → C thus describes the BG path between SOC and DPA.

In his doctrine of UG, Hirschman assumes that SOC and DPA cannot be developed simultaneously.This means that a UDC may either choose SOC over DPA or DPA over SOC.

If the country chooses the path of development via excess capacity (i.e., preference of SOC over DPA), the development path of the economy would be AA_1 BB_2C. When the economy increases SOC form A to A_1, this induces investment in DPA. The induced investment in DPA accelerates to B until balance between SOC and DPA is restored. Meanwhile, the economy is on a higher growth path. Now SOC is increased further to B_2 which induces further investment in DPA until balance is restored at C.

If the economy follows the path of development via shortage of SOC, that is, more investment is made on DPA over SOC, the development path would be AB_1 BC_1C. When DPA is accelerated to B_1, DPA will have to shift to B_1, and then to B. When DPA is enhanced further to C_1, this again creates pressure for more investment in SOC until balance is restored at C.

The next important issue is the choice of selecting the kind of imbalance that becomes highly effective (i.e., highest profitability of investment). This necessiates the knowledge of interlinkages across different sectors of the economy. Hirschman introduces the concept of *forward and backward linkages*.

An industry is said to have forward linkage effects if it prompts the setting up of new industries using its output. For example, the setting up of a steel factory results in an expansion of a variety of steel-using industries, like automobile, cycle industries. On the other hand, industries with backward linkages make use of inputs from other industries. For example, the setting up of a steel mill will create demand for coal, iron ore, and blast furnace. Usually, for consumer good industries forward linkage is rather weak while agriculture has some sort of backward linkages. In general, intermediate industries have the most linkages.

Thus, these linkages are stimuli to expansion and growth. The aim of development policy should be not to push forward simultaneously on all fronts but to select and concentrate on particular 'strategic' sectors of the economy where these interdependent linkage effects may be expected to be the strongest.

The *chief* merit of this UG doctrine is that it is a more realistic approach as far as LDCs are concerned. This is because that this approach recognises the scarcity of productive resources as an obstacle of development, rather than small-sized market as BG theorists emphasise. *Secondly*, it attaches importance to the creation of SOC by state intervention. *Thirdly*, this doctrine does not abandon the role of market mechanism. Above all, the experience of the erstwhile USSR is a pointer to the LDCs as this country witnessed a massive growth following the adoption of this growth strategy. India, too, followed this strategy during the Second Five Year Plan (1956-1961) when emphasis was given to the development of basic and key industries.

Limitations of UG Doctrine : Despite these merits, the UG doctrine is not free from defects and weaknesses as evident :

First, this doctrine recommends creation of deliberate imbalance for economic development, but remains silent on the degree of unbalance among the various sectors. The doctrine does not specify at all *where* to unbalance and *how much* in order to accelerate growth. Truly speaking, the doctrine does not talk about the composition, direction, degree, and the timing of unbalanced growth.

Secondly, the UG doctrine concentrates too much on stimuli to expansion but tends to neglect or minimise resistances caused by unbalanced growth. However, resistance may occur in many ways and in many forms. For instance, institutional bottlenecks or unsophisticated entreprenurial attitudes often act as drag on development. It may also happen that some decision-takers may make mistakes in uncertain circumstances associated with imbalances. This may result in bad investment in spite of good linkage effects. How to overcome such resistances or obstacles has not been given importance in this doctrine.

Thirdly, the strategy of UG pays less attention to agriculture. This may be suicidal to the overpopulated agricultural countries. Shortage of agricultural goods (particularly, wage-goods) can emerge as a serious constraint to the industrialisation programme of a country.

Fourthly, Hirschman emphasises on linkages as the criteria of development. But in LDCs one finds lack of interdependence between different sectors. In other words, there may be limited backward and forward linkages, thereby slowing down the process of development. Above all, linkage effects are not based on statistical data pertaining to LDCs.

Fifthly, imbalances can be a powerful source of inflationary pressure in a poor LDC where massive investments are undertaken in selected strategic sectors. Such cost and price increases, in turn, produce detrimental effects on the balance of payments of a nation, particularly if goods are price inelastic and income elastic in demand. If inflationary control measures are adopted it may cause emergence of some other untoward developments like worsening of supply position in the shortage sectors, rising bogey of unemployment, currency exchange depreciation, etc.

Finally, the UG doctrine may be of a great help if the state exercises effective control over the country. This theory then has the greater applicability in socialist countries where state directs all resources according to societal needs and invests in socially desired lines. But such is not true in an economy where control of the state over resources and investment is left with the private sector along with the governemt. It is because of the limited government control it cannot create right type of imbalances or disequilibria between different sectors of the economy. This then hampers the process of economic development.

Conclusion : There can be no end to this sort of debate and thus there are difficult to evaluate. Neither of the two doctrines is an unfailing prescription for development as these theories cannot be tested empirically. From a purely economic point of view, these two growth strategies must not be viewed as alternatives. So what is needed is the reconciliatory approach—an approach that emphasises both the BG and the UG approaches. In other words, one step towards this reconciliatory approach is to pursue unbalanced growth as a means of achieving the ultimate objective of balanced growth. An optimum strategy of development should combine some elements of both balances and imbalances.

2.6 The Strategy of Growth—(B) Agriculture vs Industry

One of the basic issues in development economics is the resource allocation among competing ends, given the scarcity of resources. First, the country has to decide which sectors need to be prioritised in the development process. This means that should policymakers decide to invest more in agriculture or in industry is a moot question. After assigning priority or preference to one sector, a closely allied decision about technology to be adopted for producing goods need to be settled. Because of interdependence between the choice of goods/sectors and the choice of technology, a country need to design whether it should opt for labour-intensive technology or the capital-intensive technology.

2.6.1 Role of Agriculture

To begin with the concept of priority or preference of one sector and one technology over another is a slippery one. For instance, A. W. Lewis once remarked that "Agriculture has been the weakest link in the development chain." On the other hand, there is another argument that suggests that agricultural productivity and output contribute towards an economy's development. Against this backdrop, the case for priority in agriculture rests on the following facts.

Since the days of David Ricardo, importance of agriculture in an economy's development is being recognised. Taking the "natural limits"—the problem of diminishing returns—in agriculture into account, Ricardo concluded that such 'limits' in agricultural production would set the upper limit to the growth of the non-agricultural sector and to capital formation for economic development.

There are four ways through which agriculture contributes towards the process of economic development as described by Simon Kuznets. These are : (i) product contribution, (ii) market contribution, (iii) factor contribution, and (iv) foreign exchange contribution.

Product contribution : The product contribution of agriculture refers to its contribution of wage-goods, that is, foodstuffs over the subsistence level to feed the labour force of urban non-agricultural sector. A growing population must be supported with increased food supply. Raising food supply through different ways has thus great importance for economic growth of a country. The annual rate of increase in demand for food in an economy is determined by

$$D = p + \eta g$$

where p and g stand for the rates of growth of population and per capita income, and η stands for income elasticity of demand for agricultural goods. Poor LDCs experience high population growth rate and a high income elasticity of demand for food. Under the circumstance, an increase in per capita income strongly increases the demand for foodstuffs/agricultural goods in these countries more than the advanced countries of the West. In Britain, agricultural revolution brought in the wake of Industrial Revolution (1760 onwards) raised agricultural productivity, provided surplus labour to the non-farm sectors, and wage-goods to support industrial expansion.

To this end, what is needed is the generation of 'marketable surplus'—a surplus of agricultural output over the subsistence needs. Marketable surplus from agriculture also tends to widen the home market for the industrial products. Of course, the demand for industrial products largely depends on farm income. Increased agricultural productivity, a growing marketable surplus, and a rising income of the agriculturists are necessary to trigger an expansion in the demands for industrial products by the agricultural sector.

Market contribution : The market contribution of agriculture to economic growth refers to the fact that the demand from agriculture acts as the source of autonomous demand for industrial goods. As a result of agricultural progress there occurs a market extension for industrial goods. Agriculture thus has linkages with the industrial sector—there is a complementarity between the two sectors. A precondition for rapid industrial growth is a rapidly expanding agricultural sector. Dr. Bright Singh asserts that increase in agricultural production and the rise in farm incomes together with industrialisation and urbanisation lead to an increased demand for industrial products. Thus, a sluggish growth in agriculture acts as a drag on industrial development.

Thus, it is evident that if agriculture itself grows, there occurs a product contrbution and when agriculture trades with other sectors, there occurs a market contribution.

Factor contribution : The factor contribution, comprising both labour contribution and capital contribution, occurs when there is a transfer of productive factors/resources to other sectors from the given sector. A overpopulated developing economy is characterised by the existence of surplus labour or disguised unemployment. Arthur Lewis, Ragnar Nurkse once suggested that in overpopulated underdeveloped countries agricultural sector—by transfering its labour resources to the modern industrial sector where they create a surplus—can contribute to growth and development. Industrial development of many of the South East Asian countries had been bolstered by cheap labour supply available in the farm sector.

Agriculture contributes substantially to the sources for capital formation. However, savings may be voluntary or forced. Voluntary saving is made by rich landlords, peasant farmers while savings may be collected by coercion as was done in the erstwhile Soviet Union and China in the past. In addition, government, by taxing away agricultural sector, may collect resources for investment. In addition, agricultural sector provides funds for capital formation through (i) transfer of labour and capital from farm sector to the non-farm sectors, (ii) export of surplus agricultural products, (iii) turning the terms of trade against agriculture by imposing price controls on agricultural goods by taxation or by using multiple exchange rates against agriculture, etc.

Foreign exchange contribution : Agriculture may be a great source of foreign exchange of a country. Foreign exchange is an important source, just like savings. Primary products producing underdeveloped countries earn foreign exchange by exporting these products. As those exports contribute nearly 60 to 70 p.c. of their export earnings, the capacity to import capital goods and machinery required for industrial development largely depend on export earnings. However, as terms of trade deteriorate against primary products in the international market, the prospect of higher export earnings is rather limited.

Egalitarian income distribution : *Finally*, agricultural growth tends to improve income distribution more in favour of small peasants. Urban, industrial sector is characterised by 'skewness' in income distribution, the concentration of income in the hands of a few small business houses. Any effort for rural development would help in reducing the rural-urban gaps. Agricultural development thus helps in improving social welfare, particularly in the rural areas. In the process, the rural masses enjoy a better way of living.

While emphasising the importance of agriculture, the World Bank in its 2007 *World Development Report* pleads for the development of agriculture in the 21st century as a fundamental instrument for both sustainable development and poverty reduction. Three-quarters of poor people of developing countries derive their livelihoods from agriculture. In this connection, the Bank considers that there are three types of countries—agriculture-based countries, transforming countries, and urbanised countries—where agricultural development along with the associated industries are 'essential' to both higher growth and the poverty reduction.

Its recommendations for agricultural development in these countries are as follows. A comprehensive approach to (i) shifting to high-value agriculture, (ii) extending non-farm activities in rural areas so as to encourage agricultural labour to reduce their dependence on agriculture for livelihoods in transforming countries of South and East Asia, the middle East and North Africa. However, for the agriculture-based countries of most of sub-Saharan Africa, it recommends strong agricultural development along with related industries as an engine of higher economic growth and the reduction of mass poverty. Lastly, in urbanised countries of mostly Latin America and Central Asia, the reduction of poverty may be initiated by helping small landholders so that these people can participate in the modern food markets. As a result, jobs are created not only in agriculture but also in agro-industrial activities.

What thus emerges from the above is that agriculture must play a great role in the transformation of a developing economy. Agriculture must be viewed as sources of (i) surpluses to support industrialisation, (ii) dynamic growth, employment, and better income distribution.

2.6.2 Role of Industry

Industrialisation offers substantial benefits that are crucial for structural transformation of LDCs. The concept of *big push* or *balanced growth* reflects deliberate industrialisation of these economies. Those who favour in giving a special priority to industry over agriculture put arguments like :

In the *first* place, agricultural productivity is hampered by poor technology and paucity of capital investment in poor LDCs. Under the circumstance, these countries must choose that sector which promises the greatest development. Indeed, modern growth and industrialisation is essential. An appropriate industrial policy can overcome the obstacles to industrialisation. Industrial growth depends on agricultural growth—an assured supply of chemical fertilisers, pesticides, farm technologies may trigger industrial growth. Again, industrial growth creates the demand for agricultural output. In this way, it creates the basis of balanced growth.

Secondly, industrial investment will stimulate further investment compared to agriculture as the industry maximises linkages—the Hirschman's concepts of *backward and forward linkages*. For instance, an iron and steel industry has very strong forward and backward linkages. The unbalanced growth doctrine implicitly but strongly recommends industrial investment.

Thirdly, it is strongly asserted that over time as agriculture is subject to diminuition, its labour-absorbptive capacity will decline. However, the employment potentiality of the industrial sector is indeed large. Although heavy industry being capital-intensive in nature cannot be a great employment provider; small and medium industries have the greater capacity to absorb labour force. Anyway, no economy can afford the luxury of remaining an agrarian one all the time; indeed no other alternative to this economy but to have industrialisation.

To be more specific, structural transformation demands industrialisation. As industrialisation develops, there occurs a shift in the composition of output from primary sector activities towards industrial activities along with a structural change in employment pattern in favour of industrial sector. This kind of structural transformation is a pointer to a higher level of development.

Fourthly, agricultural production is more cyclical and thus income receipts and tax receipts are not stable. Industrial growth more or less guarantees income stability and revenue stability to the government. Industry is also subject to cyclical ups and downs but not so like agriculture. Again, because of interdependence between agriculture and industry, the industrial output may exhibit cyclical variability. The current global recession (2008 onwards) largely faced by the USA and other European countries has somehow reduced India's export earnings.

Fifthly, industrialisation provides a firm basis in raising the share of industry in total income rapidly. In other words, progress of industrialisation is accompanied by an increase in national and per capita incomes. After examining data for 45 countries grouped into three—large countries, small countries with heavy orientation of exports of manufactured products, and small countries with a greater orientation of exports of primary products—Hollis B. Chenery and L. Taylor concluded that the share of industry rises from 16 p.c. to 37 p.c. for large countries as against a decline in the share of primary production from 45 p.c. to 12 p.c. The behaviour of small-industry oriented countries is, however, different. This study then clearly shows that large developing countries as well as small-industry oriented countries can gain a lot by developing industry.

Finally, from the sociological point of view, it can be said that industrialisation can bring about a change in the social outlook of people. With industrialisation the traditional village life gets transformed; people migrate to cities for jobs in non-farm activities. Casteism tends to vanish as educational attainment improves. Education acts as a catalyst of social change; new progressive ideas towards life occur. A new class of entrepreneurs is born, capital formation increases, technical innovations take place. All these changes produce a favourable impact on social relationship which, in fact, acts as a precursor of a new, modern, cultured, and a vibrant society.

2.6.3 Interdependence between Agriculture and Industry

In the previous two sections, we have studied first how agriculture contributes to economic development and then how industry contributes towards development. However, the issue of choice of one sector over the other remains unresolved as far as economic policy is concerned.

Truly speaking, these two sectors are not to be viewed as competitive but are complementary to each other. In practice, the futures of agriculture and industry are closely linked with each other in the sense that expansion in agriculture depends on the supply of industrial inputs and the expansion in industry is tied up with the development of the agricultural activity. J. L. Nehru observed in 1963 that agriculture is more important than industry as industry depends on agriculture. Industry which is, no doubt, important, will not progress unless agriculture is sound, stable, and progressive. Because of this interdependence these sectors are complementary, and not competitive. In the development of an underdeveloped economy, there is as such no conflict between agricultural and industrial development.

Interdependence between agriculture and industry becomes strengthened through various linkages generated in these two sectors. The three most important linkages are : production linkages, demand linkages, and saving-investment linkages.

Production linkages arise from the interdependence between agriculture and industry through the use of productive inputs. Agriculture draws some raw materials, like chemical fertilisers, pesticides, electric power, agricultural machinery and implements, etc., from the industry. Agriculture is also dependent on industry for the supply of materials for building up social and economic overheads in the agricultural sector. Further, many raw materials and inputs used in industrial production, e.g., cotton, jute, sugarcane, tobacco, etc., is supplied by the agricultural sector. Such production linkages demonstrate that a 10 p.c increase in agricultural output results in an increase in industrial output by as much as 5 p.c.

Demand linkages between the two sectors suggest that demand for one sector's product pulls demand for another sector in an upward direction. Urbanisation and industrialisation are synonymous. Under the impact of Green Revolution, agriculturists now experience rising rural incomes which has brought a change in the pattern of tastes and preferences of rural people. Increased rural income has resulted in an entry of industrial consumer goods, like TV, refrigerator, modern, car, footwear, refined sugar, edible oils, motorbikes, etc. In the urban areas, we see some sort of demand saturation of some of these products of consumer goods industries. The impact of rising urban incomes and industrialisation has a favourable impact on the demand for food, vegetables, fruits, various raw materials produced in the agricultural sector. It has been an article of faith in India that the demand stimulus for industrial expansion would likely come mainly from agriculture with low social and economic costs.

Finally, there is a savings-investment linkage between these two sectors. A self-reliant agriculture capable of exporting surplus foodgrains helps in saving scarce foreign exchange resources of the country. Now these resources can be better utilised for importing capital goods and crucial raw materials needed for industrialisation effort. As agricultural production and productivity rises above the subsistence requirement, the volume of marketable surplus increases which provides sinews of industrialisation, particularly in the rural sector. Again, the rising volume of savings and capital formation consequent upon rising farm incomes give strong stimulus to demand for manufactured goods. Investment in one sector pulls investment of other sectors up thereby accelerating overall growth rate of the economy.

Similarly, the rise in non-farm incomes leads to an increase in the demand for various agricultural products. In the process, agricultural sector becomes diversified, modernised.

Most importantly, the relative terms of trade between the two sectors affect the flow of resources from one to another sector. Terms of trade will improve for agricultural sector if over a period of time the prices of agricultural commodities move at a higher rate than the prices of manufactured articles. Thus, the terms of trade favouring agricul-

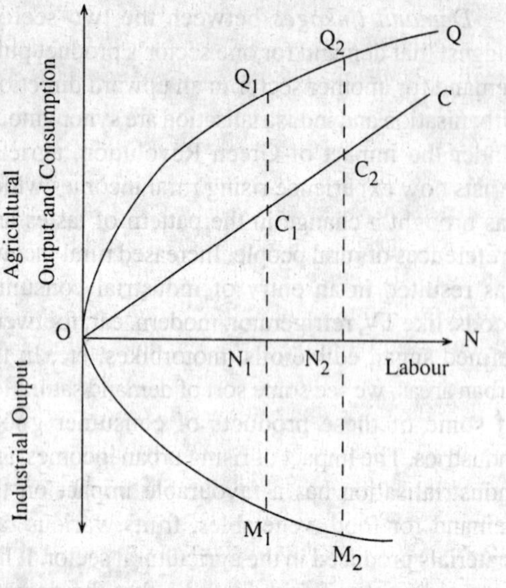

Fig. 2.2 : Interdependent Development

ture results in an increased real income and, hence, increased private saving and investment. The relative terms of trade also influence government saving and investment in these two sectors.

It is thus evident that there is an interrelationship between the two sectors and each sector influences the development of the other. How does agriculture contribute towards higher development can be explained in terms of Fig. 2.2.

Here we consider two sectors—agriculture and industry. Agricultural production and consumption are measured on the vertical axis above the origin while industrial output is measured on the vertical axis below the origin. Horizontal axis—ON axis—measures the volume of agricultural labour. Agricultural output is indicated by the OQ curve. Its shape is governed by the law of variable proportions. OC curve measures the volume of consumption of agricultural output. The difference between OQ and OC thus measures the volume of surplus generated in the agricultural sector. At ON_1 level of employment made in the agricultural sector, C_1Q_1 becomes the surplus agricultural output. Investment of this surplus generates N_1M_1 output in the industrial sector. As employment in agriculture increases to ON_2, industrial output rises to N_2M_2 consequent upon a C_2Q_2 surplus produced in agriculture. If technological change is made in the primary sector there will be more surplus and, hence, more output in the industrial sector.

In the end, we must say a few words about the problem of inter-sectoral resource allocation. To begin with, it is almost impossible to make an optimum balance between these two sectors. In many of the developing countries, agriculture no longer enjoys a pride of place, for some obvious reasons. Neo-liberal era has seen the over-emphasis on the urban, industrial sector. That is why agricultural land is now being forcibly taken away for industrial development, infrastructural developments, and so on. Against this backdrop, farmers of these economies have been shifting their attention from the agricultural sector towards non-agricultural activities. How far these two sectors will complement each other, and to what degree, is an important issue. Indeed, the failure on the agriculture front is oftern attributed to faulty agricultural policy in many developing countries, including India.

2.7 Role of Technology in Agriculture and Industry

Another controversial area of development strategy is the choice of technology in the productive sectors of the economy. Choice of technology is concerned with the question of factor proportions in productive activity : should a country opt for labour-intensive technique of production or capital-intensive technique? We are interested in knowing the role of technology in the growth process of a country.

Technology may be defined as the hardware of production—knowledge about machines and processes. But a broader definition extends to all the "skills, knowledge and procedures for making, using and doing useful things." Technology should also include the organisation of productive units in terms of scale (large or small) and ownership. The characteristics of technology chosen by a country are largely determined by the nature of the economies for which they are designed. Technology choice is determined by the labour or capital intensity of a country.

2.7.1 Role of Technology in Agriculture

The days of modern technology can be traced to the industrial revolution that increased industrial productivity manifold in some European countries. Modern technology was also introduced in the field of agriculture in these countries. Since then, with the advancement of knowledge, new technologies are being introduced across the globe rather regularly.

Unfortunately, poor LDCs fail to grow like the developed countries. They lagged far behind the developed countries in terms of technology used in both agriculture and industries. This caused low productivity in agriculture and industry.

Before the 1970s, Indian agricultural output did not rise much to meet the country's needs. Part of the increase in agricultural production could be attributed to increase in the sown area and to a slightly greater degree to increse in productivity. The mid-1960s was a disaster as far as India's agricultural sector was concerned. The country witnessed a massive shortfall in agricultural output when the vast number of people faced the twin blows of hunger and malnutrition. This then demanded innovative effort on a massive scale.

Repeated calls for action encouraged the Rockfeller and Ford Foundations to take the lead in creating an international agricultural research programme so that new technologies appropriate to the conditions of the developing countries could be adapted. Work started with the research on rice and wheat. The breeding of improved rice and wheat varieties in conjunction with the greater use of fertilisers, irrigation, 'miracle' seeds, pesticides, etc., dramatically increased output of these food crops. These were described as the 'green revolution' by the USAID administrator, W. S. Gaud.

The green revolution comprises a package of modern inputs—irrigation, improved seeds, fertilisers and pesticides. In other words, the green revolution is driven by the technology revolution—seed-fertiliser-water technology or modern technology. As a result of the application of this green revolution technology, Asia witnessed a boom in production and yield. For instance, wheat yields increased by 4.1.p.c. p.a. and rice yields by 2.5 p.c. p.a. between 1967 and 1982. It is said that Indian agriculture became more capital-intensive with the green revolution. Commenting on its success, Peter B. R. Hazell says : "Higher yields and profitability also led farmers to increase the area of rice and wheat they grew at the expense of other crops. And with faster-growing varieties and irrigation, farmers grew more crops on their land each year. This change led to even faster growth in cereal production. All these gains were achieved with negligible growth in total area planted to cereal—just 0.4 p.c. p.a."

How did agricultural growth stimulated by the green revolution in India act as a motor for the Indian economy may be confirmed by a study made by C. Rangarajan in 1982. He estimated that an increase of 1.0 percentage point in the agricultural growth rate stimulated an increase of 0.5 p.c. in the industrial output growth rate, and an increase of 0.7 p.c. in the growth rate of national income.

But the green revolution, being pro-capitalist in nature, has accentuated the problem of rural inequality. Further, technological innovations of the labour-saving variety have displaced labour. Most important worry that has become uppermost in the minds of all is the environmental sustainability of the green revolution technology.

Green revolution needs to be made pro-poor and environmentally sustainable.

2.8 Choice of Techniques in Industry

An underdeveloped economy attempting to have planned economic growth is often forced with the problem of (appropriate) choice of techniques of production. There are various alternative techniques of production in which technology may be high or low. The amount of capital investment per unit of labour varies enourmously from technique to technique. This is the problem of choice of technique.

Broadly, there are two techniques available in an economy. These are : labour-intensive and capital-intensive techniques of production. A technique that requires a high proportion of labour compared to capital or a high labour-output ratio is called *labour-intensive technique*. On the other hand, when more capital input than the labour input is employed or when the capital-output ratio is high, then we have *capital-intensive technique* of production.

Thus the problem of choice of technology really boils down to the problem of right choice of capital-labour ratio in a producing sector. In other words, the assessment of the high or low technology must take into account the shortage or surplus labour force and capital. Different techniques imply different strategies of economic development and have different implications on the performance of an economy. The techniques that yield the greatest advantages at the lowest possible cost appears to be the best indicator of the choice of techniques of production.

In simple terms, an underdeveloped country has a defintie bias in favour of labour-intensive techniques of production as labour there is relatively abundant and cheap. On the other hand, developed countries opt for capital-intensive techniques since labour there is scarce and dear while capital is both abundant and cheap. In practice, it is often observed in developing countries that the capital intensity of techniques of production is quite identical to those of advanced countries in many areas of production. For instance, the handicraft and cottage industry methods of producing consumer goods and the spade and bucket methods of constructing roads and irrigation works are the examples of labour-intensive techniques of production. Simultaneously, one also finds a greater capital-intensity or labour-saving technology used in the modern sector. Under the circumstance, because of lower labour costs and higher productivity, the net output per unit of capital may be comparatively high. Thus the choice of an (appropriate) technology is a complex one.

Before going into the intricacies of the choice of techniques of production relevant for present day developing economies, we now present 'standard' arguments for both labour and capital-intensive techniques of production.

Arguments for Labour-intensive Techniques : Should an overpopulated economy like India choose labour-intensive method of production? Arguments for such techniques are :

The *first* argument in favour of labour-intensive or capital-saving technology is its high employment potential. Poor LDCs suffer from huge unemployment problem. These countries also experience a huge army of surplus labour. By using labour-intensive industry like small-scale and handicrafts industry, employment possibilities of the unemployed labour force can be met in a greater way.

Secondly, this technique makes an equitable income distribution since this technique helps in raising the income level of a relatively large member of workers and hence poverty level gets reduced. This technique either increases employment or minimises the problem of unemployment by absorbing workers. This then increases output, consumption, etc. All these have the potentiality of spreading higher equality among masses. Thus, the roadmap for an egalitarian society is built up. Social justice—an important objective of growth and development—is ensured.

Thirdly, labour-intensive techniques are not import-dependent technologies as such. Being simple, these technologies are produced domestically. As a result, scarce foreign exchange reserves are not drained out. On the other hand, developing countries need to import capital-intensive technologies as these technologies are not manufactured in these economies. Thus, capital-intensive techniques of production fail to save scarce foreign exchange.

Fourthly, for the reduction of regional inequalities, this technique is considered to be an ideal one, since labour-intensive industries can be set up anywhere in the country. Establishment of these industries do not require large investment. Nor do these industries require social and economic infrastructures. That is why small-scale and cottage industries are set up even in rural areas. In other words, decentralisation or dispersal of industries is made possible through this technique.

Fifthly, another powerful argument in favour of labour-intensive techniques of production is that it can use local latent resources in a multifarious and varied manner. Often in rural areas and even in urban areas, one may find the presence of some skilled workers as well as small entrepreneurs who are deemed to be competent for running and managing small industries. Large-scale modern industries, however, do not entertain these local resources which are considered as 'unfit' for these industries. Thus, by building up small-scale and cottage industries, a country can utilise its latent resources in a more effective way.

Finally, underdeveleped countries suffer from shortage of capital. To fill this gap, foreign assistance is often recommended though these countries fail to attract such aid because of many reasons. Under the circumstance, a labour-saving capital-using technology can absorb very few people. This means that it would 'create small islands of high productivity whilst leaving large parts of the economy untouched'. On the contrary, labour-using technology is capable of utilising scarce capital in an optimal manner in more important areas of production, particularly consumption goods.

Arguments for Capital-intensive Techniques : Some economists like W. Galenson and Harvey Leiben-stein have challenged labour-intensive techniques of production as ideal technologies for LDCs and have made a strong plea for capital-intensive indus-tries on the following grounds :

First, the capital-intensive techniques of production will make possible a rapid rate of investment as this technology maximises productivity per worker minus consumption per worker. On the contrary, labour-intensive technology attracts more employment but at low wages. Thus there is little leftover income for savings and investment. But the capital-intensive technology has the highest 're-investment quotient'—a faster economic development appears because of high income, savings, and investment.

Secondly, since economic growth rate tends to be higher and faster under capital-intensive technology, it generates more employment opportunities over a long period of time compared to the labour-intensive techniques. Although small scale and cottage industries have the greater potential of employment of labour in the current period, capital-intensive industries open up employment opportunities in the long run on a wide scale. In other words, employment multiplier of this kind of industry is not weak as was assumed by Galenson, Liebenstein, etc.

Thirdly, economic development of any country or the sectoral activity largely depends on the availability of economic infrastructures. Capital-intensive techniques assist in the development of such infrastructures. Further, by building up infrastructural facillities, capital-intensive industries may be diversified.

Fourthly, it is strongly argued that capital-intensive plants enhance the skills and the efficiency of the workers as well as managers. In this way, it helps in removing the shortage of experience, competent and skilled personnel that an LDC experiences in its growth process. In other words, *learning by doing* argument is very strong in the case of capital-intensive technology.

Finally, mass production at a low cost is possible under labour-saving technology. Inexpensive products mean low prices. One of the main reasons towards increasing the size of a plant has been the economies of large-scale production.

What is now clear from the above discussion is that both the techniques have advantages. Some people argue : Small is beautiful, while others argue : Large is beautiful. Hence the controversy : Which technique is to be chosen?

Indeed, it is because of the conflict between employment and output, and between employment and savings in the choice of techniques, there is no 'unambiguous' answer.

The Conflict between Employment and Output : In the choice of techniques, one encounters two kinds of conflict between objectives. *First,* the maximisation of employment involves a sacrifice of output. Ultimately, this conflict boils down between present consumption and future consumption. The technique that maximises employment has a lower flow of current output. How much investment need to be made—according to Amartya Sen and Maurice Dobb—depends on the time element or the planning horizon. If an importance is attached on raising the current consumption and employment rather than the future output, the labour-intensive techniques should be chosen. On the other hand, as capital-intensive techniques of production yield a lower volume of present employment and consumption, they promise higher future output growth, employment, and consumption.

This argument can be explained in terms of Fig. 2.3. On the horizontal axis, time and on the vertical axis, output of consumption goods are measured.

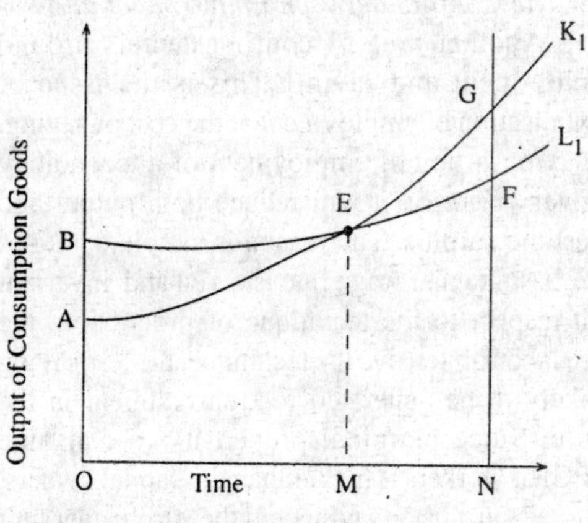

Fig. 2.3 : Choice of Techniques of Production

Here AK_1 and BL_1 curves show the flow of real consumption over time with two different techniques—the capital-intensive and the labour-intensive, respectively. The capital-intensive techniques represented by the curve AK_1 shows lower present immediate output and a higher rate of growth than the labour-intensive techniques given by the BL_1 curve. Until we reach point E, the labour-intensive techniques yield higher output than the capital-intensive techniques. So the total gap ABE has to be made up by the capital-intensive techniques in the future time. As soon as the time period ON is reached, the above gap is met by the capital-intensive techniques (AEB = EFG). Following Amartya Sen, we may call the period OM, the 'period of recovery' which gives us the time period over which the aggregate consumption levels are the same. While selecting one technique over another, the recovery period is crucial.

If we discover that this period is longer, i.e., if within the time horizon of our planning (may be 5 or 10 years), the amount of output we sacrifice to start with by adopting the more capital-intensive techniques is not recovered by the excess of output later on (i.e., after point M), the country should choose the labour-intensive technique. Before we reach OM time period, the output of consumption of goods produced by the labour-intensive technology is larger. On the other hand, after OM, the capital-intensive technology is chosen as it will yield larger flow of consumption goods—a surplus of output of EFG will arise. The surplus as found in the long period may exceed the loss found in the short period. Thus, capital-intensive techniques of production should be chosen.

The Conflict between Employment and Saving : Another area of conflict centers around employ-ment and saving. This is the issue of maximisation of employment at the cost of saving. If maximisa-tion of employment of a technology is given priority, it will reduce both output and investible surplus. The reason is simple enough : If we assume that wage rate is given and invariant with respect to the technique of production, the more labour-intensive the technique, the less saving is likely to be generated for reinvestment in the future. Since marginal prepensity to consume (MPC) of workers is higher than the capital owners, the total surplus or saving and the surplus per unit of capital invested left for re-investment will be smaller under labour-intensive technology. Conversely, the more capital-intensive the technology, the lower the level of present consumption and employment, but higher the future rate of investment, growth, and employment.

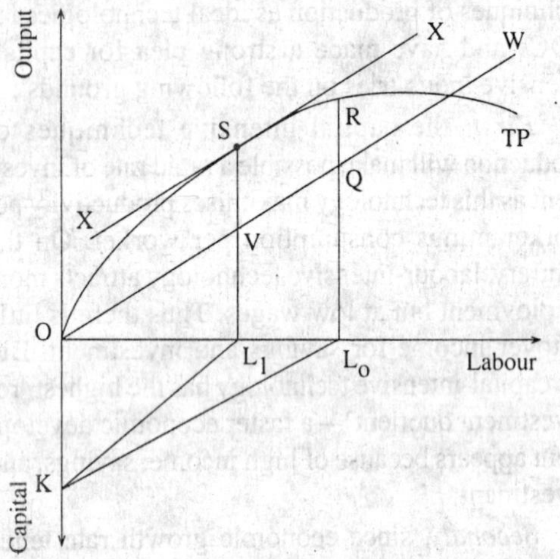

Fig. 2.4 : Employment vs Saving or Labour-intensive vs Capital-intensive Techniques

This argument may again be illustrated in terms of Fig. 2.4 used by M. Dobb and Amartya Sen. The amount of capital, OK, is assumed to be given and is measured on the vertical axis below the origin. This amount of fixed capital is combined with varying units of labour measured on the horizontal axis to produce output. Output is measured on the vertical axis above the origin. TP is the output curve which exhibits diminishing returns to labour. The line OW shows the volume of wage bill. At a fixed wage rate the wage bill proportionally increases with the quantity of variable input, labour. The difference between the TP curve and OW line measures profit or surplus. Profit or surplus or saving is maximised where a line drawn parallel to the OW line is tangential to the TP curve, i.e., point S. That is, when OL_1, amount of labour, is combined with OK fixed volume of capital, then reinvested surplus, SV, becomes the greatest. However, if the employment of labour is increased the volume of surplus will be smaller—the volume of saving and investible surplus RQ is smaller when OL_o, the amount of labour is employed. Thus, the more labour-intensive techniques maximise output and consumption in the short run, but the more capital-intensive techniques provide a greater surplus for re-investment for growth and future output and consumption.

The upshot of the current discussion on the choice of techniques is that it is not possible to make an invariable choice in favour of more labour-intensive techniques even in overpopulated countries, unless we make explicit choice between the present and the future. The more we value raising the present consumption level and current employment against future growth, the more we should go for labour-intensive techniques. On the contrary, capital-intensive technology should be favoured.

Intermediate technology : Whether a country should attach importance to labour-intensive techniques or not ultimately depends on a variety of factors, since these two techniques are not to be viewed as competitors. A country needs all the techniques available in the economy. For certain type of industries like agriculture, handicraft, and cottage industry, labour-intensive or capital-saving technology may be recommended, while, for basic and heavy industries, capital-intensive or labour-saving technology may be suggested.

Objections and counter-objections against these two techniques have led to the search for an 'intermediate technology.' Such technology is neither so advanced that it is beyond the means of LDCs, nor so primitive. Capital-intensive technology produced by the developed industrialised nations is quite inappropriate in LDCs. Again, primitive labour-intensive technology has also become obsolete as well as inappropriate even in these countries. Thus, an intermediate technology or the appropriate technology seems to be more ideal for LDCs. This technology in these countries can be employed in a more efficient manner. Adoption of 'walking on two legs' technique in China under Mao's regime is the classic example of intermediate technology.

QUESTIONS WITH ANSWER-HINTS

Long-Answer Questions

1. Trace the origin of economic planning.
   Ans. 2.2
2. What is meant by economic planning? Discuss the nature and scope of economic planning in different economic systems.
   Ans. 2.3 and 2.3.1
3. Discuss the necessity of economic planning.
   Or
   What role does economic planning play in a developing deregulated liberal economy?
   Or
   Give economical and institutional arguments towards the rationale of planning in the present framework of a liberal economy.
   Ans. 2.3.2
4. Discuss the relative arguments for and against balanced growth and unbalanced growth strategy.
   Ans. 2.5, 2.5.1 and 2.5.2
5. What is understood by balanced growth? Is this growth strategy fault-free?
   Ans. 2.5.1
6. What is meant by 'linkage effect' in economic development? Can unbalanced growth be a strategy of economic growth in developing countries?—Explain.
   Ans. 2.5.2
7. Discuss the role of agriculture in a poor developing economy as a development strategy.
   Ans. 2.6 and 2.6.1
8. Why is industrial development preferred over agrcultural development? Justify your arguments in the light of a developing economy.
   Ans. 2.6.2
9. Agriculture and industry are not to be viewed as alternatives since one sector pulls the other. How do you explain the interdependence between agriculture and industry?
   Ans. 2.6.3
10. Discuss the role of technology in promoting agricultural development of a country.
    Ans. 2.7.1
11. Should countries like India always choose labour-intensive techniques of production?
    Or
    The choice between labour-intensive and capital-intensive techniques of production

involves conflict between employment and output and between employment and saving. Explain your answer as suggested by A. Sen and M. Dobb.

Ans. 2.8

Short-Answer Questions

1. How is economic planning defined?
   Ans. 2.3
2. What is the role of planning in a mixed economy?
   Ans. 2.3.2
3. What is the 'equity' argument of planning?
   Ans. 2.3.1
4. Explain the 'market failure' argument of planning.
   Ans. 2.3.2
5. What is 'big push'?
   Ans. 2.5
6. Smallness of the market acts as an impediment to development.—Explain.
   Ans. 2.5.1
7. What is meant by 'indivisibility' on the supply and demand side of the development process?
   Ans. 2.5.1
8. Discuss two important arguments for adopting balanced growth doctrine of development strategy.
   Ans. 2.5.1
9. What is meant by unbalanced growth?
   Ans. 2.5.2
10. Define social overhead capital and directly productive activities as envisaged in the unbalanced growth doctrine.
    Ans. 2.5.2
11. Define the path of development via (i) excess capacity, and (ii) shortage.
    Ans. 2.5.2
12. Define forward and backward linkages with examples.
    Ans. 2.5.2
13. Explain two arguments against the unbalanced growth doctrine.
    Ans. 2.5.2
14. Justify giving priority to agriculture in the development process.
    Ans. 2.6.1
15. Agriculture contributes towards economic development through 'market contribution'.—Explain.
    Ans. 2.6.1
16. Justify your arguments for industrialisation of a developing economy.
    Ans. 2.6.2
17. How do you establish 'production linkage' between agriculture and industry?
    Ans. 2.6.3
18. Explain the 'saving-investment linkage' between the agrictural and industrial sectors.
    Ans. 2.6.3
19. How does technology play a role in agriculture?
    Ans. 2.7.1
20. Define labour-intensive and capital-intensive techniques of production.
    Ans. 2.8
21. Give two important arguments for and against labour-intensive technology.
    Ans. 2.8
22. Give two important arguments for and against capital-intensive technology.
    Ans. 2.8
23. What is meant by 'intermediate technology'?
    Ans. 2.8
24. What type of techniques of production would you recommend for the agricultural sector?
    Ans. 2.7.1

CHAPTER 3

Population Growth and Problems of Capital Formation

3.1 Introduction

Economics as a discipline has a long history, while development economics—a subset—is the mid-20th century product. It studies why some countries are developed and why some are poor. Its major concern is to understand why so many people across the globe live below the poverty line. Economics as a discipline attempted to explore such differences between countries. Unfortunately, classical economists like A. Smith, D. Ricardo, T. R. Malthus, etc., thought that in the long run some countries would land in a situation called 'stationary state'. To reach this situation, population increase is thought to be a by-product. But such a gloomy picture could not appear in industrial economies where it is the population growth that stimulated 'industrial revolution'. Thus, the relationship between population growth and economic development is multi-dimensional. It has been estimated that between 1960 and 2005, as population in sub-Saharan Africa grew by excess of 3 p.c., if not negative, the economic growth rate came to be pretty low. But in high income countries population growth rate during the same time came to be even less than 1 p.c., economic growth rate in these countries was much higher—not comparable to many developing countries.

One of the central objectives of this chapter is to analyse the role between population growth and economic development. Earlier, development and population growth were linked to each other. Population growth contributes to development. In the 20th centrury, population growth to be came delinked from development—especially in developing countries. Thus, the relationship of population growth to economic development is complex as well as interesting. This chapter begins with showing this kind of relationship between population growth and economic development.

This Chapter puts emphasis not only on the two dimensions of population and development but also on 'demographic transition'—the age distribution of population. Such transition then analyses dependency ratio of the population—a ratio between dependent population and working population.

In Chapter 1 we listed several factors that contribute towards development. These are : natural resources, human resources, capital accumulation, technology, and institutional environement. One of the important features of low income countries is the low level of accumulated capital. Capital accumulation helps poor countries to move on to a higher growth path. Higher standard of living enjoyed by the advanced countries is attributed to the availability of machines, buildings, and overhead capital that have accumulated over time. Another important issue that requires our attention is the mobilisation of domestic resources to augment the formation of capital. This chapter then outlines the various sources of (domestic) capital formation. However, poor developing countries seek foreign assistance to supplement domestic capital formation.

3.2 Different Views on the Role of Population Growth

Population growth plays a conflicting role in the development process of a country. It helps economic development and it retards economic development.

To the Greek philosophers, about 2,500 years ago, population growth was undesirable as it adversely affects economic development. Plato (427-347 B.C.) suggested that the member of citizens of a country should be kept fixed at 5,040 on the ground that this number is divisible by any number from 1 to 12 except 11. Aristotle (384-322 B.C.) also argued in the same vein. He desired that the country's population must not exceed beyond certain level. Sir William Petty presented an optimistic outlook on population growth. Adam Smith also regarded the growth of population as the basis of wealth. But the classical economists, especially T. R. Malthus[1], sounded an alarm bell of rising population growth in a country. However, Mathus' argument came under severe attack at the hands of Karl Marx and F. Engles.

In the following sections, we will discuss the benefits—population growth helps development—and costs—population growth slows development—of population growth.

3.3 Relationship between Population Growth and Economic Development

The relationship between population growth and economic development may be summarised in the words of Robert McNamara—the past president of the World Bank. He described it as 'the most delicate and difficult issue of our era… It is overlaid with emotion. It is controversial. It is subtle. Above all, it is immesurably complex.'

Mao Zedong once remarked that "A country's greatest wealth is its people." On the some vein, the then Prime Minister Mr. Pitt of England declared in the 18th century : "A man could enrich his country by producing a number of children, even if the whole family were paupers." All these suggest that not only there is no conflict between population growth and economic development but also an increase in population is necessary for increase in wealth and development. But, antithesis to this is the Malthusian version which regards population growth as the number one barrier to economic development. Neo-Malthusians attribute all of the world's modern problems of underdevelopment to massive population growth.

Thus, there is a conflicting role between population growth and economic development. It can act both as a stimulus and as an impediment to growth and development. Such conflicting roles suggest that the relationship between population and economic development is intricate, complex and interesting.

Benefits of Population Growth : Population growth helps the process of development in the following ways. *First*, an increasing population means an increase in the number of working population who can function as active participants in the process of economic growth and development. It is to be noted that labour, assisted by necessary tools and implements, was always and still is the greatest productive asset of nations. A growing population leads to an increase in total output. The sheer arithmetical increase in population creates work as well as incentives for production that impacts upon output and productivity quite favourably. Indeed, this argument is empirically important in addition to theoretical reasoning.

Secondly, a growing population means a growing market for most goods and services and we know that division of labour is limited by the extent of the market. A potentially expanding market may stimulate entrepreneurs to invest more and more in capital goods and machinery. Business activity will be spurred as a consequence. And more income and employment will be created in the process. Moreover, it will provide an outlet for the products of efficient, large scale, mass-production industries. The net effect may be favourable to the country.

1. Probably, T. R. Malthus was the world's first professional economist—the first economics professor of modern history and political economy in a college.

Of course the size of the domestic market of a country does not only depend on the number, but also on the per capita income level. But given the same low level of income per head, a country like India offers a more favourable environment for setting up heavy capital goods industries which depends so much on the economies of scale for their success. In contrast, a thickly populated country with a small population base such as Sri Lanka seems to be especially handicapped by the small size of its domestic market.

Population growth has been a favourable factor in stimulating growth in many a country in the last two centuries, when vast areas remained largely unsettled. Even in the USA, in the 1930s, it was apprehended that a slowing down of the rate of population growth would lead to long run (secular) stagnation. The vast secular boom in the post-industrial revolution England had been 'largely induced by the unparalleled rise in population'.

Thirdly, an arithmetic increase in population permits in reaping economies of scale in production, greater division of labour, extension of the market, etc.

The World Bank in its 1984 *World Development Report* argues : '...there is little doubt that the key to economic growth is people, and through people the advance of human knowledge. Per capita measures of income should not be used to imply that the denominator, people, contributes nothing to the numerator, total income. Nor is population growth in itself the main cause of natural resource problems—air pollution, soil degra-dation, even food availability."

Costs of Population Growth : But Malthusians and neo-Malthusians think otherwise. *First,* they argue that population growth negatively affects economic development. Their argument is based on the law of diminishing returns in agriculture. Population growth acts as a barrier to economic development since the growth of population grows never in commensurate with the growth of food supply. Actually speaking, as the rate of growth of population exceeds the rate of production, economic development is hampered. A growing population, within a limited geographical area, usually puts heavy pressure on the existing factor endowments, especially natural resources of the country. Moreover, if the society has a limited stock of capital, labour may have to be substituted for capital, in which case the production function will exhibit the law of diminishing returns. Diminishing returns may become a serious problem if population growth is rapid.

However, empirical evidence suggests that technological change—or the so-called green revolution in agriculture in different LDCs—has greatly offset the effects of diminishing returns in agriculture and the spectre of food problem and its aftermath (huger, famine, etc.,) in most of these countries has virtually vanished. So, one must not view that population growth badly affects economic development.

Secondly, based on the Indian experience, Ansle Coale and E. M. Hoover drew attention to the likely adverse effects of population growth on savings and capital formation through the following effects: the *age-dependency effect*, the *capital-shallowing effect*, and the *investment diversion effect*.

It is said that a rapid population growth causes an increase in *dependency ratio*—a high ratio of non-working population to working wage people or *active* population. When the number of dependents or the ratio of consumers (non-producers) to producers increase, there occurs a diversion of income from savings to consumption and a fall in per capita income. But anti-Mathusians talk in a different vein. They argue that many young children contribute directly to parents' income by working in farms and off-farm sectors. Further, additional mouths in the low income families tend to encourage people to work more. In this way, children themselves contribute to household and saving. Anyway, the impact on household saving can be negative, negligible or positive—the issue needs to be settled by empirical investigation.

The *capital-shallowing effect* states that a rapid population growth lowers the ratio of capital to labour or workforce thus works with less capital and consequently the poor rate of savings. This then reduces productivity of labour. As children remain engaged in productive works, the family may experience an increase in saving. Under the circumstance, the *capital-shallowing effect* may remain inoperative. High economic growth is accompanied with overall high savings ratio in many developing countries.

The *investment-diversion effect* states that, because of rapid population growth a country's scarce resources get diverted away to the so-called unproductive sectors of health, education and social services from the more productive growth-oriented sectors. This logic assumes that the expenditures on human capital are unproductive. Educated and healthy people are viewed as one of the essential ingredients of economic development. Indeed, there are high returns to investment in human capital.

Anyway, empirical research does not confirm the Coale-Hoover thesis.

Thirdly, Mathusians are convinced that population growth badly affects food supplies. To them, the chronic food problem experienced by many poor developing economies is often attributed to rapid population. It is because of 'natural limits' in agriculture population growth would overtake food supply output, thereby leading to famine, hunger, malnutrition, etc.

But the evidence tells a different story. Because of the introduction of green revolution technology in agriculture, yields have increased to such an extent that many countries, including India, have now been exporting foodgrains. Unfortunately, the present global world is highly unequal. We see an abnormally high level of malnourished children; starvation and famines occassionally visit in many countries. However, this must not be attributed to a mismatch between a high population growth and food supply. This can be referred to as the unequal distribution of purchasing power among different groups of population. Hunger and famine, according to A. Sen, is due to 'entitlement failure', and not the food availabilities as such.

Fourthly, the question of unemployment and underemployment has assumed serious proportion, particularly in LDCs, because of rapid population growth. But whether population growth is responsible for unemployment problem cannot be said definitively since no such statistical strict correlation is observed. In fact, it is the technology that determines the absorption of unemployed labour force. The experiences of Korea and Taiwan tell that economic development in these countries proceeded successfully despite high population growth.

In recent years, as agriculture is becoming more and more unprofitable, the issue of engaging surplus labour has become a concern to the Government of India. Agriculture's contribution towards GDP growth is not only falling but the absorbtive capacity of agriculture is also falling. This development, consequent upon Malhusian pressure, has been forcing many farm people to migrate to towns and urban areas in search of employment. However, this argument is a faulty one. Economic development is associated with declining importance of agriculture. Thus, the migration of the productive farm workers in other sectors needs to be attributed to the policy failure and not to the population pressure.

Finally, neo-Malthusians argue that excessive population growth and massive poverty in LDCs have greatly damaged the ecological balance by deforestation and land degradation. Consequently, these countries suffer badly from a variety of environmental hazards. Such canard is made by developed countries who are to be condemned outright for destroying ecological balance.

But today the debate has shifted from population pressure to climate change and environment—perceived as a great threat to humanity. The current ecological crisis is caused by human economic activity or anthropogenic. The way an economy is organised is rather 'inherently suicidal'. The whole world is burning fosssil fuels to drive the growth economy. Carbon dioxide emission is at its highest level. All these may be linked to a developed rich economy addicted to growth. The US economist Kenneth Boulding made the following statement : "Anyone who believes that exponential growth can go on forever in a finite world is either a madman or an economist."

Conclusion : Considering the above-mentioned plus and minus points, economists conclude that hindrances to economic development in LDCs are not to be attributed to population growth. The greatest and real obstacle to development is underdevelopment. Potentialities for development are adequate. By designining their development programmes, LDCs can raise their levels of income and living standards. Further, they argue that there is no population bomb in these countries. The myth of over-population causing underdevelopment should be given up in any analysis of economic development. It is not to be accepted that a slowing down of population increase might contribute substantially to our development prospects. So what is sauce for a goose may not be the sauce for a gander!

The moot point is that population growth may be either favourable or unfavourable to economic development, depending on where, when, and how it takes place.

Today, an international consensus has been reached. A country may strike a higher growth and development if population increases slowly. No one should exaggerate either the beneficial or the unfavourable effects of population growth on economic development. However, it is to be kept in mind three important issues. *First*, all problems of levels of living, inequality and poverty are not to be necessarily linked with high population growth. *Secondly*, population growth must involve the quality of life, and not the quantity perse. *Thirdly*, but truly, rapid population growth makes prospect for development rather remote. All these then demand an appropriate economic and social policy so as to improve the well-being of the future world populations in a sustainable way.

3.4 Effects of Economic Development on Population Growth

We should not miss the point that there is a two-way causation. Population growth affects economic development; and, in its turn, economic development affects population growth. So far, we have studied the effects of population growth on economic development. We now take up the effects of economic development on population growth.

The last two centuries have witnessed a fall in the death rate and the consequent growth of population in today's economically advanced countries. The birth rate also fell. Economic development brought in its wake higher standards of living, better food, adequate clothing and shelter, as also protection from the natural disasters of drought and famine. There also occurred improvement in medical facilities and health care. All these led to a fall in infant mortality and healthier people and longer life-expectancy. These were closely related to the economic progress that these countries were making. "In general, therefore, ... the modern increase in population in the developing countries of Europe and North America occurred along with and was really part and parcel of a more general process of rising living standards, industrialisation, and technological progress." (R. T. Gill).

When we turn to the *population explosion* problem of developing countreis, we see that these countries have shown very little economic growth. Yet their populations are expanding rapidly. These countries are importing Western technology to start modern industrialisation programmes but are unable to emulate or import the growth process itself. The spread of Western techniques of health care, sanitation and medicine to such countries has brought about sharply falling death rates and rapid population growth. But the standard of living is yet to achieve any appreciable improvement. The other accompaniments of economic development are also conspicuous by their absence.

The above point has been highlighted by Stephen Enke : "High fertility rates have the demographic effect of increasing the proportionate number of children. A country with a crude birth rate of over 40/1,000 a year is likely to have 40% of its population under 15 years of age. Youngsters under 15 years of age are significant consumers but insignificant producers. Large families including many children with consequent low incomes per family member are poor contributors to domestic saving. Low savings per capita are associated with young population and high fertility."

The point is that modern acceleration of population growth is largely attributable to the general and technological expansion of the West. But it is no longer true to assume that economic progress is a necessary condition for population expansion. Thanks to the achievements of modern science, rapidly growing numbers are the rule in most countries where poverty for the existing masses remains the most outstanding fact of economic life.

There is no doubt that population growth and the associated increase in labour force have been positive factors in stimulating economic growth. A large labour force means more productive manpower, while a larger size of population increases the potential size of the domestic market. However, whether rapidly growing labour force in developing countries exerts a positive or negative influence on economic progress depends on the ability of the economic system to absorb and productively employ these added workers. This, in its turn, is conditioned by the rate and type of capital accumulation and the availability of other complimentary factors such as managerial and administrative skills.

3.5 A Note on Malthusian Trap/Low Level Equilibrium Trap

An underdeveloped economy reels under the vicious circle of poverty. How an underdeveloped economy is caught in the low level equilibrium trap has been lucidly explained by R. Nelson. His model tries to integrate population and development theories by recognising the interdependence between population growth, per capita income, and national income growth. Nelson's thesis is based on two propositions :

(i) Nelson and H. Leibenstein put forward the proposition that population will increase when per capita income of a country rises above the minimum subsistence level. (This follows from the Malthusian theory.) But they believed that while initially population grows rapidly with a rise in per capita income, there is an upper limit to the rate of population growth, say at about 3 p.c. per annum. Beyond this limit, a rise in per capita income will not be accompanied by a further rise in the rate of growth of population. On the contrary, the rate of growth of population may even fall with every increase in per capita income. (At high levels of income, people want

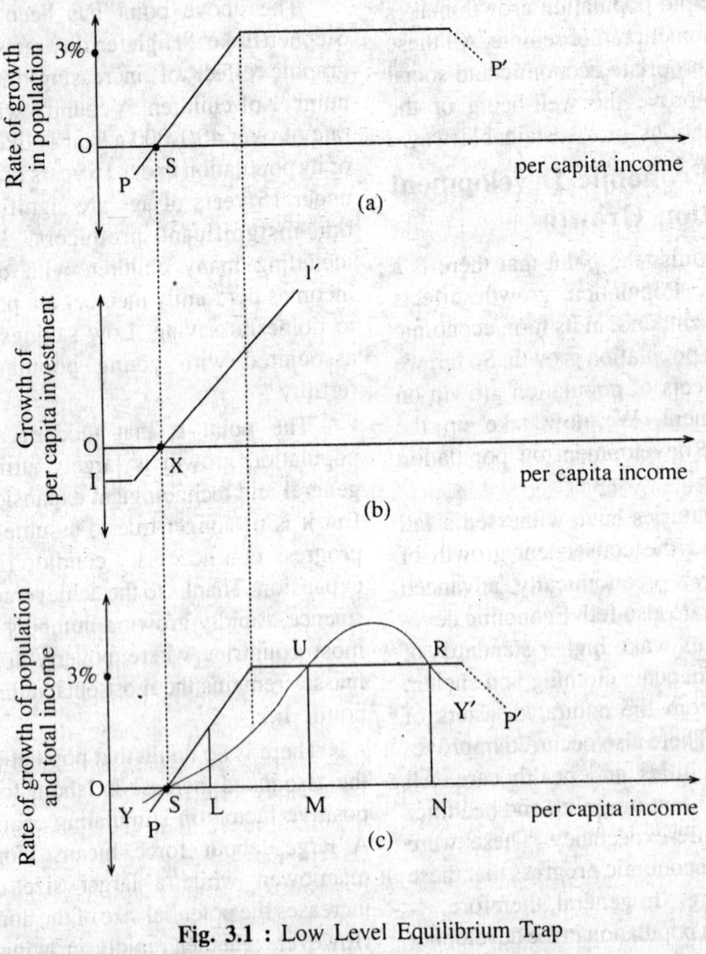

Fig. 3.1 : Low Level Equilibrium Trap

to keep the size of the family in check so as to maintain a high standard of living.)

(ii) The second proposition is based on Nurkse's concept of the vicious circle of poverty. Nurkse pointed out that at low levels of per capita income, people are too poor to save and invest much. This low rate of investment, in its turn, will result in a low rate of growth but as the per capita income rises above a certain minimum level at which there is zero saving a rising proportion of the total income will be saved and invested (because the marginal propensity to consume falls and the marginal propensity to save rises with an increase in income above a certain level). This will, ultimately, lead to a higher rate of growth in income.

Fig. 3.1 having three interconnected parts, illustrates the above argument. In Fig. 3.1(a) we measure per capita income on the horizontal axis and the rate of growth of population (in percentage term) on the vertical axis. The point S denotes the minimum subsistence level of per capita income. Below this level of income (i.e., to the left of point S) population will be decreasing, and at point S, it will remain unchanged. However, as we move to the right of S, denoting a rise in the per capita income above the subsistence level, population will increase (as is shown by the PP′ curve) until it reaches the upper limit of 3 p.c. after which it may gradually decline.

In Fig. 3.1 (b) we measure the level of per capita income on the horizontal axis, and, on the vertical axis, we measure per capita investment out of savings at different levels of per capita income. The point X denotes that level of income at which saving is zero. If income is less than this, saving and investment will be negative. Society will have to live on past capital. But as the economy moves to the right of X, denoting a rise in per capita income above the zero saving level, the per capita rate of investment, the II′ curve, will rise. And this process will continue. As we move to the right of X, a rising proportion of the total income will be saved and invested. This actually happens beyond the point at which the rate of growth in population levels off at 3 p.c.

In Fig. 3.1(c), the vertical axis measures the percentage rate of growth of income and population while the percentage rate of growth in total income at the different levels of per capita income have been shown along the horizontal axis. The point S (equal to X) on the horizontal axis represents the *low level equilibrium trap*. It denotes the intersec-tion of the PP′ curve (showing population growth) with the income growth curve YY′ at the zero rate of growth. If we start from this, for any small rise in the level of per capita income, say SL, the rate of growth of population will exceed that of total income. This will drive the per capita income back to its previous stable equilibrium level of OS.

In the language of H. Myint : "This low level equilibrium trap will be stronger the more quickly the rate of population growth responds to a given rise in per capita income and the more slowly the rate of growth in total income responds to a increase in investment, due, say, to initial population pressure on land."

Now, if it is possible somehow to raise the level of per capita income by a discontinuous jump by more than SM, i.e., if we can raise the growth rate of per capita income beyond the population barrier of 3 p.c., then we should be able to reach a new unstable equilibrium at U. This increase in per capita income, in the absence of a further rise in the rate of population growth, would then lead to a cumulative process of rising income until possibly it reached a new stable equilibrium point R with a per capita income level of ON.

This *critical minimum effort* or *big push* theory provided us a clear idea of the vicious circle of low per capita income. The origin of *big push* theories of development and the concept of a *critical minimum effeort* is the belief that, to escape from Nelson's trap, it will be necessary to raise the per capita income above OM in one go.

3.6 The Vicious Circle of Poverty and the Scarcity of Capital

Many orthodox economists explain the state of underdevelopment in terms of the so-called population explosion in developing countries. But the relationship between population growth and economic development is complex—it advances development and it retards development. Most economists argue that the poor developing countries suffer from the shortages of physical capital, savings and investment. This amounts to suggest that economic growth is a function of the 'capital formation quotient'. Further, there are quite a large number of economists who believe that poverty is the basic cause of underdevelopment. In addition, there are technological gaps in poor developing countries that also explain underdevelopment. Underdeveloped countries are also characterised by many socio-cultural obstacles.

It is, thus, clear that no single factor can be held responsible for retarding growth and underdevelopment of the poor LDCs. Many of the factors work in tandem and keep these countries in a perpetual state of underdevelopment. To break this deadlock, many economists believe that an increase in capital accumulation is a necessary—if not sufficient—condition for development. Before explaining the investment requirements to achieve a growth rate of national income and outlining the various sources of capital formation, we like to understand the notion of *vicious circle of poverty*. Ragnar Nurkse in the 1950s articulated that poverty of the poor countries may be attributed to the lack of capital formation.

The vicious circle argument : Capital accumulation is believed to be an escape route from the so-called vicious circle of poverty—a circle of low productivity, leading to a small real income and a low saving and capital accumulation leading to low productivity. The source of vicious circle of poverty can thus be traced to low productivity. The crucial issue is how the vicious circle is broken and, ultimately, turned into a 'virtuous circle'.

Anyway, continuous and rapid economic growth is a historical abnormality. Therefore, any overall approach to development must take note of the reality, i.e., the various obstacles to growth as well as the persistence of stagnation over a long period of time. The most fashionable concept here is the vicious circle of poverty—a concept introduced by Ragnar Nurkse and others. A less developed country is caught in the vicious circle of poverty.

The vicious circle argument holds that conditions in LDCs are such that economic development is impossible. To explain this vicious circle argument, one often uses the notion of a poor man. A poor man, because of very low income, is underfed and under-nourished. Underfeeding as well as under-nourishment makes him weak and becomes susceptible to sickness and diseases. A poor man then earns less as his capacity to earn is also low due to sickness or poor health. Thus, a man is sick because he is poor. Or a man is poor because he is sick.

The implication is clear. It assumes that people of less developed countries save little or nothing since they are poor. Since savings are low, investment is low. Low investment means low productivity levels, and, with low productivity levels, people will always remain poor. Other elements of poverty then appear and become self-reinforcing. For instance, low income is accompanied with poor or low level of education and health. These, in turn, fail to incentivise technological advancement. What is important is that poor countries that are strongly influenced by the vicious cycles can get caught in a *poverty trap.*

The basic logic of this vicious circle argument is that the greatest obstacle towards the development of an economy is poverty. The primary causes of underdevelopment are so intimately connected that they together form a circle which is vicious. Ragnar Nurkse explains that the vicious circle implies a circular constellation of forces tending to act and react upon one another in such a way as to keep a poor country in a state of poverty. The entire argument is summed up in Nurkse's words : "A country is poor, because it is poor." Or "Because it is poor, the country does not develop; because it does not develop, it remains poor."

The vicious circle argument is often explained from the supply side and the demand side of capital. The supply of capital is governed by the ability and willingness to save, the demand for capital is governed by the incentives to invest. Nurkse says : "On both sides of the problem of capital formation in poor countries a vicious circle exists."

Let us first explain the supply side of capital. A poor country saves little because of poor income. As a result, it experiences shortage of capital for developmental activities. Lack of capital supports the labour-intensive technique of production. This technique of production is less productive. In other words, a poor country experiences low productivity. And low income is the result of low productivity. The supply side has been aptly summarised by P. A. Samuelson : "They (the underdevelopd countries) cannot get their heads above water because their production is so low that they can spare nothing for capital formation by which their standard of living can be raised." This sort of vicious circle may be represented diagrammatically (Fig. 3.2).

Now, from the demand side of capital, one can explain the vicious circle argument. The logic is : In a poor country, demand for capital is less

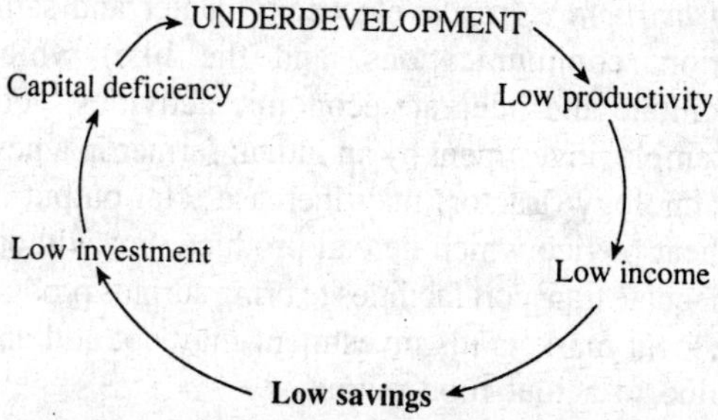

Fig. 3.2 : The Vicious Circle : Supply Side

because of low investment which is the result of low purchasing power of masses. In other words, low income means limited market opportunities. Low purchasing power or limited market for goods tells on investment—which becomes low. Low investment now spells low income. Thus, underdevelopment perpetuates and the poor country is caught in low income equilibrium. The low level of income is a point that is common to both the circles. This is shown in Fig. 3.3.

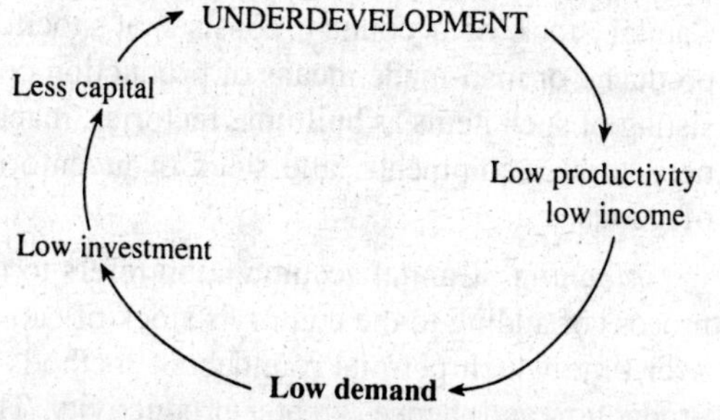

Fig. 3.3 : The Vicious Circle : Demand Side

It is thus clear that poverty is the cause of poverty and the entire logic is cumulative. In other words, poor countries are held down to their low levels of per capita incomes by "interlocking vicious circles". Self-perpetuating poverty and deprivation get transmitted from one generation to the next in a poor country. Because of poor income of poor people, children start school at a disadvantage and may receive little support from their parents. With little qualifications they cannot get decent jobs and good wages. Thus, they remain poor. "They will probably pass on to their children this inheritance of low wages, poor housing, ignorance and perhaps violence. Poverty is seen in these terms as the result of particular qualities of those in poverty, without reference to the social institutions of political structure under which it exists."

Interlocking vicious cycles may be presented in another way (see Fig. 3.4).

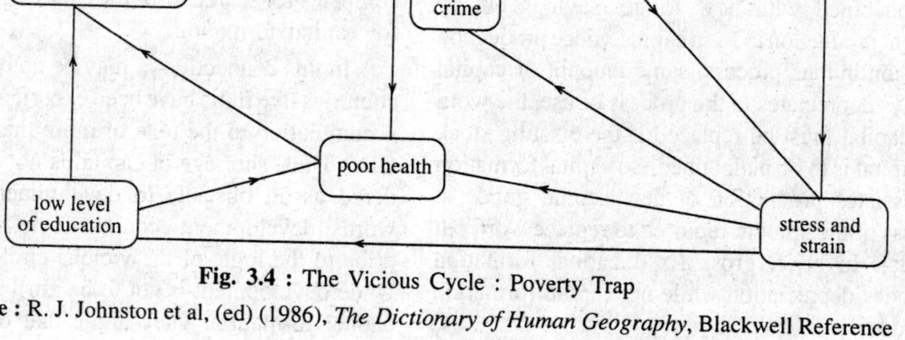

Fig. 3.4 : The Vicious Cycle : Poverty Trap

Source : R. J. Johnston et al, (ed) (1986), *The Dictionary of Human Geography*, Blackwell Reference

3.7 Capital Formation

Labour is abundant while capital is scarce in LDCs. The simplest way to view economic growth is the shifting of the production possibility boundary. Such increases in output can be attributed to either increases in the country's available resources or technical progress. The standard wheels that operate in every country are land, labour (including human capital) and capital which is defined as a produced means of production. Capital stock of a country consists of stock of produced or man-made means of production consisting of such items as building, factories, machinery, tools, equipments and stock of inventories of goods.

Meaning : Capital accumulation refers to the process of adding to the country's stock of capital over time which permits roundabout methods of production and, hence, greater productivity. This then enhances future income streams to society and consequently raises future consumption.

It is "the process of adding to our stock of machinery, tools, buildings, and so on, over time. If our stock of capital at the end of the year is larger than it was at the beginning, the difference represents the amount of capital we have accumulated during the year." It also goes by the name *investment.* Annual net investment is the addition to society's capital stock in an accounting year.

In a fundamental sense, capital formation is possible when a society produces a surplus of consumer goods sufficient to satisfy the wants of the workers engaged in producing capital, i.e., producing goods which are not themselves consumed during the period. That is to say, capital formation is the difference between production and consumption. The problem of capital formation is concerned with how to get savings out of current production to form capital. Since production is a continuous process, same amount of capital always depreciates in the process of use, the worn out capital must be replaced if the existing stock of capital is to be maintained. So capital formation necessiates production of new capital goods in excess of the amount required to replace worn out capital. In brief, gross fixed capital formation includes depreciation while net capital formation excludes it.

In the words of Todaró : "Capital accumulation results when some proportions of present income are saved and invested in order to augment future outputs and incomes." New factories, machinery, plant and equipments and materials increase the physical capital stock of a nation and these vast array of capital make it possible to expand the level of output of a country. These *directly productive investments* are supplemented by "investments in what is often known as *social and economic infrastructure* (roads, electricity, water and sanitation, communications, and the like) which facilitate and integrate economic activities." For example, investment by an Indian farmer in a new technology (tractor) may increase total output of wheat or rice which he can produce, but without adequate transport facilities to bring surplus product in local markets his investment may not add any value to actual food output.

However, capital in a country is formed by foregoing present consumption and diverting these resources to the production of future wealth. Thus, during the process of capital accumulation, one has to make a choice between present output and future output : the less a country produces for current consumption, the larger of its resources are utilised for capital formation. And, ultimately, capital formation triggers future consumption.

But LDCs are so poor that they stay at the subsistence level of consumption. It is absolutely impossible on the part of the poor people who form the majority to curtail consumption. Thus, while in developed industrial countries 20 p.c. to 30 p.c. of income are channelled into capital formation through the saving-investment process, many of the LDCs struggle hard to save and invest even 10-15 p.c. of their national income. The urgency of fulfilling immediate consumption competes for scarce resources, leaving little scope for capital formation.

In this connection, it may be noted that some countries like India have been experiencing capital accumulation to the tune of more than 30 p.c. of GDP. Thus, shortage of capital is not to be considered as an obstacle to development. In other words, development economists no longer subscribe to the logic of the vicious circle argument. Underdevelopment is not to be attributed to poor capital formation. They argue that other factors like poor quality of institutions and governance are the prime causes of failure to develop many developing countries. Even then, the importance of capital accumulation is undeniable.

3.7.1 Importance of Capital Formation

Capital accumulation plays a very important role in the process of economic development of a poor country. According to Nurkse, the vicious circle of poverty in poor LDCs can be broken through capital formation. The importance of capital formation for increasing production and productivity can be traced to the writings of early history of economic thought. In rich countries the amount of capital per head is large while in poor countries it is small. Capital accumulation sets off rich from poor countries in the modern age and the industrial era in general from the past history of the world. The importance of capital formation as a kingpin of economic development is clear from the following facts :

First, capital formation is required to provide a growing population with more necessary facilities of tools and machinery of production. All these tools and implements contribute directly to productive process. These facilities may take the form of tangible physical capital like factories, machinery, equipments in both industry and irrigation for agricultural production. It also takes the form of social overheads : investments in roads, transport and communication, health and education, etc. Economic development is impossible in the absence of these crucial elements.

Secondly, capital accumulation itself serves as an important vehicle of technical progress—the improvement in the art of production. The British industrial revolution was the product of improved technology. Technology provides the benefits of specialisation, shorter working hours, and the creation of skilled jobs, large scale production. Capital accumulation is similarly the handmaiden of technological progress. A. K. Cairncross adds : "Development as an on-going process rests on the constant injection of new technology and on the capacity to generate and absorb technical change."

Thirdly, as the facilities per head of the working population rise, it increases human skills and capabilities which are examples of human capital. Both education and measures to improve health care are two important forms of human capital formation. Education improves the quality of labour as well as the quality of physical capital. The capacity to absorb physical capital is indeed limited by investment in human capital that improves the future growth performance of an economy.

Finally, a rapid rate of capital accumulation leads to an increase in the supply of tools and machinery per worker. Output per worker can be increased if we devote more time and labour to the production of more capital goods.

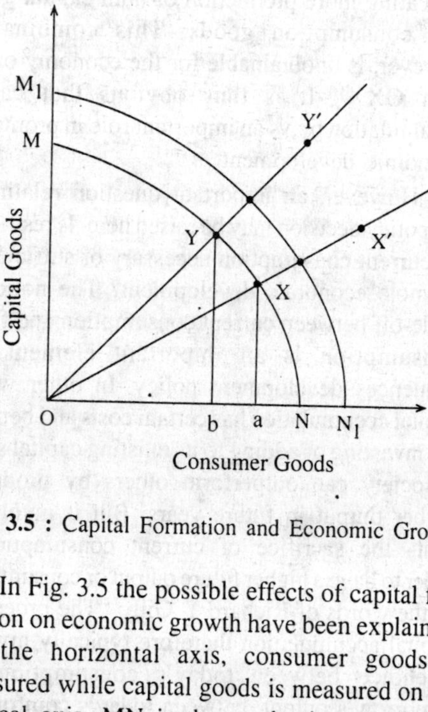

Fig. 3.5 : Capital Formation and Economic Growth

In Fig. 3.5 the possible effects of capital formation on economic growth have been explained. On the horizontal axis, consumer goods is measured while capital goods is measured on the vertical axis. MN is the production possibility boundary that an economy can produce various combinations of both the goods with the given inputs. Lines OXX′ and OYY′ represent growth paths. Obviously, OYY′ line describes a higher growth rate compared to OXX′ line. Suppose the country is initially producing at point X on the MN curve. The rate of annual consumption of consumer goods is now assumed to be OA. If productive capacity of the economy grows at 2 p.c. p.a., the production possibility frontier then shifts outwards by the same percentage to M_1N_1. If the country decides to employ its resources to the production of capital goods by the same proportion its growth path will be represented by OXX′.

But for capital formation what is required is the sacrifice of current consumption. Let consumption decline by the amount *ab*. This means an increase in capital formation. This then shifts production point to Y. Faced with more capital goods the growth rate of the country increases. After a lapse of some years, the economy's growth path will be represented by OYY′ line. Thus, a lower volume of current consumption causes a rapid economic growth rate—the production possibility frontier would then shift to point Y′ indicating more production of both capital goods and consumption goods. This combination, however, is unobtainable for the economy on the path OXX′. It is thus obvious that capital accumulation plays an important role in promoting economic development.

However, an important question relating to the policy decision may be raised here. Is restriction on current consumption necessary or sufficient to promote economic development? The notion of trade-off between current consumption and future consumption is an important element that influences development policy. In other words, capital accumulation has certain costs and benefits. By investing or adding to its existing capital stock, a society can outperform others by producing higher output in future years. But it involves a cost—the sacrifice of current consumption in order to have a higher future output or consumption. In the words of Richard T. Gill : "The process of capital accumulation therefore typically involves a choice between today's consumption and tomorrow's output, between today's comfort and tommorrow's economic growth."

3.7.2 The Processes or the Stages of Capital Formation

Capital accumulation involves the mobilisation of an economic surplus to increase the stock of future output and consumption. The question then arises : how is such capital to be created or increased, or in other words, how is capital formation accelerated? As capital formation is the result of savings, it, therefore, depends on savings out of current income. It is better to indicate the three essential stages or process of capital formation. How much capital will, in fact, be accumulated depends in the first instance on how much is saved. These stages of capital formation are : (i) creation of savings, (ii) mobilisation of savings through a wide range of different sources, and (iii) the act of investment itself, by which resources are used for increasing the capital stock.

Creation of savings : Capital formation depends first on saving—both private and government. The volume of saving or propensity to save depends on : (i) will to save, and (ii) power to save.

The desire to save or the will to save depends on a variety of motives. People want to remain prepared for unforeseen emergencies. They want to make provision for education and health. Many people save because they want to improve their position and status in life. Savings take place through the financial intermediaries. Anyway, the other motives behind the willingness to save are : (i) social and political conditions of the country, (ii) availability of financial infrastructures, (iii) the level of literacy of people while making financial transactions through financial intermediaries, (iv) the rate of interest on savings, etc.

However, the existence of the willingness to save is not sufficient to induce savings. There must also be the ability to save. Income is commonly regarded as the most important determinant of (private) saving. Governements also save out of receipts from taxation or from profit of nationalised enterprises. It also depends on the state of income distribution of a society—marginal propensity to save (MPS) is higher for the high income group while the marginal propensity to consume (MPC) is higher for the low income group. A society composed of a large number of poor people has the less potentiality in raising the aggregate savings.

It may be noted here that the volume of investment is handicapped by saving. Thus, the shortage of capital cannot be solved merely by increasing the supply of finance. The two important internal sources of saving are voluntary and involuntary. The volume of saving depends on how much an individual is willing to forego consumption. Such cut in consumption is not possible when the average income is low. In view of this, government may resort to forced saving through tax payments, inflationary policy, etc. But through taxes very little amount is collected when the community's income is low. Ability to pay taxes depends on the volume of income. Inflationary financing has dangers too.

Mobilisation or canalisation of savings : Mere creation of savings is not enough. The second stage involves mobilisation of savings for investment purposes. It depends on the existence of a well-organised banking and other financial institutions and capital market as well to serve as a conduit between savers and investors. As savers and investors are two different persons in the community, institutions like banks, postal savings bank, insurance companies, etc. help to mobilise savings of them and pass them on to investors.

Conversion of savings into capital assets : The third and the final stage of capital formation consists of actual investment of monetary savings or conversion of monetary savings into capital goods. The volume of investment depends on a variety of factors, like the size of the market (both domestic and external) for the outlet of goods and machinery produced, machinery, entrepreneurial skill, availability of critical infrastructures of power, road and transport, and, most importantly, government policies.

The role of government in the realm of capital accumulation should not be underestimated. In an LDC, the responsibility of the government in this area can never be minimised. In these countries, the rate of capital accumulation is low because of low level of income. Private businesses also exhibit their apathy towards larger investment, particularly in social overhead projects. In such situations, the government has to play a dominant role in increasing capital stock.

3.7.3 Sources of Capital Formation

Now we will concentrate on the various sources from which necessary savings can be mobilised for the purposes of investment. The sources of capital formation are primarily two—internal and external sources. The internal or domestic sources are voluntary reduction in consumption by households and enterprises, and involuntary cut in consumption through taxation, compulsory lending to the government, or inflation, absorption of underemployed labour into productive work, profits of government enterprises, etc. External sources of capital formation may come from the investment of foreign capital, restriction of consumption imports, or improvements in the country's terms of trade or good commercial policy. These sources of capital formation are :

Domestic Sources : (A) *Voluntary savings* : It has been stated that saving is necessary to fund investment. Savings in an economy comes from three sources : the household sector, the business sector, and the government. The nature of savings consists of three types—voluntary, involuntary, and forced.

Voluntary savings are the savings that come through self-imposed reductions in current consumption out of disposable income of both the household and the business sectors. Since income is the most important determinant of saving (or consumption) the voluntary reductions in consumption may not fructity if the average income is very low. It can, however, be reasonably expected that with the rise in income the marginal propensity to save will exceed the average propensity to save. Thus, in a poor country, voluntary household savings and business savings contribute little towards capital accumulation.

But, at the same time, it may be mentioned that inability to save consequent upon poor income is not a big constraint in developing countries. Voluntary reduction in consumption or an increase in saving may be made if efforts are made to attract more savings in a more productive way. For instance, various saving promotion schemes may be introduced so that people can be persuaded to save against bad days. Further, people may be induced to divert their savings made in speculative and unproductive investments like gifts of jewellery to gods into more productive as well as non-speculative activities.

However, in many poor economies, household saving is not too insignificant as it has been assumed here. For instance, gross domestic saving as a percent of GDP in India in 2008-09 stood at 32.5 p.c. of which household saving alone contributed 22.6 p.c. of GDP.

A. W. Lewis and R. Nurkse postulated that disguised unemployment is an important source of saving in LDCs. An underdeveloped economy is often characterised as a *labour-surplus* economy. Labour surplus or disguised unemployment means the existence of large population in the agicultural sector whose marginal product falls to zero. If these labour resources are transferred to the modern industrial sector, it then creates industrial surplus or profit that may be used for further growth and development. Lewis and Nurkse have suggested the use of unemployed or disguised unemployed workers in the industrial sector as well as various construction projects like road-irrigation works. In this way, additional permanent capital is formed. To quote Nurkse : "The state of disguised unemployment implies, at least, to some extent a disguised saving potential as well."

As things stand, the 'unproductive' surplus labourers on land are sustained or maintained by the 'productive' labourer engaged in the industrial sector or new capital projects. This then assumes that the transfer of labour from the rural sector is supported by productive members who do not increase their consumption. The productive labourers are thus making 'virtual' saving; they produce more than they consume. The scheme is apparently attractive as no one is required to curtail his consumption, but capital accumulation takes place via reallocation of labour. If productive peasants left behind on agriculture were to send their 'unproductive' colleagues to work on capital projects and if they continued to feed them there, then their *virtual* saving would become *effective* saving.

Thus the use of disguised unemployment for the accumulation of capital could be financed from within the system itself. This method has the obvious advantage that it makes use, at small cost, of resources that would otherwise be idle. Anyway, the potential is there, but it is difficult to apply.

(B) *Involuntary savings—Taxation* : There is another method of financing development from domestic sources is the taxation. Fiscal policy and taxation play two major roles in the financing of development. *First*, it helps in maintaining an economy at full employment so that the saving capacity of the econmy rises with the rise in per capita income. The *second* needs the designing of the tax policy in such a way that it raises the marginal propensity to save (MPS). It then appears that an appropriate taxation policy offers incentives to save and to work more.

The generation of additional saving through tax policy can take two main approaches—creation of tax incentives to encourage increased private saving and the use of tax instruments to reallocate investible resources to the public sector. If it is assumed that growth is impaired due to the lack of adequate incentives then the tax policy is to be designed in such a way that adequate concessions are granted so that incentives to work and save get boosted. But, if resources are inadequate then the poor LDCs should make effort to raise resources required for investment through taxation. Saving brought about by taxation is called *involuntary* or *forced* saving. This then forces people to consume less. Thus, taxes provide the most appro-priate instrument for increasing savings for capital formation.

However, the issue of raising revenue through taxation depends on a country's *taxation potential*. Potential of taxes in generating revenue resources depends mainly on people's income, the degree of inequality in the distribution of income, etc. For the most obvious reason, the actual ratio of tax revenue to national income is low in developing countries. Imposition of taxes in these countries results in the reduction of disposable income of taxpayers that adversely affects ability to work and save. As progressive tax rates penalise economic success it depletes potential sources of saving. Above all, if political leadership in a country is given by the rich, imposition of high tax rates on them will be wellnigh a difficult proposition. That is why agriculture in developing countries is undertaxed compared to the manufacturing and services sectors. In practice, land taxes contribute insignificant revenue.

But taxation as a method of development finance has its limits and difficulties. While involuntary savings may increase following a cut in consumption, voluntary savings may decline if people try to maintain their old consumption standards. This then reduces the volume of private savings. Moreover, all kind of taxes adversely affect the willingness and ability to work and save. Thus, while there is a great deal of necessity for raising revenues more by means of taxation, the obstacles to its effective realisation cannot be underestimated.

(C) *Inflationary finance* : If voluntary and involuntary savings are inadequate, inflationary finance then becomes the mechanism for capital accumulation. A government finances its expenditures by money creation as its revenue falls short of expenditure. When financing of expenditures by money creation is made there occurs an increase in aggregate spending. When idle productive capacity exists or if the country's resources are underemployed, increased spending may stimulate aggregate output till the full employment is reached. This kind of inflationary finance mechanism works in two ways :

First, investment can generate its saving by raising the income level when the economy operates below the state of full employment. *Secondly*, this method allows redistribution of income from poor fixed income-earners having a low MPS to rich persons with a high MPS when the economy reaches the full employment stage. As a result, aggregate savings of the community become large which can be used for capital formation to accelerate the level of development.

Most importantly, as soon as the state of full capacity is reached, deficit financing causes inflation to flare up. Inflation is now considered as the means through which resources are redistributed between consumption and investment. Deficit financing thus imposes 'forced' savings as deficit-led inflation tends to reduce consumption propensities of the community whose level of income rises less than proportionately to the increases in prices. This *forced* saving can be utilised for the production of capital goods. This then triggers economic development.

But deficit financing is self-defeating in nature as it tends to generate inflationary forces in the economy. The trouble lies with the 'dose' of inflation—a 'little' or a 'big' one. It is said that a mild inflation has an encouraging effect on national output. A high rate or an erratic rate of inflation distorts all economic calculations. It may distort the pattern of capital formation. It may encourage the flight of capital to abroad (tax-free havens) where people perk their money to have an assured profitable return on invested money. Further, in a situation of high rate of inflation, investment in plants and equipments by people becomes unattractive. On the contrary, investment tends to get channelised in diverse speculative activities. Thus funds collected through deficit financing ultimately become fewer than projected at the time of preparing deficit budget. Finally, the consequences of inflation for international trade and balance of payments also impose heavy economic costs. Because of inflation, imports rise and exports fall. Thus, a country not only looses foreign market following a fall in export but also the ability to import industrial products and capital goods suffers badly.

In view of these problems, it is argued that this kind of financing is an 'evil', but a 'necessary evil.' However, in the end, we like to add that there is conclusive evidence that inflation speeds or hampers development : growth is positively related to inflation up to a certain rate of inflation and then negatively related. To have a favourable impact of deficit financing on economic development, the magnitude of deficit financing and its phasing over the time horizon of development plan, it has to be kept within the 'safe' limits so that inflationary forces do not distort economic calculations. But it is difficult to set a 'safe' limit. Much of the success of deficit financing can be reaped if anti-inflationary policies are employed in a just and right manner.

External Sources : Most of the developing countries have to supplement domestic savings as investment in these countries exceed saving capacity. It is the foreign borrowing that supplements domestic saving to bridge the *savings-investment gap* and the *foreign-exchange gap*. In filling the saving gap or domestic resource gap, foreign capital provides the necessary capital stock. But, usually developing countries import more than what they export. To finance import, *foreign-exchange gap* needs to be bridged. This can be done by drawing foreign exchange reserves. Since developing countries fail to build up large foreign exchange reserves because of excess of imports over exports, they then rely greatly on external financing—the capital assistance provided by government-to-government economic aid, the private investment of foreign capital, and the loans from the international agencies like the IMF, the World Bank, etc.

This 'dual gap analysis', on the one hand, shows that foreign assistance helps in promoting domestic savings, and, on the other, many of the (capital) goods required for growth is required to be imported with the help of foreign assistance. Such inflow of foreign capital thus adds additional capital but also allows domestic capital to be utilised in production. In this way, it increases a country's potential for greater investment required for higher growth. Foreign investments are usually made in capital-intensive projects. It then provides direct employment to many workers and stimulates the economy by raising incomes in the process. Further, multinational corporations or companies (MNCs) not only import capital but also act as the vehicle for the transfer of advanced technology to developing countries.

But the cost of external financing may often outstrip the benefits received by the recipient countries. It is argued by many that aid is unnecessary for development. It is inimical to development by fostering foreign dependence. It weakens development effort and creates distorted consumption and production structures. Historical experience shows both successes and failures of foreign assistance in garnering resources for development. Finally, economic policy is considered as an important determinant of such external financing. Economic policy does not operate in a vacuum; however, political issues often cloud the economic logic. For instance, India's surplus generated in the pre-independent period was drained out through the channels of foreign aid and investment. National sovereignty often comes under threat from MNCs.

What emerges is that foreign aid is neither a necessary nor a sufficient condition for a country's economic development. After 1980s, we heard about 'aid fatigue'. Emphasis has now shifted from quantity to quality of such foreign development assistance.

3.8 Problems of Capital Formation in LDCs

Physical capital formation plays a very important role in the process of economic development. In fact, the level of output or GNP and its composition depends to a great extent of the amount of capital available in the country. Capital here refers to not only private physical capital such as factories, structures, transport equipments but also to social overhead capital such as bridges, highway, irrigation dams, power projects, rail, roads, etc. Economic development is not possibe in the absence of these tangible assets. Industrialisation, as also agriçultural prosperity, depend on use of modern machines and capital goods. At the same time, economic development is largely conditioned by the existence of an integrated infrastructure (or social overhead capital).

However, most LDCs find it difficult to accelerate the rate of capital formation so as to be able to achieve a faster rate of economic growth. The rate of capital formation is low for various reasons. In other words, there are various obstacles to capital formation. Such obstacles operate both from the demand side and the supply side. We may now discuss the problems of capital formation from both the sides in order to get a complete picture of what Nurkse calls the *vicious circle of poverty* (or in a broad sense, the vicious cycle of underdevelopment).

Supply of capital in LDCs : It is anybody's knowledge that due to low per capita income and widespread poverty most LDCs cannot save much. Moreover, whatever little is saved is not used for productive purposes. The proximate reason seems to be international demonstration effect. Most people in LDCs have a tendency to imitate the consumption pattern of people of advanced countries, so, when income increases, saving does not increase much. Instead, the major portion of additional income is utilised to purchase luxury goods or non-essential items of consumption. This is partly attributable to long colonial heritage and partly due to the strong desire to catch up with the West or in brief, consumerism, in no time. This is true not only of the urban people but also of the rural people.

However, things are changing of late. Some developing countries have adopted a number of measures for raising the rate of saving and have succeeded in their effort to some extent. Fiscal measures such as taxation, borrowing, including small savings schemes and deficit financing have proved to be quite effective in some countries. In certain other countries public sector enterprises have succeeded in generating surplus and have stepped up the rate of capital formation.

Another major obstacle to capital formation from the supply side is the underdeveloped or rather the fragmented nature of financial (money and capital) markets. Due to the absence of banking facilities in most parts of the rural sector and non-existence of stock exchanges, most people in rural areas cannot save much even if they desire. A major portion of saving goes waste or is utilised to purchase unproductive assets like gold and jewellery. A certain portion of saving is hoarded. Thus, it is quite obvious that only by setting up a strong and sound financial infrastructue, i.e., by establishing a strong network of commercial banks and public financial institutions or development banks (such as IFCI or IDBI), as also stock exchanges and insurance companies in rural and semi-urban areas, is it possible to mobilise inactive savings for productive purposes.

Demand for capital in LDCs : There are certain obstacles to capital formation which operate from the demand side. It is to be noted at the outset that the demand for capital is a derived demand, i.e., it actually depends on the demand for consumption goods. Thus, in a country where demand for consumption goods is large, a huge quantity of capital good is required to expand the production capacity in the concerned industries. If the demand for the product is large, producers can hope to make large profits and this will naturally induce them to make large investment in plants, equipments, machinery, etc. However, in LDCs, most people live under sub-human conditions. Moreover, the majority of the population live in rural areas and depend on agiculture as a means of livehood. In such countries adequate demand for manufactured article or industrial goods is unlikely to exist. Even people belonging to the so-called middle class do not have sufficient income to buy industrial goods. Whatever little is spent by urban and rural elites is not quite sufficient to produce adequate inducement to investors. In short, in most LDCs, the demand for non-agricultural goods and services is limited. This seems to be the main reason why there is not much demand for capital in these countries.

The fact is that the inducement to invest is limited by the narrow size of the domestic market. Nurkse, following Adam Smith's analysis of limits to division of labour set by the size of the market, first brought into focus the concept of the *vicious cycle of poverty* in 1953. He pointed out that underdeveloped countries face a shortage of purchasing power and, as a consequence, the size of the domestic markets is limited. Due to low demand for counsumber goods and services, the demand for capital is also small.

It is quite obvious that, in order to break the *vicious circle of poverty* in an LDC, it is absolutely essential to increase the inducement to invest. This can be achieved only by increasing the size of the market. According to Nurkse, the size of the domestic market cannot be increased just by artificially increasing money supply. It will have the effect of causing inflation from the demand side. The only way to increase the size of the market is to increase the productivity of reasources (or total factor productivity). The amount of output not only determines the extent or the size of the market, it also sets a limit to the expansion of the market. An improvement in factor productivity increases both the flow of goods and automatically increases income level. The increase in income automatically stimulates consumption. This, in its turn, will stimulate production further. Therefore, it is absolutely essential for LDCs to raise the productivity level—both in agriculture and in industry—if they are to break the *poverty trap*.

Productivity can be increased by using modern technology also. Adoption of modern technology is also related to capital formation because technological knowledge is often embodied in new machines and equipments. But, there is a practical problem. Most LDCs are labour-surplus countries. So the adoption of capital-intensive methods of production is likely to create the problem of unemployment—both in urban and rural areas.

3.9 Incentives for Savings

The importance of capital formation, hence, of the saving/investment rate for economic development, has been pointed out. But many developing countries score rather little in raising the rate of capital formation—thereby vindicating Nurkse's statement : "A country is poor because it is poor." But if the development record of these countries is read with all-seriousness, the low volume of capital accumulation is not to be attributed to low income or poverty of the masses. This is attributed to institutional failure and is argued today that "a country is poor because of poor policies". It is the institutional environment that influences savings and investment. Development is rather impossible without an effective government, market, and civil society. Sound state policies with good governance contribute real per capita income to go at a higher rate, and not bad policies and bad governance. Institutional change is now considered as a central force or input affecting growth and development.

By creating the incentive structure in the economy, institutions can strongly influence savings and investment. In developing countries, institutional setting is dichotomised. In the money market, one finds predominance of informal credit markets that act as a drag on development. Because of the lack of formal financial sector, lending is mostly confined to meet consumption needs. Further, because of high interest rate charged by the informal money market, total investment is discouraged. Further, the lack of formal financial institutions is an incentive on the part of the savers to put their money in real assets as opposed to the monetary assets. Obviously, in this institutional setting, investment does not pick up. Like the money market, the institution of capital market in the developing countries is also underdeveloped. A developed capital market is a prime requisite for the countries' initiative towards industrialisation as it acts as a vehicle for investment. Thus, development strategy demands an improvement in institutional ambience.

How to raise savings : It has been said that capital formation depends on (i) creation of savings, (ii) mobilisation of savings, and (iii) investment of savings. What is of great importance is how to raise aggregate savings. In developing countries, informal financial institutions play a great role in the generation of savings. In these economies, many transactions take the form of barter. People save in real assets. Moneylenders charge high interest rates while loans are mostly given to meet consumption needs of the borrowers.

Given these savings-investment patterns, banking and credit institutions need to be developed as these institutions act as stimulus to savings and investment. A large investible surplus is available only when institutional arrangements of an economy are broad and wide. The greater use of money releases both resources and helps in savings and in generating resources. A formal organised money market charges a lower interest rate which helps in raising the volume of savings.

Above all, savings in these institutions are risky and, hence, unsafe. Informal savings or deposit-accepting institutions often harass customers in one pretext or another. Some of the owners of these institutions, in the past, pulled down their shutters without returning back the hard-earned savings of the customers.

Further, lending of the formal money market is meant mainly for investment purposes and that too is available at a cheaper rate compared to the informal credit market. Thus, developing a well-organised formal banking institution is one of the first priorities to incentivise savers. Along with this, the fragmented capital market that allocates capital in a distorted and in an inefficient way also needs to be developed. Like the money market, capital market also mobilises savings of big investors and such are invested in industries, trade and commerce. It is also important that capital market should be integrated with the money market so as to have a unified interest-rate structure.

At the time of independence, both informal and formal sectors coexisted in which the former predominated. Over the years—and particularly after the nationalisation of commercial banks in 1969—the banking sector has developed in length and breadth. As a result, the volume of household savings as a percentage of GDP that stood at 9.5 p.c. of gross domestic savings in 1970-71 rose to 22.6 p.c. in 2008-09.

Further, India's capital market is now on a sound footing. That is why people are encouraged to invest their money in shares, debentures, bonds, small savings schemes, etc. To strengthen the country's monetary structure, capital formation has been made institution-elastic. Household savings are now being channelised not only through banking institutions but also through non-banking financial intermediaries like the UTI, LIC, GICI, mutual fund, special development banks, and micro-credit institutions. These institutions also promote corporate savings.

Fiscal policy and taxation also play an important role in raising savings capacity of the economy. This demands designing an appropriate tax policy so that the MPS exceeds APS. The volume of household savings depends on income level and the interest rate on savings. A higher interest rate is an incentive to the savers. But investors find little incentive to invest if banking institutions charge higher rates of interest. Thus, banks need to balance these two aspects. Further, a cut in tax rate enables individuals to save more. Higher tax rate acts as a deterrant to savings and investment. To give boost to investment, corporate tax rates may be cut; tax exemptions or tax holidays in different investment projects may be given. But often the revenue needs force the government not to adopt such soft-pedalling. However, the efficacy of getting larger resources for investment depends on the tax administration. It is the poor goverenence or laxity in tax administration that causes tax evasion—thereby frittering the country's resources away from productive investment.

Another component of gross savings is government or public savings which are generated from profits of public sector enterprises. Besides social welfare objectives, these enterprises also run on commercial basis. Profits made by public sector enterprises are reinvested. But public sector enterprises in India suffer from limitations like excess manpower, rising overhead costs, inappropriate price policy, poor management, etc. Above all, neo-liberal economic policy introduced in 1991 aims at privatisation of these enterprises. Anyway, public sector industries need to be expanded and should also run on commercial basis. What is needed is the designing of an appropriate policy so that these enterprises generate profit on a sustainable basis.

3.10 Incentives for Investment

Development in developing countries is associated with industrialisation—and industrialisation and capital accumulation go hand in hand. It is not necessarily true that an increase in savings will lead to an increase in investment. Even if investment rises the institutional prerequisites for development may be lacking. In other words, because of lack of proper investment incentives, capital formation tends to be low in the developing countries.

To push the investment rate up, the following steps need to be taken. : (i) increase in the supply of investible resources, (ii) opening up of investment opportunities. These, in turn, require favourable institutional environment, that is, primarily, an appropriate industrial policy that affects industrial investment and production.

Industrial policy focuses on lot of things other than fiscal and financial policies. It defines the scope of state participation in economic activity. It specifies the attitude of the government towards private capital (both domestic and foreign), technology import, a whole range of financial and fiscal polices which pertain to the provision of industrial finance, development of the capital market, fiscal incentives/disincentives to investment, etc. Thus, what is recommnded is the substantial role of the government. Recently, there has developed a trend of 'minimalist' government and hence economic reforms and the market is assumed to pursue the goal of efficiency. It then suggests that incentives for investment may be addressed both by the market and the state. We are not interested in elaborating the debate between market and the government.

Capital market or the share market is an important institution through which the flow of funds is generated in an economy. Share market is characterised by booms and slump consequent upon so many domestic and external factors. A boom in the share market on a sustainable basis encourages people and foreign institutional investors to participate in the market. This then pushes investment up. However, boom-slump phenomenon provides a signal for macroeconomic stability. Macroeconomic stability refers to managable fiscal deficit and the balance of payments deficit in tandem with low inflation. When such stability is ensured it encourages holding of financial assets and required funds for investment become available to the private sector. To give a boost to investment, governmental investment is also required to be steeped up—but not at the cost of fiscal slippage. To encourage investment, tax exemptions, lower rate of taxes, etc., may be given.

However, capital accumulation demands an improvement in economic and social infrastructures. Just as the productivity of physical capital depends on investment in human capital, so it depends on the infrastructural investments, say, on road, power, irrigation, etc. The need for different types of infrastructure changes with economic development. As this investment is lumpy in character, it is mostly undertaken by the government. However, inefficiency and waste may creep in such infrastructural investment. To minimise waste and to improve efficiency, commercial principles need to be applied. Managerial autonomy may be given.

Finally, foreign direct investmet needs to be pumped in to increase capital formation. This then requires liberalisation of industrial licensing policy. Reforms in the capital market are required so that foreign institutional investors can participate. Truly speaking, this requires a combination of restrictions and incentives. Government regulations may be imposed on the participation of foreign investment in certain 'key' sectors. It may also restrict foreign participation in ownership or management, limit the volume of profits, impose exchange controls on the repatriation of capital or profit. On the other hand, a slew of investment incentive measures—like protective tariffs on domestic commodities that compete with those produced by the foreign investors, exemptions from import duties on necessary equipments, machines, etc., tax concession schemes, special legislation for the protection of foreign investments and the like—may be taken up.

QUESTONS WITH ANSWER-HINTS

Long-Answer Questions

1. Discuss the relationship between economic development and population growth of a country. Give suitable illustrations from underdeveloped countries.

   Or

   Examine the effects of population growth on economic development of the developing countries.

   Or

   Does population growth act as a stimulant or a deterrent to economic development? Examine.

   Or

   Population growth has both benefits and costs.—Explain.

   Ans. 3.3

2. Point out, in brief, the effects of economic development on population growth.

   Ans. 3.4

3. Underdevelopment of a country is usually explained in terms of vicious circle of poverty. How do you explain this obstacle to development?

   Or

   "A country is poor, because it is poor." Explain this statement in terms of scarcity of capital.

   Or

   Poor countries are held down to their low levels of per capita incomes by interlocking vicious cycles.—Explain.

   Ans. 3.6

4. What is meant by capital formation? Discuss the importance of capital accumulation in the process of economic development.

   Ans. 3.7 and 3.7.1

5. The process of capital accumulation involves a choice between current consumption and future output.—Explain.

   Ans. 3.7.1

6. What is capital formation? Discuss the process or stages of capital formation. Why is the rate of capital formation low in an LDC?

   Ans. 3.7 and 3.7.2

7. State the causes of low rate of capital formation in a poor country. Suggest measures to raise capital formation in such a country.

   Ans. 3.7, 3.9 and 3.10

8. Discuss the relative merits of domestic and external sources of capital formation.

   Ans. 3.7.3

9. Elaborate the problems associated with capital formation in LDCs.

   Ans. 3.8

10. What measures do you suggest to increase savings and investment in an economy so as to accelerate the process of capital accumulation?

    Ans. 3.9 and 3.10

11. How do you explain Malthusian population trap?

    Ans. 3.5

Short-Answer Questions

1. What are the benefits of population growth?

   Ans. 3.3
2. Examine the adverse effects of population growth in terms of age-dependency effect and the investment-diversion effect.

   Ans. 3.3
3. Explain the 'vicious circle of poverty' argument from the demand and supply side of capital.

   Ans. 3.6
4. What is meant by capital formation?

   Ans. 3.7
5. Why is capital formation important? Give at least three reasons.

   Ans. 3.7.1
6. There are three stages of capital formation. Briefly explain these stages.

   Ans. 3.7.2
7. Discuss the merits and demerits of voluntary savings as a source of capital formation.

   Ans. 3.7.3
8. How do taxes contribute towards capital formation?

   Ans. 3.7.3
9. Explain inflationary finance as an important source of capital formation.

   Ans. 3.7.3
10. There are both benefits and dangers of external sources of development finance. Discuss.

    Ans. 3.7.3

CHAPTER 4

Foreign Investment and International Institutions —The IMF and The World Bank

4.1 Introduction

In an open economy, different types of foreign assistance can overcome the 'savings gap' faced by the poor developing countries. These countries can make greater contributions to investment over their savings via external assistance. In addition to savings gap, the problem of 'foreign exchange gap' arises because of unfavourable balance of payments situation. To fill in these two gaps in the development process, the role of foreign assistance is recognised.

In the resource-scarce poor developing countries much of the capital needed for growth is supplemented by many kinds of external assistance. In this chapter, we discuss various types of external assistance, and particularly private foreign direct investment (FDI) undertaken by the multinational corporations (MNCs) or transnational corporations (TNCs) and multilateral assistance from the international institutions, such as the International Monetary Fund (IMF) and the World Bank (WB).

It is argued that foreign aid or FDI makes significant constributions to economic development. However, neo-Marxist authors view foreign assistance as a tool of neo-imperialism or neo-colonialism since the motives behind such assistance go against the interests of developing countries, barring the problems associated with such assistance. Indeed, this is one of the most controversial areas in development economics. This topic is subject to varying economic, political, social, emotional, and ideological interpretations.

While emphasising the importance of international capital and international aid in all the economies irrespective of the state of devolopment, A. W. Lewis in his book *The Theory of Economic Growth* (1963) states : "Nearly every developed country has had the assistance of foreign finance to supplement its own meagre savings during the early stages of its development. England borrowed from Holland in the seventeenth and eighteenth centuries and in turn came to lend to almost every other country in the world in the nineteenth and twentieth centuries. The United States of America, now the richest country in the world, borrowed heavily in the nineteenth century and is, in tum, called upon to become the major lender of the twentieth." Despite such high regard for foreign capital in the economic development of a nation, persistent doubts over it have cast aspersion—particularly when 'strings' or 'conditionalities' are often attached to it. All these will be unfolded in the following pages.

4.2 Types of International Capital Flows

Usually, the word 'aid' is often associated with relief given to people who need it. But, foreign aid is in no way connected with 'relief'. Such aid is only 'concessional' rather than 'commercial', as such. The two major forms of international capital flows are : (i) official and private development assistance and foreign direct investment (FDI). However, the latter flows are nothing but commercial flows of private capital and are not to be treated as foreign assistance.

Any flow of capital in the form of loans or grants between governments or government agencies (bilateral flows) and through multilateral institutions (multilateral flows) like the IMF, the World Bank, etc., to less developed countries on concessional terms may be called foreign aid. Such aid is given often in a non-commercial form in the sense that it needs to be utilised for economic development and/or for influencing income distribution. The two essential characteristics of official foreign assistence are—it should be (i) concessional (and hence the name 'aid'), and (ii) non-commercial. Such official grants and loans may come in the form of currency or in kind ('food-aid' that India was forced to take in the early 1960s from the USA under PL 480). It may be added here that if foreign aid is in the form of 'pure grants', rather than loans, outright grants then do not call for any obligation for repayment. Outright grants or non-repayable loan assistance is like 'something for nothing'. This kind of assistance comes from bilateral donors, international donors, NGOs.

The most important source of international flow of financial resources to LDCs is the private foreign direct investment. This private investment is of two types : (i) FDI by MNCs (or TNCs), and (ii) foreign portfolio investment (e.g., stocks, bonds and notes). Such private foreign investment is not to be confused with foreign aid as the former flows are made on commercial purposes at non-concessional terms. In recent times, because of the growing equity and credit markets in developing countries, foreign institutional investors (FII) have been showing keen interest in purchasing equity capital, bonds extensively. In addition to this kind of direct capital investment, foreign players are participating in portfolio investment, in spite of its 'volatility' in character. It may be noted that such portfolio investment is made in accordance with the fortunes of share market index. In view of this, portfolio investment is thought of as speculative finance or hot money.

Another important form of international flow of resources is the FDI by MNCs/TNCs with headquarters in the developed countries. FDI is an investment involving the setting up of a new overseas operation or the acquisition of controlling interest in an already existing foreign company through the purchase of shares.

In addition to these official development assistance and private foreign direct and portfolio investment, a new form of international financial resource has been gaining strength in LDCs. This is the remittance of earnings by international migrants. Its magnitude has been outstripping foreign aid and portfolio flows, coming second to FDI in LDCs. Between 1990-2005, remittance flows of non-residents across LDCs to their homelands zoomed up to nearly \$200 billion. Usually, skilled workers and professionals migrate to foreign countries to enjoy larger incomes compared to their own countries. Earlier, this kind of 'brain drain' denuded local capital, etc. But its benefits through remittances have been outweighing the losses. The World Bank Reports suggest that such remittances of international migrants have reduced the poverty level in countries like Ghana, Uganda, Bangladesh, Guatemala, etc.

4.3 What is Foreign Aid?

External assistance is considered to be a major element towards the advancement of the developing countries. It is said that aid, and not trade, is the engine of growth.

The term foreign aid or external assistance or development assistance or development aid is often used synonymously, though there are certain subtle differences in their meanings. In essence, all these term refer to transfer of resources (e.g., loans, growth, technical assistance) from rich to poor countries or from international agencies like the IMF, the WB.

To start with, it is better to have a clear understanding of the notion 'foreign aid'. Any transfers of capital from one country to another cannot be treated as foreign aid. In the strict sense, all governmental resource transfers from one country to another is to be called foreign aid. And resource transfers by private foreign investors need not to be confused with aid. According to economists, any flow of capital is included within the ambit of foreign aid to LDCs if it satisfies three criteria.

Transfer of resources should be (i) developmental or charitable, (ii) non-commercial, and (iii) concessional. Thus, loans to LDCs are treated as foreign aid if they contain a "growth element".

Foreign aid or external assistance can thus be defined to include all official grants and concessional loans either in foreign currency or in kind, which aims at transfering resources from the developed countries to the LDCs fon developmental reasons.

4.3.1 Types of Foreign Aid

The two main forms of external assistance are : (i) private foreign direct investment by MNCs/TNCs and portfolio investment that comprises stock or equity holdings by non-residents in the receipient country's joint stock companies, and (ii) public and private development assistance (call it foreign aid) from governments of foreign countries and international donor agencies.

FDI is an investment involving the setting up of a new overseas operations or the mergers and acquisitions of controlling interests in an already existing foreign company through the purchase of shares and stocks. On the other hand, portfolio investment is just a transfer of capital through equity holding from one country to another.

Broadly, loans and grants are the two forms of foreign aid. Loans are required to be repaid with interest, however, on concessional terms. One may call it 'soft' loan also. However, outright grants do not have any obligation of interest payment or anything else. But grant-recipient countries sometimes may be asked to purchase commodity or 'consultancy services' from the grant-donor countries.

Secondly, foreign aid may be project and programme aid. In the words of C.P. Kindleberger : "Project aid is embodied in loans or grants that are intended to pay for specific projects. Project aid allows the donor to influence and control the uses to which aid is put. Programme aid embodies more general support, for example, for the activities of sectors as a whole such as agriculture or education, or for balance of payments support without reference to the goods being bought with the proceeds of the transfer."

Thirdly, there is *commodity aid*. It is well known that the U.S. Government provided agricultural commodities (mostly wheat) to India under PL 480 and 665 free of cost subject to the payment of transport costs in hard currency. Such commodities may serve the purpose of capital goods if through such transfer of resources in the importing country previously used in food production are shifted out of agriculture into (i) export production to provide foreign exchange to pay for imported capital goods, and (ii) capital formation, to the extent that domestic capital is in short supply. Such transfer may also replace existing purchased agricultural imports and thus release foreign exchange for buying capital or other consumption goods.

Fourthly, aid is often given in a *tied or non-tied form*. Donors often force recipients to spend their loan amount in the country where the aid originated. The result of aid-tying is two-fold. First, projects with large import content are eligible for more aid than those using domestic inputs. This imposes a permanent burden on the aid-receiving countries. Purchase of one country's products initially implies continuing demand for spare parts and ongoing technical advice on operating the imported equipment. Second, aid tied to exports from a single donor country may buy less than unrestricted ('untied') aid, if prices in the donor country are higher than elsewhere.

Fifthly, foreign aid may take a variety of physical *forms*. It may take the shape of capital goods, technical assistance, agriculture commodities or even military support. Again, aid may be either bilateral (i.e., nation-to-nation programmes of aid of particular countries) or multilateral (IMF, W. B, ADB, aid from global and regional development banks, some United Nations agencies, and aid consortia consisting of the principal donor countries and creditors of any given LDC, e.g., the 'Aid India Club'). In case of the latter, the donor countries, "surrender control over the uses of those funds and agree to abide by the decisions which they make with other members of the agency or institution."

Sixthly, foreign aid may be hard or soft loan. If repayment of loan requires foreign currency then such is called hard loan. Repayment of loan by home currency refers to soft loan. While the World Bank loan is hard loan, loan of its affiliates is soft loan.

4.4 Private Foreign Investment : Benefits and Costs of Development

It may be noted at the outset that the FDI tends to concentrate in those countries where the institution of 'governance' or the 'policy environment' is more favourable. In other words, firms engage more and more in multinational production if (i) the expectations of the rate of returns on investment are not only certain but also high; (ii) the absence of political instability or conflict and hence safety of investment prevails. The only objective which MNCs are concerned is the attainment of the goal of maximum business interests—not development of poor developing countries.

In spite of this, there has been a massive upsurge in FDI going to developing countries. The phenomenal growth of FDI in recent years can be understood from the following piece of information. Total flows of FDI in 1980 accounted for roughly $20 billion. It swelled to $ 35 billion in 1990, $ 150 billion in 2002, and $ 334 billion in in 2005. It accounts for 10 p.c. of total investment and 2 p.c. of GDP in these countries. In the following paragraphs, some pros and cons of FDI have been summarised.

Pro-FDI people believe that private foreign investment contributes towards the development of an economy. Anti-FDI group argues that it acts as the vehicle of exploitation of poor countries by the rich developed countries. Earlier, it was used by the colonial powers to exploit the colonies. To them, internal constraints like low savings and investment are not significant cause for underdevelopment. Underdevelopment or backwardness of any country is viewed as an externally-induced phenomenon. With the attainment of independence of these poor economies, foreign private investment in the developing world is now coming through MNCs/TNCs. This is the area where this kind of debate is yet to subside. In the following pages, this debate or controversy has been summarised.

Benefits of FDI

(i) *Gap-filling device* : Pro-FDI group starts with the 'two-gap model'. As a supplement to domestic (saving) gap, foreign borrowing or foreign investment may be encouraged so as to achieve faster growth. Further, such investment may also be used as a supplement to 'foreign-exchange gap'. Foreign investment thus fills these two gaps. Let the the concept of dual-gap be elaborated in terms of basic macroeconomic accounting identity of an economy :

Aggregate output and income = Aggregate expenditure

$$\text{Or, } Y = C + I + (X - M) \tag{4.1}$$

where C and I are the total (public and private) consumption and investment expenditures, respectively, while X and M represent exports and imports. Rearranging and re-interpreting the identity, we get

$$Y + M = C + I + X \tag{4.2}$$

The L.H.S. denotes sources of resources used in the economy and is matched by the R.H.S. (i.e., uses of resources in the economy or expenditure targets).

Now let us subtract C from both sides and since S (saving) is a residual element (i.e., what is not consumed is automatically saved), we define S as Y – C. Now we generate an equation that describes the two gaps:

Foreign exchange gap = Domestic savins gap,

$$\text{Or, } M - X = I - S \tag{4.3}$$

However, there may not always be exact balance between the two sides. If, for instance, the foreign exchange gap is larger than the domestic savings gap, imports will surely fall. This will retard growth to the extent that imports foil the development efforts. If, contrarily, the domestic savings gap is larger than the foreign exchange gap, planned investment could drop down to a low level indeed and this, in turn, would lower the growth rate of the economy.

Most LDCs are unable to raise their savings rates sufficienctly to permit a high rate of investment that is needed to meet its growth goals as reflected by the savings gap. Moreover, an LDC is in dire need to import capital goods and industrial materials to sustain development effort, but it cannot finance such imports from its normal export earnings. This is called the 'trade gap'. It is believed that these gaps can be covered by foreign resources. Thus this dual gap model suggests that if foreign-exchange gap is too big, it refers to the role of foreign assistance to supplement both domestic resource gap (i.e., domestic saving) and foreign exchange gap.

Foreign investment, in fact, plays a two-fold role in this respect. It permits a country either (a) to invest more and thus cover the domestic saving-investment gap, or (b) to import strategic goods which it is unable to finance by normal export earnings. To the extent that these constraints really do limit economic development, foreign invest-ment helps promote growth in LDCs. Today, FDI accounts for about 10 p.c. of total investment and 2 p.c. of GDP in developing countries.

In addition to the 'dual-gap', the role of FDI in filing up 'the technological gap' is undeniable. MNC is the important channel through which newer and newer technologies with their practical knowledge and skilled workers are put in developing countries. Introduction of modern technology is the result of research and development. MNCs of the Western world are relentlessly making effort in the introduction of newer technologies. Even the smaller MNCs of South Korea, Taiwan have been developing modern technologies compatible with LDC environments. Some of these have been using old or recently rejected technologies of MNCs of developed countries and are doing remarkable jobs for making them suitable for LDCs. Anyway, FDI increases productivity via technology transfer. The multiplier effect of FDI spreads from one sector to the others.

(ii) *Investment package* : FDI brings to the recipient country not only capital and foreign exchange but also a distinctive package of critical industrial inputs (production technology) and technological knowledge, administrative organisations (managerial skill, R & D, etc.,) which are in short supply in LDCs. Within the framework of foreign investment, modern technology and foreign knowledge enters the LDC world. Thus, a reverse 'brain drain' and 'technology drain' take place from rich to poor countries through MNC investment. In addition, it helps labour to learn new skills and the knowledge gained by these workers that get transmitted to other set of labour group who might be employed later by domestic firms. In other words, knowledge externality tends to flourish, thereby raising productivity level.

(iii) *Employment creation* : The inflow of foreign capital not only raises productivity of labour but also allows a large labour force to be employed. Foreign capital is often justified for the expansion of the manufacturing and tertiary sectors. The inflow of foreign capital thus enables a country to develop or build a foundation of heavy industries and social overhead capital. As these expand, employment opportunities tend to develop. In addition, such investment also creates indirect employment through various backward and forward linkages. G. M. Meier asserts : "The international flow of capital can thus be interpreted as an alternative to labour migration from the poor country..." Rural sector characterised by the presence of disguised unemployment may be absorbed in advanced industrial sector.

Foreign investment in one industry may encourage domestic investment by reducing costs or by creating demand in other industries. Profits may then rise and lead to expansion in these other industries. This then triggers employment in these industries. A whole series of domestic investment may thus be linked to foreign investment.

(iv) *Mobilisation of financial resources* : Foreign investment not only fills up the savings gap, trade gap, technology gap but also the revenue gap. One of the important objectives of business of MNCs is profit maximisation. Indeed, profitability is a fundamental determinant of (foreign) investment. LDC Governments may earn huge revenue by taxing MNC profits or royalties. This fiscal benefit then enables these governments to reinvest these financial resources for development projects.

(v) *Export earnings* : It is argued that FDI may improve the export capability of the LDCs. By introducing newer and newer products and modern technology suited to the country's requirements, MNCs may be able to export a large part of their output. As a result, export earnings may go up and foreign exchange position may improve.

Costs of FDI

Most of the above-noted advantages of foreign investment are unreal. Its costs are enormous as FDI has both serious economic and political implications.

Following arguments against FDI may be advanced :

(i) *Adverse effects on gap-filling* : The gap-filling arguments—the savings gap, the foreign exchange gap, the investment package gap, and the revenue gap—are subject to serious scrutiny.

Instead of filling saving-investment gap, private foreign investment actually lowers both domestic saving and investment rates by choking off competition through exclusive production agreements made with most countries. Often, MNCs fail to reinvest much of their profits and repatriate the same to the parent companies.

As far as foreign exchange gap is concerned, the benefits are largely cornered by the developed countries. Foreign investment in the long run reduces foreign exchange earnings on current and capital accounts. As far as export potentiality as well as willingness to export their products in the foreign markets are concerned, MNCs are never so generous enough and pursue restrictive business practices on the contrary. It then suggests that the MNC exports constitute a very small proportion. Further, import of both capital goods and intermediate goods, on the one hand, tends to worsen the current account balance and, on the other hand, repatriation of royalties, profits, dividends, management fees, etc., results in the deterioration of the capital account. Thus, the prospects of having an improved foreign exchange position are rather bleak.

Investment packages that foreign investment allows do not necessarily develop local resources. Often local resources and skill get distorted. Since MNCs are most powerful business entity, the terms and conditions for their investments often become unfair. Some of the package elements are redundant in poor LDCs but MNCs force host governments to accept all these in a packaged form.

As far as filling up of revenue gap is concerned, very little is earned because of tax concessions, investment allowances, tariff protection, and, most importantly, dishonest practices. Meanwhile, they succeed in repatriating huge profits thereby denuding capital.

(ii) *Inappropriate technology* : Private foreign capital is attractive as it provides new technology, new processes. Unfortunately, this argument loses strength as MNCs transfer technology to the LDCs that is inappropriate for them. Since modern technology is largely capital-invensive its employment potential is pretty low. These technologies have been developed according to the needs of the developed countries. Further, this kind of technology does not have large linkages with the other sectors of the economy. Above all, this modern technology creates long-run dependence on imported equipments and associated inputs. Technological dependence ultimately leads to financial dependence. Technology import encourages investment in capital goods sector. In other words, increase in investment leads to a growth in capital goods imports. Thus, industrialisation effort of LDCs based on imported technology puts a great burden on the trade balance and the balance of payments of these countries.

(iii) *Dualistic economic structure* : It is alleged that FDI encourages dualistic economic structure. Through private foreign investment modern sectors are developed and that co-exists with the traditional, backward sectors. This modern sector is engaged in the production of elite goods. In the process, foreign investment for the local market excludes local manufacturers. In this way, inappropriate products are then produced. Ultimately, income inequalities tend to widen.

In this age of consumerism, MNCs are attracted to produce those goods that are demanded by elite people. It is because of commodity fetishism, poor people are even driven by the 'demonstration effect'. These people imitate the Western consumption styles so that they can 'appear in public without being ashamed or feeling disgraced'. Such tendency is getting strength more and more in urban areas. Anyway, the changed consumption pattern is not only undesirable but also nutritionally harmful.

[*In this connection, the behaviour of Nestle′—the Swiss confectionary giant—in the marketing of processed baby food milk all over the globe may be referred here. WHO recommends breast milk rather than tinned milk. Further, the prevention of such powdered milk is dependent on the availability of good drinking water, sterile bottles, mixing equipments, etc. Unfortunately, no LDCs satisfy all these conditions. In spite of the strong condemmation by the WHO, Nestle′ has been supplying Third World families with baby milk formula and operating in an unethical way. Indeed, MNCs run their business in such a way that they are 'above the law'. Likewise, violating the laws, the Coca-Cola company has been supplying cold drinks in many LDCs.*]

(iv) *The issue of profit* : Private foreign investment comes through MNCs. Obviously, MNCs invest in those areas where profit is the largest. What is wrong is the volume of profits earned. Not necessarily, big profits are due to efficiencies of MNCs over their LDC business enterprises. It is argued that if an MNC makes an investment worth 1 dollar in host countries, it will return home with at least 7 dollars.

(v) *The issue of environmental damage* : Today, MNCs are often accused of encourageing some of their firms so as to dump 'dirty' activities/ industries in poor developing countries where lack of environmental consciousness and environmental laws dealing with such activities are not properly enforced. Indeed, poor LDC governments are extremely fearful of losing foreign exchange. The Union Carbide gas leak in 1984 is a pointer to this argument.

This sort of earning of profit by MNCs is equivalent to 'gift'. That is why some people prefer foreign borrowing over FDI. As far as borrowing is concerned, there is obligation of repayment of borrowed money with interest. FDI calls for unlimited obligations—repatriation of profit to the headquarters. Ultimately, balance of payments position tend to become negative unless the volume of investment flows rise regularly over the long run.

(vi) *The issue of sovereignty of nations* : *Finally*, MNCs not only gain over local assets and jobs but also exert enormous influence in such a way that a country's political independence is threatened. Past experience of many of these countries suggests the subjugation of national sovereignty in the guise of foreign investment. There is a saying : Flag follows foreign capital. To some, MNCs are believed to be the tools of exploitation, or instruments of promoting economic neo-colonialism. Some others, however, call them 'lackeys of capitalism'.

MNCs often try to influence the political parties and various institutions through 'donations', bribes, and illegal gratification. There have been instances in MNCs that often attempt to subvert political process of the host countries :

In the *first* place, the International Telephone and Telegraph (ITT)—a US MNC that produces electronic appliances—had been accused of overthrowing the communist government of Chile headed by President G. S. Allende in 1973.

Secondly, the Bhopal Gas Tragedy of December 1984 caused by the US-owned Union Carbide plant at Bhopal occurred 'as the result of slipshod management and a breakdown of safety procedure, water got into a tank of methyl isocyanate (MIC), a deadly cynide gas, heating it and causing its escape as a gas. It killed in the end almost 15,000 people; this was the worst ever industrial disaster.'

Conclusion : Thus, it emerges from the abovenoted pros and cons of FDI on LDCs' economic development that it provides a range of conflicting arguments. That is why a love-hate attitude towards FDI prevails in these economies. These countries need foreign investment to increase their potentials for more and more investment. However, the losses emerging out of FDI are viewed from ideological and political perspectives. However, some of the costs of FDI can be minimised if LDCs can impose restrictions on profit repatriation, performance requirements, technology transfer, damages on environment, etc. However, the success of these measures largely depend on the bargaining powers of the host-country governments.

An international code of conduct may be evolved to control the undesirable as well as unacceptable activities of MNCs so that the conflicting objectives of MNCs and LDC operations can be conciliatory. This is not an easy task. At least, we can hope for the best. Virtually all countries have abandoned central planning and embraced market forces. Under the circumstances, these countries have liberalised their policies to accommodate more FDI.

As M. P. Todoro and S. C. Smith add : "Whether the net outcome will be more positive for development than in the past remains to be seen. It is to be hoped that ways can be found in which MNC profits and broad-based national development can be served simultaneously."

4.4.1 Meaning and Size of MNC

External dependence of poor LDCs arises because the bulk of FDI is done by the MNCs/ TNCs.

Table 4.1 : GDP vs MNC Sales

	Country	GDP ($ million)	MNC	Sales ($ million)
1.	Denmark	1,74,363.0	General Motors (USA)	1,76,558.0
2.	Poland	1,54,146.0	Wal-Mart (DO)	1,66,809.0
3.	South Africa	1,31,127.0	Exxon-Mobil (DO)	1,63, 881.0
4.	Israel	99,068.0	Royal Dutch/Shell (Netherlands/UK)	1,05,366.0
5.	Ireland	84,861.0	IBM (USA)	87,548.0
6.	Malaysia	74,634.0	Siemens (Germany)	75,337.0
7.	Chile	71,092,0	Hitachi (Japan)	71,858.0
8.	Pakistan	59,880.0	Sony (DO)	60,052.7
9.	New Zealand	53,622.0	Honda Motor (Germany)	54,773.5
10.	Hungry	48,355.0	Credit Suisse	49,362.0

Source : Manfred B. Steger (2003), *Globalization : A Very Short Introduction;* OUP

There is a controversy regarding the definition of MNCs. Usually, MNCs are defined as firms that enjoy management rights and controls in at least *two* countries. Others say that the number of such firms that control assets in at least *six* countries is to be called MNCs. What is important is that only enterprises that undertake at least *one* FDI project in which it enjoys management rights and control are to be called the MNC.

FDI is an investment involving (i) green-field investment—the creation of new production facility abroad; and (ii) the mergers and acquisitions of controlling interest in an already existing foreign company through the purchase of shares and stocks. It may be noted that such controlling right depends on the volume of share of equity of a foreign business and that too varies from country to country. Foreign affiliates can be minority-owned (10 to 50 p.c. of equity capital), majority-owned (between 50 p.c. and less than 100 p.c.), and wholly-owned (100 p.c.) affiliates.

United Nations prefers the term transnational corportions (TNCs) to MNCs since a firm's business operations from a single home country are extended beyond national frontiers.

On the basis of this definition, the United Nations Conference on Trade and Development (UNCTAD) estimated that in 2002 there were about 64,000 MNC firms as against 50,000 in 2000 with more than 8,70,000 affiliates. Enterprises like General Motors, Wal-Mart, Exxon-Mobil, Mitsubishi, and Siemens belong to the 200 largest MNCs which account for over half of the global industrial output. All these corporations maintain headquarters in North America, Europe, Japan, and South Korea. One of the largest MNCs—Royal Dutch Shell of Netherland—has subsidiaries in 116 countries. In terms of sales, the largest MNC is General Motors. In 2000, sales figure of General Motors exceeded Denmark's GDP figure of that year. Table 4.1 compares the strength of MNCs, measured in terms of sales and the country's GDP.

As far as power and influence of MNCs over production and export of agricultural commodities produced in LDCs is concerned, only 3 US-based MNC firms control more than one-half of global banana trade, 5 European companies control 90 p.c. of tea sold in the developed countries. Anyway, total FDI flows that constituted nearly $ 150 billion in 2002 shot up to $ 334 billion in 2005 to developing countries. Out of this total FDI, 10 countries of South America and South-East Asia received as high as 80 p.c. of such investment.

We conclude this section in the words of M. B. Steger : "No doubt, the growing power of TNCs has profoundly altered the structure and functioning of the international economy. These giant firms and their global strategies have become major determinants of trade flows, the location of industries, and other economic activities around the world. As a consequence, TNCs have become extremely important players that influence the economic, political, and social welfare of many nations."

4.5 Foreign Aid—The Debate

In addition to FDI to close the dual-gap, another source of foreign exchange needed for LDCs' development is the public or official developmental assistance, commonly known as foreign aid or external assistance.

Case for Foreign Aid

Foreign aid is a hotly debated topic in LDCs. One group of people (both the Left and the Right) argue that LDCs must not seek foreign aid as it is not an essential component of growth. Often, China and Japan are considered as 'role-model' since the contribution of foreign assistance towards the development of these two Asian economies is minimal. They argue that aid is an instrument that sponsors neo-imperialism. Since such foreign economic aid in recent past came to be linked with military aid and political and military movements in poor low-income countries. Some even argue that the developed countries need to concentrate on the typical domestic problems of LDCs, such as poverty, hunger, inequality, malnutrition, etc. The other group do not believe in such exaggeration in the dangers of aid as propounded mainly by the Left. These group argue that foreign aid can play a vital role in helping LDCs to promote economic and social development.

Here we will now present economic rationale (rather than political and moral or humanitarian rationale) for foreign aid.

First the macroeconomic role of aid can be modelled in terms of a 'two-gap model'. LDCs are usually characterised by shortage of resource—a shortage of savings over investment. This 'resource gap' is called a 'savings gap'. This kind of internal imbalance in the macroeconomy of a developing country leads to an external imbalance of imports exceeding exports. This kind of 'resource gap' is called the 'foreign exchange gap' or 'trade gap'. These gaps or bottlenecks can be filled up by an inflow of capital from abroad through loans, or foreign development assistance or private foreign investment. In other words, foreign aid supplements LDCs low domestic savings and low foreign exchange reserves. Thus, foreign aid permits a country to invest more than what it is able to save.

Furthermore, with the aid of foreign assistance, a country can import more than what it is capable of financing by its own exports. Thus, the resource constraint that stands in the way of development of LDCs can be greatly removed if foreign assistance is sought for.

Secondly, aid fills up 'technological gap' and 'manpower gap' of the developing countries. These countries are technologically poor. But by importing foreign technologies alone, prosperity will not flow. It requires high-end manpower that is also scarce in LDCs. This demands aid in the form of manpower transfers. These technological and manpower gaps work in the same way as the financial gap filling process works.

For instance, the green revolution of the mid-1960s was driven by a technology revolution. It is a product of agricultural research programme conducted by the Rockefeller and Ford Foundations that helped to transfer and adopt scientific advances to many developing countries. This brought in substantial increase in output of food grains in many Asian and African countries.

Thirdly, foreign aid by supplementing inadequate domestic savings, foreign exchange, and the transfer of technology and manpower can help to build up a country's infrastructure of roads, airports, power stations, health centres, schools and colleges, shelter, a clean and pure water supply, etc. In this way, it helps increase the investment level that produces a big multiplier effect. As a result, social returns of foreign aid become higher than its costs. External economies of aid are thus believed to be stronger.

Finally, Anne Krueger gives a different reason for aid—aid by multilateral agencies provide policy dialogue that help LDCs to sort out their macroeconomic and structural imbalances. She says that the recipient country may be asked by the donor agencies to change its macroeconomic policies in the course of the dialogue.

However, aid will flow to that country which agrees to the policy change recommen-dations. "Regardless of the influence used, foreign assistance could certainly become a means of speeding policy reform in developing countries." This policy package advice subject to conditionally may thus cause some good to LDCs.

Anyway, foreign aid is thus not undesirable for development. At a micro level, aid has a positive impact.

Case against Foreign Aid

Against these economic arguments, P. T. Bauer has pointed out that foreign aid is neither a necessary nor a sufficient condition for any country's development. As far as recent experiences of Hong Kong and Singapore and past experiences of Japan and England are concerned, foreign aid is not a necessary tool for development as these countries developed without any substantial foreign aid. On the other hand, it is not sufficient because evidences galore where little development has occurred in spite of large foreign aid. Thus, foreign aid may not produce large economic benefits.

Let us first consider extreme left view relating to aid. It is argued by Marxists that trade perpetuates dependence as it destroys self-reliance, props up authoritarian regime, and prevents economic development. It may not be out of place here to remark that in 1980 foreign aid as a percentage of GNP for oil importing LDCs accounted for less than 2 p.c. Thus, says Deepak Lal : "Given the smallness of the sums relative to GNP, total investment, or even the government budget in most developing countries, it would be strange if so much evil could flow from so little."

Secondly, whether aid has fulfilled the positive macroeconomic role has not been statistically verified. It is feared that aid may displace savings, particularly public sector savings. Above all, aid may produce some undesirable effects on the balance of payments of a country as this leads to drainage of foreign exchange reserves by way of royalty, dividends, etc., to be paid to the donor countries. Further, some macroeconomic studies have failed to show a systematic relationship between aid and economic growth. Aid serves other purposes apart from promoting economic growth. Aid also brings inappropriate technologies.

Thirdly, whether foreign aid is a growth-promoting instrument (device) crucially depends upon the uses to which it is put. Foreign aid fosters capital accumulation by reducing its scarcity and thus making possible higher output. Thus, in the end, it promotes growth. However, this happy result cannot be ensured if aid is used for maintaining or even raising current consumption (rather than being devoted to capital formation).

Rather, foreign aid may result in an ultimate lowering of the recipient's long-term growth rate. The U.S. PL 480 aid had laid the inevitable impact of hampering the growth of the agricultural sector through dumping (putting cheap crop into the market of LDCs thereby discouraging the growth of domestic production of food and primary commodities). If, instead, such aid could take the shape of imports of machinery it would bridge the technology gap in LDCs and could render a considerable help to the primary sector by restoring its longterm health and ensuring its permanent viability.

Finally, because of foreign aid LDCs are often caught with substantial debt repayments. External debt grows in magnitude in these countries when foreign loans are used to finance an excess of imports over exports and interest payments on existing debt. Further, the "conditionality" clause of loans of multilateral agencies is the most worrying aspect of foreign aid. This seriously attacks the sovereignty of nations as well as promotes politicisation since a few major industrial countries (mainly the USA) are the most strong decision-makers in shaping the Fund-Bank programmes. In view of these strong reactions against foreign aid, leftists argue that aid leads to the extension of international Western style capitalism and supports the political motives of the strong neo-colonial powers. Thus, when aid serves political interests, the economic benefits of aid are lost.

Conclusion : It may be noted at the end that there are certain things which foreign aid cannot do. Experience has shown that foreign aid cannot right all social wrongs or solve every economic problem of a developing country. It cannot bring about instant progress. A country's economic develop-ment depends, ultimately, upon its own people, their participation and suitable long-term economic planning. It is not true that countries receiving aid grow at a much faster rate than countries without aid. Neverthless, it is also true that aid plays an economically useful role in poor countries.

4.6 Global Governance and International Institutions

In the 1950s and 1960s, development economists were talking about growth of GNP over time in terms of 'capital fundamentalism'. This means that higher GNP growth is to be accomplished or vicious circle of poverty can be broken through capital accumulation and industrialisation. In this process, government or planning mechanism has had a great role to play. An activist government can improve growth and welfare of the people. But as the confidence in government action in improving living standards and well-being was shaken, the emphasis was placed upon 'market fundamentalism' by the neo-liberal school in the 1980s and 1990s. But as there is government failure so there is market failure.

Although different countries have grown at different rates over the last 50 years, the preconditions for development are not uniform in terms of institutions. Markets depend on a set of public institutions. Markets can flourish if institutional environment is friendly. Institutions refer to both formal and informal rules and regulations that not only dictate the functions of the state, but also govern those of private entitles. In brief, it is defined as the arrangements that govern collective undertakings. Thus, institutions are public goods.

Institutional economics attributes underdevelopment in terms of institutional failures. Institutional strengthening assumes an important role and acts as a complement to macroeconomic policy changes. In development theory and practice, there has been a growing recognition of the importance of formal and informal institutions. Again, institutions may be local and global. Good institutions provide good governance. Government acts as the builder and provider of institutions for the market economy. Here we will highlight the importance of international institutions. For the purpose of global governmance, several international institutions have been created over the last 65 years or so as a 'means of achieving collective objectives that could not be accomplished by acting individually.'

As the challenges of the reconstruction of the European economy and the resurrection of the global economy became uppermost after the termination of the Second World War, new international institutions in the name of the United Nations, the International Monetary Fund, the World Bank (or the International Bank for Reconstruction and Development—IBRD) were set up with the aim of achieving higher and better development and greater coordination of international efforts.

4.6.1 Background to the Establishment of the Bretton Woods System

The international monetary system, as defined by the 'rules of the game', has gone through many changes since the beginning of the 20th century. It may be noted that the international trading environment is largely governed by the exchange rate policy.

An exchange rate connects the price system of trading nations since this (special) price shows the relationship between all domestic prices and all foreign prices. Exchange rate management policy has great implications for macroeconomic environment. There are many types of exchange rate policy options. Important among these are : fixed, flexible, and managed exchange rates. The international monetary system, however, is not in a stable state as the abovenoted three kinds of exchange rates evolved and prevailed at different times.

The international monetary system before the World War I (1870-1914) comprised the *gold standard system*. Under this system, government does not intervene in the foreign exchange market and follows a policy of keeping the exchange rate of its currency at a fixed rate. Under this system, currencies of different nations were convertible into gold. With the outbreak of the World War I, the gold standard system failed and the currencies were exchanged at floating rates. However, the United Kingdom went for restoration of the gold standard (1927-31).

But some authors convincingly argued that the re-establishment of the gold standard brought in the Great Depression of the 1930s and the associated financial problems. As a result of these developments, countries one after another went for (competitive) devaluations. All these brought the collapse of the gold standard system and, ultimately, disrupted the international economic order. Most of the countries then adopted nationalistic policies to avoid further disruption. Protectionist measures were undertaken—thereby resulting in a decline in world trade.

It was against this background that plans for a new world trade and monetary order were worked out in the USA during the World War II to prevent the repetition of the 1930s. Two plans were drafted in the early 1940s—one by J. M. Keynes of the U.K. Treasury and another by Harry Dexter White of the US Treasury to provide a permanent and acceptable framework for international transactions. The overriding objectives of the new monetary system to be evolved were the stabilisation in exchange and the promotion of free trade. These objectives were to be achieved through the creation of a permanent international institution.

Ultimately, the White Plan, instead of the Keynes Plan, prevailed as the USA became economically more powerful than the U.K. Anyway, in the spirit of international cooperation, a conference in July 1944 of 44 non-communist nations at Bretton Woods in the state of New Hampshire, U.S.A, led to the creation of the IMF and the International Bank for Reconstruction and Development (now called World Bank). Together these two form the Bretton Woods institutions. From then, the international monetary system moved into the Bretton Woods pegged exchange rate system (1945-71) under the auspices of the International Monetary Fund (set up in July 1944). These two institutions are, indeed, complementary. The IMF is responsible for short-term balance of payments aid and the World Bank is responsible for long-term project-related development aid.

4.6.2 Creation of the IMF : Objectives and Functions

The origin of the IMF goes back to the days of international chaos of the 1930s. During the Second World War, plans for the construction of an international institution for the establishment of monetary order were taken up. At the Bretton Woods Conference held in July 1944, delegates from 44 non-communist countries negotiated an agreement on the structure and operation of the international monetary system. The Articles of Agreement of the IMF provided the basis of the international monetary system. The IMF commenced financial operations on 1 March 1947, though it came into official existence on 27 December 1945, when 29 countries signed its Articles of Agreement (its charter). Today (May 2012), the IMF has near-global membership of 188 member countries. Virtually, the entire world belongs to the IMF. India is one of the founder-members of the Fund.

Objectives

Article 1 of the Articles of Agreement (AOA) spell out 6 purposes for which the IMF was set up. These are :

I. To promote international monetary cooperation through a permanent institution which provides the machinery for consulation and collaboration on international monetary problems.

II. To facilitate the expansion and balanced growth of international trade, and to contribute thereby to the promotion and maintenance of high levels of employment and real income and to the development of the productive resources of all members as primary objective of economic policy.

III. To promote exchange stability, to maintain orderly exchange arrangements among members, and to avoid competitive exchange depreciation.

IV. To assist in the establishment of a multilateral system of payments in respect of current transactions between members and in the elimination of foreign exchange restrictions which hamper the growth of world trade.

V. To give confidence to members by making the general resources of the Fund temporarily available to them under adequate safeguards, thus providing them with the opportunity to correct maladjustments in their balance of payments, without resorting to measures destructive of national or international prosperity.

VI. In accordance with the above, to shorten the duration and lessen the degree of disequilibrium in the international balance of payments of members.

All these objectives of the IMF may be summarised : to promote international cooperation; to facilitate the expansion and balanced growth of international trade; to promote exchange stability; to assist in the establishment of a multilateral system of payments; to make its general resources available to its members experiencing balance of payments difficulties under adequate safeguards; and to shorten the duration and lessen the degree of disequilibrium in the international balance of payments of members.

Functions

The principal function of the IMF is to supervise the international monetary system. Several functions are derived from this. These are : granting of credit to member countries in the midst of temporary balance of payments deficits, surveillance over the monetary and exchange rate policy of member countries, issuing policy recommendations. It is to be noted that all these functions of the IMF may be combined into three. These are : regulatory, financial, and consultative functions

Regulatory function : The Fund functions as the guardian of a code of rules set by its (AOA—Articles of Agreement).

Financial function : It functions as an agency of providing resources to meet short term and medium term BOP disequilibrium faced by the member countries.

Consultative function : It functions as a centre for international cooperation and a source of counsel and technical assistance to its members.

The main function of the IMF is to provide temporary financial support to its members so that 'fundamental' BOP disequilibrium can be corrected. However, such granting of credit is subject to strict *conditionality*. The conditionality is a direct consequence of the IMF's surveillance function over the exchange rate policies or adjustment process of members.

The main conditionality clause is the introduction of structural reforms. Low income countries drew attraction of the IMF in the early years of 1980s when many of them faced terrible BOP difficulties and severe debt repayment problems. Against this backdrop, the Fund took up 'stabilisation programme' as well as 'structural adjustment programme'. Stabilisation programme is a demand management issue, while structural programme concentrates on supply management. The IMF insists member countries to implement these programmes to tackle macroeconomic instability. Its main elements are : (i) application of the principles of market economy; (ii) opening up of the economy by removing all barriers of trade; and (iii) prevention of deflation.

The Fund provides financial assistance. It includes credits and loans to member countries with balance of payments problems to support policies of adjustment and reform. It makes its financial resources available to member countries through a variety of financial facilities. It also provides concessional assistance under its poverty reduction and growth facility and debt relief initiatives. It provides fund to combat money-laundering and terrorism in view of the attack on the World Trade Centre of the USA on 11 September 2001.

In addition, technical assistance is also given by the Fund. Technical assistance consists of expertise and support provided by the IMF to its members in several broad areas : the design and implementation of fiscal and monetary policy; institution-building, the handling and accounting of transacions with the IMF; the collection and retirement of statistical data and training of officials.

Maintenance of stable exchange rate is another important function of the IMF. It prohibits multiple exchange rates.

It is to be remembered that unlike the World Bank, the IMF is not a development agency. Instead of providing development aid, it provides financial support to tide over BOP difficulties to its members.

4.6.3 Organisation and Management of the IMF

Like many international organisations, the IMF is run by a Board of Governors, an Executive Board and an international staff. Every member country delegates a representative (usually heads of central banks or ministers of finance) to the Board of Governors—the top link of the chain of command. It meets once a year and takes decision on fundamental matters such as electing new members or changing quotas.

The Executive Board is entrusted to the management of day-to-day policy decisions. The Board comprises 24 executive directors who supervise the implementation of policies set by the member governments through the Board of Governors.

The IMF is headed by the Managing Director who is elected by the Executive Board for a 5-year term of office.

Rights and obligations, i.e., the balance of powers in the Fund is determined by a system of quotas. Quotas are decided by a vote of the Board of Governors. Quotas or subscriptions roughtly reflect the importance of members in the world economy. It is the quota on which payment obligations, credit facilities, and voting rights of members are determined.

4.6.4 Financial Structure of the IMF

The capital or the resources of the Fund come from two sources, viz., (i) subscription or quota of the member nations, and (ii) borrowings.

Each member country is required to subscribe an amount equivalent to its quota. It is the quota on which payment obligations, credit facilites, and voting right of members are determined. As soon as a country joins the Fund, it is assigned a quota which is expressed in Special Drawing Rights (SDRs). At the time of formation of the IMF, the quota of each member was made up of 25 p.c. in gold or 10 p.c. of its net official holdings of gold and US dollars (whichever was less). Now this has been revised. The capital subscriptions or quota is now made up of 25 p.c. of its quota in SDRs or widely accepted currencies (such as the US dollar, euro, the yen or the pound sterling) instead of gold and 75 p.c. in country's own currency. The size of the Fund equals the sum of the subscriptions of members. Total quotas at the end-August 2008 were SDR 217.4 billion (about $341 billion).

The Fund is authorised to borrow in special circumstances if its own resources prove to be insufficient. It sells gold to member countries to replenish currency holdings. It is entitled to borrow even from international capital market. Though the Articles of Agreement permit the Fund to borrow from the private capital market, till today no such use has been made by the IMF.

4.6.5 Special Drawing Rights (SDRs)

The Special Drawing Rights (SDRs) as an international reserve asset or reserve money in the international monetary system was established in 1969 with the objective of alleivating the problem of international liquidity. The IMF has two accounts of operation—the General Account and the Special Drawing Account. The former account uses national currencies to conduct all business of the fund, while the second account is transacted by the SDRs. The SDR is defined as a composite of five currencies—the Dollar, Mark, Franc, Yen and Pound. The SDRs are allocated to the member countries in proportion to their quota subscriptions. Only the IMF members can participate in SDR facility.

SDRs being costless, often called paper gold, is just a book entry in the Special Drawing Account of the IMF. Whenever such paper gold is allocated, it gets a credit entry in the name of the participating countries in the said account. It is to be noted that SDRs, once allocated to a member, are owned by it and operated by it to overcome BOP deficits. Since its inception, there have been only four allocation to SDRs—the first in 1970, and the last in 2008-09—mainly to the developing countries.

4.6.6 Essentials of the Bretton Woods System

Both the IMF and the World Bank were conceived at the Bretton Woods Conference in 1944. The international monetary system is governed by the IMF. The original intention of the Fund was the stabilisation of the world economy providing shortterm loans to member countries in case of temporary BOP difficulties. Today, it acts as a development agency as it has shifted its focus of attention to macroeconomic policies so as to lay a basis for sustainable growth and poverty reduction in poor income countries.

The IMF began its operation under its original charter from 1947-71. The founders of the Bretton Woods System wanted to remove the disadvantages of the gold standard system or the 'fixed' exchange rate system as well as the 'instability' and uncertainty of completely 'flexible' exchange rate system. In other words, the System would aim at achieving a stable exchange rate and at lessening the duration and reducing the degree of BOP disequilibrium. The Bretton Woods System that evolved during 1947-71 came to be known as 'fixed but adjustable exchange rate' system. It also came to be known as 'par value system' or the'pegged exchange rate' system. Under this System, members were required to establish the parity of their currencies in terms of gold or dollar and then to maintain the values of their currencies within 1 p.c. of its par value (±1). The Articles of Agreement, however, provided an alteration of the par values, subject to the Fund's approval. Such changes in the parity of the exchange rates (that is, devaluation or revaluation) could be approved if the country could justify its BOP to be in 'fundamental disequilibrium'.

Thus the Bretton Woods System was indeed a compromise between a short run stability of exchange rates and the long run flexibility. Hence the name 'stable but adjustable' exchange rate system.

To fulfil its obligations to maintain the values of currencies within 1 p.c. of par value, the second condition that required to be fulfilled was the creation of a pool of international reserve asset. It involved a system of quotas and drawing rights. SDRs represented a major innovation in 1967 to ease the problem of international liquidity.

The third element of the Bretton Woods System was the prohibition of exchange controls that many nations made frequent use of as a means of dealing with their BOP problems. The Bretton Woods System prohibited the use of exchange controls on current account but allowed exchange controls on capital account transactions.

Between 1945 and 1958 the world economy saw a serious disequilibrium—a surplus in the US BOP vis-a-vis the rest of the world. The result was acute dollar shortage. However, by 1958, a situation of dollar surplus in consequent upon the BOP deficit in the USA emerged. In the process, a classic 'crisis of confidence' over the dollar came out. Chronic US BOP deficit caused massive dollar outflows in 1971 when foreign exchange markets were flooded with dollars. The consequences were far-reaching—foreign exchange markets were closed for brief periods; despite prohibition nations emphasised exchange control mechanisms; countries allowed their currencies to float temporarily. All these brought some embarrassing situations in the world economy. On the one hand, tremendous enthusiasm by all the nations to dollar sales and, on the other, foreign central banks (except the Federal Reserve Bank of the USA) showed utter disinclination in dollar purchase. By August 1971, the par value system broke down. The United States devalued dollar by 8.6 p.c. in December 1971. This could not prevent BOP deficit from falling. On the contray, speculation in dollar become so strong that, again, the US currency was devalued in 1973.

Anyway, it was against this background that the Bretton Woods System was abandoned in 1972. By March 1973, the IMF introduced managed floating exchange rate system.

4.6.7 Instruments of IMF Lending and Loan Conditionality

The IMF Articles of Agreement clearly state that the resources of the Fund are to be used to give temporary assistance to members in financing BOP deficit on current account. Of course, the financial assistance provided by the Fund is loan. The following technique is employed : If a country calls on the Fund it buys foreign currencies from the IMF in return for the equivalent in the domestic currency. This, in legal and technical terms, is called a 'drawing' on the Fund. The technique, therefore, suggests that the IMF does not lend, but sells the required currency to the members on certain terms. This unique financial structure of the Fund clearly suggests that the Fund's resources cannot be lent for long time. It is meant to cover short run gaps in BOP.

The IMF's unique financial structure does not allow any member to enjoy financial assistance over a long time period. The total amount that a country is entitled to draw is determined by the amount of its quota. A member is entitled to draw an amount not exceeding 25 p.c. of its quota. The first 25 p.c. called the 'gold tranche' ('tranche' a French Word meaning slice) or 'reserve tranche' can easily be drawn by countries with BOP problems. This 25 p.c. of the quota is the members' owned reserves and therefore no conditions are attached to such drawings. This may be called 'ordinary, drawing rights; even the Fund cannot deny its use. However, no interest for the first credit tranche is required to be paid though such drawings are subject to repayment within 3-5 years period.

The 'credit tranche' of 100 p.c.—each equalling 25 p.c. of a member's quota—are also available subject to the IMF approval and, hence, 'conditional'.

Originally, it was possible to borrow equal to 125 p.c. of one's quota. At present, borrowing limit has been raised to 450 p.c. of one's quota which must be redeemed within five years.

Borrowing methods used by the Fund are :

(i) *Stand-by Arrangements* : This method of borrowing has become the most normal form of assistance by the Fund. Under this form of borrowing, a member state obtains the assurance of the Fund that, usually over 12-18 months, requests for drawings of foreign exchange (i.e., to meet short-term BOP problems) up to a certain amount will be allowed if the country concerned wishes. However, the stand-by arrangements can be extended up to 3 years while repayments are required to be made within 3-5 years of each drawing. The term "stand-by" here means that, subject to conditionality, a member has a right to draw the money made available, if needed. In most cases, the member does, in fact, draw.

(ii) *Extended Fund Facility (EFF)* : Stand-by arrangements to stabilise a member's BOP run usually for a period of 12-18 months. Developing countries suffer from chronic BOP problems which could not be remedied in the short run. Such protracted BOP difficulties experienced by the LDCs were the result of structural imbalances in production and trade. It then necessitated an adjustment programme and redemption scheme of longer duration. In the 1970s, the Fund recognised this idea and built up the EFF in 1974. The EFF is designed to provide assistance to members to meet their BOP deficits for longer period (3-4 years) and in amounts larger in relation to their quotas. Repayment provisions of EFF cover a period of 4-10 years. However, conditions for granting loans are very stringent. Drawings on this account since 2000 stand at over 50 billion dollar in SDRs.

(iii) *Compensatary Financing Facility* (CFF) : Apart from the ordinary drawing rights, there are some 'special finances' windows to assist the developing countries to tide over BOP difficulties. CFF, introduced in 1963, is one such special drawing provision. Its name was changed to Compensatory and Contingency Financing Facility (CCFF) in 1980, but the 'contingency' was dropped in 2000. Under it, members were allowed to draw up to 25 p.c. of its quota when CFF was introduced. It can now draw up to 45 p.c. Since the mid-1990s, this has been the least-used facility.

(iv) *Structural Adjustment Facility (SAF) and the Enhanced SAF (ESAF)* : In 1986 a new facility—the SAF—was introduced for the benefit of low income countries. It was increasingly realised that the so-called stringent and inflexible credit arrangements were too inadequate to cope with the growing debt problems of the poorest members of the Fund. In view of this, SAF was introduced which stood quite apart from the monetary character of the Fund. Under it, credit facilities for economic reform programmes are available at a low interest rate of 0.5 p.c compared to 6 p.c. for most Fund facilities. Loans are for 10 years with a grace period of five and a half years. LDCs facing protracted BOP problems can get assistance under SAF provided they agree to undertake medium-term structural adjustment programmes to foster economic growth and improve BOP contidions. An extended version of SAF—ESAF—was introduced in 1987. The ESAF has been replaced by a new facility, called Poverty Reduction and Growth Facility in 1999.

What emerges from the structural adjustment facility is that the IMF's loan is now available to member countries in support of policy programmes. It now insists on the supply side policy 'as a condition' for assistance, in addition to loans meant for short-term BOP difficulties.

(v) *Poverty Reduction and Growth Facility (PRGF)* : The PRGF that replaced the ESAF in November 1999 provides concessional lending to help the poorest member countries with the aim of making poverty reduction and economic growth —the central objectives of policy programmes. Under this facility, low-income member countries are eligible to borrow up to 140 p.c. of its quota for a 3-year period. Rate of interest that is charged is only 0.5 p.c and repayment period covers $5^1/_2$-10 years, after disbursement of such facility. However, financial assistance under this facility is, of course, 'conditional'.

(vi) *Supplemental Reserve Facility (SRF)* : This instrument provides additional short-term financing to member countries facing exceptional BOP difficulties because of a sudden and disruptive loss of market confidence reflected in capital outflows of countries concerned. Consequent upon the eruption of East Asian financial crisis, the SRF was introduced in 1997.

Till date (March, 2012), the top three largest borrowing nations are Greece, Portugal and Ireland from the IMF.

Strings of conditionality : It is to be remembered here that the IMF lending is conditional. Further, the IMF lending is temporary ranging from 1 year to 3 years. Repayment period varies from country to country and from one facility to another. Repayment under PRGF for low income countries is 10 years with a $5^1/_2$ year grace period on principal payments.

The IMF may be viewed as both a financing and an adjustment-oriented international institution for the benefit of its members. The distinguishing features of the Fund loans are their cost and certain macroeconomic policy conditions. These conditionality requirements range from rather general commitments to cooperate with the IMF in setting policies to formulating a specific, quantified plan for monetary, trade, and fiscal policies.

The IMF practice of tying loans to conditions reflects the dominant influence of the capitalist world. The strings of conditionalities as well as the policy of sanctions that came to the fore in the early 1960s made this international organisation the most controversial institution. This is because of the fact that the conditions set by the Fund cannot constitute a standard solution for deficit countries to the Fund's finances. By attaching conditions to credit facilities, the Fund has assumed the role of a 'neo-colonist'. Some say that the IMF has been acting as 'a rubber stamp for the desires of the US administration'.

The conditionality is always intended to restore internal and external balance and price stability. While formulating specific performance criteria (often referred to as 'conditional loans' that is, 'at the point of a gun'), the Fund prepares 'stabilisation' programme and 'adjustment' programme which member states will be required to adopt to tackle macroeconomic instability. The programme design involves monetary and fiscal policy measures so that structural adjustment (i.e., reforms aimed at changing the structure of both production and consumption) takes place. Stabilisation is generally regarded as a precondition of structural adjustment policies[1]. Thus, stabilisation and structural programmes not only includes monetary and fiscal policies but also exchange rate policy (i.e., devaluation), liberalisation or deregulation, privatisation, reforming institutions to carry governments' new role, freeing markets to determine prices, reforming the labour sector. Almost all stabilisation programmes intend to curb effective demand.

4.6.8 Working of the IMF

There are two phases in the working of the IMF over the last 65 years. The first phase covers the period late 1940s (i.e., 1947) to 1971. This phase is popularly known as the 'Bretton Woods System'. The IMF system or the Bretton Woods System provides for exchange rate stability in the short run but allowed for the possibility of exchange rate adjustment when a country experienced 'fundamental' disequilibrium in its BOP accounts. Thus, the pegged exchange rate was adjusted in accordance with the IMF. Hence the name 'adjustable peg system'.

As the system was the source of some major problems, it was abandoned in 1971 and more flexibility was introduced in the monetary system. In other words, the demise of the Bretton Woods System made room for the floating exchange rate regime, requiring changes in the role of the IMF. After prolonged negotiations (1973-78), the IMF started its second-leg journey in 1978.

---

1. Structural adjustment programmes were invented after the collapse of the Bretton Woods System. Economic thinking and policies and reforms to be applied in poor countries are referred to as Washington Consensus. This Concensus is based on neo-classical economic thinking. The term Washington Consensus was coined in 1989 by John Williamson. It is so-called because many governmental, private sector, and inter-governmental economists of the Fund-Bank are Washington-based. The core elements of SAPs are : (i) belief in the efficacy of market forces, (ii) deregulation, liberalisation, and privatisation, (iii) trade liberalisation instead of protectionism. With the collapse of the socialist states, the Washington Consensus received tremendous encouragement from the twin sisters.

The decade of the 1970s saw massive borrowing by the developing countries. It rose to $600 billion by 1982. Meanwhile, the rise in interest rates in the USA from 1979 and the appreciation of dollar caused tremendous difficulties to the developing countries in servicing their debts. On the other hand, the switch to the floating exchange rate system coincided with the deteriorating economic conditions in the industrialised countries. Debt crisis that emerged in many developing countries had a dramatic effect. Mexico—a Latin American country—announced its failure to honour debt obligations. The IMF now played a crucial role to put the international financial system in order. It came in for mobilisation of additional financial resources so as to reduce the debt burden. As a result of this and other related measures, many countries regained access to the international banks and creditors and the severity of the debt problem moderated considerably in Latin America in the early 1990s.

With the break up of the Soviet Union in 1989, a new category of countries, especially the erstwhile communist countries, joined the IMF. The IMF now came forward to assist countries undergoing transition from a centrally planned economy to a market-oriented economy. Privatisation is indeed a crucial element of the transition process. That is why the IMF is providing financial assistance and technical support for the development of sound economic management and the privatisation of state enterprises.

In 1997, the East Asian financial crisis began when the currencies of the 'Asian tiger' economies (South Korea, Singapore, Hong Kong, Taiwan) plummeted, and the stock market crashed. Rescue packages were launched by the IMF under strong authority conditions.

Achievements : From this balance sheet of the working of the IMF, we are now in a position to evaluate its performance over the last 65 years or so. First, we state the achievements of the Fund.

The IMF acts both as a financing and an adjustment-oriented international institution for the benefit of its members. It has been providing financial assistance to the deficit countries to meet their temporary disequilibrium in BOP.

The Fund aims at promoting exchange rate stability. In its early phase, the Fund made arrangements of avoidance of competitive exchange depreciation.

It has made an attempt to solve the problem of international liquidity. To create international liquidity, Special Drawing Rights (SDRs)—an artificial currency—were created in 1969 as foreign exchange reserves to benefit the developing countries in particular. SDR allocations are made to member countries to finance the BOP deficits.

It is an institution through which consultation in monetary affairs takes place in an ongoing way. It acts as a forum for discussions of the economic, fiscal and financial policies of member countries, keeping the BOP problems in mind. Previously, the poorest developing countries did not receive adequate treatment from the Fund. But from 1980s onwards—when the debt crisis broke out in poor countries—the Fund decided to divert its financial resources to these countries.

In 1980s, centrally planned economies were not hitherto members of the Fund. With the collapse of the Soviet Union in 1989, ex-communist countries became members of the Fund and the Fund is providing assistance to these countries so as to instil the principles of market economy. It has decided to finance resources to combat terrorism and money-laundering.

Finally, the IMF has assisted its members in the formulation of appropriate monetary, fiscal, and trade policies.

Failures : Despite these achievements, its failures are glaring. In other words, its success is, on the whole, limited. There are some serious charges against this institution that cannot escape attention. These are :

The Fund provides short-term finance to its members to tackle BOP disequilibrium. For this purpose, it adopted an adjustable peg system in the first phase of its life. But it failed to establish a stable exchange rate. Its role in controlling the competitive exchange depreciation policies adopted by the members was subject to serious scrutiny, although it was created to avoid devaluation as a BOP measure as much as possible. Truly speaking, the IMF is incapable of taking independent policy decisions. It complies with the 'order' of the superpowers. Further, it has minimal influence over the policy decisions of the major industrial powers. In these cases, its mandate to exercise 'firm surveillance' over some influential members or superpowers is virtually meaningless—it has no influence over the US deficits or European interest rates.

Secondly, the Fund imposes conditions on the poor countries while sanctioning loans. Now, it is ignoring its central concern—exchange rate management and the BOP problems. It is now championing the issue of 'market principle'. It suggests poor developing countries to cut expenditure-borrowing-subsidy, raise prices of state enterprises, privatisation of state-owned enterprises, etc. If such measures—most popularly known as structural adjustment progammes—are adopted only then the IMF credit would follow. It is said that the third world debt crisis is due to the Fund policies and working.

Thirdly, the Fund has failed to eliminate foreign exchange restrictions imposed by its members that hamper the growth of trade.

In view of these, the developing countries are blaming the IMF for their economic malaise. It is said that the IMF has outlived its mission and the time has come for it to go into oblivion. Sixty-five years is long enough!

4.6.9 Role of the IMF in Economic Development of LDCs

Being a central institution of international monetary system, the IMF works for global prosperity by promoting a balanced expansion of world trade. The IMF not only operates as a BOP adjustment institution but also a BOP financing institution. The IMF system provides for exchange rate stability in the short run but allows for exchange rate adjustment if a country faces 'fundamental' disequilibrium in its BOP accounts. Hence the name 'adjustable peg system' that lasted till 1971 since its birth. Till the mid-60s of the 20th century, some progress had been achieved in the direction of international cooperation and compliance with the Fund's Articles of Agreement. Continuous drop in its gold reserves and chronic BOP deficits resulting in a crisis of confidence of dollar forced the USA to abandon the convertibility of dollars into gold in 1971. This is called breakdown of the Bretton Woods System that seriously raised questions about the role of the IMF in the provisioning of international finance. Floating exchange rate system thus introduced caused severe hardships to the LDCs. Meanwhile, many LDCs faced serious BOP deficits because of a world recession, the first oil shock in the form of recoketing fuel prices, and a falling exports of LDCs.

Earlier, that is before 1971, the bulk of the Fund's resources was used to maintain the value of currencies of the developed world. The Fund had been also marginalised by the actions of the G-7 and regional trading blocks. However, with the change in the exchange rate system, the role of the IMF also underwent a change. It shifted its focus of attention to the developing countries in the late 1970s. In the 1980s, it became more generous in providing resources to the countries in difficulty. Since then, both the IMF and the World Bank have been helping ex-communist countries to build a market economy, though the IMF was created primarily as an institution for the promotion of international monetary stability. The founding fathers of the Fund expected that it would poke its nose in the affairs of the LDCs and, lately, of the former communist countries.

Today, the Fund is being labelled as an 'anti-developmental' institution, as far as structural adjustment lending is concerned. The IMF now serves the needs of global finance instead of the needs of global stability. The use of conditionality and the direct 'surveillance' on macroeconomic policy by the Fund is suggestive of increasing involvement in the LDCs' development process.

Drawings from the EFF, SRF, PRGF, etc., are available if the member countries agree to a stabilisation programme. The IMF focuses mainly on a country's macroecomomic stability as well as structural adjustment programme that influences its macroeconomic performance. Conditionalities are attached when member countries opt for drawings from the abovenoted sources of the Fund. Structural adjustment programmes (that includes not only stabilisation programmes associated with monetary and fiscal policy measures, but also trade liberalisation, privatisation, globalisation, freeing markets to determine prices, reforming institutions, to carry government's new role, and so on) are said to be preconditions for securing Bank-Fund loans. Its adverse impacts on the LDCs are varied and numerous.

First, SAP was justified as necessary to the LDC world as it would enable them to repay their debt to banks of advanced countries. By the late 1980s, more than 70 LDCs had to swallow the SAP medicine. But its impact on growth of these countries was negative. As many as 77 p.c. of countries saw the most significant decline in their per capita incomes. In Latin America, during the 1960s and 1970s, income grew by 75 p.c. when these economies were relatively closed, but during the 1980s, income grew by 61 p.c. only. Average incomes in sub-Saharan Africa actually contracted.

Latest research data (2006) for 98 countries during 1970-2000 revealed a negative impact of the IMF programmes on the per capita income growth of 1.7 p.c. p.a. Another study (1991) of 40 countries showed negligible growth in GDP, marginal increase in export growth and the BOP situation and a decline in investment. The IMF aims at tackling BOP disequilibrium but does little to learn the root causes of such disequilibrium.

Secondly, the costs of adjusting to greater openness of the LDC economy are shouldered mainly by the poor. The Fund recommends privatisation so as to offset government failure. It is said that the government-run enterprises are inefficient. Bureaucracies are corrupt. Thus by 'freeing the markets', competitive efficiency could be improved. But the costs of such adjustment programmes are expensive. Indeed, globalisation has triggered both poverty and inequality. Today's world see the "billionaires of capitalists" and the exponential growth of poverty-stricken, malnourished people.

In compliance with the IMF demand, in Argentina during 1976-87, employment in public administration was down by 11.5 p.c. and in State enterprises by 18.9 p.c. In India, during the stabilisation period 1991-99, growth rates in employment in the organised sector declined form 1.44 p.c. to 0.84 p.c. and further to –0.31 p.c. during 1994-2006. The inevitable consequence of this is the rise in the number of unemployeds and poor people. "In the eyes of some, the acronym IMF stands for (I)inflation, (M)isery and (F)amine!" (A.P. Thirlwall).

Again, the IMF introduced economic shock therapy measures in command economies. All these comprised the introduction of capitalism in Russia and other former Soviet-bloc countries and hence a shift from the state-led development to market-led development.

Thirdly, Joseph Stiglitz has accused the IMF of promoting an agenda of 'market fundamentalism' thereby injuring the country's social fabric. The Fund emphasises fiscal discipline—cuts in government expenditures and subsidies—so as to pursue a free market economy philosophy. But because of cuts in government expenditures and various subsidies on basic necessities and a rise in the price of public services, vulnerable people bore the major brunt. Following cuts in subsidies on food products, milk prices in Chile went up by 400 p.c., bread by 367 p.c., potatoes by 850 p.c. and carrot by 1,589 p.c. in 1975—the average rate of inflation there was 340 p.c. Many LDCs saw their indicators of standard of living—infant mortality, life expectancy, adult literacy, primary school enrolment, per capita calorie supply, etc.—falling to an unimaginable proportion. The Fund is unresponsive to "adjustment with a human face".

Fourthly, structural adjustment conditionality is often criticised for the third world debt crisis. Borrowing-dependent third world countries in the 1970s and 1980s went for private commercial bank loans—thereby causing accumulation of external debt and ballooning of debt service payments. Faced with this crisis, many of the LDC countries approached the IMF for borrowing to avert the risk of default. It then invented the structural adjustment lending, provided conditionalities imposed by the Fund-World Bank are respected by the borrowing nations. This debt burden also caused severe BOP crises in many countries. The Fund-Bank do not find incentives to close exchange gap; rather they decapitalise LDCs.

Finally, the Fund often brings political and social unrest. Many of the policy measures suggested by the Fund (e.g., subsidy cut, labour retrenchment, golden handshake, etc.) caused widespread strikes, riots, etc., in many countries. Actually, finding no other alternatives, these countries had to swallow the bitter painful SAP medicine. One author has remarked that the Fund 'has overthrown more governments than the military'! Social unrest consequent upon strict conditionalities brought more chaos, rather than solution. Argentina faced military takeover in 1976, Brazil in 1964, Chile and Uruguary in 1973, Turkey in 1960, 1971, and 1980. Military coups do not deserve the name 'stabilisation' and 'structural adjustment', in any case!

Conclusion : Anyway, actions and policies of the Fund are designed not in accordance with the interests of the third world countries but to encourage the logic of capitalist expansion. The major shareholders of the IMF, mainly the USA, are not interested in sharing power with developing countries. It is the quota restriction that allows the USA to enjoy overwhelming power and status in the shaping of Fund policies. Whenever some people batted for developing countries and criticised the Fund-Bank activities, they experienced pressure from the USA. For instance, the former chief economist of the World Bank, the Nobel Laureate Joseph Stiglitz, remarked that the basic motive of the Fund-Bank was to serve the interest of the Wall Street through the US Treasury. Before facing the step for sacking Stiglitz from the World Bank at the initiative of the US Treasury, Stiglitz resigned from the post in January 2000. The IMF is truly 'a proxy for the USA' as remarked by the *New York Times*.

4.6.10 IMF vis-a-vis India

India is one of the founder members of the Bretton Woods institutions. The IMF provides short-term financial assistance to the members so as to enable them to tide over BOP short run situation. To ease the problem of international liquidity, SDRs were created in 1969. The SDRs are allocated to the members in proportion to their quotas. India borrowed both financial and other assistance from the IMF quite a number of times under several lending provisions of the Fund.

Although India borrowed from the Fund immediately after independence, her dependence on it for financial assistance became critical during the Second Five Year Plan (1955-56 to 1960-61) when she witnessed a sharp fall in her foreign exchange reserves. She borrowed $200 million to meet the crisis. As the BOP crisis remained precarious she again borrowed $250 million in 1961. As there was no sign of improvement in the BOP position, India devalued her currency in 1966 to the extent of 36.5 p.c.—allegedly on the advice of the IMF.

India again made a huge borrowing from the IMF in 1981 to tide over the BOP difficulties following the second oil price rise made by the OPEC and the large volume of trade deficit. Under the borrowing arrangement with the IMF, India agreed to draw SDR 5 billion, over a three year period. As BOP situation as well as economic conditions improved, actual drawing from the Fund was only SDR 3.9 billion, rather than SDR 5 billion.

The situation again deteriorated in the late 1980s and early 1990s when foreign exchange reserves—for two weeks' imports as against the generally accepted 'safe minimum reserves' of three month equivalent—position were terribly unsatisfactory. Several face-saving measures were taken by the Government, but with little or no achievements. The then Government headed by P. V. Narasimha Rao entered an agreement with the IMF to borrow from it. In August 1991, the Government applied for a standby loan of $ 2.3 million for a 20-month period. For this, a letter of intent was issued. In this letter, India promised to launch several structural reforms in the coming years. In other words, conditionality clause was incorporated by the IMF against such loans. The economic reforms of 1990s in India are said to have been introduced at the instance of the IMF-World Bank.

India has been receiveing benefits from the Fund from time to time. Quite a large number of time, India got financial accommodation from the Fund to cover deficits in BOP. As the IMF and the World Bank are inseparable twins, membership in the former is a prerequisite for membership in the latter. This is why India receives various kinds of help for various development projects from the World Bank. The Fund provides technical expertise and support to India in various broad areas—particularly fiscal and monetary policy. Its staff frequently exchange views on India's BOP situation, fiscal situation, exchange rate problems, etc., and suggest appropriate remedies to the problems. Thus, India gains from the Fund.

However, conditionality clause of the IMF loan in recent years is subject to serious debate.

Measures suggested by the Fund in the early years of the 1990s involved serious stress and strains. The IMF medicine—devaluation of Indian currency, reduction in budgetary and fiscal deficit, cut in government expenditure and subsidy, import liberalisation, industrial policy reforms, trade policy reforms, banking reforms, financial sector reforms, privatisation of public sector enterprises, etc.,—involved some costs that are mostly unwarranted. Inspite of the use of IMF medicine since 2007, India has been facing recession in industries. Unemployment problem is on the rise. Public sector enterprises are facing extinction. Number of people living below the poverty line is on the rise. It is true that the BOP problem is not so serious today than what it was 10 or 15 years ago, but debt burden is not showing any sign of abatement. Deb-service payment rose from $ 8.2 billion in 1992 to $ 15.4 billion in 2009. However, debt-servicing ratio during the period 1992-2010 declined from 30.1 p.c. to p.c.

Anyway, the IMF prescriptions on India as well as on other countries present a mixed picture of failures and successes. Some of the measures adopted were urgently called for. One such measure is the creation of a free, competitive economy. The IMF has to be credited for the creation of competitive economy. Still more has to be done. But, in the process, it has generated enough problems. We must not brush aside these as transitional problems. These problems are to be tackled promptly.

4.7 The World Bank

The World Bank (WB) was originally created as the International Bank for Reconstruction and Development (IBRD) in 1944 along with its twin, the IMF. Together they came to be known as the 'Bretton Woods' twin sisters'. When it was set up it was decided that this international bank would assist in the economic reconstruction of the World War II-damanged European economies. In early 1946 this international bank launched its carrer as the multilateral development bank and since then the IBRD came to be known as the World Bank. Its headequarters is located in Washington, opposite the IMF building, and it lies as the next door neighbour of the White House.

Functions

Being twin sisters, membership in the IMF is a prerequisite for membership in World Bank (188 countries in May, 2012).

The Bank performs the following functions :

I. To assist in the construction and development of the territories of its members by facilitating investment of capital for productive purposes, including the 'restoration of economies destroyed or disrupted by war', and the encouragement of the 'development' of productive facilities and resources in less developed countries.

II. To promote private investment and long run balanced growth of international trade and BOP equilibrium by means of guarantees or participation in international loans and investments.

III. To arrange loans made or guaranteed by it, so that more useful and urgent projects receive preference.

IV. To provide finance to projects from its own capital, funds raised by it and by participating with other members.

In addition, the Bank provides advice and expertise. It now puts more emphasis on institutional technical assistance and infrastructure assistance. Over the years, it has been able to generate and disseminate policy relevant knowledge. Today, it has been concentrating more on this asset rather than financial resources. This organisation is now called the 'knowledge bank'.

Objectives

The purposes and objectives are constantly changing. For instance, in the early years, the Bank's investment concentrated on infrastructural build-up like power, transport, communications and irrigation. During the late 1960s and 1970s, the Bank went on financing agricultural projects more actively—particularly in the promotion of cash crops. However, in the 1980s, agricultural lending declined drastically.

Meanwhile, the WB decided to put emphasis on the alleviation of poverty in less developed countries in the late 1960s and 1970s. During Robert McNamara's Presidency (1968-81), the WB made a radical change in emphasis—the reduction of rural poverty as well as urban poverty. Since then all the Presidents reiterated the commitment to fight poverty, enhance growth with sustainability. It also introduced structural adjustment programmes (SAPs) in developing countries so that not only macroeconomic stability can be attained but also structural reforms aimed at accelerating growth can be undertaken. It has shifted its emphasis from the financing on specific projects towards non-project linked programmes. It works in developing economies with the focus of helping the poorest people and the poorest countries. For all its clients, the Bank emphasises the need for

(i) investing in people, particularly through basic health and education;
(ii) focussing on social development, governance and institution-building as the major elements of poverty alleviation;
(iii) strengthening the ability of the governments to deliver quality services with greater efficiency and transparency;
(iv) protecting the environment;
(v) supporting and encouraging private business development and long-term planning.

Through its loans, policy advice, and technical assistance, the WB supports a broad range of programmes aimed at reducing poverty and improving living standards in the developing world including the achievement of the Millennium Development Goals (MDGs) by helping countries develop an environment for investment, jobs, and sustainable growth. The WB works with government agencies, non-governmental organisations (NGOs), and the private sector to formulate various assistance strategies.

4.7.1 The IMF and the World Bank—Similarities and Differences

Both these institutions are called Bretton Woods institutions. They have the same membership—no admission to the World Bank without the IMF membership. The management structure of the Bank is largely similar to that of the Fund. Voting rights in these institutions depend primarily on capital contribu-tion of the member countries.

But there are same fundamental differences between these two institutions. Basically, the Fund is a monetary institution while the Bank is a developmental institution. The main concern of the IMF is to reform the international monetary system. It grants credit to member countries to correct temporary BOP deficit. It pledges to maintain a stable exchange rate. The WB, on the other hand, was set up for financing war-damaged economies of Europe caused by World War II. As soon as the Marshall Aid programme was rolled out in meeting resource needs of Europe, the Bank shifted its focus to developing countries and came to be known as the 'World Bank'. Being a development institution, it finances long and medium term development programmes. That is, the IMF's main concern is *macro* element while the Bank focuses on *micro* aspects of development.

In recent years, the Bank has shifted its attention from project financing to economic reform packages. However, both these institutions provide conditional loans—the structural adjustment loans (SALs). The Bank took up this lending in 1980 through the stabilisation programme with conditionalities which were adopted by the IMF in the 1970s. Today, we observe overlapping activities of these institutions. The Bank is now moving to macro issues and the Fund now shapes policies for the developing and ex-communist countries to build up a market economy. Today, in a variety of areas, both these institutions are cooperating—one intrudes into the domain of the other. Cooperation between these institutions is observed 'in supporting governments in implementiong poverty reduction strategies in low income countries, providing debt relief for the poorest countries, and assessing the financial sectors of countries.' In view of these developments, it has now become increasingly difficult to identify the differences between these institutions.

4.7.2 A Critical Evaluation of the World Bank Activities

The WB offers two basic types of loans—investment loans for the support of econo-mic and social development projects, and development policy loans to support countries' policy and institutional reforms. The WB grants loans only to the developing countries (and not all the 188 members) annually at nearly $ 20 billion a year usually for a period of 15 to 20 years for the purpose of building roads, dams, and other physical capital that contribute to their economic development. Its lending rate is somewhat low and is fixed every six months. The Bank offers hard currency loans. It accepts hard currency at the time of repayment. The Bank functions as an agent on the international capital markets for countries which are unable to obtain sufficient loans on concessional terms. Its loan provisions are : (i) project loans, (ii) sectoral loans, and (iii) structural adjustments loans (SALs).

The Bank provided $ 24.7 billion loans in the fiscal year 2008, with Africa receiving 23 p.c. of the total; Latin America and the Caribbean 19 p.c.; East Asia and Pacific 18 p.c.; South Asia 17 p.c.; Europe and Central Asia 17.4 p.c.; and Middle East and North Africa 6 p.c. With Bank support—both lending and advice—governments are reforming their economies and strengthening the entire financial and banking systems.

Tte World Bank has made remarkable success in achieving its basic objectivess over the last 65 years or so. Its concern for developing countries deserves special attention. It has taken up various poverty-reduction strategies and poverty-focused lending. Bank programmes give high priority to sustainable, social and human development and strengthened economic management. Latin American experience suggest that, during the 1980s and 1990s, inflation rate declined in Mexico, Panama, Costa Rica, Bolivia, Argentina, except Brazil. Further, because of trade liberalisation programme, the share of exports to GDP in these countries rose to 21.3 p.c. in 1993 from 14 p.c. in 1980. Still then, the modus operandi of the Bank has come in for sharp criticisms.

One of the serious charges against the WB loan is its structural adjustment lending or policy-based lending. The essence of SAL is loans disbursed in exchange for policy reforms like trade liberalisation, privatisation, financial sector reforms, tax reforms, etc. But various studies have shown that SALs have failed miserably in establishing a basis for healthy economic and social development in debtor countries. In most of the developing countries, average incomes, investment, import, etc., have fallen drastically. Unemployment and inflation have become major problems. Number of people living below the poverty line does not show any declining trend in these countries. On the contrary, global poverty has increased and its activities are alleged to be detrimental to the environment, public health, and cultural diversity. It seems two institutions now need urgent reforms.

Among the developing countries, the Latin American experience is too hard to digest. After the adoption of SAPs, average incomes fell by 10 p.c., and investment declined from 23 p.c to 16 p.c. of national income during the 1980s. According to a WB estimate, the poverty ratio increased marginally from 15.53 p.c.. to 15.67 p.c. and the number of poor people rose from nearly 64 million to 78 million. Many of the Latin American countries experienced the process of deindustrialisation—causing a massive increase in the number of unemployeds. Import liberalisation policy resulted in an increase in imports of stable food like rice, corn, etc. These costly imports lowered the living standards of masses. The case of sub-Saharan Africa is worst where nearly all children under-5 are malnourished.

A final word about the social and environmental damage caused by the WB project lending is a matter of grave concern. The '*Sobradinho Dam*' in Brazil displaced quite a good number of poor families from their homes and livelihoods, but they had never been compensated. The '*Singrauli Super Thermal Power Plant*' in central India resulted in a massive displacement of the local population from their places—about 49,000 in 1994. During a visit of a WB study team in the Singrauli region in 1993, a number of houses in Nimidam were bulldozed and oustees were forced to move without adequate arrangement. The gigantic investment in this project has resulted in a variety of problems in the area : severe air pollution from coal and ash dust leading to high rates of pulmonary diseases, unemployment, inadequate compensation, inadequte housing, pollution of drinking water, etc. Thus 'adjustment with a human face' has come under strict scrutiny.

It is also said that the World Bank is an instrument that serves the interests of the USA as well as the Western countries. Its functioning lacks transparency.

Thus, the World Bank has not come up to the expectations of many of the developing countries.

QUESTIONS WITH ANSWER-HINTS

Long-Answer Questions

1. What is meant by foreign aid? What are the benefits and costs of development of private foreign investment?

   Ans. 4.3 and 4.4

2. Do you think that the benefits of private foreign direct investment are more beneficial to the developing countries than the costs generated by such investment?
   Ans. 4.4
3. What are international capital flows? What are its types? Mention different types of aid received by the developing countries.
   Ans. 4.2 and 4.3.1
4. What are the arguments for and against foreign aid?
   Ans. 4.5
5. What do you mean by multinational corporations? How do these organisations fill up different types of 'gaps' or deficiencies experienced by the less developed countries?
   Ans. 4.4 and 4.4.1
6. What are the objectives and functions of the International Monetary Fund?
   Ans. 4.6.2
7. Briefly point out the different lending provisions of the IMF. What are the loan conditionalities?
   Ans. 4.6.7
8. What is meant by the Bretton Woods System? What are its essential elements? Why was it abandoned?
   Ans. 4.6.6
9. Make a brief assessment of the working of the IMF.

   Or

   What are the major achievements and failures of the IMF during its career?
   Ans. 4.6.8
10. Discuss the role of the IMF in the economic development of developing countries.
    Ans. 4.6.9
11. Discuss the role played by the IMF in shaping India's development.
    Ans. 4.6.10
12. What are the functions and objectives of the World Bank?
    Ans. 4.7
13. Discuss the role of the World Bank in the economic development of developing countries.
    Ans. 4.7.2

Short-Answer Questions

1. What are the types of foreign aid?
   Ans. 4.3.1
2. Distinguish between foreign aid and foreign investment.
   Ans. 4.3 and 4.3.1
3. Explain the dual-gap hypothesis.
   Ans. 4.4
4. What is MNC? Do you have any idea about the size of MNCs?
   Ans. 4.4.1
5. What are the major objectives of the IMF?
   Ans. 4.6.2
6. Write a note on Fund-Bank loan conditionality.
   Ans. 4.6.7.
7. Briefly discuss the major functions of the World Bank.
   Ans. 4.7. (v)
8. Mention the different types of international capital flows.
   Ans. 4.2
9. How does FDI fill up the 'technological gap'?
   Ans. 4.4 (i)
10. How does FDI by MNC promote dualistic economic structure?
    Ans. 4.4 (See *Costs of FDI.*)
11. Discuss one important argument for foreign aid.
    Ans. 4.5
12. What is the Bretton Woods System?
    Ans. 4.6.6
13. What are the loan conditions?
    Ans. 4.6
14. What do you mean by the structural adjustment programmes?
    Ans. 4.6.9
15. What is Special Drawing Rights?
    Ans. 4.6.5
16. Brifly point out the similarities and differences between the IMF and the World Bank.
    Ans. 4.7.1

CHAPTER 5 Gender and Economic Development

5.1 Introduction

Development economists of the earlier years could not recognise the important role played by women or the activities of female labour in the economic and social development of communities and countries. These people discussed the relationship between population growth and economic development, but not the role of women. Indeed, gender did not receive as a crucial concept in both economic theory and development economics. The most likely reason is that women are engaged in non-market work.

The Nobel Prize winning economist Gary S. Becker in 1965 pointed out that women spend non-market time in home/household production (hidden market). Goods thus produced in the home are not exchanged in the market; rather these are consumed by the members of the family. Over countries, it is seen that women specialise in unpaid household production while male members only work in market. Becker and others argue that this kind of labour division based on sex is made to lower the earnings and status of women in the society relative to men. In other words, gender inequality is then transmitted from family to the broad areas—the labour market.

With the development of this idea came '*economics of gender*'. The role of women is changing. The importance of women is receiving greater attention. The decade of 1975-85 was declared as the 'United Nations Decade for Women'. The year 2001 was declared as the 'Year of Women's Empowerment'. *The Human Development Report*, 1995, said "Human Development, if not engendered, is endangered." Human development demands gender equity. But in the contemporary world, we observe very serious gender inequality in economic and social arrangements.

This chapter focuses on different forms of gender inequality and deprivations. However, women's development is impossible without their empowerment. In other words, inequalities need to be addressed by the empowerment of women to achieve equality and equity with men in society. To measure the living standards of a nation, the UNDP has invented an index called *Gender-related Development Index* (GDI). In addition, another index called *Gender Empowerment Measure* (GEM) is used to measure the extent of inequality in gender empowerment. These two indices have also been touched upon in this chapter.

It may be noted that gender equality—rather than gender inequality—matters for development. A country with greater gender equality can improve labour productivity, enhance development outcomes for the future generation. In addition, institutions can be made for vocal and representative where gender in equality persists. Empowering women is a step in this direction. That is why it is said that gender equality is an instrument for development.

5.2 Multiple Roles of Women

It may be noted that while 'sex' is biologically determined, gender is socially or culturally determined. In most of the societies, women are devalued while male members' activities are highly respected. All domestic labour like caring and maintenance of the family is thought to be as 'non-work', as contrasted to men's paid labour.

Gender inequality between men and women is quite compatible with the structure of patriarchy. This has given rise to innumerable social fetters. Thus, gender inequality is not only an economic issue; but its social-political implications are substantial indeed.

It may be noted that gender relations are fundamentally about power. Women's work involves three components : biological role or reproductive role (i.e., child bearing) social reproduction (i.e., child rearing and nurturing all members of the family, household activities, and some community management in free time), and market-based production. These works are simultaneously performed by women while men are involved in market-based activity. Since men enjoy income earning capacity, they exercise more power in the partiarchal society. Contrarily, women enjoy less power and status as they are engaged in non-income earning household activity. Further, even if they earn in the labour market, their earnings are relatively less to men.

One conclusion that can be safely made is that women 'produ ' more than what the male counterparts do, but that remains either unpaid/ 'invisible' or underpaid. On the contrary, they are subject to all kinds of deprivations and exploitation; it is a collection of disparate interlinked problems. Gender inequality and injustices are the most common 'natural' phenomena that has been ruling over our social life over centuries. Their role is 'secondary' in a partiarchal society in spite of the the multiple roles played by them.

5.2.1 Different Forms of Gender Inequality

Gender is a word that focuses on empowering women in their relationship with men. It enables women to become self-reliant. Once the process of empowering women gets strength, gender roles get modified leading to a better state of human development and inclusive growth.

Gender-based inequality or the discrimination between sexes stems from the patrilineal character of most societies. Gender inequality is not a homogeneous phenomenon in the sense it appears in many different forms. However, the different faces of gender inequality are indeed overlapping; some type of inequality tends to encourage and sustain other kinds of inequality. For example, women lack decision-making power in the family for which primarily low level of educational achievement is responsible. This then affects 'investment' in children and household welfare—an example of "family public good". A vicious cycle of inequality then sets in. Gender inequality is thus the archetypical 'inequality trap'.

Here we explain the different faces of gender inequality :

(i) *Women work longer than men* : In most of the societies the malestream is the main stream who argues that women have comparative advantage in household non-market production, like cooking and cleaning for the family that can be called emotional and prersonal cairing work. Based on this thinking, household jobs are then asymmetrically distributed. Women are more valued in home. Men are specialised in market-based production. Thus, being the bread-earners, males enjoy both power and status.

It may be then concluded that women's activities serve primarily as inputs into the family's well-being. In addition, women of poor families are subject to dual burden of home-labour and market work for cash earnings.

[*Low status and power of women may thus be attributed to the 'functional theory'. This theory says that in such a sex-based division of labour system one observes a built-in disadvantage for women in non-household jobs or comparative advantage in household activities. Hence the inequality between sexes. Some experts explain gender-based inequality in the perspective of 'conflict theory'. In the capitalist society, labour market is such that it creates one set of jobs with poor salary and long working hours (e.g., construction workers) for women and a better one for male counterparts. This amounts to saying that women belong to the 'minority' group. This kind of boundary triggers discrimination between sexes.*]

Nearly 70 p.c. of food production is prepared by women. An average Indian woman spends at least 4 hours a day or 16 p.c. of their life time in the kitchen and 2-4 hours in a day for child-bearing and child rearing. These are all non-market household activities. In addition, market-based works are done by women to supplement family income.

Today, women represent 40 p.c. of the global labour force and 43 p.c. of the world's agricultural labour force. Most importantly, because of the reduction in fertility rate in many developing countries, women's participation in paid job has been rising in these countries. This, of course, is suggestive of reduction in gender gaps as time advances. It is revealed from the *World Development Report 2012* that the gender gap in work participation has been narrowed from 32 p.c. to 26 p.c. between 1980 and 2008.

In Fig. 5.1 the contributions of both men (in terms of work-hours) and women in market-based activities and non-market activities in both developed and develping countries have been shown to understand the dynamics of gender disparity. We see almost a uniform pattern of gender dispariry in time spent per minute in a day in both the developed and developing countries. Male-bias in job allocation (both home-based and market based) in different countries has been shown in Fig. 5.1.

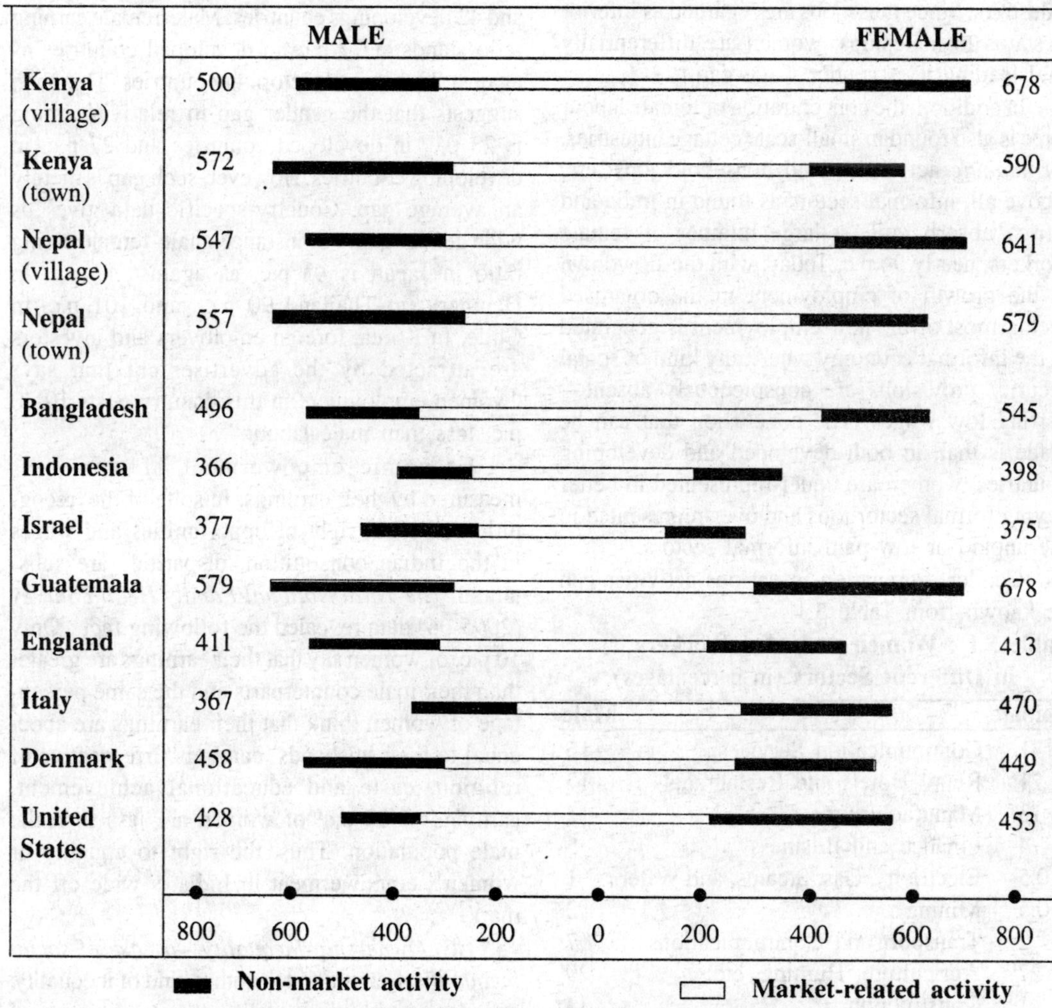

Fig. 5.1 : Gender Inequality : Economic and Household Works

(ii) *Inequality in employment and earnings* : Historically, men have greater participation in work outside home than women. But women (particularly of poor households) share unequally household duties in addition to economic production. Thus they work longer than males. This kind of 'division of labour' may be seen as the 'accumulation of labour' on women, as described by Amartya Sen. Household activities are often viewed as 'sedentary activities' which require less 'calorie' to gain energy.

As women shoulder household responsibilities, they tend to work mostly in a narrow range of occupations, called 'female industries'—textiles, clothing, electronics, food and beverages, etc., where wages are ususlly lower than in other industries. Since these jobs are regarded as inferior in status to male jobs, women are differentially paid leading to a gender wage gap.

In addition, the concentration of female labour force is also found in small-scale cottage industries, *biri-making* activities, paid household jobs, etc. Above all, informal sectors as found in India and Africa absorb quite a large number of female workers, nearly 94 p.c. Today, with the slowdown in the growth of employment in the organised sector, most of the new employment is generated in the informal economy where any kind of social security provisions are conspicuously absent—barring low wages. The conclusion that can be made is that, in both developed and developing countries, women are under-represented in better paying formal sector jobs and over-represented in the unpaid or low-paid informal sectors.

Gender segregation in various activities can be known from Table 5.1.

Table 5.1 : Women and Men Workers in Different Sectors (in percentages)

Female		Male
31	Communication Services	16
21	Retail Hotels and Restaurants	17
13	Manufacturing	12
4	Finance and Business	5
0.5	Electricity, Gas, Steams, and Water	1
0.5	Mining	2
2	Transport and Communications	7
27	Agriculture, Hunting, etc.	29
1	Construction	11
100	**All sectors / All occupations**	**100**

Source : *World Development Report*, 2012

As far as earnings are concerned, women are discriminated againt male workers not only in the informal sector but also in administrative or business and commerce, as well as professional jobs. The following table highlights the 'gender gap' relating to earnings between the sexes in both developed and developing countries :

Table 5.2 : Relative Earnings of Male and Female Workers

Male-female earning ratio	Gender gap
Developed countries (N = 19) 0.77	0.23
Developing countries (N = 42) 0.73	0.27

The table depicts the wage gap between male and female workers for 19 developed countries and 42 developings countries. Male-female earning ratio stands at 77 p.c. in developed countries as against 73 p.c. in developing countries. This then suggests that the gender gap in relative earning is 23 p.c. in developed countries and 27 p.c. in developing countries. However, such gap is merely an average gap. Country-specific data gives us wide gender gap. For instance, male-female earing ratio in Japan is 43 p.c. as against 47 p.c. in Denmark, in Thailand 90 p.c., and 101 p.c. in Chile. In Korea, foreign employers and investors are attracted by the advertisement that says "women employment in this country costs 10-20 p.c. less than male labour."

Economic empowerment of women is measured by their earnings. In spite of the recognition of equal right of opportunities and wages in the Indian constitution, disparities are substantial. *The Third National Family Health Survey (2005-06)* data revealed the following fact : Only 10 p.c. of women say that their earnings are greater than their male counterparts and the same percentage of women think that their earnings are about equal to their husbands' earnings. Irrespective of religion, caste and educational achievement, earnings of 80 p.c. of women are less than the male population. Thus, the right to equality or women's empowerment in India is wide off the mark.

(iii) *Ownership inequality—a case of social inequality* : Let us turn to another kind of inequality, called ownership inequality—a classic case of social inequality. In most of the societies, ownership over property and means of production rests mainly on male members. The law of inheritance provides such ownership rights on male child. Such denial coming out of hierarchical dualism within the family not only reduces the voice of women but also prevents them from participating in commercial, economic and social activities. This kind of social deprivation means absence or lack of capability. Or because of 'capability deprivation', women are subject to various kinds of exploitation and unfreedoms. Social inequality distorts the process of development. Unfortunately, ownership inequality in any country is not of recent origin. In her earlier life, a woman comes under the influence of her father, then husband as she enters a married life, and, finally, under sons—ownership right over property is skillfully avoided. A Telegu proverb corroborates this understanding :"Bringing up a daughter is like watering a plant in another's courtyard."

(iv) *Survival inequality* : Another crudest form of gender disparity is the unusually high mortality rates of women, though biologically, women live longer than men! Thus, more boys than girls are born everywhere leading to a 'deficit' of women and a 'surplus' of men. In developed countries because of absence of gender-bias in health care and nutrition, women outnumber men. In Europe and in North America, 105 or more girls are born per 100 boys. Such high female-male ratio (1.05) in these countries is attributed to a high gendered survival rate in different age groups.

But in developing countries, women receive less care and support than men. There is a strong 'son preference'. There is a male-bias in food allocation. Women require fewer calories than men; women's calorie intake constitutes 29 p.c. less than men. Average nutritional intake of Indian women is just 1,400 kilocalories daily against the nutritional requirement of 1,600 kilocalories—the barest minimum. Further, they eat less, even leftover foods after consumption of other members of the family and the guests, and sleep less for the family's welfare. Indian women are thus malnourished. This is how 'marginalisation of women' has been going on in a male-structured society since immemorial times.

Further, developing countries not only show 'pro-boy preference' but also exhibit a strong anti-female bias. Because of this attitude towards women, mortality rates of women are higher than men in developing countries.

The concept of 'missing women' as stated by Amartya Sen may be linked to this kind of anti-female bias relating to care and medical attention. Low female male ratios in Asian and North African countries is another way of explaining 'missing women'. If these countries showed the female-male ratios as observed in Europe and the North American countries, these countries would have millions more women.

Missing women is a rough estimate of the quantitative difference between the 'actual' population sex ratio and the 'expected' population sex ratio in the absence of discrimination between sexes. If 'actual' ratio exceeds the 'expected' ratio, then the excess is called the 'missing women'. Sen has demonstrated that had female-male ratio of Asia and North African countries were equal to Europe and America, then, in 1986, China would have gained 4.40 crore excess women, India 3.70 crore, and all the countries of Asia and Africa would have a total of more than 10 crore. These are the 'missing women'. In 2001, the number of missing women in India went up to 3.91 crore while in China it declined to 4.09 crore. During this time, actual gender ratio in India came to 1.072 against an expected ratio of 0.993.

Let us have a look at India's current state of gender ratio. India's female-male ratio has been becoming more and more adverse as the census figures suggest. Female : male ratio that stood at 927 in 1991 rose to 933 in 2001, and further to 940 in in 2011. However, this ratio is 1,084 in Kerala and 618 in Daman and Diu in 2011. But if we look at the child sex ratio, the picture that emerges is really a mind-boggling one and a cause for great concern. Child sex ratio (0-6 years) that stood at 945 girls per 1,000 boys in 1991declined to 927 in 2001, and further to 914 in 2011. This diminishing trend of girl child clearly suggests that some girl children are never born nor have the opportunity or scope to survive longer. In its Report, the United Nations International Children's Emergency Fund (UNICEF) claimed that 7,000 fewer girls are born in India everyday, a figure higher than the global average. The conclusion that one makes from this notion of 'missing women' in India is the strong gender bias or gender disparity.

As per the World Bank's estimate (*World Development Report,* 2012) globally excess female deaths after birth (women who would not have died in the previous year had they lived in high income countries) in developing countries and 'missing' girls at birth account every year for 3.9 million women below the age of 60. Out of this, 2/5ths of them are never born.

But why has such gender imbalance been increasing in developing countries? In Europe and America, males outnumber females at birth but women outnumber men as the female-male ratio (of around 1.05) tells. On the contrary, in the third world countries, because of high mortality rates of women, male population becomes large. Abundance of women in advanced countries may be related to premature death, a high propensity to smoking and a larger involvement in violent activities of men. The bias towards boys over girls explains the 'missing women' mystery. Because of significant anti-female bias in health care and other social influences relevant for survival, female infanticide that goes on is one good reason for 'missing women'. Another reason that has become even popular among the educated Indians is the sex-selective abortions to eliminate female fetuses. Ths has become possible because of 'high-tech sexism'. It is practised largely in East Asia (China, and South Korea) Singapore, Taiwan, etc., and even in India and other countries of South Asia.

This 'natality inequality' indicates that parents want the newborn child to be a boy. This sort of 'son preference' in male-dominated societies is not only strong among poor illiterate parents but also among urban educated rich parents! This bias is linked to the increasing devaluation in social status and disempowerment of women in male-structured societies.

(v) *Gender bias in the distribution of education and health* : Health and education—the two major forms of human capital—are related to economic development. Human capital gets accumulated as a society advances in education. The contribution of human capital towards Japan's remarkable economic progress attracts our attention. Improvement in health capital also improves the return to investments in education, and vice versa.

However, one finds a huge education and health gaps between developed and developing countries. In recent times, despite a large increase in economic advancement in Asia and Africa, these countries lag far behind the developed countries in terms of educational attainment—particularly in respect of women's education. Gender disparity not only hinders economic progress but also exacerbates social inequality. There is enough statistical evidence that the rate of return on women's education is higher than that on men's. It is the mother's education that improves child health and nutrition. It has the potentiality of breaking the vicious circle of poverty and inequality. Education of women is directly related to poverty reduction.

In spite of this, male-child bias in third world countries of Asia is palpable. Such bias can be attributed to the following facts. *First,* being the breadwinner, male child is considered as an 'insurance bond' of the family. *Secondly,* male child provides security during old age. *Thirdly,* a male child is deemed to be an asset as it enables parents to garner huge dowry/gift at the marriage time. All these speak about anti-female bias. During marriage of a girl, there occurs a leakage of money from the parents to give dowry to the bride.

Above all, investment in women's education is not worthwhile as ultimately a girl child after marriage considers welfare of her husband's family. Unless this mindset changes gender disparity will continue. To remove such gender gap in education. the role of women's education is undesirable.

Anti-female bias in education gets reflected in male-female literacy rate, gross enrolment rate in elementary education (Class I-VIII), dropout rates among girl students.

Male-female literacy rate in India has increased from 75.26 p.c.-53.67 p.c. in 2001 to 82.14 p.c.-65.46 p.c. in 2011, thereby reflecting an educational gender gap of almost 17 p.c. Such disparity becomes larger if the adult male-female literacy ratio is taken into account. Currently, adult literacy rate for women is roughly 54 p.c. This means that slighltly more than half of female population can read and write—a pathetic figure indeed! Because of lower importance given to education, there has been a deterioration in India's Human Development Index ranking. It slipped from 126th among 117 countries in 2006 to 134th in 2011.

Boys-girls' gross enrolment rate in 2009 at the primary level came to 115 p.c. and 111 p.c. For China, it is 111 : 115. Further, dropout rate among girls in India is the highest. Several reasons are advanced to explain the huge gender disparity in dropout rates. *First* is the low level of education of poor parents. *Secondly,* because of low level of education, child marriage at barely 13 or 14 years is a common sight in Indian states, though the legal marriage age for women is 18 years. One in every 4 girls in India and one in every 5 girls in Nepal is married by the age of 15. Fifty p.c. girls of Bihar (having a literacy rate of 32-33 p.c. in 2001), Rajasthan, Uttar Pradesh and Madhya Pradesh are married at or before the age of 16.

This sorry state of affairs in women's education indicate poor state of health. Because of early marriage, poor Indian women's child-bearing age starts earlier. It results not only in frequent pregnancies but also creates problems in caring for the newborn child. Maternal mortality rate per 1,00,000 live births during 2004-09 account for 254 in India as against China's 34 only. Frequent pregrancies, in addition, at a low age leads to high percentage of anemic women. 63-85 p.c. of married women of West Bengal, Orissa, Bihar, Assam, and Arunachal Pradesh give birth to underweight baby. One sees gross deprivation in having a nutritious food and adequate care during pregnancy. Nearly 46 p.c baby suffers from underweight that raises the risk of having poor health and poor development of brain. Ultimately, all these lead to high infant mortality rate. 30 p.c. women die p.a. due to child birth and pregnancy-related causes. 38 p.c. of all HIV positives are women. Further, women suffer from illness more than men. Besides anti-female bias, poor women are deliberately denied basic health care facilities. When they suffer from diseases male members make a plea that a visit to a physician or hospital of a female member may lead to a postponement of the entire day's household jobs, including preparation of food for the family.

(vi) *Gender inequality in freedom expression*: Let us talk about gender inequality beyond economic issues or factors. Women are not only subject to income or asset inequality but also in terms of freedom and power deprivation of women goes beyond one's imagination. They lack not only economic freedom at home because of absence of autonomy in household decisions, limited or complete absence of property ownership rights and the poor wages earned but also lack any freedom in airing opinions over education of children. In some backward poor societies the right of women giving opinion is completely denied. Such unfreedoms, however, are not uncommon even among the educated elites who enjoy enormous power and authority in the male-dominated society. Historically, this sort of low socio-economic status of women has been continuing nowadays. In addition, one finds tremendous apathy in awarding political power and authority—that is participation in administrative decision-making and political decision-making—to women. In fact, women are underprivileged and are politically marginalised in many countries. Democracy then falters.

In many countries, voting rights to women has been granted, gender inequality, nevertheless, is rather widespread. Although many heads of states of many South Asian countries are women, women's representation in political institutions are indeed minimal. In government offices, administrative decision-making power rests solely on male members. India, however, is fortunate in having 50 p.c. seat reservations for women in gram panchayats in the year 2009. If these are implemented seriously, democracy and participation of women will foster. Public discussion and participation, interaction of all citizens then can act as catalysts of social change.

But, as in the processes of development and governance in many countries, women are marginalised, the goal of empowerment of women is jeopardised. At the same time, as women's agencies are rather active in India, some sort of politicisation of gender has been taking place and often women have become successful in having their genuine rights. Human capabilities can expand if women are assured of economic and political freedom. Such capability expansion is not hindered by poor income. With the expansion of capabilities of women, not only self-confidence gets a stimulus but also women increase their social status.

A final word of caution. Only by guaranteeing participation in elections, socio-politico-economic freedom of expression of women cannot be ensured. This is, however, not sufficient to remove the shackles of women's unfreedoms. What is important is the effective implementation of democratic procedures and norms. This requires reforms in the political field. The main opposition here, as usual, comes from the male members of the society. Gender inequality is an ultimate outcome of any patriarchal society. Only by empowering women, this social and economic barrier of gender inequality cannot be broken. This requires education of women. Effectiveness of political participation of women depends on the state of education. Thus, education acts as a great social change.

(vii) *Gender inequality in respect of violence and victimisation* : Finally, anti-female bias starts before the girl child is born (consequent upon sex-specific abortions) and this attitude of the society a female member carries throughout her life. It is because of the unequal sharing of income, property, household benefits (health and nutritional deprivation), women are subject to both physical and sexual violence—the opposite of freedom, and an extreme form of coercion. This is common for both poor and not too much uncommon in rich countries as well as among rich people. One in three women in the word is beaten or raped during her lifetimes.

Dowry harassment is considered as an 'instrumental use' of violence. Dowry death is the most serious form of domestic violence. Wife beating is not uncommon. Sexual violence is an obnoxious form of human rights violation. In addition, with the increase in poverty level, trafficking of women and children for sexual exploitation has become a high-profit-low-risk trade for those who organise it. There are many causes of such violences but physical prowess of men, dynamics of power and injustice, low or absence of education of women seem to be the most cogent reasons for gender inequality and subordinate status of women globally.

Economic independence and social emancipation through creating ability to earn income and gainful employment outside the home, guaranteeing ownership rights, literacy in education is of great importance. Empowerment value of all these is difficult to ignore. All these empower women. Through women's empowerment, patriarchal dominance and male monopoly of violence and the exploitation of women can be broken. And, above all, women's education can only destroy the institution of 'housewifisation' of women's labour through marriage and through work legislation.

5.2.2 Desirability of Gender Equality

No country treats men and women on the same platform. Gender inequality is found in key areas of economic and political decision-making and participation. We have talked about adverse effects of gender-based inequality. *Human Development Report, 2005* categorically asserted that "Human Development, if not engendered, is endangered". Gender equality promotes economic growth, strengthens democracy, improves governence, and reduces poverty and insecurity. Gender education gap, for instance, induces inequalites in many dimensions of social well-being. Thus, closing the gender gap is desirable on the following grounds.

First, studies from developing countries categorically show that the rate of return of female (basic) education is much higher than the rate of return on public infrastructure projects. In this situation, the importance of universal primary education is very significant. It is because of low level of education and religious beliefs the 'son complex' among parents rules in the Indian society. Early marriage is another bane of the Indian society. Poverty forces many people to get their daughters married much before the marriagable age.

Women's education alone can remove the social taboos. Through education, child-bearing time is not only delayed but also fertility rate tends to decline. It is because of low literacy rate of Indian rural women that the trend of declining birth rate is not found. There is a close relationship between women's literacy and reproductive capacity. Women having male child is a way out of eternal emancipation or '*nirvana*' or salvation of the soul. Such mindset is also prevalent even among educated persons in the Indian society. Only education can bring about a change in such mindset. Citing the importance of universal primary education, Ashok Mitra remarked that spending money worth rupees ten for contraceptives and family planning publicity is equivalent to spending worth rupee one for universal primary education.

Secondly, expansion of women's education acts as a catalyst of social change. In Asia, overabundance of men and deficit of women is explained by the concept 'missing women'. The so-called anti-female bias can be removed through education. It is the poorer treatment of girls that largely explains 'missing women'. Mother's education and a pro-female bias can wipe out this social malaise. Again, in many backward societies, male child is considered as an 'insurance bond'as he gives security to parents during old age. On the contrary, a female child requires dowry upon marriage but aims at improving the well-being of husband's family. Education alone can remove this kind of anti-female mentality bias.

Thirdly, increasing women's education helps not only in raising farm and firm productivity but also results in greater labour force participation, late marriage, lower fertility and improved health care and education of children—both sons and daughters of next generation. Income alone cannot bring such a favourable change. An educated women is better placed to liberate herself from the economic dependence on men. Besides economic participation, women need to participate in political decision-making so that the governance structure is improved. Women's voices are not only to be respected in the family but also in political decision-making. Those who lack basic education cannot have access to information. In such a situation, women will be put at a greater risk relative to men. Education enables ones to get independent access to information. An educated woman can protect herself against exploitative work conditions, poor wages, and even physical violence. Thus, the empowerment value of education of women is enormous.

Fourthly, women's education can turn the 'vicious' cycle of poverty and inequality into a 'virtuous' one. Amartya Sen says that poverty traps can be removed through the expansion of primary education and basic health care. In other words, with the expansion and distribution of social opportunities, human capabilities can be improved.

Fifthly, the strong correlation beteween increasing number of educated mothers and improved child health and nutrition stimulates human capital. This then produces multiplier effects on the quality of a nation's human resources for many generations to come.

Thus, gender unequality is more than deprivation of women. Achieving greater gender equality involves a process of active social change. Amartya Sen says that "Women's power and initiative can uplift the lives of all human beings—women, men and children."

5.3 Policies to Reduce Gender Gap

It is indeed true that there has been a great change for the better is being noticed across the globe. Improvements in women's education, health, labour force outcomes, and rights have taken place largely in the last two decades in low income countries. What these countries achieved over the last 40 years, as far as reduction in gender gap is concerned, it took even a century in the developed countries. All these changes have been bringing about gender equality gains.

Many policies may be designed for greater gender equality. Gender inequality, as we have seen, is not a homogeneous one. Therefore, choosing and designing policy intervening or the purpose of reducing gender gaps need simultaneous attacks on many fronts. One of the important pockets of disadvantage faced by women is education and partly in health. Thus the two gender gaps—education gap and health gap—can be minimised at the first instance through rising incomes. But higher incomes do not always enable ones to enjoy better education and health goods. Actually speaking, what is most demanding is the better service delivery especially to the poor and other disadvantaged groups. It is because of poor service delivery (e.g., access to schools for primary education and health centres for basic health care) educational and health outcomes are pretty low in poor developing countries. These services need to be provided not only efficiently but also be accessible to poor people. In this direction, what may be suggested is the provisioning of clean water and sanitation waste removal, etc. A clean piped water supply can reduce child mortality by 5 to 7 p.c.

In the first instance, therefore, gender gaps in human capital can be closed by increasing access to education among boys and girls, especially of the disadvantaged group. Education can improve labour productivity. It provides better outcomes for their children across generations. Education increases access to economic opportunities, strengthens voice of the voiceless and women's agency. However, accessibility to better educational facilities depends on the financial strength of a government. Many governments of poor countries pay little attention on the plea of shortage of fund. The ground reality is lack of commitment. What is required is both demand (e.g., conditional cash transfers, midday meal scheme, etc.), and supply-side interventions (such as building of schools and other logistics of learning inputs) by the government. All these will increase enrolment rate and reduce dropout rates.

The *second* policy measure should address improving public health through provisioning of clean piped water, sanitation and waste disposal so as to reduce the burden of diseases like diarrohea, infectious diseses, etc. All these require public investment in health sector. Larger budgetary allocations need to be made in this sector. To encourage enrolment of girls and to discourage dropout rates one may recommend stipends for girls.

The *third* policy that is often recommended is the removal of gender bias in politics by enabling women's access to public offices. In 1993, by an amendment of the Constitution of India, a gender quota of 1/3rd has been made reserved for women. Various survey reports conducted by experts reveal that this provision has increased women's leadership in Indian villages. As a result of this kind of exposure of women, quality of public goods available to the villages has improved. Further, bribes are, as such, not given to the council heads where seats are reserved for women. Anyway, this political empowerment of women has a salutary effect in reducing educational and social inequality and discrimination between the two sexes. Further, this kind of women leadership can reduce structural violence (both domestic and sexual).

Conclusion : However, there is a huge gap between rhetoric and reality. It is indeed true that globally one understands the steady increase in awareness of the need to empower women through various social, economic and political measures as well as broader access to basic health, education, nutrition, human rights, etc. But the progress in this directtion is not only slow but also highly patchy. Gender disparities exist in every dimension. To measure gender inequality, the World Economic Forum in 2006, in its report, introduced '*global gender gap index*' (GGGI). As usual, this index ranks countries according to their gender gaps.

The GGGI for Iceland increased from 0.7813 in 2006 to 0.8530 in 2011. In terms of ranking, Iceland stands first among 135 countries. India ranks 113th whose index stood at 0.6190 in 2011. Bangladesh ranks 69th, China stands 61st, Sri Lanka 31st.

5.4 Gender-related Development Index (or GDI) and its Indicators

According to Amartya Sen, economic development needs to be defined in terms of 'entitlement' and 'capability'. By entitlement we mean a set of alternative commodity bundles that an individual can command through the totality of rights and obligations that one faces. Thus, entitlement generates 'capabilities' that represent a person's freedom to achieve various functioning combinations. In other words, capability is essentially one of freedom. And, by ecomomic development, Sen suggests capability expansion or expansion of freedoms. For instance, poverty is a failure to achieve certain minimum capabilities. Unfreedoms like hunger, malnutrition, poverty, poor health, economic insecurity, poor schooling and health care, etc., generate inequalities. Despite remarkable growth, a vast section of population of the contemporary society is deprived of basic freedoms. One such unfreedom is gender bias.

Though HDI incorporates some aspects of human development, inequalities in opportunities between men and women are missed out in HDI. Because of gender bias in health care, mortality rates of women are high compared to men. It is the adverse sex ratio as observed in Asia and North Africa which is attributed to 'missing women' concept. Above all, in respect of allocation of health care, schooling, food and nutrition, the neglect of women is rampant. All these reflect gender-related inequality.

With the advancement of economic progress as well as social progress, such clear cut bias against women should have declined. Unfortunately, such trend is on the rise. Capability deprivation results in gender inequality. Through sex-selective abortion, female fetuses are eliminated so that no female child is born. In 1998, as a resuit, for the world as a whole, shortfall of women

Table 5.3 : Goalposts for Calculating the GDI

Indicator	Maximum value	Minimum value
Female life expectancy at birth (years)	87.5	27.5
Male life expectancy at birth (years)	82.5	22.5
Adult literacy rate (%)	100	0
Combined gross enrolment ratio (%)	100	0
Estimated earned income (US $)	40,000	100

relative to men exceeded 100 million. This is called 'missing women'. The 2012 *World Development Report,* puts this figure to 3.9 million in low income countries. Substantive freedoms that a male member enjoys are denied to female member. For example, women eat less and get little medical attention. Educational gender gap is also perceptible. Women have no or little power or authority over any household decision-making process. Outside the home, women are politically marginalised. All these reflect gender disparity.

To measure the extent of this disparity or inequality, the UNDP in 1995 took a new initiative to construct an index called 'gender-related development index' (GDI). In addition, in order to close this gap, women used to be empowered. To measure the extent of empowerment of women, the UNDP devised 'gender empowerment index' (GEI) also in 1995.

The HDI measures achievements in human development in terms of three indicators, but ignores differences between men and women. Gender differentials in achievement are studied with the index called GDI. Like the HDI, GDI measures achievements in the same three dimensions and variables in respect of men and women. These three dimensions may now be recapitulated : (i) a long and healthy life, as measured by life expectancy at birth; (ii) knowledge, as measured by the adult literacy rate and the combined primary, secondary and tertiary gross enrolment ratio; and (iii) estimated earned income measured by US $.

Before calculating GDI, an index requires to be created for each of these dimensions. To calculate these dimension indices, minimum and maximum values for female and male indices in each dimension are calculated in accordance with the following formula :

$$\text{Dimension index} = \frac{\text{actual value} - \text{minimum value}}{\text{maximum value} - \text{minimum value}}$$

GDI

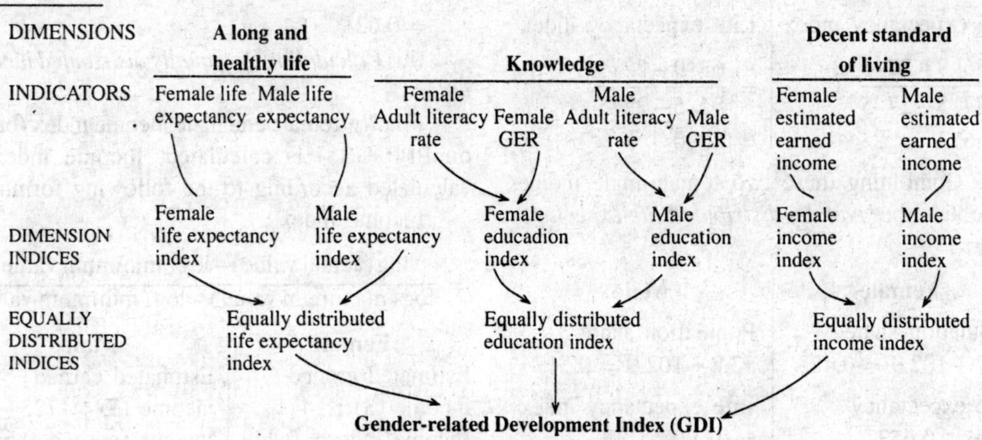

Fig. 5.2 : GDI

the gender disparity, lower the GDI. Countries that have achieved some success in expanding capabilities for both men and women will have higher GDI. A country having a GDI less than 0.500 indicates larger gender disparity.

How GDI is understood has been presented in terms of Fig. 5.2.

5.4.1 How is GDI Constructed?

In HDI, the life expectancy index at birth of a country is calculated. But in the case of GDI, life expectancy at birth for both male and female are calculated. After determining life expectancy at birth for male and female, these are combined in a way that 'penalises' differences in achievement between men and women. The index thus obtained is called '*equally distributed life expectancy index*'. The formula of this index is :

Equally distributed index = {[female population share (female index $^{1-\varepsilon}$] + [male population share (male index $^{1-\varepsilon}$)]}

ε measures the inequality aversion. In the GDI, ε is assumed to be equal to 2. If $\varepsilon = 0$ then GDI equals HDI. As ε tends to infinity gender inequality widens.

The calculation procedure of GDI involves the following four steps :

(i) *Calculating the equally distributed life index* : Out of 102.9 crore Indian population in 2001 census, male members (53.2 crore) exceeded female members. Life expectancies at birth for Indian women and men were 66.9 years and 63.9 years. Thus,

Female	Male
Life expectancy index $= \frac{66\cdot9-27\cdot5}{87\cdot5-27\cdot5} = 0.657$	Life expectancy index $= \frac{63\cdot9-22\cdot5}{82\cdot5-22\cdot5} = 0.690$

Combining these two female-male indices we obtain the '*equally distributed life expectancy index*'.

Female	Male
Population share : 49.7 ÷ 102.9 = 0.483	Population share : 53.2 ÷ 102.9 = 0.517
Life expectancy index : 0.657	Life expectancy index = 0.690

The equally distributed life index = $\{[0.483\,(0.657^{-1})] + [0.517 + (0.690^{-1})]\}^{-1} = 0.674$

(ii) *Calculating the equally distributed education index* : *First,* the adult literacy rates for women and men are determined. *Secondly,* the combined primary, secondary and tertiary gross enrolment ratios for women and men are calculated.

Female	Male
Adult literacy rate : 53.7 p.c.	Adult literacy rate : 75.3 p.c.
Adult literacy index : 0.537	Adult literacy index : 0.753
Gross enrolment ratio : 58	Gross enrolment ratio : 66
Gross enrolment index : 0.580	Gross enrolment index : 0.660

Now we will calculate the education index for both women and men. To do this, two-thirds weight to the adult literacy index and one-third weight to the gross enrolment index are assigned to obtain both female and male education indices.

Education index = 2/3 (adult literacy index) + 1/3 (gross enrolment index)

Female education index = 2/3 (0.537) + 1/3 (0.753) = 0.551

Male education index = 2/3 (0.753) + 1/3 (0.660) = 0.722

Finally, the female and male education indices are combined to obtain the equally distributed education index :

Female	Male
Population share : 0.483	Population share : 0.517
Education index : 0.551	Education index : 0.722

Equally distributed education index

$= \{[0.483(0.551)^{-1}] + [0.517\ (0.722^{-1})]\}^{-1}$

$= 0.628$

(iii) *Calculating the equally distributed income index*

Finally, female and male income index (based on PPP US\$) is calculated. Income index is calculated according to the following formula.

Income index

$$= \frac{\log(\text{actual value}) - \log(\text{minimum value})}{\log(\text{maximum value}) - \log(\text{minimum value})}$$

Female	Male
Estimated earned income (\$) : 1471	Estimated earned income (\$) : 4723
Income index = 0.449	Income index = 0.643

Combining the female and male income indices, we calculate equally distributed income index :

Female	Male
Population share : 0.483	Population share : 0.517
Income index : 0.449	Income index : 0.643

Equally distributed income index = {[0.483 (0.449^{-1})] + [0.517 (0.643^{-1})]}$^{-1}$ = 0.532

(iv) Calculating the GDI

GDI is simply the unweighted average of the three indices. Thus,

GDI = 1/3 (life expectancy index) + 1/3 (education index) + 1/3 (income index)

= 1/3 (0.674) + 1/3 (0.628) + 1/3 (0.532)

= 0.611

5.4.2 Gender Empowerment Measure (GEM)

In developing countries, as women are subject to various forms of inequality they are caught in 'inequality trap.' This gender inequality, being undesirable, needs to be closed. This requires empowerment of women. In this respect, women themselves have to come forward. In other words, empowerment of women is linked to the 'agency of women'. Amartya Sen, while emphasising the importance of women's agencies for securing gender justice and hence social progress, argues that gender inequality does not decline automatically with the process of economic growth.

In this respect, activities of women's organisations and other forms of agency that promote, say, female labour force literacy, female literacy, demographic change, etc., are of crucial importance, as far as empowerment of women is concerned. Empowering does not come from above; it has to come from the grassroots level. When this happens, women's empowerment then influences positively on the lives of both women and men and children. This then brings about both development and social progress.

Five elements of women's empowerment are : (i) education, (ii) ownership rights over property and assets, (iii) position and status of women in the labour market, (iv) opportunities to work, and (v) familiar and societal attitude regarding women's employment. For overall development of a society, empowerment of women is prerequiste.

The *Human Development Report, 1995* focusing on women's opportunities rather than their capabilities introduced '*Gender Empowerment Measure*' or GEM. This index is constructed highlighting the three key areas : (i) political participation and decision-making power as measured by the percentage shares of parliamentary seats of both female and male, (ii) economic participation and decision-making power, as measured by two indicators—percentage shares of positions as legislators, senior administrators and managers of both sexes and women's and men's percentages shares in professional and technical positions, and (iii) power or authority over economic resources, as measured by contributions of earned income of both women and men. GEM is simply the average of these three indices. The essence of GEM has been shown in Fig. 5.3.

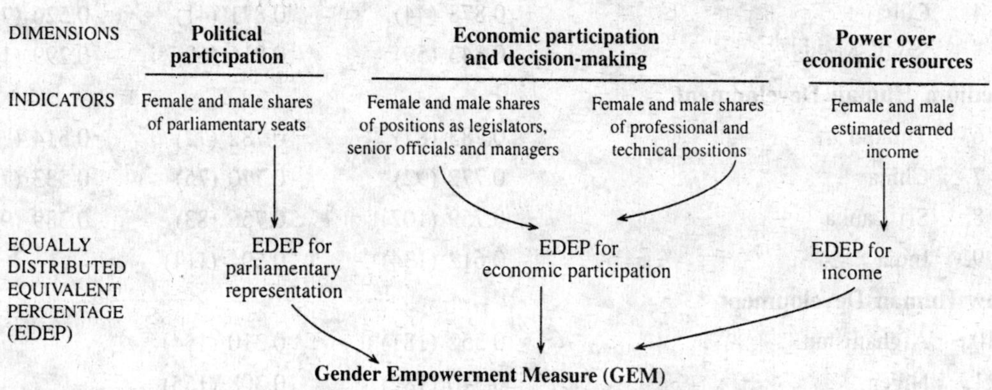

Fig. 5.3 : GEM

HDI, GDI and GEM : If human developmentt of a country exhibits higher degree of gender inequality, GDI becomes less than HDI. Although female and male not only live within a family and cooperate each other, yet one observes huge disparities in their achievements and, hence, greater deprivation of women. Such adverse state of women gets reflected in GDI. Despite the same potentials, women's education index is lower than men's education index in many countries of the world. Because of neglect of women in health care and nutrition, women are vulnerable in respect of life expectancy index. Given the same level of work, women labour learn less than the male counterpart. GDI addresses these malaise. GEM addresses both economic and political participation and decision-making power.

These two indices—GDI and GEM—are highly important. GDI reflects gender gap—the larger the gender gap the larger the inequality. This kind of social choice is highly undesirable. Women's agencies, however, highlight both the GDI and GEM. These agencies then compel government to change policies and programmes so as to give effective freedom to women. More and more expansion of women's agencies and the gradual and positive transformation of gender relations associated with it are emerging as one of the powerful sources of social change in contemporary India.

Gender inequality is not only to be viewed as a social failure; it also contributes to other social failures. By giving more freedom to women, barriers of inequality can be removed. Here women's agency is a great mover of development—social justice can be achieved through the active agency of women, says Amartya Sen.

In terms of HDI, GDI and GEM, Norway ranks 1st and 2nd, respectively. In terms of GEM Germany's performance is better (9th) than in terms of GDI (20th) or HDI (22nd), as is revealed in Table 5.4. India stands at 134th in respect of HDI, but she is better placed in terms of GDI (114th). Cuba and Saudi Arabia have great success in HDI, but both the countries fail rather largely in respect of GEM. One interesting observation may be put here. In most of the Middle East countries though educational attainment index is on the high side, women's economic and political participation and decision-making power is low. This reflects some sort of 'gender paradox'.

Table 5.4 : Selected Values of HDI, GDI and GEM of Some Countries

	HDI	GDI	GEM
Very High Human Development			
1. Norway	0.971 (1)	0.961 (2)	0.906 (2)
2. United States	0.956 (13)	0.942 (19)	0.767 (18)
3. Germany	0.947 (22)	0.939 (20)	0.852 (9)
High Human Development			
4. Cuba	0.878 (44)	0.871 (41)	0.526 (75)
5. Saudi Arabia	0.843 (59)	0.816 (60)	0.299 (106)
Medium Human Development			
6. Thiland	0.783 (87)	0.782 (72)	0.514 (76)
7. China	0.772 (92)	0.770 (75)	0.533 (72)
8. Sri Lanka	0.759 (102)	0.756 (83)	0.389 (98)
9. India	0.612 (134)	0.594 (114)	
Low Human Development			
10. Afghanistan	0.352 (181)	0.310 (154)	
11. Niger	0.340 (182)	0.308 (155)	

Source : *Human Development Report, 2009* [Figures in bracket denote ranking of countries.]

It may be noted that HDI ranking in 2009 is made out of 182 countries while GDI and GEM rankings are made out of 155 countries.

With the introduction of GDI, a serious debate and controversy arose relating to its reliability and usefulness in making comparisons between countries. Taking such controversies into account, the *Human Development Report 2010* proposed a new index—Gender Inequality Index (GII)—so as to address the shortcomings of GDI. This new experimental measure contains three dimensions—reproductive health, empowerment, and labour market participation.

5.4.3 A Note on Gender Inequality Index (GII)

As HDI does not capture a complete picture of evolution of human development, a broader vision for measuring human development was considered by the UNDP in the *2010 Human Development Report*. This report introduced three multi-dimensional measures of inequality. These three measures are : (i) Inequality adjusted HDI (IHDI), (ii) Gender Inequality Index (GII) in place of GDI, and (iii) Multi-dimensional Poverty Index (MPI).

the *HDR Report 2010* introduced one index only—the GII.

As is evident from Fig. 5.4, one observes three dimensions measuring inequality—reproductive health, empowerment, and labour market—and five indicators that address unequality in those dimensions. There are two indicators of reproductive health, two for empowerment, and one for the labour market.

1. Reproductive health : (a) maternal mortality, and (b) adolesent fertility.
2. Empowerment : (a) Parliamentary representation, and (b) educational attainment (secondary level and above).
3. Labour market : (a) labour force participation.

The issues of GII may be highlighted in terms of Fig. 5.4.

The GII explains the loss in potential human development due to inequality between male and female achievements in the three dimensions of

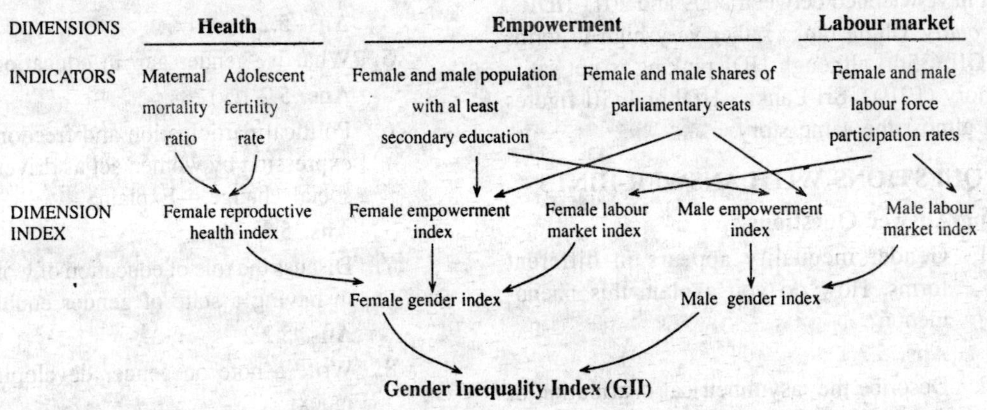

Fig. 5.4 : Gender Inequality Index (GII)

GDI and GEM were introduced in 1995. The former considered gender inequalities in the HDI dimensions, while the latter focused on political participation, economic participation and power over economic resources. As these two indices failed to provide a valid and reliable gender index, reproductive health, empowerment, and labour market participation. Its value varies between 0 and 1. If men and women fair absolute equality the index becomes 0. Greater the inequality in achievements between men and women, the index tends to 1.

5.5 Selected Values of HDI and GII for Some Countries

Very High Human Development	HDI	GII
1. Norway	0·943 (1)	0·075 (6)
2. United States	0·910 (4)	0.299 (47)
3. Germany	0·905 (9)	0·085 (7)
High Human Development		
4. Cuba	0·0776 (51)	0·337 (58)
5. Saudi Arabia	0·770 (56)	0·646 (135)
Medium Human Development		
6. Thailand	0·682 (103)	0·382 (69)
7. China	0·687 (101)	0.209 (35)
8. Sri Lanka	0·691 (97)	0·419 (74)
9. India	0·547 (134)	0·617 (117)
Low Human Development		
10. Afghanistan	0·398 (172)	0·707 (141)
11. Niger	0·295 (186)	0·724 (144)

Source : *Human Development Report, 2011*

Two highly contrasting results are obtained from the Table 5.5. *First,* in terms of HDI, the United States ranks 4th; but the GII figure (47th) is not encouraging. Similar conclusion holds for Saudi Arabia where the gaps between HDI and GII have widened between 2009 and 2011 HDRs. *Secondly,* China ranks rather very high in terms of GII (35th) although HDI ranking is not satisfactory (101st). Sri Lanka's HDI and GII figures tell almost the same story.

QUESTIONS WITH ANSWER-HINTS

Long-Answer Questions

1. Gender inequality appears in different forms. How do you explain this phenomenon?
   Ans. 5.2.1
2. Describe the asymmetrical distribution of domestic activities and inequality in employment and wage earnings between men and women in a male-dominated society.
   Ans. 5.2.1(i)
3. How do you explain survival inequality between men and women? Explain your answer taking India's example.
   Ans. 5.2.1(iv)
4. In the allocation of food, education, and health one observes pro-male bias. Do you agree with this view?
   Ans. 5.2.1(v)
5. Why is gender equality desirable?
   Ans. 5.2.2
6. What is meant by gender-related development index? What are its indicators? How is GDI constructed?
   Ans. 5.4 and 5.4.1
7. Discuss the importance of constructing gender empowerment index. How is it constructed?
   Ans. 5.4.2

Short-Answer Questions

1. Explain the concept of 'missing women'?
   Ans. 5.2.1(iv)
2. How do you describe male-bias in both domestic and outside the home job allocation?
   Ans. 5.2.1(i)
3. Describe survival inequality between male and female.
   Ans. 5.2.1(iv)
4. Discuss the reasons behind the male child bias as found in many third world countries.
   Ans. 5.2.1(iv)
5. What is 'gender gap in education'?
   Ans. 5.2.1(v)
6. Political participation and freedom of expression by women act as drivers of social change.—Explain.
   Ans. 5.3
7. Discuss the role of education of women in having a state of gender equality.
   Ans. 5.2.2
8. Write a note on gender development index.
   Ans. 5.4
9. Write a note on gender empowerment measure.
   Ans. 5.4.2
10. How is GDI constructed?
    Ans. 5.4.1
11. What are the three key areas of GEM?
    Ans. 5.4.2
12. How is GII constructed?
    Ans. 5.4.3

INTERNATIONAL ECONOMICS

CHAPTER 6 International Trade : Theory, Policy, and Balance of Payments

6.1 Introduction

International trade is a branch of exchange of goods and services between different countries. Such exchange between nations arises because demand for goods and services of all countries are not only different but also supplies of these goods are different as every country has different potentialities to produce them. By exchanging goods and services every country tries to gain something. That is why it is said that international trade is mutually beneficial. Although international trade is just an extension of internal trade still the former is different from the latter.

This chapter attempts to answer a fundamental question : Why does trade occur? To answer this question we will take the help of a theory suggested by economists like Adam Smith and David Ricardo. Ricardo's comparative cost theory, developed in the first quarter of the 19th century, still can explain the causes behind the emergence of trade. This chapter also explains the schematic balance of payments accounts of a country. It also recommends remedies of adverse balance of payments. This chapter also deals with the exchange rate mechanisms, such as fixed and flexible exchange rates.

6.2 Why Do We Need a Separate International Trade Theory?

International trade theory is simply an extension of general economic theory on international setting. Thus, international trade theory is a branch of exchange theory where exchange relationship develops between nations, rather than between regions. A region is a geographical subdivision of a country. Trading relationship that develops between regions of the same country is called internal trade. When exchanges and trading relationship grows between nations or countries we have international trade. Anyway, such exchange between regions take place because of specialisation of a region. In other words, regional specialisation is the basis of domestic trade. Similarly, the basis of international trade is the specialisation or division of labour or cooperation.

If the basis of any trade is specialisation then why should there be a separate international trade theory? If international trade is just simply a logical extension of internal trade then why should there be a distinction between inter-regional trade and international trade?

There are several reasons to study international trade theory rather than a general trade theory :

Different monetary systems : First is the independent monetary system. Each country has its own currency and own banking system. Within a region the same currency unit prevails. But for making international transactions domestic currency is of no use. Further, a foreign exchange rate (i.e., the rate at which one currency, say rupee, is exchanged for another currency, (say dollar) has an important bearing on exports and imports. As a result, one country may gain while others may loose. However, different regions while carrying on their business/trading activities, remain insulated from such change. Or a change in the value of domestic currency will affect the entire nation uniformly.

Independent trade policies : *Secondly,* trade policies differ from country to country. Trading or exchange relationship is strongly governed by the trade policy of a country. Trade policy is concerned with either relaxation or control of trade with the objective of garnering large volume of benefits of trade, since trade involves costs as well. But, domestically, a uniform regional trade policy is pursued. There may be control or restrictions of the movement of goods within a country, but these are different from international controls.

Differences in the degree of mobility of resources : *Thirdly,* a vast difference exists in the degree of mobility of resources between countries. It is said that resources are mobile domestically but immobile internationally. Inputs like labour and capital are free to move or to choose their own areas of activity within a country. But such is not an easy thing in the international arena where immigration laws, citizenship requirements, etc., come into play to prevent the movement of labour. Similarly, capital flows are also restricted between nations for the obvious reasons. No such restrictions or controls are placed on their movement within countries.

Different socio-political conditions : *Finally,* socio-political environment varies from country to country, although such environment is uniform within a country. Market for commodity transactions between different nations is largely governed by its own geographical boundaries, social institutions and customs, habits, choice, etc. Within a country, one observes same social and economic institutions and business customs. Throughout the world, a uniform set of socio-political environment can never exist.

However, all these are not sufficient reasons for the emergence of trade. For instance, if a unique currency system prevails between different nations, trade may also emerge. When this is the case, economically speaking, we do not find any differences between internal trade and international trade. In this connection, one can cite the introduction (1999) of a uniform currency—called 'euro'—among the 16 (out of 27 member states of the European Union) members of the European Union. In these 16 countries 'euro' is being utilised, but trading relationship has not stopped. Further, in today's world, where market principles are the guiding star, most of these countries follow almost uniform free trade policies. If this is the case, international trade is not to be distinguished from internal trade. But the principal feature which makes it necessary to treat international trade as a separate issue is the factor immobility between different countries. Lack of mobility of labour and capital has an important bearing on the nature of international trade.

For all these reasons, economists have also specialised in this branch of economics and a vast body of international trade theory has been developed by these specialist economists. Thus, there is no logic to have a uniform trade theory for both international and inter-regional trade.

6.3 Need for International Trade Or, Relationship between Trade and Development

In today's global economy, international trade is at the heart of development. Nations—developed or underdeveloped—trade with each other because trade is mutually beneficial. In other words, the basic motivation of trade is the gain or benefit that accrues to nations. In a state of autarky or isolation, benefits of international division of labour do not flow between nations. It is advantageous for all the countries of the world to engage in international trade. However, the gains from trade can never be the same for all the trading nations. Thus, benefits or gains from trade may be inequitable; but what is true is that "some trade is better than no trade".

There is, however, a strong debate around the role of trade in the development of mainly less developed countries. Historically, there was a consensus amongst many people that trade acts as an 'engine of growth' (in the 19th century and early 20th century). But in the 1950s, evidence showed that benefits of trade did not accure to the LDCs; trade was beneficial to the developed countries only. Here this debate will be focused.

Benefits of trade : Virtually, every nation finds it advantageous to trade with other nations. They are linked to one another, in varying degrees, by trade flows and financial networks that surround the globe. Benefits of trade are summarised here :

The major advantage of trade is that it enlarges the scope of trade. In other words, trade begets trade. Gains from trade accrue from specialisation, i.e., division of labour. Division of labour and specialisation within a country make necessary a greater amount of exchange, so greater division of labour necessiates an extension of trade. Specialisation is the logical offshoot of exchange among nations. Thus, a greater variety of products in larger quantitics may be available. This means that we have both 'production gain' and 'consumption gain'. Every country produces maximum goods on the basis of comparative advantage. By exchanging these goods, nations can consume more than before trade. It was Adam Smith who first pointed out the advantages of trade in reaping the advantages of specialisation and the economic benefits flowing from it, viz., an improvement in production and productivity and, hence, national wealth/ income of every participating country.

Secondly, a similar gain from trade, called 'vent for surplus', has been illustrated by Adam Smith. International trade increases the level of productive activity by stimulating efficient utilisation of resources. Countries may then experience surplus produce. Smith then argued that trade was a means of disposing of surplus produce for exports. Thus, trade 'vents' a surplus productive activity that would otherwise go unsold in the absence of trade.

In the words of Samuelson, P.A. and Nordhaus, W.D. "Canadians could drink no wine, Americans could eat no bananas, and most of the world would be without jazz and Hollywood movies."

Thirdly, there are three other kinds of gains from trade : (i) those that remove the narrowness of domestic market, induce innovations, achieve the full advantages of economies of large scale production and increase productivity, (ii) those that make savings and capital accumulation easier, and (iii) those that acquire new knowledge, new ideas and cultures, new skills and entrepreneurship and dissseminate technical knowledge.

Fourthly, empirical evidence suggests that trade can boost productivity which, in turn, raises the incomes and standards of living even of poor developing countries. The link between trade and productivity, being a potential one, can be identified with exports and imports. This is what makes trade a powerful 'engine of growth'.

Finally, trade is not only considered as an important 'engine of growth', but it can also contribute to poverty alleviation by expanding markets, making larger investments in various fields, creating jobs, raising productivity which, in turn, raise incomes of the poor people.

For all these reasons, it is said that 'trade is an engine of growth'. There is no reason for any country to remain in isolation.

Disadvantages of trade : The 'trade engine' theory lost its 'fuel' in the developing countries after the World War II. Some economists suggested that gains from trade can never be unambiguous for all the trading countries—both developed and developing. Thus, the message runs : free international trade is harmful for the poor developing countries.

Raul Prebisch, Hans Singer, Gunnar Myrdal argued in the 1950s that the gains from trade are biased—rich countries gain at the expense of the poor countries. Their arguments are as follows : Poor LDCs are, by nature, primary goods producing countries while rich countries are producers of manufactured articles. Former buys manufactured goods from the latter countries by exporting their primary goods at low prices or at unfavourable terms of trade. Thus, these countries pay more to the developed countries for their imports while developed countries pay less to the developing countries for their imports. In other words, gains from trade largely accrue to the developed countries.

Secondly, some leftist economists argue that trade results in 'dependent development'. In other words, trade between rich and poor nations is exploitative in nature. These economists argue that underdevelopment of poor countries is to be explained in terms of external factors, rather than internal factors. Historically, colonial countries of the past—say Asia, Africa and Latin America—did not have economic independence where

European capitalist imperialist powers ruled. From these colonies, capitalist countries drew their economic resources and filled their coffers simply by exploiting them. This is called 'development of underdevelopment' as a deliberate consequence of free international trade.

Danger of dependence is often explained in the following way. A country may face economic depression if its international trading partner suffers from it and then it spreads from one country to another. The Great Depression that emanated during 1929-30 in the US economy swept all over the world and all countries suffered badly even if their economies were not caught in the grip of Depression. Such overdependence becomes catastrophic duing war.

Further, commercial rivalries resulting from trade may lead to war.

Conclusion : Against this backdrop, one must not jump to a conclusion that poor LDCs must not trade with anyone, particularly the developed nations. This is highly unrealistic since no country—whatever the size and whatever the level of development—is self-sufficient. Thus, for surival, trade is essential. All countries trade. To reap the maximum advantages of trade, right trade policies need to be adopted. In addition, cooperation among all countries can promote more benefits from growth.

6.4 Why Nations Trade : The Classical Trade Theory

Why do different countries trade with each other? As trade benefits them, they trade with each other. Why does gain from trade arise? The gain from trade arises because of specialisation in production and division of labour. Individuals specialise in certain products. Same is true for the countries. That is why each country is interested in exchanging its own specialised products for non-specialised products. But which products should a country specialise in? Classical economists answered this question.

According to the classical writers, differences in cost form the basis of trade. Differences in cost may be of two types : (i) absolute cost diference, and (ii) comparative cost difference. In 1776, Adam Smith argued that the absolute cost difference or absolute advantage is the basis of trade. But another classical economist, David Ricardo, went a step forward in 1817 to search the basis of trade in terms of comparative cost difference or comparative advantage. Smith argued that a country will export that commodity in which it has an absolute advantage and import that commodity in which it has an absolute disadvantage. According to Ricardo, a country will produce and export that commodity in which it has a comparative advantage and will import that commodity in which it has a comparative disadvantage.

In explaining their trade theory, classicists made the following assumptions :

- There are two countries, two commodities, and one factor; i.e., a 2 × 2 × 1 model.
- The labour theory of value holds. Classicists argued that labour is the only productive input as far as the value of a commodity is concerned. The value of a commodity is determined by the amount of labour embodied in it. Thus, production cost is measured in terms of labour costs only.
- Production function obeys constant returns to scale. In other words, output per unit of labour is constant over all relevant ranges of the production function.
- Inputs, although mobile domestically, are completely immobile internationally.
- Transport cost is zero.
- Free trade policy is pursued.

6.4.1 Adam Smith's Absolute Advantage Doctrine

According to Adam Smith, it is the difference in absolute production cost that causes the emergence of trade. A country has an absolute advantage over another country in the production of a good if it can produce it at a lower cost. It would, thus, be advantageous for the country if it specialises in the production of a cheapest good. Smith argued that a country would produce and export that commodity in which it has an absolute advantage or lower cost and import that commodity in which it has an absolute disadvantage or higher cost.

The following example will help explain Smith's absolute cost difference. Let us assume that there are two countries, A and B, that produce two goods X, and Y, which require labour for their production. Further, suppose that country A takes 1 day's labour to produce 3 units of X and 2 units of Y. Country B produces 4 units of X and 1 unit of Y by the same labour cost. Clearly, country A has an *absolute advantage* in the production of Y since it can produce it at a lower cost than country B and country B has an *absolute advantage* in the production of X.

Country A in 1 day's labour produces	3 units of X and 2 units of Y
Country B in 1 day's labour produces	4 units of X and 1 unit of Y

In the absence of trade (i.e., under autarky or no trade), in country A, 3 units of X will exchange for 2 units of Y and in country B, 4 units of X will exchange for 1 unit of Y. Thus, internal and domestic exchange ratio between two goods of country A is 3 : 2 and for B it is 4 : 1. Country A will now benefit if it can produce and export good Y to buy more than 2 units of Y. Similarly, country B will gain more by producing and exporting X from A by buying more than 4 units of X. Clearly, both countries will gain. Anyway, trade is mutually beneficial since it increases both production and consumption.

Because of trade, production of both X and Y will increase in the following pattern :

	Good X (units)	Good Y (units)
Country A	–3	+2
Country B	+4	–1
Net increase in output	+1	+1

Thus, international trade is mutually beneficial. Global output and consumption of both X and Y have increased by at least 1 unit in each country.

6.4.2 David Ricardo's Comparative Advantage Doctrine

Ricardo has demonstrated that absolute cost advantage is not a necessary condition for the two countries to gain from trade. Instead, he concluded that trade would also benefit both the nations if comparative costs differ. To him, comparative difference in cost is a sufficient condition for trade to emerge. Ricardo's doctrine states that a country will export that commodity in which it has a comparative advantage and import that product in which it has a comparative disadvantage.

The following example suggests that the developed country A has an *absolute advantage* in the production of both goods X and Y. Neverthless, country A can gain from trade with the less developed country, B, because the former has a *cost advantage* or a *comparative advantage* in the production of Y over X. In contrast, the poor country B has a *comparative advantage* in the production of X.

Country A in 1 day's labur produces	6 units of X and 3 units of Y
Country B in 1 day's labour produces	4 units of X and 1 unit of Y

In other words, in country A good Y is *relatively less expensive* compared to country B. Similarly, in country B good X is *relatively less expensive* than country A.

Pre-trade exchange ratios for A and B are 1 X for 2 Y (i.e., 6 for 3) and 1 X for 4 Y. In other words, Y is cheaper in A while X is cheaper in B. So, A should export Y while B should export X, each specialising in that commodity in which it has a comparative advantage.

Before trade, let us assume that country A transfers all labour from the production of X to the production of Y in which its pre-trade opportunity cost (1 : 2) is lower and country B shifts all labour from the production of Y to the production of X in which its pre-trade opportunity cost (1 : 4) is lower. As a result, production of X will decline in country A by 6 units while production of Y will increase by 3 units.

At an international exchange rate of 1 : 3 (lying between two domestic exchange rates of 1 : 4 and 1 : 2), country A will now export 3 units of Y and import 9 units of X. Before trade, country A consumed 6 units of X, and after trade it consumes additional (9 – 6 = 3) units of X. This is called 'gains from trade'.

Likewise, country B gains from trade. As country B transfers labour from Y-production to the X-production, Y output declines by 1 unit. But as labour is transferred to the X-production, X-output rises by 4 units. Country B now trades with A at an exchange rate of 1 : 3 by exchanging 1 unit of X for 4/3 = $1^1/_3$ units of Y. As a result of trade, country B consumes additional $^1/_3$ unit of Y. This is known as 'gains from trade'. The result will be :

	Good X (units)	Good Y (units)
Country A	–6	+3
Country B	+8	–2
Net increase in output	+2	+1

We have learnt that the internal terms of trade in country A and in B is 1 : 2 in country A and 1 : 4 in B. Both countries will now gain from this specialisation in trade if exchange rate or post-trade terms of trade lies between two internal or domestic exchange rates, i.e., between 1 : 2 and 1 : 4. Let the international terms of trade be 1 : 3. At this new exchange rate, A will specialise in the production of Y. Now, by exporting Y, it will bring more X. As soon as country A transfers labour from X-production to the Y-producton and country B from Y-production to the X-production, there occurs complete specialisation. This kind of specialisation results in more global output.

Thus, Ricardo's comparative cost doctrine demonstrates the basis of trade, direction of trade and gains from trade.

Graphical Representation of Ricardo's Doctrine

Ricardo's doctrine of comparative cost can also be explained in terms of production possibility curve that gives the maximum producible amount of commodities (say, wheat and cloth) that an economy can produce. RS is the production possibility curve of a DC and BH is of an LDC. Since constant cost conditions prevail, the production possibility curve is a straight line—implying constant opportunity costs of production. The slope of this line indicates constant domestic or pre-trade price or constant terms of trade (TOT). The pre-trade terms of trade or the exchange rate in DC is 1 wheat for 2 cloth, i.e., 1W : 2C, and that for LDC it is 2W : 1C. This is indicated by the production possibility curves RS and BH for both DC and LDC, respectively. RS has a slope of 1W : 2C $\left(\text{or } \frac{1}{2}\right)$ and BH has a slope of 2W : 1C $\left(\text{or } \frac{2}{1}\right)$.

Let P be the production and consumption point of the DC before trade. Since the DC has a comparative advantage in cloth production, after trade it will produce at point S. Thus, it produces cloth only, and no wheat. The DC experiences a complete specialisation in the production of cloth. Similarly, the LDC's pre-trade production and consumption point is N. After trade, its production point shifts to B implying that it specialises in the production of wheat. Thus, trade enables each country to produce more than what it produces domestically.

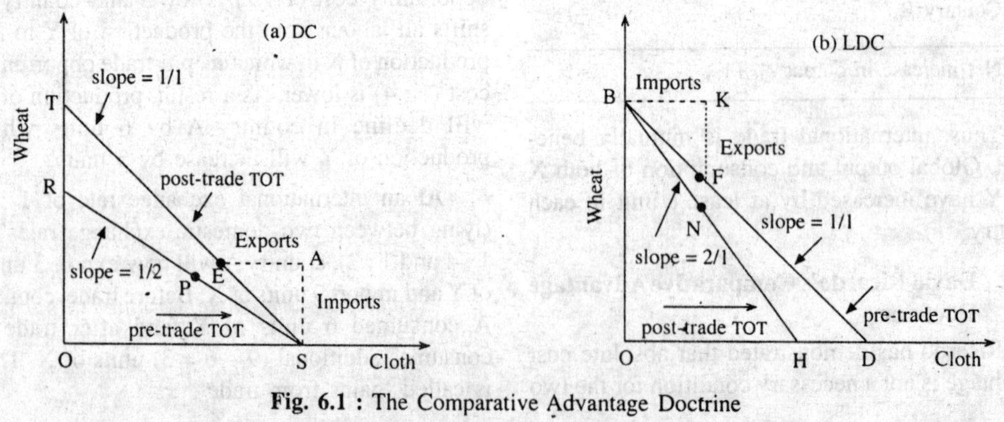

Fig. 6.1 : The Comparative Advantage Doctrine

For simplicity's sake, we are assuming that the international terms of trade or the post-trade exchange rate is 1W : 1C—an intermediate rate that exists between 2W : 1C and 1W : 2C. To demonstrate this new exchange ratio, we have drawn line TS in Fig. 6. 1(a) whose slope is

1W : 1C $\left(\text{or } \frac{1}{1}\right)$, and BD in Fig. 6.1(b)

whose slope is also 1W : 1C$\left(\text{or } \frac{1}{1}\right)$. This new terms of trade line enables each country to consume more. Consumption point of DC shifts to point E on the TS line. This means that DC now consumes more of cloth and more of wheat. It exports its surplus cloth production EA to buy AS amount of wheat. Similarly, as a result of trade, LDC's consumption point shifts to F. This means that it sells its excess production KF amount of wheat to buy KB of cloth from the DC. At point F, LDC consumers, of course, get more of both wheat and cloth.

Thus, trade enables each country to specialise in the production of a commodity in which it has a comparative advantage. Further, trade enables each partner to consume more.

Remember that Ricardo did not specify the exact terms of trade at which trade would take place. His terms of trade ratio lies between the two domestic terms of trade ratios. The exact ratio that would govern trade was left undetermined.

Limitations : This theory has been criticised on many grounds. Important criticisms against this theory are :

Unrealistic assumption of labour theory of value : *Firstly,* one of the fundamental assumptions of the classical trade theory is the labour theory of value. This theory states that the relative costs of production are determined by the labour costs alone. Their assumption of the labour theory of value seems to be unrealistic in explaining the cause of trade. Modern economists have discarded the labour theory of value and employed opportunity cost theory. Opportunity cost theory rescues Ricardo's doctrine without altering its basic conclusion.

Assumption of perfect competition does not hold : *Secondly,* this theory also assumes that there shall be perfect competition. But there are many examples of 'market failures'. Thus, inefficiencies emerge. Under the circumstance, trade may push a country below the production possibility curve. P. A. Samuelson and W. D. Nordhaus then doubt over the conclusion of the comparative cost doctrines. When depressionary condition in an economy prevails or when the price system malfunctions because of environ-mental or other reasons, we cannot be sure that countries will gain from trade.

Differences in comparative costs not explained : *Thirdly,* Ricardo could not explain why do comparative costs differ between countries. Answer to this question was given by Eli F. Heckscher and B. Ohlin who suggested that differences in factor endowments and factor-intensity give rise to differences in comparative costs.

Let us assume that country A uses more capital in the production of a commodity than country B. If the use of capital per unit of labour in country A is higher, then country A is a capital-abundant country. On the other hand, let us assume that the country B is a labour rich country. In our example, we have seen that country A specialises in the production of Y as it has comparative advantage in Y-production. Since country A is a capital-intensive country, Y-production here becomes more capital-intensive. Likewise, country B has comparative advantage in the production of X. Being a labour-rich country, country B's production of X becomes more labour-intensive. Heckscher and Ohlin argue that a country will specialise in the production and export those goods whose production requires a relatively large amount of the factor in which the country is relatively well-endowed (i.e., the more abundant factor). Country A—the capital-rich country in this example—specialises in the production of Y (comparative costs of Y are cheaper). Since country B is a labour-abundant country, its comparative costs are lower in X-production and, hence, it exports X for Y. Thus, differences in factor endowments and factor intensity explain differences in comparative cost. Ricardo simply took for granted that labour cost ratios differ.

Exact terms of trade undetermined : *Fourthly,* Ricardo could not determine the exact terms of trade or the exchange rate at which trade takes place. Ricardo's terms of trade (TOT) would lie between the countries' pre-trade terms of trade; but the exact ratio was left undetermined. This gap was filled by the classical author J. S. Mill by introducing the concept of 'reciprocal demand' in trade theory. Ricardo's model concentrates on the supply (or cost) side and, hence, it neglects the demand side.

Zero transport cost is inconceivable : *Fifthly*, Ricardo neglects transport cost just for simplicity. It is true that transport costs are important in determining the exchange rate. Supporters of Ricardo's doctrine have adequately demonstrated that transport costs do not affect comparative cost doctrine.

Trade is multi-lateral and multi-good : *Sixthly*, for simplicity's sake, Ricardo's model is the 2 × 2 × 1 model. But if we apply Ricardo's theory in case of more than two countries and more than two commodities, conclusions of the doctrine remain virtually unaltered.

Environmental argument against comparative cost theory : *Finally*, the assault against the comparative advantage theory in recent times has come from environmentalists. These people argue that in the name of free trade many companies, particularly MNCs, destroy natural resources of a country where they produce. Further, these companies often dump their pollutants in oceans or dump their banned products in the market of developing countries. In the eyes of the environmentalists, trade needs to be restricted so that the harmful effects arising out of trade in harmful environmental products can be minimised.

Conclusion : In analysing his trade doctrine, Ricardo started with the unreal world. Some of the writers fit this theory in the real world without altering its fundamental conclusions. Some of his assumptions were questionable. Modern writers removed those assumptions and refined this doctrine. Only the gaps in the Ricardian model have been filled up by the modern writers. A doctrine propounded about 200 years ago is even now respected by all, possibly because of its originality.

6.4.3 Extending Ricardo's Doctrine : (i) Many Commodities but Two Countries

Ricardo's doctrine has been criticised on the ground that the doctrine is confined only to two commodities and two countries. Critics argue that the doctrine has limited applicability since today's trade is multilaterial. Further, the number of traded goods is not two but many. But Ricardo's disciples have successfully demonstrated that comparative cost doctrine can even be applied in the case of more than two commodities and more than two countries. Let us see how trade takes place when the two countries trade with more than two goods.

For simplicity's sake, let us assume that there are two countries A and B who trade seven commodities. These commodities have been arranged in a comparative advantage sequence. Country A has the tendency to specialise in commodities shown on the right hand side of Fig. 6.2.

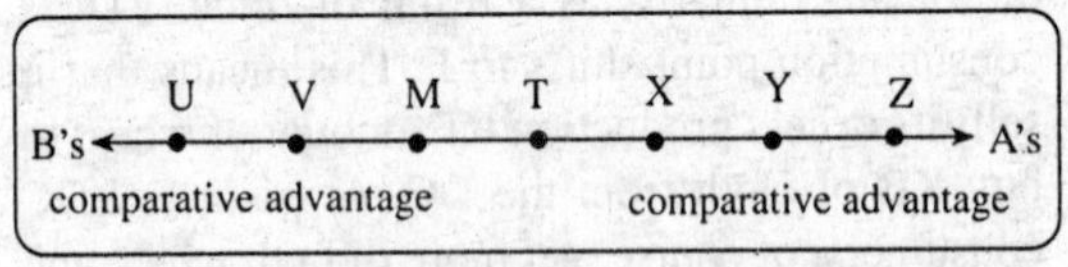

Fig. 6.2 : Extending Comparative Costs

Similarly, country B has the greatest comparative advantage in U, its advantage in Y or Z is not so large. If now trade opens up, B will export larger U and A larger Z. But what about other goods?

Whether a country will export more of other commodities depends on the strength of the international demand and the TOT. If Y is demanded more by country B, then country A would specialise in its production and produce less in which it has a comparative disadvantage, say good V. Thus, comparative cost is again the basis of trade in the case of many commodities.

6.4.4 Extending Ricardo's Doctrine : (ii) Many Countries but Two Commodities

The comparative cost doctrine is equally applicable in a multi-country model. Suppose, there are four countries A, B, C, D who trade with two goods X and Y. For simplicity's sake, let B, C, and D be described as a single group of countries. Thus, for convenience, we have two countries—A and the rest of the world who trade goods X and Y on the basis of comparative cost differences. This assumption makes this extended Ricardian model into a 2 × 2 × 1 model.

6.4.5 Extending Ricardo's Doctrine : (iii) Multi-countries, Multi-commodities

Ricardo's doctrine has also an applicability in a multi-country, multi-commodity framework. Let there be three countries—both LDCs and developed countries—A, B and C that exchange goods X, Y and Z with each other. Country A exports X to country B, country B exports Y to country C, and country C exports Z to country A. The arrowheads in Fig. 6.3 suggest that trade is a one-way traffic. This means that no country exports to another country. But it is not so since export of one country is the import of another country. What is true is that country B pays A for its export good X in country C, country C pays B via country A, and so on. Thus, trade takes place between many countries and many commodities. One must not forget that in reality trade patterns are more complex that what has been presented here.

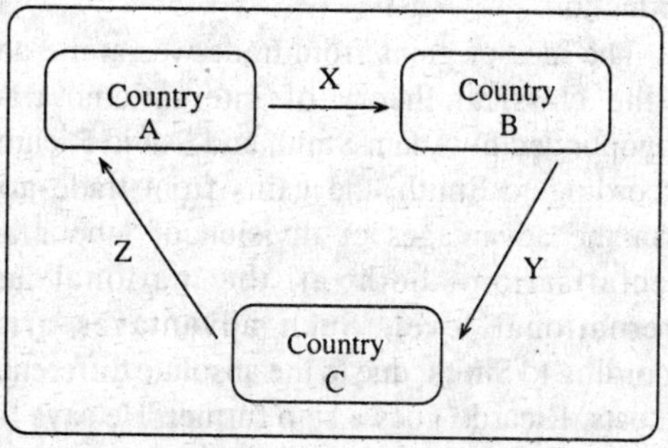

Fig. 6.3 : Extending Comparative Costs

6.5 The Concept of Terms of Trade and Reciprocal Demand

Specialisation and exchange benefit all the trading partners. Because of complete specialisation in the production of the commodities in which countries have comparative advantages—as suggested by Ricardo, global production becomes larger. Now, if every country trades with each other, every country will gain from such exchanges. However, such gain from specialisation and exchange depends on the terms of trade (TOT). It refers to the quantity of imports that exports buy. It is measured by the ratio of export price to import price. It is the ratio at which a country can export or sell domestic goods for imported goods.

Let P_x be the price of export good and P_m be the price of import good. Thus, the (barter or commodity) TOT are defined as $\frac{P_x}{P_m}$.

In the real world, where countries export and import a large number of goods, TOT are computed as an index number :

$$\text{TOT} = \frac{\text{index of export prices}}{\text{index of import prices}} \times 100$$

$$\text{or TOT} = \frac{P_x}{P_m} \times 100$$

To calculate the index of export and import prices, we choose a base year and the current period. A base period index of export and import price is 100. Thus, TOT for the base year is 100. Suppose export price index rises to 120 and import price index rises to 110. Thus,

$$\text{TOT} = \frac{120}{100} \div \frac{110}{100} \times 100 = 109$$

TOT rise to 109. This means that a unit of exports will buy 9 p.c. more imports than the old TOT. TOT thus improves. A fall in the TOT, on the other hand, implies unfavourable TOT in the sense that the country concerned will now use more exports to buy the same quantity of imports.

On which factors the TOT depend? Answer to this question was unknown to Ricardo. In other words, Ricardo could not locate the exact TOT at which trade takes place. This is because of the fact that Ricardo concentrated on the cost or the supply side of production and ignored demand conditions. Anyway, Ricardo suggested that the TOT would settle in-between two domestic cost ratios. We explain first the Ricardian notion of TOT and then Mill's concept of reciprocal demand.

Let us assume that the internal or domestic cost ratio in country A is 1 X for 1.5 Y, and, in country B, it is 1 X for 2 Y. This domestic cost ratio suggests that country A has a comparative advantage in X while country B has a comparative advantage in Y. Thus, A and B will trade with each other. But what would be the TOT at which both will trade? Ricardo argued that international TOT would lie somewhere between 1 : 1.5 and 1 : 2 and both the countries would stand to gain.

It was J. S. Mill who successfully determined the exact TOT by introducing the concept of reciprocal demand. In other words, actual TOT depends on the relative prices of X and Y after trade takes place. Or TOT depends upon the strength of the world supply and demand for each of these two commodities. This is what Mill called reciprocal demand. These relative prices will depend upon the strength and elasticity of each country's demand for the other country's product or upon reciprocal demand. If the TOT lie very close to 1 : 1.5, then country A would gain very little and she would not offer much X for export. However, at this TOT, country B would gain quite a large amount since it would demand more X by offering less Y. Consequently, country B's demand for imports of X would exceed country A's supply of exports of X, and so the price of X in terms of Y would rise. As the TOT rises to 1 : 1.6; 1 : 1.7, etc., country A offers more X to buy more Y, while country B demands less Y to buy X. In this way, a particular TOT would prevail at which the value of each country's export equals its value of imports. In this way, reciprocal demand is equated in the two countries at the international TOT.

Thus, TOT lies between the upper and lower limits of domestic cost ratios of the two countries. Equilibrium or international TOT brings equality between export and import. At the equilibrium TOT, world output equals world consumption. But the gains to both the countries need to be equal. However, more favourable the TOT to any country, greater is the welfare of a country. A tariff imposed on importables may, however, bring TOT in favour of the tariff-imposing country. However, if the tariff rate exceeds the optimum tariff rate, gains from trade may reduce even though TOT may be favourable. Thus, a favourable TOT does not necessarily increase welfare of a nation. Still then, TOT must not be adverse.

6.6 Gains from Trade

Nations—developed or underdeveloped—trade with each other because trade is mutually beneficial. In other words, the basic motivation of trade is the gain or benefit that accrues to nations. In the case of autarky or isolation, benefits of international division of labour do not flow between nations. It is advantageous for all the countries of the world to engage in international trade. However, the gains from trade can never be same for all the trading nations. Some countries may reap a larger gain compared to others. Thus, gains from trade may be inequitable but what is true is that "some trade is better than no trade".

In simple words, gain from trade refers to extra production and consumption effects that countries can achieve through international trade. These gains are, thus, of two types : gain from exchange and gain from specialisation in production.

The idea of gains from trade was at the core of the classical theory of international trade propopunded by Adam Smith and David Ricardo. According to Smith, the gains from trade arise form the advantages of division of labour and specialisation—both at the national and international level. Such advantages arise, according to Smith, due to the absolute differences in costs. Ricardo goes a step further. He says that trade contributes "to increase the mass of commodities, and therefore, the sum of enjoyments ..." Ricardo adds that the gain from trade consists in the saving of cost resulting from obtaining the imported goods through trade instead of domestic production.

Ricardo's comparative cost thesis may be applied to establish the existence of gains from trade. In other words, gain from trade depends on the comparative cost conditions. Comparative cost doctrine suggests that trade can provide benefit to all countries if they specialise in the production of those goods and, hence, export them in which they have comparative advantage. A country, thus, specialises in production and export in accordance with its comparative advantage. Ricardo's trading nations acquire complete specialisation in production. As a result, global output becomes larger than under autarky. Trade also enables each country to consume more than under isolation. Thus, there is a production gain and a consumption gain arising out of international trade. Such gains cannot be reaped in the absence of trade.

However, in determining the exact volume of gains from trade, Ricardo's doctrine is incomplete. For this, what is required is the determination of the actual terms of trade or exchange rate at which trade would take place. The rate at which one commodity (say, export good) is exchanged for another commodity (say, import good) is called terms of trade. Or what import the export buys is called the TOT. Of course, export (and, hence, import) varies with the change in TOT.

This concept of TOT was introduced in the literature by J. S. Mill by introducing the concept of reciprocal demand. By reciprocal demand we mean demand of each country for the other's goods. On the basis of the principle of reciprocal demand, Mill determined a final TOT at which trade between two nations takes place. At the final TOT, goods demanded by one country are equal to the goods demanded by the other, or one country's supply or the export of good must equal the other country's demand for that good. Thus, TOT is an index of measuring a country's gain from trade. As a result, if a poor, small, less developed country (LDC) trades with a large, rich, developed country's (DC) autarkic or domestic cost ratio, then the LDC will acquire all the gains from trade. If the actual TOT lies between two domestic cost ratios then gains from trade will accrue to both the countries.

However, gains from trade depend on the

i. relative strengths of elasticity of demand for export and import of goods;
ii. size of the country;
iii. changes in technology;
iv. supply of goods traded; etc.

In general, greater the inelasticity in the foreign demand for exports and greater the elasticity of foreign demand for imports, greater will be the gains from trade.

Further, trade leads to increased competition. Competition enhances efficiency. LDCs gain largely in this competitive world. Improved research and technology of the developed world flow in these countries. Openess to trade supports technological upgrading via learning. Evidence on learning and technological upgradation is observed in many activities, mainly in the manufacturing and service sectors. Larger output and productivity increases indeed can occur not only in the manufacturing sector, but also in other sectors in which technological ugrading of the advanced countries is embodied. In addition, variety of products becomes available to consumers. All these suggest that trade is an 'engine of growth'.

However, gains from trade can never be unambiguous for all the countries. Sometimes, TOT may turn adverse against poor LDCs. Further, trade policy is often designed by the advanced countries in such a way that it reduces benefits of the LDCs from trade. Possibly, due to this fact it is said that free trade is better than restricted trade. Of course, restricted trade has merits too. By imposing a tariff, a poor country can even improve its TOT and, hence, can obtain benefits from trade.

6.7 Trade Policy : Free Trade and Protection

What should be the appropriate trade policy or commercial policy of a country? The issue was first raised by the classical authors. However, they were the champions of free trade. The two giant advocates of free trade—Adam Smith and David Ricardo—about two hundred years ago argued that free flow of goods and services, i.e., unrestricted trade, would be beneficial. As a result of free trade, each country specialises in production in which it has a comparative advantage. This will enable each country to reap gain from trade. After the Second World War (1939-1945), commercial policy underwent a change when the wave of protectionism swept all over the world. It was argued at that time that though some trade is better than no trade, there is no reason to suppose that free trade is the best.

A new question thus arose : Can protected trade cause a gain from trade? LDCs after the World War II, by imposing tariffs and duties, made an attempt to secure maximum benefits from international exchange of commodities. This kind of governmental intervention in trade policy is known as 'inward-oriented trade strategy' or 'biased against trade strategy'. But the last quarter of the 20th century saw the revival of free trade or 'outward-oriented trade strategy' all over the globe as protection failed to provide enough gains which the countries required. Actually speaking, a strong wind was then blowing in favour of free trade. The International Monetary Fund (IMF) and the World Bank also came forward to encourage the free trade philosophy. However, the debate between free trade and protection is yet to die down. In this section, we will touch upon the main issues of free trade and protection.

6.7.1 Trade under Free Trade

The trade theory (both the absolute advantage and comparative advantage theory) assumes the existence of free trade. Here we want to explain how do free trade influence domestic production, consumption, and import. Such may be explained with the aid of demand-supply mechnism.

In Fig. 6.4, the curves DD and SS are the demand and supply curves of say, Indian consumers and producers, respectively. These two curves intersect each other at point E. Thus the pre-trade price prevailing in India is OP. However, as soon as this particular commodity goes outside the

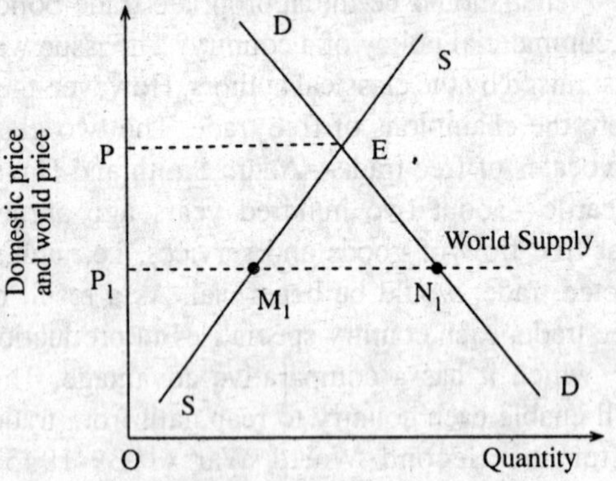

Fig. 6.4 : Trade under Free Trade

country where price is determined in the world market, it becomes lower than the domestic price OP. Let the world price be OP_1 (<OP). Now in the absence of tariff and with the opening of trade, the price in India (OP) becomes equal to the world price (OP_1). But, why? Since trade is free, the foreign country would then export in the Indian market where price is higher than the global price. It is because of competition between the countries price would then fall to OP_1 in the Indian market.

Note that at this lower price, Indian producers would reduce supply from PE to P_1M_1 while domestic demand would increase by M_1N_1. The horizontal line represents the supply curve for import. This is a perfectly elastic supply curve. Anyway, with the opening of trade, the supply-demand gap to the tune of M_1N_1 is to be met by imports from the foreign country.

The essence of the argument is that the strength of Indian demand for imports and supply of domestic good determine this volume of trade. In other words, it is the demand and supply that determines the volume of trade under free trade.

6.7.2 Free Trade: Arguments and Counter-arguments

International trade that takes place without barriers such as tariff, quotas, and foreign exchange control is called free trade. Thus, under free trade, goods and services flow between countries freely. In other words, free trade implies the absence of governmental intervention on international exchange among different countries of the world.

There are many arguments for free trade :

Arguments for Free Trade

Advantages of specialisation : Fristly, free trade secures all the advantages of international division of labour. Each country will specialise in the production of those goods in which it has a comparative advantage over its trading partners. This will lead to an optimum and efficient utilisation of resources and, hence, economy in production.

All-round prosperity : *Secondly*, because of unrestricted trade, global output increases since specialisation, efficiency, etc., make production large scale. Free trade enables countries to obtain goods at a cheaper price. This leads to a rise in the standard of living of people of the world. Thus, free trade leads to higher production, higher consumption and higher all-round international prosperity.

Competitive spirit : *Thirdly*, free trade keeps the spirit of competition of the economy. As there exists the possibility of intense foreign competition under free trade, domestic producers do not want to lose their grounds. Competition enhances efficiency. Moreover, it tends to prevent domestic monopolies and free the consumers from exploitation.

Accessibility of domestically produced goods and services : *Fourthly*, free trade enables each country to get commodities which it cannot produce at all or can only produce inefficiently. Commodities and raw materials unavailable domestically can be procured through free movement even at a low price.

Greater international cooperation : *Fifthly*, free trade safeguards against discrimination. Under free trade, there is no scope for cornering raw materials or commodities by any country. Free trade can thus promote international peace and stability through economic and political cooperation.

Free from interference : *Finally*, free trade is free from bureaucratic interferences. Bureaucracy and corruption are very much associated with unrestricted trade.

In brief, restricted trade prevents a nation from reaping the benefits of specialisation, forces it to adopt less efficient production techniques and forces consumers to pay higher prices for the production of protected industries.

Samuelson, P. A. and Nordhaus, W. D. argue that restricted or protected trade (opposed to free trade) 'prevents the forces of comparative advantage from working to maximum advantages.'

Arguments against Free Trade

Despite these virtues, several people justify trade restrictions. Following arguments are often cited against free trade :

Advantageous not for LDCs : *First,* free trade may be advantageous to the advanced countries but not to the backward economies. Free trade has brought enough misery to the poor, less developed countries, if past experience is any guide. India was a classic example of colonial dependence of UK's imperialistic power prior to 1947. Free trade principles have brought colonial imperialism in its wake.

Destruction of home industries/products : *Secondly,* it may ruin domestic industries. Because of free trade, imported goods become available at a cheaper price. Thus, an unfair and cut-throat competition develops between domestic and foreign industries. In the process, domestic industries are wiped out. Indian handicrafts industries suffered tremendously during the British regime.

Inefficiencey becomes perpetual : Free trade cannot bring all-round development of industries. Comparative cost principle states that a country specialises in the production of a few commodities. On the other hand, inefficient industries remain neglected. Thus, under free trade, an all-round development is ruled out.

Danger of overdependence : *Fourthly,* free trade brings in the danger of dependence. A country may face economic depression if its international trading partner suffers from it. The Great Depression that arose in 1929-30 in the US economy swept all over the world and all countries suffered badly even if their economies were not caught in the grip of the then Depression. Such over dependence following free trade also becomes catastrophic during war.

Penetration of harmful foreign goods : *Finally,* a country may have to change its consumption habits. Because of free trade, even harmful commodities (drugs, etc.,) enter the domestic market. To prevent such, restrictions on trade are required to be imposed.

In view of all these arguments against free trade, governments of less developed countries in the post-Second World War period were encouraged to resort to some kind of trade restrictions to safeguard national interest.

6.8 Protection : Arguments and Counter-arguments

By protection we mean restricted trade. Foreign trade of a country may be free or restricted. Free trade eliminates tariff while protective trade imposes tariff or duty. When tariffs, duties and quotas are imposed to restrict the inflow of imports then we have protected trade. This means that government intervenes in trading activities. Thus, protection is the anti-thesis of free trade or unrestricted trade. Government imposes tariffs on an ad valorem basis or imposes quotas on the volume of goods to be imported. Sometimes, export taxes and subsidies are given to domestic goods to protect them from foreign competition. These are the various forms of protection used by modern governments to restrict trade.

Now an important question arises : What forces the government to protect trade? What are the chief arguments for protection? Can protection deliver all the goods that a nation needs? These questions are raised often because quite a large number of people regard foreign competition with suspicion. Such hostility against free competition often gets reflected by the campaigns to "buy home-produced goods".

Arguments for Protection

The concept of protection is not a post-Second World War development. Its origin can be traced to the days of mercantilism (i.e., the 16th century). Since then, various arguments have been made in favour of protection. The case for protection for the developing countries recieved a strong support from Argentine economists R. D. Prebisch and Hans Singer in the 1950s. All these arguments can be summed up under three heads : (i) fallacious or dubious arguments, (ii) economic arguments, and (iii) non-economic arguments.

Non-economic arguments make a trade-off between national objectives of a country and economic welfare. In this category, national objectives (e.g., defence preparation) are more important than a nation's overall output and economic welfare.

(i) Fallacious Arguments

Fallacious arguments do not stand after scrutiny. These arguments are dubious in nature in the sense that both are true. This argument is based on a misunderstanding of economic logic. 'To keep money at home' is one such fallacious argument. By restricting trade, a country need not spend money to buy imported articles. If every nations pursues this goal, ultimately global trade will squeeze.

(ii) Economic Arguments

Infant industry argument : Perhaps the oldest as well as the cogent argument for protection is the infant industry argument. When an industry is first established its costs will be higher. It is too immature to reap economies of scale at its infancy. Workers are not only inexperinced but also less efficient. If this infant industry is allowed to grow independently, surely it will be unable to compete effectively with the already established industries of other countries. Thus, an infant industry needs protection of a temporary nature. Given time to develop an industry, it is quite likely that in the near future it will be able to develop a comparative advantage, withstand foreign competition, and survive without protection. It is something like the dictum : *Nurse* the baby, *protect* the child and *free* the adult. Once an embryonic industry gets matured it can withstand competition. Competition improves efficiency. Once efficiency is attained, protection may be withdrawn. Thus, an underdeveloped country attempting to have rapid industrialisation needs protection of certain industries.

If we look at the history of the recent past, we see how this infant industry argument has been vindicated. India during the 1960s and 1970s followed import-substituting strategy of industrialisation. This strategy is based on this infant industry argument. The country's industrial base was poor when India got her independence. Thanks to the introduction of the said strategy, India has become a self-reliant country now than what she was in the 1960s and 1970s. In the early stages of industrialisation, many developing countries opted this strategy.

However, in actual practice, the infant industry argument, even in LDCs, loses some strength. Some economists suggest production subsidy rather than protection of certain infant industries. Protection, once granted to an industry, continues for a long time. On the other hand, subsidy is a temporary measure since continuance of it in the next year requires approval of the legislature. Above all, expenditure on subsidy is subject to financial audit. Thus, protection is something like a "gift".

Secondly, protection saps the self-sufficiency outlook of the protected industries. Once protection is granted, it becomes difficult to withdraw it even after attaining maturity. That means infant industries, even after maturity, get 'old age pension'. In other words, infant industries become too much dependent on tariffs and other countries.

Thirdly, it is difficult to identify potential comparative advantage industries. A time period of 5 to 10 years may be required by an industry to achieve maturity or self-sufficiency. Under the circumstances, infant industry argument loses force.

In view of these criticisms, it is said by experts that the argument "boils down to a case for the removal of obstacles to the growth of the infants. It does not demonstrate that a tariff is the most efficient means of attaining the objective." Further, these people argue that the market principle should be adopted to select the industries to be protected.

These counter-arguments, however, do not deter us to foster the growth of infant industries in less developed countries by means of tariff, rather than subsidies.

Diversification argument : As free trade increases specialisation, so protected trade brings in diversified industrial structure. By setting up newer and variety of industries through protective means, a country minimises the risk in production. Comparative advantage principle dictates narrow specialisation in production. This sort of specialisation is not only undesirable from the viewpoint of economic development, but also a risky proposition. Efficiency in production in some products by some countries (e.g., coffee of Brazil, milk products of New Zealand, oil of Middle East countries) results in over-dependence on these products. If war breaks out, or if political relations between countries change, or if recessionary demand condition for the product grow up abroad, the economies of these industries will be greatly injured. Above all, this sort of unbalanced industrial growth goes against the spirit of national self-sufficiency. Protection is the answer to this problem. A government encourages diverse industries to develop through protective means.

However, a counter-argument runs. Politics, rather than economics, may be the criterion for the selection of industries to be protected in order to produce diversification at a reasonable cost. But, one must not ignore economies of protection.

Employment argument : Protection can raise the level of employment. Tariffs may reduce import and, in the process, import-competing industries flourish. In addition, import-substituting industries—the substitution of domestic production for imports of manufactures—develop. The strategy of import-substituting industrialisation promotes domestic industry at the expense of foreign industries. Thus, employment potential under protective regime is quite favourable. In brief, tariff stimulates investment in import-competing and import-substitution industies. Some investment produces favourable employment multiplier.

But, cut in imports following import-substituting industrialisation strategy may ultimately cause exports to decline. Above all, tariff is not an efficient instrument in creating more employment opportunities in an economy. It is strongly argued that the monetary and fiscal policy are the most important means of increasing employment potentiality in an economy.

Balance of payments argument : A deficit in the balance of payments (BOP) can be cured by curtailing imports. However, imports will decline following a rise in tariff rate, provided other trading partners do not retaliate by imposing tariff on a country's export. Import restrictions through tariff may be uncalled for if the balance of payments crisis becomes chronic. In view of this and other associated problems of tariff, it is said that tariff is a second-best policy.

Anti-dumping Argument : Usually, we hear about unfair competition from firms of low-cost countries. One particular form of unfair competition is dumping which is outlawed by international trade pacts, such as the World Trade Organisation (WTO). Dumping is a form of price discrimination that occurs in trade. Dumping occurs when a country sells a product abroad at a low price because of competition and at a high price in the home market because of monopoly power. In other words, dumping is a kind of subsidy given to export goods. This unfair practice can be prevented by imposing tariff. Other-wise, workers and firms competing with the dumped products will be hit hard.

Strategic trade advantage argument : It is argued that tariffs and other import restrictions create a strategic advantage in producing some new products having potential for generating some net profit. There are some large firms who prevent entry of new firms because of the economies of large scale production. Thus, these large firms reap pure profits over the long run during which new firms may not dare enough to compete with these established large firms. Thus, the large scale economies themselves prevent entry of new firms.

But as far as new products are concerned, a new firm may develop and market these products and, ultimately, reap substantial profit. In the end, successful new firms producing new products become one of the few established firms in the industry. New firms showing potential for the future must be protected. "If protection in the domestic market can increase the chance that one of the protected domestic firms will become one of the established firms in the international market the protection may pay off."[1]

All these economic arguments are then based 'on market power or macroeconomic imperfections'.

(iii) Non-economic Arguments

National defense argument : There are some industries which may be inefficient by birth or high cost due to many reasons and must be protected. This logic may apply to the production of national defence goods or necessary food items. Whatever the cost may be, there is no question of compromise for the defence industry since 'defence

1. Lipsey and Chrystal : *An Introduction to Positive Economics*, ELBS.

is more important than opulence'. Dependence on foreign countries regarding supply of basic food items as well as defence products is absolutely unwise.

However, objections against this argument may be cited here. It is difficult to identify a particular item as a defence industry item because we have seen that many industries—from garlic to clothespin—applied for protection on defence grounds. Candle stick-maker (for emergency lighting) and toothpick-makers (to have good dental hygiene for the troops) demanded protection at different times at different places! A nation which builds up its military strength through tariff protection does not sound convincing. Thus, tariff is a second-best solution.

Arguments against Protection

There are some good 'side-effects' or 'spillover effects' of protection. This means that it produces some undesirable effects on the economy and the basic objective of protection can be attained rather in a costless manner by other direct means other than protection. That is, protection is never more than a second-best solution.

First, protection distorts the comparative advantage in production. This means that specialisation in production may be lost if a country imposes tariff. All these lead to squeezing of trade. *Secondly*, it imposes a cost on the society since consumers buy goo‸ at a high price. *Thirdly*, often weak declining industries having no future potential stay on the economy under the protective umbrella. *Fourthly*, international tension often escalates, particularly when tariff war begins. Usually, a foreign country retaliates by imposing tariff on its imports from the tariff-imposing country. Once the retaliatory attitude (i.e., 'beggar-thy-neighbour policy') develops, benefits from protection will be lost. Under the circumstance, the argument that a tariff improves terms of trade of the tariff-imposing country loses potency. Ultimately, tariff war ensues. *Finally*, protection encourages bureaucracy. Increase in trade restrictions means expansion of governmental activity and, hence, rise in administrative cost. Bureaucracy ultimately leads to corruption.

Conclusion : The classical golden age of free trade no longer exists in the world. But, free trade concept has not been abandoned since the case for free trade is the strongest in the long run. Protection is a short term measure. Thus, the issue for public policy is the best reconciliation of these two perspectives so that gains from trade (may be free or restricted) become the greatest.

In recent times, most countries (153) are the members of the World Trade Organisation (WTO) which favours more free trade than restricted trade. This philosophy gathered momentum in the Dunkel Draft and the General Agreement on Tariffs and Trade (GATT) negotiations. The aims of the GATT (now abolished) and now the WTO are trade liberalisation rather than trade restriction.

6.8.1 Tariff vs Quotas

Governments of different countries have to intervene in the area of international trade for both economic and non-economic reasons. Such intervention goes by the name of protection. Protection means government policy of according protection to the domestic industries against foreign competition. There are various instruments or methods of protection which aim at raising exports or reducing imports. Here we are concerned with those methods that restricts import.

There are various methods of protection. The most important methods of protection are : tariff and quotas. A tariff is a tax on imports. It is normally imposed by the government on the imports of a particular commodity. On the other hand, a quota is a quantity limit. It restricts imports of commodities physically. It specifies the

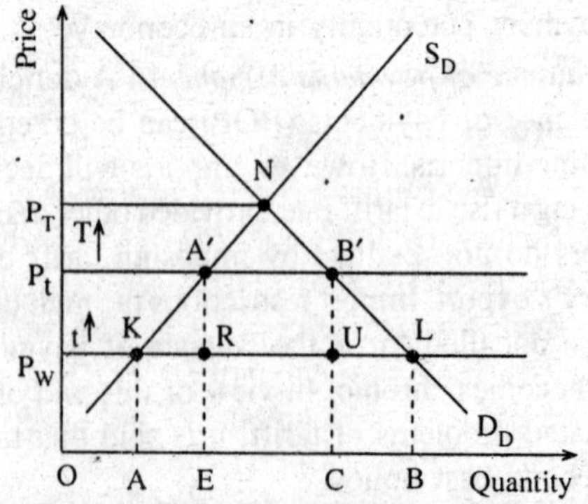

Fig. 6.5 : Effects of Tariff and Quotas

maximum amount that can be imported during a given time period.

We can now make a comparison between tariffs and quotas in terms of partial equilibrium or demand-supply approach. Fig. 6.5 illustrates the effects of tariffs. The domestic supply curve is represented by the S_D curve while the demand curve is given by the D_D curve. These two curves intersect each other at point 'N'. And the price that is determined is known as the autarkic price or pre-trade price (P_T). If trade is free, the international price that would prevail is assumed to be P_W. At the international price P_W, a country produces OA but consumes OB and the country, therefore, imports AB.

Now, if a country imposes a tariff = t per unit on its import (small-sized arrow), immediately the price of the product will rise to P_t by the amount of tariff. This may be called 'non-prohibitive tariff.' This increase in price has the following effects.

Since tariff raises the price, consumers buy less. Now consumption declines from OB to OC. This is called the *consumption effect* of tariff. The second effect is the *output effect or protective effect*. Tariff raises domestic output from OA to OE; this is because higher price induces producers to produce more. The third effect is *import-reducing effect*—as tariff is imposed or tariff rate is increased import declines from AB to EC. The fourth effect is the *revenue effect* earned by the government. The government revenue is the volume of import multiplied by the volume of tariff, i.e., the area A′B′UR. It is a transfer from the consumers to the government. However, if a tariff equal to 'T' were imposed, the price would have increased to P_T. Consequently, imports would drop to zero. Such a situation is called 'prohibitive tariff' (big-sized arrow) that chokes off all imports.

6.8.2 Effects of Quotas

Quotas are similar to tariffs. In fact, they can be represented by the same diagram. The main difference is that quotas restrict quantity while tariffs work through prices. Thus, a quota is a quantitative limit through imports. If an import quota of EC (Fig. 6.5) amount is imposed then price would rise to P_t because the total supply (domestic output plus imports) equals total demand at that price. As a result of this quota, domestic production, consumption, and imports would be the same as those of the tariffs. Thus, the *output effect, the consumption effect and the import restrictive effect* of tariffs and quotas are exactly the same.

The only difference is the area of revenue. We have already seen that a tariff raises revenue for the government while quotas generate no government revenue. All the benefits of quotas go to the producers and to the lucky importers who manage to get the scarce and valuable import permits. In such a situation, quotas differ from a tariff. However, if import licences are auctioned-off to the importers then the government would earn revenue from the auction. Under these circumstances, the effects of quota and tariff are equivalent.

6.8.3 Advantages of Quotas

Quotas are superior to tariffs on the following grounds :

Foreign exchange implication : The main advantage of quotas is that it keeps the volume of imports unchanged even when demand for imported articles increases. It is because quotas make the completely elastic (horizontal) import supply curve completely inelastic (vertical). But a tariff permits imports to rise when demand increases, particularly if the demand for imports becomes inelastic. Thus, a quota leads to greater foreign exchange savings compared to tariff (which may even lead to an increase in foreign exchange spending because imports may rise even after tariff).

Precise outcome : Another advantage of a quota is that its outcome is more certain and precise, while the outcome of a tariff is uncertain and unclear. This is so because the volume of imports remains unchanged if a quota is imposed. But this is not so in the case of a tariff.

Flexibility : *Finally*, Ingo Walter argues that "quotas tend to be more flexible, more easily imposed, and more easily removed instruments of commercial policy than tariffs. Tariffs are often regarded as relatively permanent measures and rapidly built powerful vested interests which make them all the more difficult to remove."

6.8.4 Disadvantages of Quotas

But its disadvantages are nonetheless unimportant :

Corruption : Quotas generate no revenue for the government. However, if the government auctions the right to import under quotas to the highest bidder then quotas are similar to tariffs. But quotas lead to corruption. Usually, officials charged with the allocation of import licences are likely to be exposed to bribery. Under this situations tariffs are preferable to quotas.

Monopoly profit : *Secondly*, quotas create a monopoly profit for those with import licences. This means that consumer surplus is converted into monopoly profits. Thus, a quota is likely to lead to a greater loss of consumer welfare. If a tariff is imposed, domestic price will be equal to import price plus tariff.

Monopoly growth : *Thirdly*, allied to this disadvantage of quotas is that quotas are much more restrictive in effect as it restricts competition. Thus, quotas may ultimately lead to concentration of monopoly power among importers and exporters.

Distortion in trade : *Finally*, a quota has the tendency to distort international trade much more than tariffs since its effects are more vigorous and arbitrary.

Thus, we will have to make a choice between a tariff and a quota. A tariff is usually considered a less objectionable method of trade restriction than an equivalent quota. A tariff permits imports to increase when demand increases and, consequently, the government is able to raise more revenue. In contrast, a quota is less obvious and more likely to remain in force for an indefinite period. For all these reasons, a tariff, while objectionable, is still preferable to a quota. The WTO condemns quotas.

6.9 What is Balance of Payments?

The balance of payments (henceforth BOP) is a consolidated account of the reciepts and payments from and to other countries arising out of all economic transactions during the course of a year. In the words of C. P. Kindleberger : "The balance of payments of a country is a systematic record of all economic transactions between the residents of the reporting and the residents of the foreign countries during a given period of time." Here by 'residents' we mean individuals, firms and government. By all economic transactions we mean individuals, firms and government. By all economic transactions we mean transactions of both visible goods (merchandise) and invisible goods (services), assets, gifts, etc. In other words, the BOP shows how money is spent abroad (i.e., payments) and how money is received domestically (i.e., receipts). Thus, a BOP account records all payments and receipts arising out of all economic transactions. All payments are regarded as debits (i.e., outflow of money) and are recorded in the accounts with a negative sign and all receipts are regarded as credits (i.e., inflow or money) and are recorded in the accounts with a positive sign. The International Monetary Fund defines BOP as a "statistical statement that subsequently summarises, for a specific time period, the economic transactions of an economy with the rest of the world."

6.9.1 Components of BOP Accounts

According to the broad nature of the transactions concerned, the BOP of a country is divided into two main parts : (i) the current account, and (ii) the capital account. The other part is official reserve account.

The Current account : The current account of BOP includes all transaction arising from trade in currently produced goods and services, from income accruing to capital by one country and invested in another and from unilateral transfers—both private and official. The current account is usually divided in three sub-divisions.

The first of these is called visible account or merchandise account or trade in goods account. This account records imports and exports of physical goods. The balance of visible exports and visible imports is called balance of visible trade or balance of merchandise trade [i.e., items 1(a), and 2(a) of Table 6.1].

The second part of the account is called the invisibles account since it records all exports and imports of services. The balance of these transactions is called the balance of invisible trade. As these transactions are not recorded—in the customs office—unlike merchandise trade we call them invisible items. It includes

Table 6.1 : The Schematic BOP

A. Current Account

1. Merchandise Trade

(a) Visible exports, (b) Visible imports.

2. Invisible Trade

(a) Invisible exports, (b) Invisible imports.

3. Other Flows

(a) Investment income, (b) Unrequited transfers.

B. Capital Account : (a) Long term capital transactions,

(b) Short term capital transactions.

C. Balancing Item

Net Errors and Omissions.

D. Official Reserve Account

freights and fares of ships and planes, insurance and banking charges, foreign tours and education abroad, expenditures on foreign embassies, transactions out of interest and dividends on foreigners' investment and so on. Items 2(a) and 2(b) comprise services balance or balance of invisible trade.

The difference between merchandise trade and invisible trade (i.e., items 1 and 2) is known as the *balance of trade.*

There is *another* flow in the current account that consists of two items [3(a) and 3(b)]. Investment income consists of interest, profit and dividends on bonus and credits. Interest earned by a US resident from the TELCO share is one kind of investment income that represents a debit item here. There may be a similar money inflow (i.e., credit item). Unrequited transfers include grants, gifts, pension, etc. These items are such that no reverse flow occurs. Or these are the items against which no quid pro quo is demanded. Residents of a country received these cost-free. Thus, unilateral transfers are one-way transactions. In other words, these items do not involve give and take unlike other items in the BOP account.

Thus the first three items of the BOP account are included in the current account. The current account is said to be favourable (or unfavourable) if receipts exceed (fall short of) payments.

The Capital account : The capital account shows transactions relating to the international movement of ownership of financial assets. It refers to cross-border movements in foreign assets like shares, property or direct acquisitions of companies' bank loans, government securities, etc. In other words, capital account records export and import of capital from and to foreign countries.

The capital account is divided into two main subdivisions : short term and the long term movements of capital. A short term capital is one which matures in one year or less, such as bank accounts.

Long term capital is one whose maturity period is longer than a year, such as long term bonds or physical capital. Long term capital account is, again, of two categories : direct investment and portfolio investment. Direct investment refers to expenditure on fixed capital formation, while portfolio investment refers to the acquisition of financial assets like bonds, shares, etc. India's investment (e.g., if an Indian acquires a new Coca-Cola plant in the USA) abroad represents an outflow of money. Similarly, if a foreigner acquires a new factory in India it will represent an inflow of funds. Thus, through acquisition or sale and purchase of assets, capital movements take place. Investors then acquire controlling interests over the asset. Remember that exports and imports of equipment do not appear in the capital account. On the other hand, portfolio investment refers to changes in the holding of shares and bonds. Such investment is portfolio capital and the ownership of paper assets like shares does not ensure legal control over the firms.

[In this connection, the concepts of capital exports and capital imports require little elaboration. Suppose, a US company purchases a firm operating in India. This sort of foreign investment is called capital import rather than capital export. India acquires foreign currency after selling the firm to a US company. As a result, India acquires purchasing power abroad. That is why this transaction is included in the credit side of India's BOP accounts. In the same way, if India invests in a foreign country, it is a payment and will be recorded on the debit side. This is called capital export. Thus, India earns foreign currency by exporting goods and services and by importing capital. Similarly, India releases foreign currency by importing visibles and invisibles and exporting capital.]

Statistical discrepancy—errors and omissions : The sum of A and B (Table 6.1) is called the basic balance. Since BOP always balances in theory, all debits must be offset by all credits, and vice versa. In practice, it rarely happens—particularly because statistics are incomplete as well as imperfect. That is why errors and omissions are considered so that the BOP accounts are kept in balance (Item C).

The Official reserve account : The total of A, B, C, and D comprise the overall balance. The category of official reserve account covers the net amount of transactions by governments. This account covers purchases and sales of reserve assets (such as gold, convertible foreign exchange and special drawing rights) by the central monetary authority.

Now, we can summarise the BOP data :

Current account balance + Capital account balance + Reserve balance = Balance of Payments

(X – M) + (CI – CO) + FOREX = BOP

X is exports,

M is imports,

CI is capital inflows,

CO is capital outflows,

FOREX is foreign exchange reserve balance.

6.9.2 Distinction between BOP and BOT

The BOP of a country is a systematic record of all economic transactions between the residents of the home country and the residents of the rest of the world during a given year. By all transactions we mean exports and imports of both goods and services, unrequited transfers as well as capital movements. Thus, the BOP of a country is a complete picture of its international transactions. On the other hand, the 'balance of trade' (henceforth, BOT) is the difference between visible exports and visible imports. This difference is also called marchandise balance or balance of visible trade. Similarly, one obtains the balance of invisible trade which represents the difference between invisible exports and invisible imports. The difference between a nation's exports of goods and services and its imports is called balance of trade in goods and services or 'balance of trade.' Whether invisibles are included or not in the BOT, it is clear that the BOP is a broader concept than BOT. BOT is classified into balance of visible and invisible trade.

The BOT is said to improve when exports of visible items (and invisible items) rise more than or fall less than imports of visible items (and invisible items). Conversely, the trade balance deteriorates. A country's BOP to be is and favourable if its total receipts exceed total payments.

An important point to note is that there may be a BOT deficit but a BOP surplus, or vice versa. In other words, a trade deficit does not necessarily imply that a country is losing its foreign reserves—the difference is accounted by long term capital movements.

6.9.3 BOP always Balances

A nation's BOP is a summary statement of all economic transactions between the residents of a country and the rest of the world during a given period of time. A BOP account is divided into current account and capital account. Former is made up of trade in goods (i.e., visibles) and trade in services (i.e., invisibles) and unrequited transfers. Latter account is made up of transactions in financial assets. These two accounts comprise BOP.

A BOP account is prepared according to the principle of double-entry book keeping. This accounting procedure gives rise to two entries—a debit and a corresponding credit. Any transaction giving rise to a receipt from the rest of the world is a credit item in the BOP account. Any transaction giving rise to a payment to the rest of the world is a debit item.

The left hand side of the BOP account shows the receipts of the country. Such receipts of external purchasing power arise from the commodity export, from the sale of invisible services, from the receipts of gift and grants from foreign governments, international lending institutions and foreign individuals, from the borrowing of money from the foreigners or from repayment of loan by the foreigners.

The right hand side shows the payments made by the country on different items to the foreigners. It shows how the total of external purchasing power is used for acquiring imports of foreign goods and services as well as the purchase of foreign assets. This is the accounting procedure.

However, no country publishes BOP accounts in this format. Rather, by convention, the BOP figures are published in a single column with positive (credit) and negative (debit) signs. Since payments side of the account enumerates all the uses which are made up of the total foreign purchasing power acquired by this country in a given period, and since the receipts of the accounts enumerate all the sources from which foreign purchasing power is acquired by the same country in the same period, the two sides must balance. The entries in the account should, therefore, add up to zero.

In reality, why should they add up to zero? In practice, this is difficult to achieve where receipts equal payments. In reality, total receipts may diverge from total payments because of : (i) the difficulty of collecting accurate trade information; (ii) the difference in the timing between the two sides of the balance; and (iii) a change in the exchange rates, etc.

Because of such measurement problems, resource is made to 'balancing item' that intends to eliminate errors in measurement. The purpose of incorporating this item in the BOP account is to adjust the difference between the sums of the credit and the sums of the debit items in the BOP accounts so that they add up to zero by construction. Hence the proposition 'the BOP always balances'. It is a truism. It only suggests that the two sides of the accounts must always show the same total. It implies only an equality. In this book-keeping sense, BOP always balances.

Thus, by construction, BOP accounts do not matter. In fact, this is not so. The accounts have both economic and political implications. Mathematically, receipts equal payments but it need not balance in economic sense. This means that there cannot be disequilibrium in the BOP accounts. A combined deficit in the current and capital accounts is the most unwanted macroeconomic goal of an economy. Again, a deficit in the current account is also undesirable. All these suggest that BOP is out of equilibrium. But can we know whether the BOP is in equilibrium or not? Tests are usually three in number : (i) movements in foreign exchange reserves including gold, (ii) increase in borrowing from abroad, and (iii) movements in foreign exchange rates of the country's currency in question.

Firstly, if foreign exchange reserves decline, a country's BOP is considered to be in disequilibrium or in deficit. If foreign exchange reserves are allowed to deplete rapidly it may shatter the confidence of people over the domestic currency. This may ultimately lead to a run on the bank.

Secondly, to cover the deficit a country may borrow from abroad. Thus, such borrowing occurs when imports exceed exports. This involves payment of interest on borrowed funds at a high rate of interest.

Finally, the foreign exchange rate of a country's currency may tumble when it suffers from BOP disequilibrum. A fall in the exchange rate of a currency is a sign of BOP disequilibrium.

Thus, the above (mechanical) equality between receipts and payments should not be interpreted to mean that a country never suffers from the BOP problems and the international economic transactions of a country are always in equilibrium.

6.10 Foreign Exchange Rate

Meaning : If a Kashmiri shawlmaker sells his goods to a buyer in Kanyakumari, he will receive in terms of Indian rupee. This suggests that the domestic trade is conducted in terms of domestic currency. Within the country, transactions are, then, simple and straight-forward. But if the Indian shawlmaker decides to go abroad, he must exchange Indian rupee into Jap yen or dollar or pound or euro. To facilitate this exchange form, banking institutions appear. Indian shawlmaker will then go to a bank for foreign currencies. The bank will then quote the day's exchange rate—the rate at which Indian rupee will be exchanged for foreign currencies. Thus, foreign currencies are needed for the conduct of international trade. In a foreign exchange market comprising commercial banks, foreign exchange brokers and authorised dealers and the monetary authority (i.e., the RBI), one currency is converted into another currency.

A (foreign) exchange rate is the rate at which one currency is exchanged for another. Thus, an exchange rate can be regarded as the price of one currency in terms of another. An exchange rate is a ratio between two monies. If 5 UK pounds or 5 US dollars buy Indian goods worth Rs. 400 and Rs. 250 then pound-rupee or dollar-rupee exchange rate becomes Rs. 80 = £1 or Rs. 50 = $1, respectively. Exchange rate is usually quoted in terms of rupees per unit of foreign currencies. Thus, an exchange rate indicates external purchasing power of money.

A fall in the external purchasing power or external value of rupee (i.e., a fall in the exchange rate, say for Rs. 80 = £1 to Rs. 90 = £1) amounts to depreciation of the Indian rupee. Consequently, an appreciation of the Indian rupee occurs when there occurs an increase in the exchange rate from the exsisting level to Rs. 78 = £1. In other words, the external value of rupee rises. This indicates strengthening of the Indian rupee. Conversely, the weakening of the Indian rupee occurs if external value of rupee in terms of pound falls.

Remember that each currency has a rate of exchange with every other currency. Not all exchange rates between about 150 currencies are quoted since no significant foreign exchange market exists for all currencies. That is why exchange rate of these national currencies are quoted usually in terms of the US dollars and euros.

6.10.1 Determination of Exchange Rate

Now two pertinent questions that usually arise in the foreign exchange market are to be answered now. *First*, how is the equilibrium exchange rate determined, and *secondly*, why does exchange rate move up and down?

There are two methods of foreign exchange rate determination. One method falls under the classical gold standard mechanism and another method falls under the classical paper currency system. Today, gold standard mechanism does not operate since no standard monetary unit is now exchanged for gold. All countries now have paper currencies not convertible to gold. Under inconvertible paper currency system, there are two methods of exchange rate determination. The first is known as the purchasing power parity theory and the second is known as the demand-supply theory or the balance of payments theory. Since today there is no believer of purchasing power parity theory, we consider only demand-supply approach to foreign exchange rate determination.

Demand-Supply Approach of Foreign Exchange

Or, BOP Theory of Foreign Exchange Rate Determination

Since the foreign exchange rate is a price, economists apply supply-demand conditions of price theory in the foreign exchange market. A simple explanation is that the rate of foreign exchange equals its supply. For simplicity, we assume that there are two countries : India and the USA. Let the domestic currency be rupee. The US dollar stands for foreign exchange and the value of rupee in terms of dollars (or conversely, the value of dollars in terms of rupee) stands for foreign exchange rate. Now the value of one currency in terms of another currency depends upon the demand for and the supply of foreign exchange.

Demand for Foreign Exchange

When Indian people and business firms want to make payments to the US nationals for using US goods and services or to make gifts to the US citizens or to buy assets there, the demand for foreign exchange (here dollar) is generated. In other words, Indians demand or buy dollars by paying rupee in the foreign exchange market. A country releases its foreign currency for buying imports. Thus what appears in the debit side of the BOP account are the sources of demand for foreign exchange. Larger the volume of imports, greater is the demand for foreign exchange.

The demand curve for foreign exchange is negative sloping. A fall in the price of foreign exchange or a fall in the price of dollar in terms of rupee (i.e., dollar depreciates) means that foreign goods are now more cheaper. Thus, an Indian could buy more American goods at a low price. Consequently, imports from the USA would increase—resulting in an increase in the demand for foreign exchange, i.e., dollar. Conversely, if the price of foreign exchange or the price of dollar rises (i.e., dollar appreciates) foreign goods will now be expensive leading to a fall in import demand and, hence, fall in the demand for foreign exchange. Since price of foreign exchange and demand for foreign exchange move in opposite directions, the importing country's demand curve for foreign exchange is downward sloping from left to right.

In Fig. 6.6, DD_1 is the demand curve for foreign exchange. In this figure, we measure exchange rate expressed in terms of domestic currency that costs 1 unit of foreign currency (i.e., dollar per rupee) on the vertical axis. This makes the demand curve for foreign exchange negative sloping. If the exchange rate is expressed in terms of foreign currency that could be purchased with a 1 unit of domestic currency (i.e., dollar per rupee), the demand curve would exhibit positive slope. Here we have chosen the former one.

Supply of Foreign Exchange

In a similar fashion, we can determine the supply of foreign exchange. Supply of foreign currency comes from receipts for its exports. If the foreign nationals and firms intend to purchase Indian goods or buy Indian assets or give grants to the Government of India, the supply of foreign exchange is generated. In other words, what the Indian exports (both goods and invisibles) to the rest of the world is the source of foreign exchange. To be more specific, all the transactions that appear on the credit side of the BOP account are the sources of supply of foreign exchange.

A rise in the rupee-per-dollar exchange rate means that Indian goods are cheaper to foreigners in terms of dollars. This will induce India to export more. Foreigners will also find that investment is now more profitable. Thus, a high price or exchange rate ensures larger supply of foreign exchange. Conversely, a low exchange rate causes exchange rate to fall. Thus, the supply curve of foreign exchange, SS_1, is positive sloping.

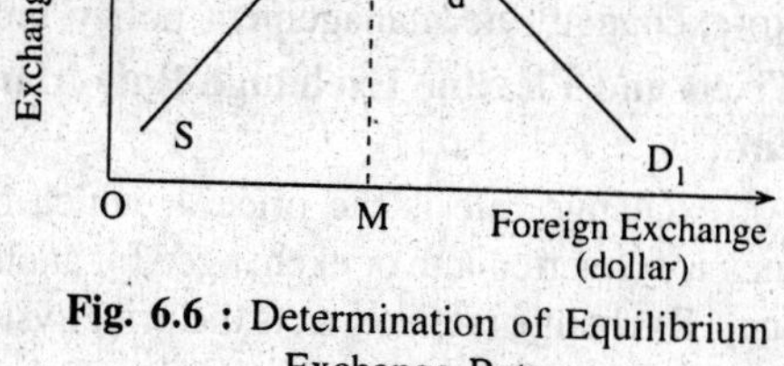

Fig. 6.6 : Determination of Equilibrium Exchange Rate

Now we can bring both the demand and supply curves together to determine foreign exchange rate. The equilibrium exchange rate is determined at that point where the demand for foreign exchange equals the supply of foreign exchange. In Fig. 6.6, DD_1 and SS_1 curves. intersect at point E. The foreign exchange rate thus determinded is OP. At this rate, quantities of foreign exchange demanded (OM) equals quantity supplied (OM). The market is cleared and there is no incentive on the part of the players to change the rate determined. Note that at the rate OP, (say, Rs. 50 = \$1) demand for foreign exchange is matched by the supply of foreign exchange.

If the current exchange rate OP_1 (suppose, pc 55 = \$ 1) exceeds the equilibrium rate of exchange (OP), there occurs an excess supply of dollar by the amount 'ab'. Now the bank and other institutions dealing with foreign exchange, wishing to make money by exchanging currency, would lower the exchange rate to reduce excess supply. Thus, exchange rate will tend to fall until OP is reached. Similarly, an excess demand for foreign exchange by the amount 'cd' arises if the exchange rate falls below OP, i.e., OP_2. Banks would then experience a shortage of dollars to meet the demand. The rate of foreign exchange will rise till demand equals supply.

The exchange rate that we have determined is called a floating or 'flexible exchange' rate. (Under this exchange rate system, the government does not intervene in the foreign exchange market.) A floating exchange rate, by definition, results in an equilibrium rate of exchange that will move up and down according to a change in demand and

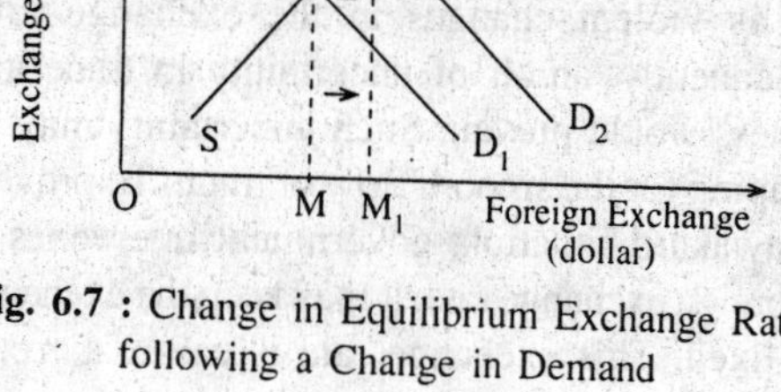

Fig. 6.7 : Change in Equilibrium Exchange Rate following a Change in Demand

supply forces. The process by which currencies float up and down following a change in demand or a change in supply forces is thus illustrated in Fig. 6.7.

Let us assume that national income rises. This results in an increase in demand for imports of goods and services and, hence, demand for dollar rises. This results in a shift in the demand curve from DD_1 to DD_2. Consequently, exchange rate rises as determined by the intersection of the new demand curve and supply curve. Note that dollar appreciates while rupee depreciates.

Similarly, if the supply curve shifts from SS_1 to SS_2 as shown in Fig. 6.8, the new exchange rate thus determined would be OP_2. If Indian goods are exported more following an increase in national income of the USA, the supply curve would then

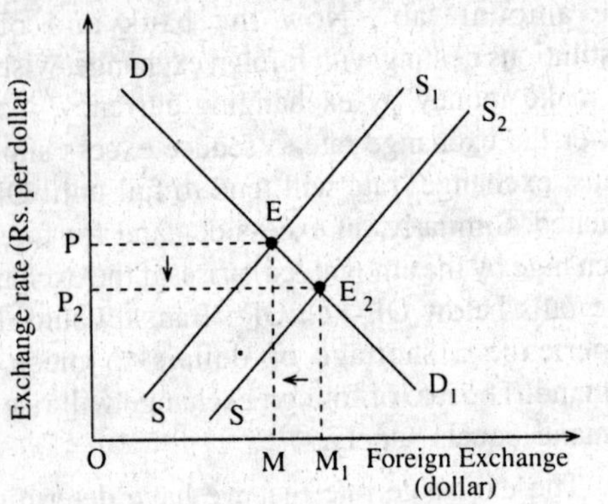

Fig. 6.8 : Change in Equilibrium Exchange Rate following a Change in Supply

shift rightward. Consequently, dollar depreciates and rupee appreciates. New exchange rate is settled at that point where the new supply curve (SS_2) intersects the demand curve at E_2.

This is the balance of payments theory of exchange rate determination. Wherever government does not intervene in the market, a floating or a flexible exchange rate prevails. Such a system may not necessarily be ideal since frequent changes in demand and supply forces cause frequent as well as violent changes in the exchange rate. Consequently, an air of uncertainty in trade and business would prevail. Such uncertainty may be damaging for the smooth flow of trade. To prevent this awakard situation, government intervenes in the foreign exchange rate. It may keep the exchange rate fixed. This exchange rate is called a 'fixed exchange' rate system where both the demand and supply forces are manipulated or calibrated by the central bank in such a way that the exchange rate is kept pegged at the old level.

Often 'managed exchange rate' is suggested. Under this system, exchange rate as usual is determined by the demand for and the supply of foreign exchange. But the central bank intervenes in the foreign exchange market when the situation demands to stabilise or influence the rate of foreign exchange. If rupee depreciates in terms of dollar, the RBI would then sell dollars and buy rupee in order to reduce the downward pressure in the exchange rate.

6.11 Exchange Rate Management Policy

Although a nation's BOP always balances in the accounting sense, it need not balance in an economic sense. An unbalance in the BOP account has the following implications. In the case of a deficit : (i) foreign exchange or foreign currency reserves decline, (ii) volume of international debt and its servicing mount up, and (iii) the exchange rate experiences a downward pressure. It is, therefore, necessary to correct these imbalances.

BOP adjustment measures are grouped into four : (i) protectionist measures by imposing customs duties and other restrictions, quotas on imports, etc., aim at restricting the flow of imports, (ii) demand management policies—these include restrictionary monetary and fiscal policies to control aggregate demand [C + I + G + (X – M)], (iii) supply-side policies—these policies aim at increasing the nation's output through greater productivity and other efficiency measures, and, finally, (iv) exchange rate management policies—these policies may involve a fixed exchange rate, or a flexible exchange rate or a managed exchange rate system.

As a method of correcting disequilibrium in a nation's BOP account, we attach importance here to exchange rate management policy only.

Fixed and Flexible Exchange Rate Management

An exchange rate is the price at which one currency is converted into or exchanged for another currency. Exchange rate connects the price system of two countries since this (special) price shows the relationship between all domestic prices and all foreign prices. Any change in the exchange rate between rupee and dollar will cause a change in the prices of all American goods for Indians and the prices of all Indian goods for the Americans. In the process, equilibrium in the BOP accounts will be restored.

Every government has to make international decisions of what type of exchange rate it wants to adopt. This means that government will have to decide how its own currency should be related to other currencies of the world. For instance, it may choose to fix the value of its currency to other currencies of the world so as to adjust its BOP dificulties, or it may choose to allow its currency to move free against other currencies of the world so as to adjust its BOP difficulties. This means that there are two important exchange rate systems—the fixed (or pegged) exchange rate, and the flexible (or fluctuating or floating) exchange rate.

These two exchange rates have been tried and tested in the past. Fixed exchange rate system had been tried by the IMF during 1947-1971 when this system was abandoned. After 1971, the world's exchange rate became a flexible one or a floating one. Truly speaking, the exchange rate that is being followed by the IMF now is known as the 'managed floating system', or the 'managed flexibility'.

(A) Fixed Exchange Rate

A fixed exchange rate is an exchange rate that does not fluctuate or that changes within a predetermined rate at infrequent intervals.

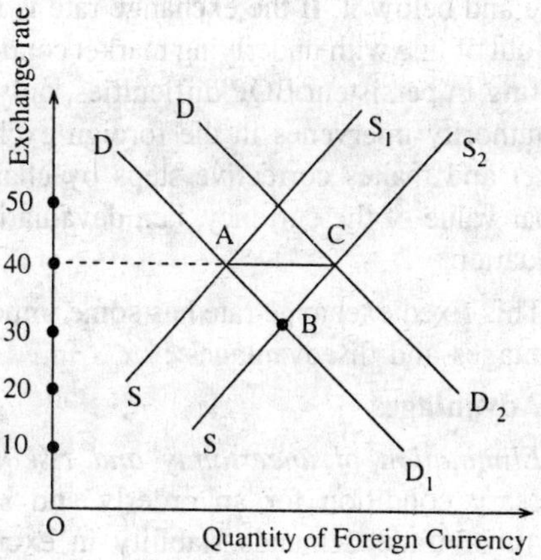

Fig. 6.9 : Fixed Exchange Rate Mechanism

Government or the central monetary authority intervenes in the foreign exchange market so that exchange rates are kept fixed at a stable rate. The rate at which the currency is fixed is called par value. This par value is allowed to move in a narrow range or 'band' of ± 1 per cent. If the sum of current and capital account is negative, there occurs an excess supply of domestic currency in the world markets. The government then intervenes using official foreign exchange reserves to purchase domestic currency.

Fixed or the pegged exchange rate can be explained graphically. Let us suppose that India's demand for US goods rises. This increased demand for imports causes an increase in the supply of domestic currency, rupee, in the exchange market to obtain US dollars. Let DD_1 and SS_1 be the demand and supply curves of dollar in Fig. 6.9. These two curves intersect at point A and the corresponding exchange rate is Rs. 40 = \$1. Consequently, the supply curve shifts to SS_2 that cuts the demand curve DD_1 at point B. This means a fall in the exchange rate. To prevent this exchange rate from falling, the Reserve Bank of India will demand more rupee in exchange for US dollars. This will restrict the excess supply of rupee and there will be an upward pressure in exchange rate. Demand curve will now shift to DD_2. The end result is the restoration of the old exchange rate at point C.

Thus, it is clear that the maintenance of fixed exchange rate system requires that foreign exchange reserves are sufficiently available. Whenever a country experiences inadequate foreign currency reserves it won't be able to purchase domestic currency in sufficient quantities. Under the circumstances, the country will devalue its currency. Devaluation refers to an official reduction in the value of one currency in terms of another currency.

(B) Flexible Exchange Rate

Under the flexible or floating exchange rate, the exchange rate is allowed to vary to international foreign exchange market influences. Thus, government does not intervene. Rather, it is the market forces that determine the exchange rate. In fact, automatic variations in exchange rates

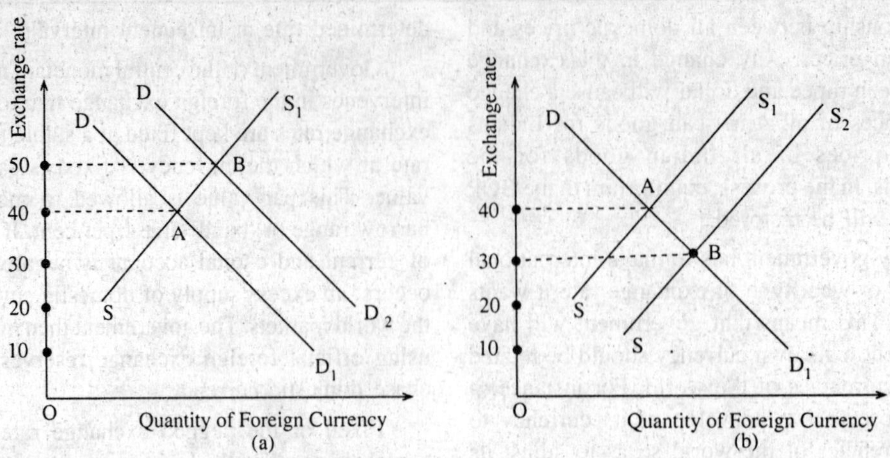

Fig. 6.10 : Flexible Exchange Rate Mechanism

consequent upon a change in market forces are the essence of freely fluctuating exchange rates. A deficit in the BOP account means an excess supply of the domestic currency in the world markets. As price declines, imbalances are removed. In other words, excess supply of domestic currency will automatically cause a fall in the exchange rate and BOP balance will be restored.

Flexible exchange rate mechanism has been explained in Fig. 6.10 where DD_1 and SS_1 are the demand and supply curves. When Indians buy US goods, there arises supply of dollar and when US people buy Indian goods, there occurs demand for rupee. Initial exchange rate—Rs. 40 = \$1—is determined by the intersection of DD_1 and SS_1 curves in both the Figs. 6.10(a) and 6.10(b).

An increase in demand for India's exportables means an increase in the demand for Indian rupee. Consequently, demand curve shifts to DD_2 and the new exchange rate rises to Rs. 50 = \$1. At this new exchange rate, dollar appreciates while rupee depreciates in value [Fig. 6.10(a)].

Fig. 6.10(b) shows that the initial exchange rate is Rs. 40 = \$1. Supply curve shifts to SS_2 in response to an increase in demand for the US goods. SS_2 curve intersects the demand curve DD_1 at point B and exchange rate drops to Rs. 30 = \$1. This means that dollar depreciates while Indian rupee appreciates.

(C) Managed Exchange Rate

Under this heading, floating exchange rates are 'managed' partially. That is to say, exchange rates are determined in the main by market forces, but the central bank intervenes to stabilise fluctuations in exchange rates so as to bring 'orderly' conditions in the market, or to maintain the desired exchange rate values.

6.11.1 Advantages and Disadvantages of Fixed Exchange Rate System

Under the fixed exchange rate system, the exchange rate between currencies is fixed or pegged at a certain value. That is to say, currencies are assigned a fixed par value by the monetary authority in terms of other currencies of the world. The exchange rate remains unchanged over a long period. Under this system of exchange rate, however, exchange rate is allowed to move in a narrow range around that par value, say 1 p.c. above and below it. If the exchange rate is found to be out of line with underlying market conditions resulting in persistent BOP difficulties, only then the authority intervenes in the foreign exchange market and makes corrective steps by changing the par value of the currency, i.e., devaluation or revaluation.

This fixed exchange rate has some important advantages and disadvantages :

Advantages

Elimination of uncertainty and risk : The necessary condition for an orderly and steady growth of trade demands stability in exchange rate. Any undue fluctuations in exchange rate cause problems to the plans and programmes of both exporters and imports. In other words, incomes of export-earners and the cost of imports of the importers tend to become uncertain if the exchange rate fluctuates. This uncertainty can be removd by a fixed exchange rate method. Further, the risks associated with international trade and investment get minimised largely if exchange rates are not allowed to vary.

Speculation deterred : As exchange rate remains unchanged for a fairly long period of time, people expect that such rate would not change in the immediate future. This then eliminates speculation in the foreign exchange market.

Further, as stability in the exchange rate over longish period eliminates the threat of speculation, it discourages the flight of capital. In a world of free fluctuating exchange rate, the danger of the flight of capital is rather high as this kind of exchange rate induces people to speculate. As exchange rates remain fixed, traders have a sense of confidence that international payments can be made safely without the danger of losses.

Prevention of depreciation of currency : In poor developing countries, one experiences BOP difficulties of a permanent type. Under the circumstances, any frequent changes in exchange rate will tend to aggravate the BOP crisis, like continuous depreciation of home currency in terms of currencies of other countries. In other words, unstable exchange rates result in depreciation of currencies. This can be prevented by the stable exchange rate.

Adoption of responsible macroeconomic policies : Stable exchange rate sysem prevents government from adopting irresponsible macroeconomic policies like devaluation of currencies. Above all, under the fixed exchange rate system, deflationary policies can even be pursued to tide over the BOP deficit, even without bringing any change in domestic policies.

Attraction of foreign investment : Exchange rate stability may encourage foreigners to perk their investible funds in a country. If the exchange rate changes rather frequently, it will deter them to invest in a country. Of course, such foreign investment having multiplier effect leads to higher economic growth.

Anti-inflationary : Fixed exchange rate system is anti-inflationary in character. If exchange rate is allowed to decline, import goods tend to become dearer. High cost import goods then fuels inflation. Such a situation can be prevented by making the exchange rate fixed.

Disadvantages

Speculation encouraged : In fact, uncertainty and, hence, speculative activities, tend to get a boost even under the fixed exchange rate system. Under a fixed rate system, if a country faces huge BOP deficit then the possibility of speculation gets brightened. If the speculators can guess that such BOP deficit will persist in the days ahead and the authority may go for a cut in foreign exchange rate then these people will be more enthusiastic to sell domestic currencies in the foreign exchange market. If such sale of home currencies continue for a longer period, the central bank will then be forced to reduce exchange rate, instead of keeping it at the old fixed rate. Under the circumstance, speculators go on buying home currencies where exchange rates have been reduced. This will make these people to earn profit. The Bretton Woods System of the IMF collapsed in 1971 because of such speculation made with the US dollars.

Adequacy of foreign exchange reserves : For the effectiveness of a stable exchange rate, the necessary condition is the adequacy of holding, foreign exchange reserves. Poor developing countries find it difficult to maintain an adequate volume of foreign exchange reserves. Speculators then anticipate currency devaluation in advances if BOP needs to be corrected. Before 1970, fixed exchange rate, in fact, prevailed because of low volume of global trade and, hence, low volume of foreign exchange reserves.

Internal objectives of growth and full employment sacrificed : When countries experience large and persistent deficits or 'fundamental disequilibrium' in BOP, they are down with the foreign exchange reserves. Countries then opt for devaluation of their currencies and take some internal measures to reduce their deficits. These harsh internal measures tends to contract economies. But the fallouts of these measures are rising prices and rising unemployment. These then reduce economic growth. Thus, fixed exchange rate—in the ultimate analysis—go for currency depreciation that results in lower economic growth and higher unemployment coupled with high inflation—the two most undesirable and unpleasant macro-economic variables not liked by anyone.

International competitive environment by-passed : The continuous changes in international competitive environment do not get reflected under the fixed exchange rate system. Thus, to make the home product more competitive in the foreign market, what is required is the change in domestic economic policies so that the country's export products get larger foothold in the foreign market. In other words, the fixed exchange rate system fails to gloss over the international competitive environment.

This kind of exchange rate developed after the World War II. The International Monetary Fund set up by the Bretton Woods Agreement of 1944 came into operation in March 1947. The period 1947-1971 came to be known as 'fixed but adjustable exchange rate system' or 'par value system' or the 'pegged exchange rate system' or the 'Bretton Woods System'. As the Bretton Woods System collapsed, this exchange rate was abandoned in 1971. Several stop-gap measures were taken but uncertainty and confusion in the exchange rate systems continued. Ultimately, in 1973, the world's exchange rate system came to be known as the 'managed floating'—in the sense that currencies tend to float more or less freely in the foreign exchange market.

6.11.2 Advantages and Disadvantages of Flexible Exchange Rate System

Under the flexible or floating exchange rate, exchange rates between currencies are freely determined in the foreign exchange market and are allowed to rise (appreciation) or fall (depreciation). This exchange rate system also has advantages and disadvantages.

Advantages

Automatic adjustment in BOP : The chief merit of the freely fluctuating exchange rate is that the BOP disequilibrium gets corrected automatically with the change in exchange rate. If a BOP deficit arises, there would be an excess supply of home currency leading to a fall in exchange rate simply by the market forces of demand and supply. This causes export goods cheaper and import goods dearer. As a result, export tends to rise while imports tend to decline—thereby removing deficit in in the BOP account. Similarly, supply in the BOP account means excess demand for home currency and, thus, rise in the exchange rate. This, in turn, encourages imports and discourages exports. As a result, the BOP accounts will reach equilibrium by the same logic. Thus, this exchange rate makes an automatic adjustment in the BOP crisis of an economy and that too without governmental intervention.

No collusion between internal-external objectives : Surplus and deficit in the BOP accounts get corrected if foreign exchange rate falls and rises, respectively. In a regime of fixed exchange rate, the removal of BOP deficit requires the adoption of internal policies like fall income and price level. In other words, pegged exchange rate requires a change in domestic macroeconomic policies like deflationary policies of price and output reduction. But, under flexible exchange rate system, a government can adopt independent monetary policy. In other words, under this system of exchange rate, internal balance could be maintained by the government. It is further argued that, as it is a self-adjusting mechanism to restore BOP equilibrium, a government can put more effort in tackling internal problems of inflation, unemployment, etc.

Absorption of sudden shocks : In a flexible exchange rate, the domestic economy remains insulated from external shocks and pressures. Under this system, the threat of 'importing inflation' from outside the country is minimum. In other words, price feedback effect is imperceptible.

Minimum buffer of foreign exchange reserves : Since exchange rate is not pegged under the floating arrangement of exchange rate, the central bank of a country need not hold adequate foreign exchange reserves as a buffer against unforeseen developments in international trade.

Disadvantages

Uncertainty and confusion : Flexible exchange rate and trade presents an atmosphere of uncertainty and confusion in trade and investment. Susceptibility to uncertainty is greater as soon as exchange rate fluctuates freely. Suppose an Indian has despatched an export 'invoice' to the foreign buyers. But the Indian exporters do not know at what price foreign currency will be converted into Indian currency. This kind of uncertainty hampers trade. However, such uncertainty can be largely minimised through forward exchange contracts. The uncertainty involved in this kind of exchange rate may cause trading community to lose some confidence in the system.

Hampering investment : Unregulated free-floating exchange rate often discourages foreign investment as exchange rate becomes erratic and, hence, destabilising. Because of the uncertainty associated with this exchange rate involving profit and loss implications of foreign investment deals, a country might experience decumulation of capital. Hence—it is destabilising in effect.

Risk, instability, and speculation : Flexible exchange rate encourages wide speculation since foreign exchange prices are not known in advance as in fixed exchange rate. It is because of speculation there occurs disruptive hot money flows. To put it elaborately, it can be argued that when the exchange rate tends to decline, speculators anticipate that such would continue to decline further and the possibility of the flight of money to another country will brighten. This will then cause a further fall in the exchange rate. Thus, greater the speculation against a currency, the deeper the economic crises.

However, economists are not unanimous about this kind of speculation associated with the flexible exchange rate system.

Inflationary in character : By nature, flexible exchange rate is inflationary. As soon as the exchange rate falls, automatically, consequent upon the BOP deficit, import goods become expensive. High cost of imported goods then fuels inflationary tendencies. As depreciation of a currency makes import costlier, the domestic economy faces both demand-pull and cost-push inflationary pressures.

It is because of these drawbacks of the freely fluctuating exchange rate that countries attach importance to 'managed exchange rate' with their central banks buying and selling currencies in the foreign exchange market so as to moderate the degree of fluctuations as far as practicable.

Conclusion : We close this section after reviewing the two types of exchange rate—fixed and flexible. The natural question that arises from this discussion is : Which system is the better one, or which system should a country opt for?

B. O. Sodersten says that the answer to this question largely depends on the circumstances. It depends on the characteristics of the economy. It should change as the economy changes. Value judgements too are also involved, and, ultimately, the answer depends on 'values and views of a political nature.'

QUESTIONS WITH ANSWER-HINTS

Long-Answer Questions

1. If international trade is an extension of internal trade, then why do we need a separate international trade theory?

   Or

   Compare internal trade with international trade.

   Ans. 6.2

2. Discuss the factors that give rise to a separate theory of international trade.

   Ans. 6.2

3. Show the relationship between international trade and economic development.

   Or

   Benefits of trade outweigh costs of trade. Discuss.

   Ans. 6.3

4. Explain, with either suitable examples or graph, the theory of comparative costs.

   Or

   Trade between two countries arises only when comparative costs of producing commodities vary. Discuss.

   Or

   Illustrate Ricardo's comparative cost doctrine to explain the basis of international trade.

   Or

   Production is generally less efficient in less developed countries than in developed countries. Yet they engage in trade. Why?

   Or

   Explain and criticise Ricardo's theory of international trade.

   Ans. 6.4 and 6.4.2

5. Discuss the basis of international trade and point out the limitations of the classical theory of comparative advantage.
Ans. 6.4, 6.4.1 and 6.4.2

6. What will happen to Ricardo's conclusion on trade if there are (i) many commodities, but two countries, (ii) many countries, but two goods, and (iii) multicountries and multi-commodities?
Ans. 6.4.3, 6.4.4 and 6.4.5

7. What are terms of trade? How are they determined? What are the factors that determine terms of trade?
Ans. 6.5

8. Discuss the nature of gains from trade.
Or
What are the gains from trade? How are they determined?
Ans. 6.6

9. What is free trade? Discuss the arguments for and against free trade.
Ans. 6.7.1 and 6.7.2

10. Explain critically the economic grounds on which developing countries prefer protection.
Ans. 6.8(ii)

11. Discuss and evaluate the following arguments for tariff : (i) the infant industry argument, (ii) diversification argument, and (iii) the strategic trade advantage argument.
Ans. 6.8(ii)

12. What do you mean by tariffs and quotas? Compare their impacts. Point out the advantages and disadvantages of quotas.
Ans. 6.8.1-6.8.4

13. What is balance of payments? What are its different components? Explain your answer with a tabular illustration of the balance of payments account of a country.
Ans. 6.9 and 6.9.1

14. What is balance of payments? What is balance of trade? Distinguish between balance of payments and balance of trade.
Ans. 6.9 and 6.9.2

15. Balance of payments always balances. Discuss the statement.
Ans. 6.9 and 6.9.3

16. What is meant by foreign exchange rate? How is it determined in a country?
Ans. 6.10 and 6.10.1

17. Write a note on the exchange rate management policy.
Ans. 6.11

18. What is meant by the 'fixed exchange rate system'? What are its advantages and disadvantages?
Ans. 6.11(A), 6.11.1

19. Define 'flexible exchange rate system'. Make out a case for and against this exchange rate system.
Ans. 6.11(B), 6.11.2

Short-Answer Questions

1. Give an argument to demonstrate that trade promotes development.
Ans. 6.3

2. Gains from trade are not reaped by poor developing countries.—Explain.
Ans. 6.3

3. What is Ricardo's comparative cost theory?
Ans. 6.4.2

4. What are the two important assumptions of Ricardo's cost theory?
Ans. 6.4.2

5. Define terms of trade.
Ans. 6.5

6. Mention two factors that determine terms of trade.
Ans. 6.5

7. What is meant by reciprocal demand?
Ans. 6.5

8. What do you meant by protective trade?
Ans. 6.8

9. What is meant by the 'infant industry argument' of protection?
Ans. 6.8(ii)

10. What are quotas?
Ans. 6.8.2

11. What is the revenue effect of tariff and quotas?
Ans. 6.8.1 and 6.8.2

12. Define balance of payments.

    Ans. 6.9 or 6.9.2

13. What is balance of trade?

    Ans. 6.9.2

14. When does a country's balance of trade becomes unfavourable?

    Ans. 6.9

15. Define fixed exchange rate.

    Ans. 6.11

16. Define flexible exchange rate.

    Ans. 6.11

17. What is 'managed flexibility'?

    Ans. 6.11

18. Give two advantages of the fixed exchange rate.

    Ans. 6.11.1

19. Mention two advantages of the flexible exchange rate.

    Ans. 6.11.2

STATISTICS

CHAPTER 7

Basic Concepts

7.1 Introduction : Origin and Development of Statistics

Today, statistics or more specifically statistical method is used extensively in almost all phases of human endeavour. In ancient times, it dealt with the affairs of the state, like collection of information (or data) regarding population and property or wealth of the state so as to subserve political purposes of rulers. Today, its influence has spread to various areas, such as agriculture, business, economics, medicine, biology, education, electronics, sociology, psychology, political science, and many other branches of science and technology.

The origin of the word *statistics* may be traced to the Latin word '*status*' or the Italian word '*statista*' from or the German word *'statistics'*, meaning political state. As time progressed, the idea behind the word *statistics* has undergone a phenomenal change. Over time, the character of information as provided has been extended to any particular sphere of human activity. Statistics as statistical data forms the backbone of many discipline. By *statistical data* we mean numerical statement of facts while *statistical methods* deal with information of the principles and techniques used in collecting and analysing such data.

7.2 Meaning of Statistics

The word '*Statistics*' was first introduced by a German Scholar, Gottfried Achenwall, in the middle of the 18th century. From the very name, it is felt that it must be related to the administrative functioning of a state supplying facts regularly and quantitatively regarding its various fields of administration. Today, *statistics* as a separate discipline from mathematics is closely associated with almost all branches of education and human endeavour which are mostly numerically representable. In modern times, it has innumerable and varied applications both qualitatively and quantitatively.

To be more precise, statistics refers to classified facts that represent the conditions of the people in a state especially those facts which can be stated in numbers or in any tabular or classified arrangements. One of the widely accepted definitions came from Horace Secrist. He defines *statistics* as, "By *statistics* we mean aggregate of facts, affected to a marked extent by a multiplicity of causes numerically expressed, enumerated or estimated according to reasonable standards of accuracy, collected in a systematic manner for a predetermined purpose and placed in relation to each other." This definition reveals the following characteristics of statistics.

(i) Numerical data should be aggregate of facts. Single fact or isolated facts or unrelated figures do not constitute statistics.

(ii) Data should be affected to a marked extent by multiplicity of causes. For instance, data on malnutrition is affected not only by poverty but also by a host of other factors like hygienic rules, etc.

(iii) Data should be numerically expressed.

(iv) Data should be enumerated or estimated with accuracy as far as practicable.

(v) Data should be collected in a systematic manner.

(vi) Data should be collected to serve a predetermined purpose.

(vii) Data should be placed in order in relation to each other.

Croxton and Cowden defined statistics as "the science which deals with the collection, analysis and interpretation of numerical data"

7.3 Statistics and Economics

Various concepts of economic theory, such as functional relationship among variables are usually stated in terms of algebra, symbols, calculus and so on. To analyse various social and economic phenomena, economic theory can be better studied and analysed in terms of 'appropriate' numbers. Such numbers, that is, statistics presents facts on the basis of a mass of figures. It helps comparison of facts. It establishes relationship between variables like price and quantity demanded or quantity supplied, global warming and agricultural output, money supply and price level and so on. Thus, economics as a discipline is linked up with statistics on many occasions. Today, we see that economic growth in India is hampered by faulty policies and better economic policymaking largely depends on the availability of improved data or statistics. Businessmen also find statistics as an indispensable tool in their regular activities. The study of modern economics requires mathematical and statistical foundation. With the development of mathematics and statistics over the passage of time, econometric methods have been developed. We thus see wide applications of *statistics* in various fields.

7.4 Data—Its Classification

Information on any field, when expressed qualitatively and / or quantitatively, is called data and they are usually classified into two main categories—primary and secondary data, depending on their origin or source. Information when collected directly from the desired field for the use of a predetermined purpose is called the *primary data* e.g., heights and weights of the students in a class. It can thus be used with much confidence because of its direct nature of collection. The primary data are usually published by the authorities who are directly responsible for its collection. However, it requires enough manpower, time and money to make the process successful.

Secondary data, on the other hand, are the data already collected by an individual or an agency for a specific purpose and used afterwards for a number of other purposes. The data so obtained from that origin are then conveniently compiled up by an investigator to meet his or her own specific needs. Such data are usually collected by an authorised agency for one particular purpose and then it is officially published and again used by other individuals or agencies to serve their own purposes and in that sense these data are not original in nature.

For example, we often use Census (data collected every after ten years with the government effort) reports to accomplish, support and supplement our studies. These are, no doubt, secondary data used by the researchers of various fields. The most important and remarkable advantage here is that it requires less manpower and time and as a result less costly to complete the entire procedure. But, in practice, it frequently contains a number of errors due to erroneous transcription, faulty rounding-off (up or down), etc., and, therefore, less dependable in nature for the researchers. The investigators and the scholars working with them should therefore be much careful while using them in their own fields. It is, therefore, quite clear that the data which are initially primary in nature at the origin for one use becomes secondary in qualities and character for other uses.

Therefore, the distinction between primary and secondary data is one of degree only. A particular data may be primary in the hands of data collecting authority but may be secondary to other people using them afterwards. Prof. H. Secrist in this context says : "The distinction between primary and secondary data is largely one of degree. Data which are secondary in the hands of one party may be primary in the hands of another."

However, the method of collection of primary data and secondary data must not be identical in nature because, in the former case data are collected originally while, in the latter case, data are to be taken up in the nature of compilation.

There exists various methods for the collection of the primary and secondary data. Choice of the exact method depends largely on the nature, object and scope of statistical investigation.

Advantages of primary data : It is usually preferable to use primary data because of the following reasons : *First*, it generally contains a detailed description and information of the definition for the terms used. *Secondly*, since secondary data are second-hand data or 'finished products', an element of error may creep in afterwards. This may then give some misleading information. Primary data cannot have such errors. *Thirdly*, in the primary data precise definition of the terms used is given and the scope of the data is clearly mentioned. Finally, collecting primary data often include the method or procedure followed and any approximation used so that one can find its limitations. On the contrary, secondary data usually lack such information.

Despite these advantages of primary data, secondary data are extensively used particularly when a large number of items are required.

The secondary data seems to be of minor importance, specially when collection of primary data is much expensive and time-consuming.

Secondary data invariably give less meaning of the statistics and frequently present no explanation other than the captions and footnotes in the tables. In fact, some information are usually suppressed in secondary data.

Advantages of secondary data : Practically, there are various advantages in using secondary data. *First*, cost of collection of data is less. That is why data produced by the Government, companies and various organisations are readily available. *Secondly*, one obtains a great variety of data on a wide range of subjects. *Thirdly*, much of the secondary data available has been collected for many years and, therefore, it can be used to study the trends. *Fourthly* and most importantly, secondary data is of great value to the government, business world and industry and also for research organisations. Again, secondary data help the government in making present policy decisions and also planning for future economic policies.

Limitations of secondary data : In spite of all these advantages of secondary data, one must use it with enough caution. *First*, the method employed for the collection of such data is often unsatisfactory. That is why, secondary data in most cases, is subject to transcribing errors (i.e., errors occurring due to wrong transcriptions of the primary data). *Secondly*, secondary data are really mere estimates and not the facts. In view of this, secondary data suffer from estimating errors. *Thirdly*, scrutiny of the secondary data is obviously essential since errors may creep in due to unwanted bias. This is because of the fact that often fictitious figures are recorded unknowingly in secondary data. In this sense, secondary data are not only inaccurate but also incomplete and inadequate. Without detailed scrutiny of the secondary data one must not be advised to use them.

Precautions for using secondary data : Since secondary data is second-hand data, one must know as much about it as possible. In other words, certain precautions are to be taken before using secondary data so that the data become really helpful to the government or the researcher.

Secondary data users must consider the following points :

(i) the scope and object of enquiry for which the data were originally collected;

(ii) the proper methods of collecting such data;

(iii) the period (normal or unusual time) and the area covered for collection;

(iv) the reliability, integrity and dependability of the data collectors engaged;

(v) precise definitions of the terms used and their units of measurement considered while the data were collected;

(vi) interpreting the data, especially when figures collected for one purpose are used for other fields.

Thus, one can say that secondary data first should be reliable. There are various ways of testing such reliability of the data. *Secondly*, secondary data should be used in such a manner that they can suitably serve the purpose of investigation and experimentation. *Finally*, in addition to reliability and suitability of the data, it should be declared adequate and accurate as far as practicable.

7.4.1 Examples of Primary and Secondary Data Sources

There are various sources of primary and secondary data in our country. Some of them are listed below.

Primary data sources. 1. The Reserve Bank of India Bulletin (issued monthly and annually).

[It contains information on current economic and financial review and review of India's balance of payments position, economic indicators of currency and banking, industrial production, prices, etc.]

2. Journal of Trade and Industry, published by the Directorate of Industrial Statistics.

3. Indian Textile Bulletin (monthly), published by the Textile Commissioner.

4. Annual Report of the Chief Inspector of Mines, published by the Chief Inspector of Mines, Dhanbad. This journal contains information on the production, consumption, import and export of coal, gold and petroleum.

5. Indian Labour Journal (monthly). Labour statistics regarding wage, employment, trade union, industrial disputes, etc., are available in this journal published by the Labour Bureau, Ministry of Labour.

Sources of secondary data : 1. "The Statistical Abstract of the Indian Union", published by the Central Statistical Organisation (CSO). It is an annual review volume.

2. Monthly Abstract of Statistics published by the CSO. This journal contains notes, reports and government notifications relating to trade, commerce, industry, import and export, control regulations, tariff, etc.

3. Annual statements on the Foreign Trade of India given by the government.

4. Annual Report of the IMF, the World Bank (IBRD), UNDP's Human Development Reports and reports of other international organisations.

7.4.2 Methods of Collecting Primary Data

Primary data are the data that are collected directly from the field of inquiry. As these data are original in nature, they can be collected through the use of four common methods. They are : (i) direct personal observation or investigation, (ii) indirect oral investigation, (iii) questionnaires sent by mail, and (iv) schedules sent through paid investigators.

We shall briefly discuss these methods in order :

Direct personal observation or investigation :

So far as the name suggests, the investigator himself/herself collects data personally from the concerned sources through observation. Such data collection may either be based on complete enumeration or sample based. For instance, while collecting data on death rate in city hospitals, an investigator may collect data about death rates, both sex-wise and class-wise to serve his or her research purpose. This is called complete enumeration. But if the investigator intends to study death rates caused by 'Tuberculosis', then he or she narrows his or her field of enquiry. This is called sample based method of data collection.

Anyway, as far as intensive investigations are concerned, this method yields quite reliable information for further analysis. Further, information collected in this way is to be considered as original. But it is much time consuming as well as expensive. But, for extensive investigations, this method is unsuitable. In this sense, in a narrow field, this method can only be employed to obtain good results. Finally, this method may cause trouble if the investigator is biased. If information collection often involves personal prejudices or biased-ness, it would give us wrong conclusions.

Indirect oral investigation : As direct sources may be a source of embarrassment to investigators and interviewees, one may rely on indirect sources also to collect such data. *Under this method, the investigator collects information from the respondents who are directly or indirectly associated with the information sought for.* Persons who are supposed to have information about the problems are questioned and interrogated in many ways. On the basis of the answers recorded on pre-determined questions, investigator compiles data. Various commissions and committiees of enquiry usually collect their data through this method. It goes without saying that the reliability of these data depends largely on the integrity of persons selected for giving evidence. Usually, one may observe over-enthusiastic as well as under-enthusiastic informants. Thus, the selection of the right person is indeed an important task.

Questionnaire sent by mail : Another method of collecting primary data is collection through questionnaire sent by mail. The investigator prepares a list of questions pertaining to the nature of the problem under investigation. The printed questions may be sent by mail to some selected persons with the request for their replies by return mail.

Information or data gathered in this way is less expensive. Further, the area of investigation can be made reasonably wider in a comparatively short period of time.

But, one can express doubt about the reliability or accuracy of such data. Informants usually give information casually. Some sort of indifference or apathy may exist even among the selected persons towards such questionnaire method. As a result, the data may often become unsatisfactory and hence require cross checking.

Schedules sent through investigators : This method is widely used, particularly, in market research. Here paid investigators, or the so-called 'enumerators' are employed for data collection. *Enumerators* carry schedules and *approach politely to the informants for giving their impressions relating to schedules designed for the purpose. The investigators fill-up the schedules on the spot on the basis of the replies made.* The data thus collected are fairly dependable.

This method is much popular and yields better results. But the availability of satisfactory data largely depends on the honesty, integrity and personality of the investigators. However, to ensure integrity of the investigators, requisite special training is often imparted to them. For instance, during the decennial census of the population of the country, investigators are first trained properly to collect data on population and other relevant matters.

Procedures for collecting statistical data : It has been already mentioned that the statistics compiled from secondary data are known as secondary statistics. Various sources for obtaining secondary data can be classified into two broad categories, published sources and unpublished sources. Published sources of secondary data come from the Union Government, State Governments, semi-government organisations, private corporate bodies, trade associations as well as international agencies. In addition, not all data are required to be published. Data from internal records of goverment or private agencies or researches done by academicians are often not published.

There are two recognised techniques of collecting data : the census method or the complete enumeration method and the sample method or the partial enumeration.

Census method : The data which are collected by the investigator himself is called primary data. Census data can be thought of as primary data. *When the data collector or investigator collects data or information about each and every item in the population and other related areas, it is known as census method. As this method deals with the investigation of the entire population, it is also called complete enumeration method.* If a survey covers 100 p.c. population, it is called a census method. In other words, here each and every item or unit constituting the 'entire population' or 'the universe' is selected for statistical enquirey. If a statistical enquiry is conducted to study the nature and pattern of urbanisation, then the universe consists only of the urban population of India. This method is called complete enumeration method because information from each and every unit belonging to India's urban population is collected.

Merits : *First*, for an extensive study (however expensive it may be) this method is considered to be an ideal one. For example, in the population census, we obtain quite a large number of key information, such as birth rate, death rate, infant mortality rate, literacy rate, ratio of urban-rural population, trend on urbanisation and so on.

Secondly, accuracy in the results is obtained. The data collected are more accurate and reliable under this census method since information are gathered from various angles. However, reliability in data and their accuracy in results are surely obtained provided enumerators do their work honestly and sincerely.

Demerits : *First*, being extensive in nature, the complete enumeration method is much *expensive* since a considerable amount of money, time, and labour are demanded and involved.

Secondly, this method is often not *feasible or practicable* because the concept of the 'universe' is hypothetical. Since 'universe' is the basis of data collection, its applicability becomes very much limited. This method cannot be met with urgency. This means that if an urgent statistical information for the entire population for policy purposes is needed, this method will surely be less helpful. In other words, it is too cumbersome and inefficient to obtain a complete picture of the target population.

Thirdly, in the census method, often large number of *non-sampling errors* creep in. This means that results obtained may not be uniform.

Sample Survey Method

Instead of the census method, data analysts often consider a portion or a sample of the population. *If a sample population*—instead of full survey of a population—*is investigated then we have sample survey method or portion enumeration method. A sample is anything less than a full survey of a population*. For example, liquor consumption among college and university students is to be investigaed. For this purpose, a small number of students following a particular prescribed technique will be picked up (sample drawn) and their habits for consumption of liquor will be investigated. The primary objective of such sample enquiry is to estimate some characteristics of the population from which the sample is selected.

Merits : Sample survey method has many advantages over census method. That is why this method is more popular than the latter method. In the words of A. C. Rosander, "If carefully designed, the sample is not only considerably cheaper but may give results which are just accurate and sometimes more accurate than those of a census technique."

This method is preferable for the following reasons :

First, since only a part of the population is investigated under this method, it takes *less time, less money and less labour*. There is saving in time also since sampling enquiry requires less fieldwork, tabulation and data processing than a full survey method. Sample survey method can be conducted when the investigatiors face the problem of budget constraint. It is cheaper to collect information from a sample group. However, for conducting the entire enquiry, small group of investigators or specialist investigators are paid huge amount and employed but the output is much more. That is why it is also said that this method results in reduced unit cost of enquiry.

Secondly, conclusions and results obtained from this method are more accurate and reliable as fewer or chosen sample units are surveyed. Trained personnel are usually employed to collect data and investigate the problem. Above all, these people use sophisticated and latest designed techniques so that results become more accurate and reliable. Further, it is true that sampling errors cannot be avoided, but such errors are easier to estimate and control.

Thirdly, the small sample data provide a good *benchmark* for the entire population.

Finally, from the administrative point of view, the sample method is considered as an ideal one as the organisaton as well as administration consider the process practically more convenient. Administrative network does not usually require to be considerably elaborate or extensive.

7.5 Classification of Data and Its Various Types

Data collection is just one aspect of descriptive statistics. Data usually collected during the course of investigation is not only unorganised and raw but also large in quantity. These data normally do not provide information that one needs. Once the data are collected statisticians engage themselves in classifying (i.e., compilation and tabulation) these statistical information. By classification of data we mean the process of arranging data so that these can be analysed for a predetermined purpose of the analysers. Mere information collection is not at all significant. Classification of data that is, the process by which data are arranged or grouped into homogeneous classes and categories is thus required to know the scope and purposes of data so that statistical analysis becomes possible and intelligible to all. Usually, an investigator classifies data on households on the basis of their age, sex, education, income, expenditure, nature of jobs, etc.

Statistical information are usually classified under four following aspects—

(a) qualitative aspect;
(b) quantitative aspect;
(c) time-dimension or time-chronological data and
(d) geographical or (spatial) locational aspect.

When the data collected are in the form of non-unquantifiable criterion or property, it is called qualitative form of data e.g., occupation of people in a region of a country, the standard of their educational attainments, health and religion, etc. Conversely, if the data are collected strictly in terms of conveniently measurable numerical units (length, weight or time following scientific (centimeter, gram, second or foot, pound, second) systems, it will surely possess some quantitative property e.g., different income tax rates imposed on various income earning classes by the Government. Besides these two, data on a particular aspect are also collected at different periods, called the 'time series' data e.g. : Price fluctuations during the last 5-year Planperiod in our country. And, finally, data on many aspects are also gathered from different locations of a country, they are called the spatial data, widely used in geographical studies. For 'example, to implement grassroots inclusive regional planning, we require data on average rainfall in various places of our country; they are also called the cross-section' data in statistical terminology.

7.6 Variable and Attribute

Statistical information (or data), as we know, are usually numerical or quantitative in nature. However, at the time of collecting information on a particular aspect, we also consider qualitative variations of the items under study over time or space. To realise the very nature and the changing behaviour of those non-numerical information, we often subdivide or segregate them distinctly under various mutually disjoined categories and then assign the number of items taken in each division and represent them understandably in a systematic, complete and comprehensive tabular form. The non-numerical qualitative character of the items considered is termed as an '*attribute*'. They can, however, be classified under a number of required disjoined classes afterwards to serve our various statistical enquiries. For example, religion of a group of people, grade obtained by the students in a class-test, the nature of common transport in a city, etc., belongs to this category. An attribute thus cannot be measured cardinally or numerically.

A specific quality possessed by an individual person, object or item of a population is called a *characteristic* of the individual. Height of a person, age, nationality are examples of characteristics which may be measurable or nonmeasurable. Measurable characteristics are those which are expressed numerically in terms of some units. A measurable characteristic of an item makes it a *variable.*

Variable (or variate), is thus an item which is basically numerical in character and because of its quantitative nature its variations can easily be shown or counted. For example, marks obtained in English by the students in this year in M.P. Examination of a school, clothes produced in a mill in the last month, labour hours rendered by an individual in a factory in the last week, teaching hours of a private tutor devoted for an individual student at home, etc. On the other hand, a non-measurable characteristic is a qualitative phenomenon, e.g., religion, caste, nationality, etc. We call such characteristics as attributes.

7.7 Presentation of Data

After collecting the required data for a specific purpose from any of the selected sources already mentioned (primary or secondary), the next important task for a statistician is to represent them in a suitable manner quite conveniently so that it becomes easily understandable even for the illiterates. The usual conventions in this context to exhibit such information systematically and understandably on different occasions are the following :

(a) Textual presentation,

(b) Tabular presentation,

(c) Graphical or Diagrammatic presentation.

(a) *Textual presentation* : Here, with this device, we try to represent the collected data, its nature and behaviour, completely literally in terms of a lucid and precise language so that people from all categories or professions can realise the situation and the reality. It is, no doubt, much difficult for the investigators to extract the true picture and the important properties of the data through it. So collected, the presentation should be brief and considerably precise having logical sequences. Official reports are usually prepared in this fashion.

For instance, India's infant mortality rate (i.e., deaths per 10,000 live births) in 2000 was 69. It declined to 50 in 2009. Again, the growth rate of eight core sector industries declined to 2.1 p.c. in August 2012 from 3.8 p.c. in August 2011, owing to contractions in output of crude oil, natural gas, fertilisers and cement. This kind of data presentation encounters same problems. By nature the text is not only lengthy but also difficult to grasp, particularly if the text contains a long list of information.

(b) *Tabular presentation* : Here, the technique is to represent the data through a complete and comprehensive statistical table and the method so followed is known as tabulation. The table, so constructed, must include all the given information. It should be simple enough and be presented in a concise format and in that sense preparation of an ideal table is definitely a fair art. An orderly and systematic presentation of numerical data in rows and columns are presented in the form of a self-explanatory table so as to clarify the problem under consideration.

A complete table must possess the following parts in an order :

(i) *Table number* : At the very beginning the table must contain a particular number at the top for its identification and ready reference for future purposes.

(ii) *Title* : A brief statement signifying the nature of information lying inside the table should be there next to the table number.

(iii) *Stub* : It will exist at the extreme left part of the table and will express the specific issues taken horizontally in rows.

(iv) *Caption* : It is vertically placed at the upper part of the table in columns. Each column must have a definite number and the unit in which the figures are noted inside.

(v) *Body* : It represents the most important part of the table and usually placed at the middle of the entire table expressing several numerical contents of it.

(vi) *Footnote* : Further explanation on any item already included in the table, if felt necessary afterwards, will be shown here. This will surely help us to understand the matter more clearly.

(vii) *Sources of information* : And, finally, at the bottom of the table, we must not forget to mention categorically the name of the original source (if possible with the chapter and the page number) from where the information are made available. The source, of course, should be unquestioningly authentic in nature and the specific period during which the data are collected must be mentioned. A hypothetical example of an ideal table showing its different parts is given below :

It may be mentioned here that there is no ideal method of tabulation. Nevertheless, some general rules are required to be followed :

Table 7.1 : Different Parts of a Table

(i) Table Number, (ii) Title,

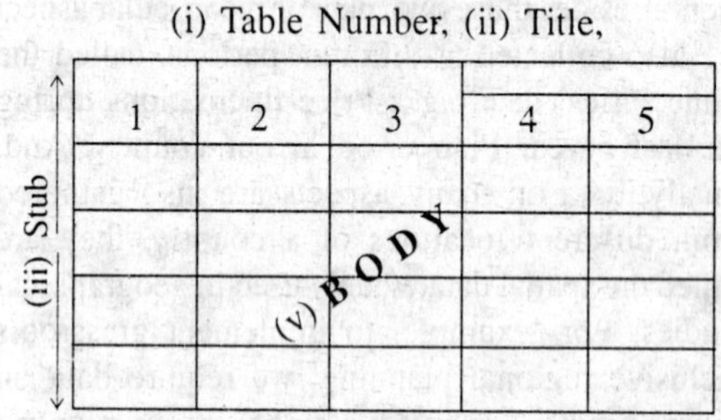

(vi) Footnote, if any, (vii) Source

First, units of measurement (e.g. height in cm), generally shown at the top of columns, must be shown clearly. *Secondly,* the table should be well-balanced in length and breadth. A long table may give inaccurate information. *Thirdly,* unnecessary details should be avoided as far as practicable. If possible, small tables showing unnecessary information may be constructed separately.

7.7.1 Types of Tabulation

The usual techniques of tabulation are :

(a) Simple tabulation, and

(b) Complex tabulation.

Information on a single variable showing only one important property when expressed in a tabular form is called simple tabulation. Conversely, a table can also consider more than one variable with a number of separate properties exhibited therein is called complex tabulation. Let us prepare at this stage two separate tables (simple and complex) with the aid of an imaginary data set.

(a) Simple Tabulation

Statistical tables, to make them easily understandable, are very often represented simply in the following manner called simple tabulation.

Table 7.2 : Age Distribution of the Children

Age Group (Yrs)	No. of Children
3 — 5	20
5 — 8	09
8 — 10	10
10 — 12	07
12 — 15	04
Total	50

Table 7.2 is an example of simple tabulation where data are shown through a simple or one-way table. From this one way table, one obtain answer to questions about one characteristic feature of data only. In other words, simple tabulation gives information about one independent question.

On the other hand, complex tabulation, also called two-way table, shows splitting up of data in two or more categories so as to provide information about one or more sets of interrelated questions. If the number of children in accordance with age-groups shown in table 7.2 is split up or further divided sex-wise, the table becomes a two-way complex table. This has been shown in Table 7.3 below where the number of children has been divided again not only sex-wise, but also resident-wise between male and female children.

7.8 Population, Sampling and Complete Enumeration

In section 7.4.2 we have mentioned two types of data collection. One is the complete enumeration method, and the other is a sample-based one. It reduces the field of enquiry into a narrow range. If one decides to count the number of smokers in the city of Kolkata, then it is practically impossible to do so. In such case, smaller pockets (at least 15 p.c. of the total prescribed in sampling theory) are to be chosen which bears the characte-ristics of the smokers of Kolkata. Thus, the smokers of Kolkata is the *population here*, while smaller pockets taken are the *samples*. So, samples are the true representatives of the *population*.

All these terms population, sample and complete enumeration—are much recognized and widely used in statistical literature today, specially in the field of Statistical enquiry and investigation.

Sampling : Notionally, sampling denotes the choice or sellection of a part of the aggregate statistical material that helps in obtaining information about the whole, such aggregate information is called *population* or *universe*. The selected elements together which is used to ascertain the characteristics of population, is referred to as *sample*.

(b) Complex Tabulation

Complex tables exhibiting a number of separate information simultaneously are usually represented in the following way :

Table 7.3 : Age Distribution of the Students

Age group	Male children		Total (A)	Female children		Total (B)	Grand total (A+B)
	Residents	Non-residents		Residents	Non-Residents		
3—5	4	8	12	4	4	8	20
5—8	3	3	6	2	1	3	9
8—10	3	3	6	2	2	4	10
10—12	4	0	4	2	1	3	7
12—15	3	1	4	0	0	0	4
Total	17	15	32	10	8	18	50

In a situation when we are interested to study a particular property of a variable having large number of units or observations on it, then it is practically not possible for an individual investigator or agency to investigate all those data supplied to them separately. In this context statisticians safely prescribe for a short-cut technique known as *sampling* to reach the goal. The entire information or data available in this respect is called the population and the prescribed part of it which is possible and practicable to investigate distinctly by an investigator, is called a sample drawn on the population. Statisticians in this respect usually advice us to consider at least 15 per cent of the available information from the total population for statistical enquiry so as to derive the results much closer to reality. For example, : while studying the economic condition and standard of living of the weavers of Nadia, West Bengal, it was not practically possible for me to contact and approach all those weaverse succe-ssively. It is then suggested to locate a few important regions in which these weavers are residing and investigate a selected part of them with a complete and comprehensive Questionnaire. The method, thus followed, is called 'stratified sampling'.

We define a variable as a phenomenon which assumes several values at different periods and places, called the time-series and the cross-section data on the variable. Variables are usually classified under two broad headings :

(a) Discrete or discontinuous variable

(b) Continuous variable

(a) When a given variable, having quantitative character, assuumes only certain selected and isolated values in its own range of variation, we call it a discrete variable, e.g., number of teachers in different schools in the district of Bankura, level of income of the families residing in a particular locality of the district, etc.

(b) A variable that can assume any value within its own range of variation, is called a continuous varible. For example, height of an individual at different ages, atmospheric temperature and pressure recorded in the laboratory of a region, etc. Here, it is to be noted that apparent discreteness in the values of the variable may arise due to instrumental defects or limitations and the errors thus arises needs correction afterwards.

The data so collected become useful for many purposes effectively so as to represent the ground level reality. However, 'sampling' has a number of techniques of its own often adviced in various situations by the experts depending on the nature of information available and the purposes to be served.

Primarily, the two commonly used techniques very often followed in this respect for collecting the desired samples are—

(a) deliberate or purposive selection of samples

(b) random selection of samples

The other methods usually followed on specific occassions by the researchers and others of various fields for selecting their useful samples are—

(i) systematic sampling

(ii) stratified sampling (with one, two or three and more stages)

(iii) multi-staged sampling

However, selection of samples and calculation with them may involve several mistakes (numerical inaccuracy) and errors (methodical inaccuracy) which needs correction afterwards.

Further detailed discussion on various techniques of sampling are not included in our present prescribed syllabus. So we are leaving it at this stage for this particular topic.

Complete Enumeration : If the investigators engaged are able to collect information from each and every unit of the entire population, the method so followed, will be known as "complete enumeration" or "the census method". For example, to determine the average wage of the labourers working in a factory, we take into account wages of all the labourers separately under this method and then find the actual average. However, this method requires enough time, money, manpower and finally an effective network and efficient organisers when the population is large enough. That is why, this method is not much popular and unhesitatingly prescribed by the statisticians of today in normal situations. When the total number of units in an entire population is not large enough and a specific property of the population is to be studied carefully, collection of data through this method becomes very much effective but on many other occations the method is not practicable.

7.8.1 Advantages of Sampling Over Complete Enumeration

Sampling methods undoubtedly have a number of additional advantages over complete enumeration. Let us mention some of them systematically below :

(i) In any sampling method we consider only a small part of the entire population available and hence it requires less time, money and manpower. Complete enumeration, on the other hand, of course require all these factors in large quantities and therefore this method is more expensive.

(ii) While adopting sampling technique a few selected and sufficiently trained efficient investigators on that field are engaged who can successfully collect the required information from the large population through a well-designed and quite comprehensive questionnaire prepared earlier following the "cross-checking" method. Naturally, the data so obtained are much dependable for the researchers and for other users also. Complete enumeration can never produce such data within that limited time and monetary expenses.

(iii) As far as errors in both the methods are concorned, the sampling technique usually contains sampling errors to a small extent. For the complete enumeration procedure, instead of sampling errors, non-sampling errors are much predominant here and it thus affects the results of the required investigation much significantly and drastically.

(iv) While adopting any sampling technique, the nature and the magnitude of sampling errors are distinctly measurable afterwards with the aid of the 'probability theory' and hence all necessary efforts to minimise those errors can easily be taken in advance. Conversely, complete enumeration do not have any such sampling error but the huge non-sampling errors involved there are not at all traceable afterwards and hence numerically not measurable through the 'probability theory' and it thus affects the entire investigation procedure quite significantly.

(v) In some practical situations, complete enumeration procedure can never be followed. A suitable example in this respect may be, to examine the quality of tea by a tea-taster in a tea producing company, the taster can only enjoy the various samples of tea separately and finally offer his or her own opinion.

Because of the above advantages of sampling over complete enumeration, sampling techniques are much more popular and widely used in different disciplines today. However, for a particular population where the units contained in it are completely different in their own characteristics, the complete enumeration procedure will give us better results.

7.9 Points to be Remembered while Preparing a Statistical Table

Construction of a decent as well as meaningful table is definitely an art and hence before preparing any complete and comprehensive statistical table, we must keep in mind the following aspects :

(a) The table should be properly balanced in the sense it should neither be too long and nor too short with ambigious and clumsy items.

(b) The data under consideration must be shown in proper order with systematic and logical sequences.

(c) The items to be compared must be arranged closely so as to make the required comparison easily understandable.

(d) The units in which the figures are measured must be indicated clearly at the top of the respective rows and columns.

(e) In many cases, to make further calculations easier, the totals of rows and columns are to be shown at the bottom and at the end of each column and row.

(f) If the number of rows and columns are large enough, they are to be shown with separate numbers for further references at the end of each row or at the top of each column.

(g) The table must have a simple, brief and self-explanatory title.

(h) The table must not include large number of abbreviations.

7.10 Graphical or Diagrammatic Representation of Statistical Data

Besides textual and tabular presentations of statistical data, the third and perhaps the most attractive and commonly used popular modern device to exhibit any data in a systematic manner is to represent them with suitable and appropriate diagrams and pictures. The usual and effective means in this context are : graphs, charts, pictures, etc. and they are really and surely capable of depicting some important features of the data which they individually are not able to exhibit. Selection of the appropriate diagram actually depends on the nature of the raw data available and the purpose or the area in which it will be applied. However, only certain limited information can be supplied through a particular diagram and as such each diagram has certain specific limitations of its own.

A few commonly used diagrams applied on different occassions in various disciplines today are the line diagram, bar diagram, ogive, pie diagram and the pictogram (as prescribed in the syllabus).

It may be noted that diagrammatic representations of statistical information is appealing to the eyes. Hidden facts may also be detected once such information are presented graphically. Further, graphs of statistical data clearly bring out the relative importance of different figures, the trend or tendency of the values of the variables involved can be studied too.

7.10.1 Line Diagrams

This kind of a diagram becomes suitable for representing data supplied chronologically in an ascending or descending order. Usually, it shows the behaviour of a variable over time. Successive values of a variable at different periods or places are plotted as separate points on a two dimensional plane and the locus of all those points joined together form a continuous line segment, called *line diagram*. While tracing out such a diagram, the usual convention is to show the successive values of the variable under study along the vertical axis in an increasing order and the time dimension along the horizontal axis. It should carefully be noted that none of the two axes be too long or too short with respect to each other. This is very much necessary mainly to avoid unpredictable and wide fluctuations in the given values of the variable. The origin or the (0, 0) point at the left hand corner should clearly be mentioned so as to discard wrong impression on the process of drawing.

Two or more (but finite number of) line segments can also be drawn on the same quadrant when information on different variables over the same period or time are simultaneously represented using the same unit of measurement along the same axis. We can thus draw a number of line-diagrames for different data series on the same quadrant. They can distinctly and attractively be displayed on a screen for presentation with various colourful lines. When the values of the variable under consideration change at a constant rate over the same successive time intervals, the dia-gram will take the shape of a straight line. Other-wise, it will represent various concave, convex or irregular curves when viewed from the origin. Let us now represent a common line diagram below—

Example 7.1 : Line diagrams showing total values of Exports and Imports during 1987-96 have been presented in Fig. 7.1. This figure has been drawn on the basis of data shown in Table 7.4.

Table 7.4 : Foreign Trade of India during 1987-96 (units in Rs. crores)

Year	Value of Export	Value of Import
1987—88	301	243
1988—89	295	226
1989—90	309	230
1990—91	260	184
1991—92	276	168
1992—93	184	85
1993—94	158	89
1994—95	166	160
1995—96	182	177

Two separate line diagrams showing fluctuations in the values of exports and imports of India during (1987—96) are shown below :

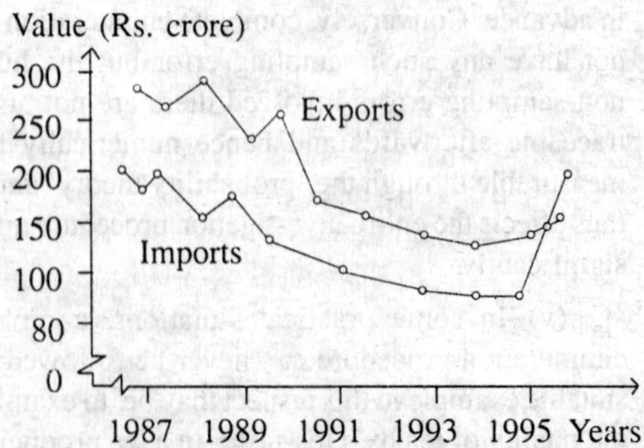

Fig. 7.1 : Line Diagrams

In the diagram drawn above the successive years from the table are shown horizontally and the corresponding values of export and import are shown vertically and the points are located separately on the plane from the middle of the respective years and the locus of those points exhibit the trend along the line diagrams.

7.10.2 Bar Diagrams

It is another wellknown useful statistical weapon to represent raw data decently. This device is applied specially in a situation where the given data can be classified on the basis of a non-measurable criterion e.g., standards of college education in different states of India at the present time. This is very often called cross-section data. More precisely, a bar graph is formed as a collection of rectangles having the same width or breadth placed successively at equal distance. Practically, the height of each bar placed vertically represents the value of the variable on the identical class interval shown horizontally. Usually, these bars are placed either vertically on the horizontal axis or horizontally on the vertical axis and they are thus known as vertical bar chart or horizontal bar chart. Conventionally vertical bar charts are formed with the time series data. Actually speaking, no formal rule as to how much space to be given in between the two bars is there. If necessary, no space in between two bars can be given. In some other cases, suitable and resonable gaps in-between two bars may also be allowed. Let us imprint simple and suitable examples of bar diagrams below :

(a) Simple Vertical Bar Diagram

Volume of population in a number of states in India in 2001 are given below—represent the data with the aid of vertical bars.

Table 7.5 : Volume of Population in Five Different States in India in 2001

States :	Andhra	Bihar	Mahr.	U.P.	W.B.
Popn. (lakh) :	434	564	503	889	444

Fig. 7.2 Shows population of a number of 5 States in India in a particular year (2001) :

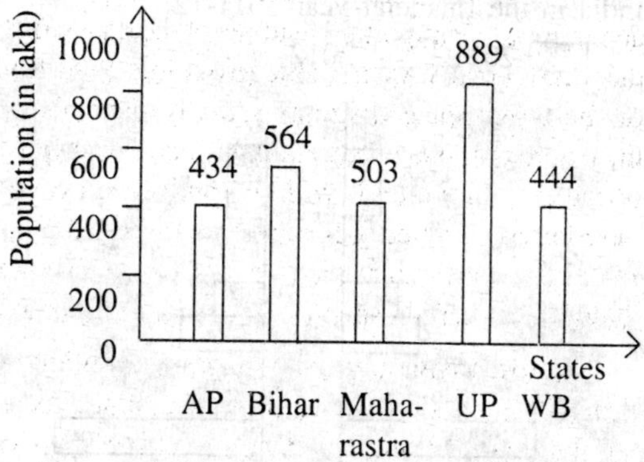

Fig. 7.2 : Vertical Bar Diagram

(b) Horizontal Bar Diagram

Volume of production and profit of five different organisations operating under a particular industry with separate productive capacities are given below for the two successive years 2011 and 2012.

We represent the information through an ideal bar diagram. Here Fig. 7.3 is drawn below on the basis of Table 7.6. We have chosen this horizontal bar diagram to facilitate comparison of performances of 5 organisations for the years 2011 and 2012, respectively.

Table 7.6 : Production and Profit of Five Different Organisations in 2011-12

Organi-sation	2011		2012	
	Production (Thousand)	Profit (Rs. Thousand)	Prodn. (Thou.)	Profit (Rs. Thou.)
A	12	11	14	11
B	06	5.5	06	06
C	25	26	27	30
D	02	1.8	1.5	1.2
E	07	64	07	07

Horizontal bars show production (in thousand) and profit (Rs. thousand) of five organi-sations of India in the financial year 2011-12.

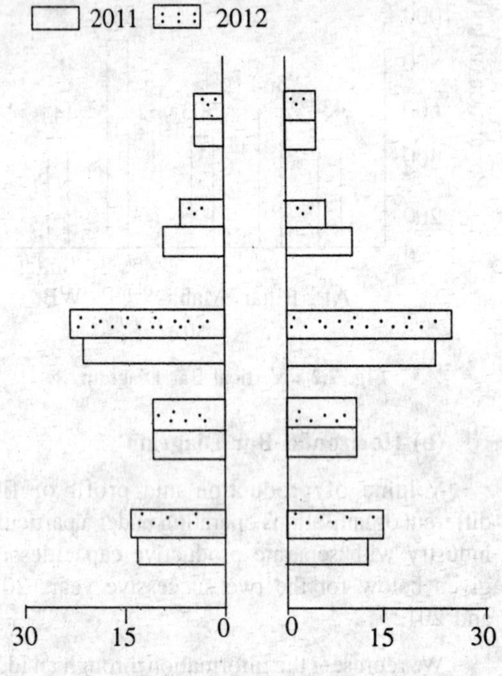

Fig. 7.3 : Horizontal Bar Diagram

(c) Multiple or Component Bar Diagram

These diagrammes are used in a situation where two or more related categories are to be compared simultaneously.

Consider the following example :

Labour employment and their percentages in 2000 and 2010 in a factory is given below. Represent them in terms of mutiple or component bar diagrams.

Table 7.7 : Sex-wise Labour Employment in a Factory in 2000 and 2010

Labour	Numbers		Percentages	
Employm.	2000	2010	2000	2010
Male	350	300	35	15
Female	400	1200	40	60
Boys	150	100	15	05
Girls	100	400	10	20
Total	1000	2000	100	100

Component bar diagrams show number of labourers of different categories and their respective percentages for the years 2000 and 2010.

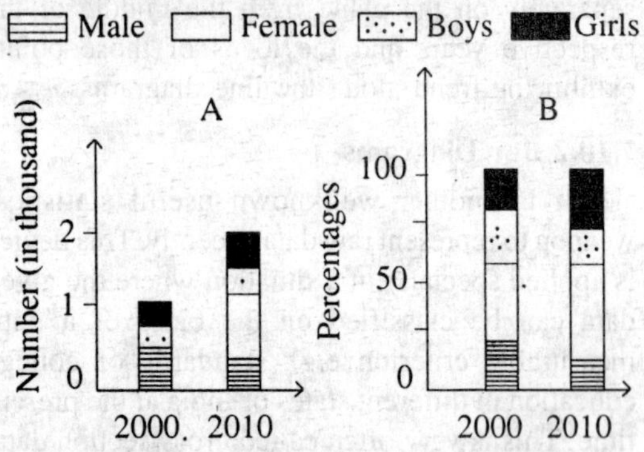

Fig. 7.4 : Component Bar Diagram

7.10.3 Pie Diagram

It is another effective statistical device to represent quantitative data obtainable on many occassions simply and diagramatically. When the various parts of the values of a variable possesses different properties then to express the inherent relationship among them and also with the aggregate value of the variable, piediagram possibly is the best device. Here, the aggregate value of the variable is expressed as the total area of a circle with a reasonable radius. The entire area in the circle is subdivided into a number of parts by several radii which are separately related to the total area of the circle and also maintain the same proportional relation with the angle at the centre.

For drawing it correctly, we convert the particular given values of the variable as a percentage of the total value of the variable. As the angle at the centre is 360°, it is supposed to express 100 p.c. value of the variable where 1 p.c. value of the variable is equivalent to an angle of 3.6° at the certre. We can thus easily convert the individual given values of the variable into the required angles at the centre. Then we draw a complete circle taking any standard radius and put the angles found from the numerical exercise separately at the centre. Each separate part in the circle signifies a particular section of the data. Let us represent a simple pie diagram below constructed with the usual method prescribed and followed for its computation by converting the following information into that diagram.

Example : Expenditure incurred by the **Planning Commission of India** on Education in the last 5-year economic plan.

Table 7.8 (A) : Educational Expenditure in the Last Five-year Economic Plan

Stages of education	Total expenditure (in Rs. crores)
I. Primary	209
II. Secondary	88
III. Higher Education	82
IV. Others	39
Total	418

Let us first convert the given data into respective percentages and then into the required angles to be shown at the centre in two more columns and represent them in the following way :

Table 7.8 (B) : Calculation for Drawing Pie Diagram

Stages of education	Total expenditure (Rs. crores)	Percentage (%)	Angle at the centre (°)
I. Primary	209	50	180.0
II. Secondary	88	21	75.6
III. Higher Education	82	20	72.0
IV. Others	39	09	32.4
Total	418	100	360.0

Here, angle at the Centre = Percentage × 3.6.

Pie diagram drawn below on the basis of Table 7.8 (B) shows expenditure on education at various stages in the last 5-year economic plan.

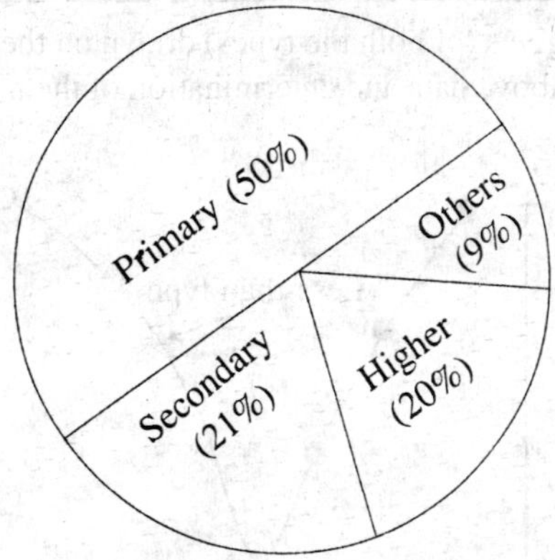

Fig. 7.5 : Pie Diagram

7.10.4 Ogive or Cumulative Frequency Polygon

An ogive is another statistical tool primarily used for finding out different quartiles in a distribution. From such a device we can also identify the number of observations lying above or below a certain value of the concerned variable.

This kind of a diagram is drawn for a frequency distribution of a continuous variable in terms of cumulative frequencies of both the types (more than or less than type). While drawing this diagram we consider the given values of the variable horizontally and the corresponding cumulative frequencies (of either type) vertically. Cumulative frequency of less than type is zero for the lowest given value of the variable and similarly cumulative frequency of greater than type is zero for the heighest value of the variable considered. Using the data available from a production organisation, Ogives of both the types are drawn below for our ready reference.

Table 7.9 : Determination of Median Wage by Drawing Ogives of Both the Types

Wages	Cumulative Frequency	
	less-than type	more-than type
30·0	0	50
40·0	06	44
50·0	20	30
52	25	25
60·0	40	10
70·0	47	03
80·0	50	0

Ogives (of both the types) drawn on the basis of the above data and determination of the median wage :

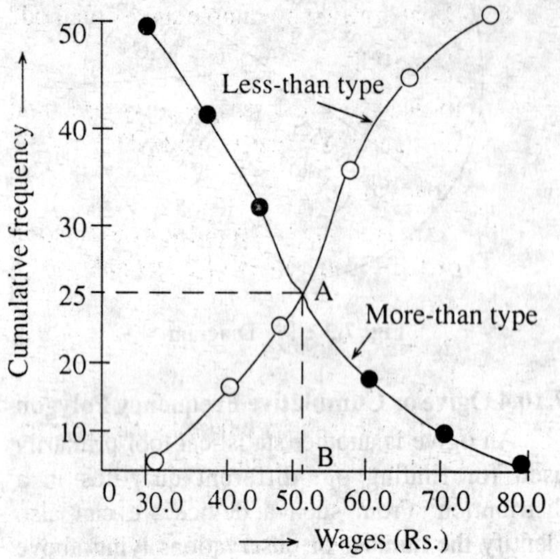

Fig. 7.6 : Diagrammatic Determination of Median Wage

Here, being the middle-most value of the given wage rates, the median wage is found OB (= Rs. 52) because only at this wage rate the two cumulative frequency curves intersect at point A representing two cumulative frequencies (less-than and greater-than) of both the types exactly equal (AB = 25) with each other. Hence, the median wage is OB = Rs. 52·00.

QUESTIONS WITH ANSWER-HINTS

Long-Answer Questions

1. Define 'Statistics' as a separate discipline of science and its various uses today.

   Ans. 7.1

2. Compare and explain with examples—(a) qualitative and quantitative nature of a variable, (b) discrete and continuous variables.

   Ans. 7.2

3. Give the definitions of the following—frequency of the value of a variable, proportionate frequency, cumulative frequency, class-frequency.

   Ans. 7.7

4. Construct a complete frequency distribution in a tabular form with the following information.

18·6	33·4	25·3	27·8	30·6	31·9	33·0	26·3	24·9
20·0	26·2	28·1	33·1	37·5	22·5	39·1	32·9	33·8
32·5	34·6	32.7	9·5	38·5	29·6	25·3	49·5	30·1
26·9	33·8	36·0	38·.0	27·5	32·3	34·2	23·1	34·7
34·1	38·6	25·9	40·6	58·5	29·3	36·8	27·1	24·9
25·4	52·6	27·9	29·0	31·6				

   Ans. Consult 7.7

5. Describe the method of preparing a complete frequency distribution in a tabular form from a set of disordered data.

   Ans. 7.10

6. Give your arguments in favour of graphical presentation of data and also mention its limitations.

   Ans. 7.10

7. What are line, bar and pie-diagrams? Describe the method of drawing such diagrams from a set of given data.

   Ans. 7.10.1, 7.10.2, 7.10.3

8. Mention and discuss the components to be presented while preparing a complete statistical table.

   Ans. 7.7

9. What is cumulative frequency? What are its usual types? Mention clearly their usefulness and methods of computation.

   Ans. 7.10.4

10. What are 'ogives'. How can you draw such curves? Draw ogives of both the types from the following information representing marks obtained in an examination.

Marks obtained	0-20	20-40	40-60	60-80	80-100
No. of students	8	10	16	14	9

   Ans. Consult 7.10.4

Write Short Notes on :

(a) Population, (b) sample, (c) questionnaire, (d) horizontal and vertical bars, (e) time-series and cross-section data, (f) sources of a data set, (g) tabulation of data, (h) continuous and discrete variables, (i) numerical and methodical errors of calculation, (j) variable and attribute, (k) sampling and non-sampling errors.

Ans. Do yourself (consult our text).

Short-Answer Questions

1. What is meant by primary data?

   Ans. 7.4

2. What is secondary data?

   Ans. 7.4

3. Point out two important advantages and disadvantages of primary data.

   Ans. 7.4.1

4. Mention two important advantages and disadvantages of secondary data.

   Ans. 7.4.1

5. Give two separate examples of primary and secondary data sources.

   Ans. 7.4.1

6. Mention the methods of collecting primary data.

   Ans. 7.4.2

7. What is census method of collecting data?

   Ans. 7.8.1

8. What is meant by sample survey method?

   Ans. 7.8

9. In what respects sample survey method is superior to census method?

   Ans. 7.8.1

10. What is meant by frequency distribution of the given values of a variable?

    Ans. 7.7

11. Define 'tabulation'.

    Ans. 7.7

12. Point out with an example the different components of a complete table.

    Ans. 7.7(b)

13. Define caption and stub of a table.

    Ans. 7.7(b) (iii and iv)

14. What is complete enumeration?

    Ans. 7.8 (last part)

CHAPTER 8

Measures of Central Tendency

8.1 Introduction

Statistical data are often condensed to a large extent by classification and tabulation. All statistical investigations are carried out with a definite purpose in view. After the proper arrangement of classification and tabulation, one can analyse and interpret statistical data. However, for analysis and interpretation of statistical data mere tabulation is not enough, especially when comparison of two or more series of data are needed. The most important characteristic that describes or summarises a set of data is its single representative value or location or central tendency. The single representative value is called an *average*, and it is often called *a measure of central tendency.*

Statistics is an important tool very often used in economic analysis. To start with, we consider the average or central value that lies between the highest and the lowest values of the data. This average is usually located at the centre or the middle of the observations. This average or single value is the representative of all the items. Or, it is the point of location around which the individual values cluster.

According to Croxton, F. E. and Cowden, D. J., "An average value is a single value within the range of the data that is used to represent all of the values in the series. Since the average is somewhere within the range of data, it is sometimes called a measure of central value.

In our chapter 7, we have discussed condensation of data due to classification and tabulation. The current chapter is prepared for computing *average* or more specifically *measures of central tendency.*

8.2 Meaning and Concept of the Term Central Tendency

Many problems in economics and management involve frequency distributions. In frequency distributions, one encounters certain values that occur frequently while other values less frequently. To be more specific, in many frequency distributions, the tabulated values show smaller frequencies at the beginning and at the end and larger or higher frequencies at the middle of the distribution. This indicates that the typical values of the variable lie nearer the central part of the distribution and other values cluster or group around these central values. This behaviour of the data about the concentration of the values in the central part of the distribution is called central tendency (or location) of data.

A variable, as we know, possesses a number of observations which changes over time (called time series data) or space (called cross section data). If we examine the whole set of observations much carefully and quite intensively, we find that these values have a general tendency to cluster around a central or a typical value existing almost in the central position. The particular value so identified is called the central value and the phenomenon is noted as the central tendency of the variable. Averages of several types computed are the usual measures of such tendency of a given variable.

Usually, we are familiar with three following types of the central tendencies of a variable, namely—the *mean*, *median* and *mode* from the available values of the given variable. Again, means are of three categories—the Arithmetic Mean (AM), the Geometric Mean (GM) and the Harmonic Mean (HM).

We can represent them in the following way—

8.2.1 Classification of the Measures of Central Tendency of a Variable within a Particular Range of Variations

We usually apply the following devises to quantify such tendency of a given variable appearing with a number of separate values :

Three Orders of Measurement of Average

Measurement of the first order	Measurement of the second order	Measurement of the third order
↓	↓	↓
Measures of Central tendency	Measures of Dispersion	Measures of Skewness and Kurtosis

Let us classify the measures of central tendency in the following format :

Central Tendency

Mean	Median	Mode

Mean ↓

Arithmetic Mean (AM)	Geometric Mean (GM)	Harmonic Mean (HM)

Types of Central Tendency

(a) Mean—(i) arithmetic mean

(ii) geometric mean (iii) harmonic mean

(b) Median, (c) Mode for grouped (having frequencies) and ungrouped (without having frequencies) data.

Summation Notation (Σ) : The Symbol Σ is the Greek capital letter *sigma* denoting sum. Let the symbol x_i (read *x subscript i*) denote any of the values $x_1, x_2, x_3, \ldots, x_n$ assumed by a variable x. The letter *i* stand for any of the number 1, 2, ..., n is called a *subscript.*

If $x_1, x_2, \ldots, x_n$ be the n number of values of a variable x, then their sum from i = 1 to i = n is shortly written as $\sum_{i=1}^{n} x_i$

Or $\Sigma x_i = x_1 + x_2 + x_3 + \ldots + x_n$ is also denoted by Σx or $\Sigma_i x_i$ or Σx_i. Similarly, the sum of $w_1x_1 + w_2x_2 + \ldots + w_n x_n$ is denoted by

$\sum_{i=1}^{n} w_i x_i$ or simply Σwx or $\Sigma w_i x_i$.

8.3 Mean

The mean or the arithmetic average of a set of values of a variable is the value obtained after dividing the sum of all the values of the given variable by their number. The arithmetic mean is usually of two types :

(a) simple arithmetic mean, and

(b) weighted arithmetic mean.

8.3.1 Simple AM

The most commonly used measure of central tendency is the arithmetic mean. It is defined as being equal to the sum of numerical values of each and every observation divided by the total number of observations. In other words, it is calculated by adding together the values of the items in the set of observations and dividing the total by the number of items or observations. The arithmetic mean is defined symbolically as

$$\bar{x} = \frac{x_1 + x_2 + \ldots + x_n}{n} = \frac{\sum_{i=1}^{n} x_i}{n} = \frac{\Sigma x}{n} \ldots (8.1)$$

In equation (8.1), $\bar{x}$ (read *x bar*) is the *mean* or the *arithmetic mean.*

It is the representative value of all the observations given on a variable.

Example 1 : Find the average wage of the ten labourers working in a small industrial unit in a village :

X : 88, 72, 33, 29, 70, 54, 86, 91, 57, 61

Solution : The required sum of the wages of those ten labourers is :

$$\sum_{i=1}^{10} x_i = 88 + 72 + 33 + 29 + 70 + 54 + 86 + 91 + 57 + 61 = 641$$

Therefore, the mean or (average wage) is :

$$AM = \frac{\Sigma x_i}{n} = \frac{641}{10} = 64.1$$

(i = 1,2, ..., 10)

It is clear from equation (8.1) or example 1 that if x_1, x_2, etc, occur with frequenceies, say f_1, f_2 etc., then the AM becomes

$$\bar{x} = \frac{x_1f_1 + x_2f_2 + \ldots + x_nf_n}{f_1 + f_2 + \ldots + f_n} = \frac{\sum_{i=1}^{n} x_if_i}{\sum_{i=1}^{n} f_i}$$

$$= \frac{\Sigma xf}{\Sigma f} = \frac{\Sigma xf}{N} = \ldots \quad (8.2)$$

when $N = \Sigma f$ is the total frequency or the total number of observations.

Example 2 : If the grades of 16 students in an examination were 55, 68, 36, 28 and 85 occur with frequencies 3, 2, 4, 6 and 1 respectively, calculate AM.

Solution : The Arithmetic Mean is calculated on the basis of equation (8.2).

$$\bar{x} = \frac{55(3) + 68(2) + 36(4) + 28(6) + 85(1)}{3 + 2 + 4 + 6 + 1}$$

$$= \frac{698}{16} = 43.62$$

Example 3 : The following marks are obtained by the II-yr. students in a class-test out of 10. Score of one examinee was detected missing and included afterwards and the average calculated was 3. Determine the score of the last examinee.

1, 1, 0, 2, 0, 3, 0, 4, 8, 6, 5.

Solution : Due to inclusion of one additional examinee in the process, the total number of examinees became 12 and hence their total marks should be $12 \times 3 = 36$.

Again, sum of the marks obtained by the previous 11 students was 30.

Therefore, the score of the last one was 36–30 = 6.

8.3.2 Weighted AM

The arithmetic mean attaches equal importance to all the items or observations. Truly speaking, all such observations may not attract same importance or weightage. Some observations may receive greater weightage compared to others. For example, greater weights are assigned to our daily needs (say, food) and lesser weights are given to luxury goods in our family budget. Such importance attached to different items with figures (or numbers) according to their priorities is called weights. When the mean is expressed with respective weights one obtains weighted AM. This kind of mean is frequently used for studying various economic problems.

If $x_1, x_2, \ldots, x_n$ be the values of a variable x and $w_1, w_2, \ldots, w_n$ be their respective weights, we then obtain weighted AM as,

$$\bar{x} = \frac{x_1w_1 + x_2w_2 + \ldots + x_nw_n}{w_1 + w_2 + \ldots + w_n} = \frac{\Sigma xw}{\Sigma w} \ldots \quad (8.3)$$

Note the similarity between the equations (8.2) and (8.3). Hence equation (8.2) can be considered as the weighted AM with weights $f_1, f_2, \ldots, f_n$.

Example 4 : Find the weighted AM of the four given numbers 92, 125, 180 and 80 having their respective frequencies 12, 7, 6 and 9.

Solution : The weighted AM of the four given numbers with their own frequencies can be expressed as :

$$\bar{x} = \frac{x_1f_1 + x_2f_2 + x_3f_3 + x_4f_4}{f_1 + f_2 + f_3 + f_4}$$

$$= \frac{\sum_{i=1}^{4} x_if_i}{\sum_{i=1}^{4} f_i} \text{ or } \bar{x}\, N = \Sigma f_ix_i \qquad [\text{Here } N = \Sigma f_i = 34]$$

$$= \frac{92 \times 12 + 125 \times 7 + 180 \times 6 + 80 \times 9}{12 + 7 + 6 + 9}$$

$$= \frac{1104 + 875 + 1080 + 720}{34} = \frac{3779}{34} = 111$$

Example 5 : Compute the arithmetic mean of the following wage earning group of labourers.

Table 8.1 : Computation of Arithmetic Mean

Age groups	No. of wage earners
14—15	60
16—17	140
18—20	150
21—24	110
25—29	110
30—34	100
35—39	90

Solution : To compute the desired Arithmetic Mean we first prepare the following table :

Table 8.2 : Determination of Arithmetic Mean

Class intervals	Mid values (x)	Deviations from 22.5 (x)	Frequency f_i	$f_i x_i$
14—15	14·5	– 8	60	– 480
16—17	16·5	– 6	140	– 840
18—20	19·0	– 3·5	150	– 525
21—24	22·5	0	110	0
25—29	27·0	4·5	110	– 49·5
30—34	32·0	9·5	100	950
35—39	37·0	14·5	90	1350
Total			760	905

Here a = 22·5, N = Σf = 760, x = X–22·5

The required arithmetic mean

$$= a + \frac{\Sigma x_i f_i}{N}$$

$$= 22{\cdot}5 + \frac{905}{760}$$

$$= 22{\cdot}5 + 1{\cdot}19$$

$$= 23{\cdot}69$$

8.3.3 Composite Mean from Two Separate Groups

When two separate groups containing n_1 and n_2 observations with their respective arithmetic means $\bar{x}_1$ and $\bar{x}_2$ are given for a variable then the composite mean of those two groups together can be determined from the following relation :

$$\bar{x} = \frac{n_1\bar{x}_1 + n_2\bar{x}_2}{N}$$

where N = n_1+n_2.

$\bar{x}$ here represent the composite or common mean for the two given groups together.

Example 6 : Calculate the composite mean of the salaries of the employees of two different departments of an organisation.

Table : 8.3 : Calculation for Composite Mean

Characteristics	Groups		Composite groups
	I	II	
No. of observations	n_1=90	n_2=70	N=160
Mean salary (Rs.)	$\bar{x}_1$=250	$\bar{x}_2$=200	$\bar{x}$=?

Solution : We use the above relation and determine the required average as—

$$N\bar{x} = n_1\bar{x}_1 + n_2\bar{x}_2$$

or $160\,\bar{x} = 90 \times 250 + 70 \times 200$

$$= 22{,}500 + 14{,}000 = 36{,}500$$

$$\therefore \bar{x} = \frac{36{,}500}{160} = 228{\cdot}11$$

8.3.4 Important Properties of AM

(a) Sum of a set of given observations is equal to the product of their number of observations and the AM.

Symbolically,

(i) $\Sigma x_i = N\bar{x}$ (for simple AM) and (ii) $\Sigma f_i x_i = N\bar{x}$ /where $N = \Sigma f_i$ (for weighted AM)

(b) The sum of the deviations of a set of observations from their AM is always zero.

(i) $\Sigma(x_i - \bar{x}) = 0$, (ii) $\Sigma f_i\ (x_i - \bar{x}) = 0$

where $\bar{x} = \sum_{i=1}^{n} \frac{\Sigma xi}{n}$ or $\bar{x} = \Sigma f_i x_i/N$

(c) If the two variables x and z are related in the manner z = ax + b for each x = x_i where a and b are two given constants then,

$$\bar{z} = a\bar{x} + b$$

Again, if $y = \frac{x - c}{d}$ where c and d are constants, then $\bar{x} = c + d\bar{y}$

(d) For the two separate groups of observations n_1 and n_2, the composite mean is :

$N\bar{x} = n_1\bar{x}_1 + n_2\bar{x}_2$ where $N = n_1+n_2$

and it can be generalised for any number of groups as $N\bar{x} = \sum_{i=1}^{n} n_i\bar{x}_i$ where $N = \sum_{i=1}^{n} n_i$

(e) The sum of the squares of diviations of a set of observations will be the minimum when deviations are taken from their AM.

Symbolically,

(i) $\sum(x_i - A)^2$ is the minimum where A is any guessed or assumed AM (which may be any number)

(ii) $\Sigma f_i(x_i–A)^2$ is the minimum where A = weighted AM

8.3.5 Advantages and Disadvantages of AM

According to the renowned statistician and author of this discipline G. U. Yule, arithmetic mean is a satisfactory average. It has the following *advantages* :

(a) It is easily understandable.
(b) It is easily and exactly computable.
(c) It is suitable for algebraic treatment.
(d) It remains free from sampling fluctuations.
(e) Its calculation involves all the values of the given variable.
(f) It can rigidly be defined.
(g) It is safely usable and expressable in all situations.

However, arithmetic mean is not free from any disadvantages. Some of them are mentioned below :

(a) The arithmetic mean from a set of given observations is not identifiable only through observations.

(b) It is not correctly computable when a single observation is missing or rejected from the given data set.

(c) It can never be calculated correctly unless the entire observations on the given variable are supplied at a time.

(d) The arithmetic mean attaches greater importance to bigger items while smaller items receive lesser attention.

(e) It is to be kept in mind that it is not a locational average as such. It needs only mathematical calculations.

(f) Finally, the simple arithmetic mean suggests only a numerical figure and nothing else.

However, the arithmetic mean is a common type of primary statistical tool and widely used in various statistical analyses. Today, it is used as a very popular representation of central tendency of a variable and hence used frequently for several analytical purposes.

8.4 Geometric Mean (GM)

The geometric mean like the AM is also a calculated average. However, it is another kind of statistical device to identify the central tendency of a variable having a finite number of observations. More precisely, for a set of n-observations, it is determined as the n-th root of their product.

Symbolically, GM of the observations of a variable (x) having—

(i) $G = \sqrt[2]{x_1 \cdot x_2}$ (two observations)

(ii) $G = \sqrt[3]{x_1 x_2 x_3}$ (three observations)

GM (for n-observations together of the variable x) of a set of n-positive numbers x_1, x_2, ..., x_n is the n-th root of the product of those numbers.

$$GM = \sqrt[n]{x_1 x_2 x_3 \cdots\cdots x_n} \quad \ldots\ldots (8.4)$$

$$= \left(x_1 x_2 x_3 \cdots x_n\right)^{1/n} \quad \ldots\ldots (8.4.1)$$

Example : Calculate the GM of 3, 6 and 24

Here, GM $= \sqrt[3]{3 \times 6 \times 24} = \sqrt[3]{432} = 7.56$

Weighted GM

It should be borne in mind that if the number of observations is more than 3, as demonstrated earlier, then computation becomes very difficult and tedious. In view of this kind of a problem, it is recommended to use logarithms. In other words, logarithms are used to simplify calculation when the number of observations is large enough. In order to calculate the GM we often use

$$\log GM = \frac{\log x_1 + \log x_2 + \ldots + \log x_n}{n}$$

$$= \frac{1}{n}\Sigma \log x \quad \ldots\ldots (8.5)$$

If x_1, x_2, ..., x_n occur with frequencies (or weights) f_1, f_2, ..., f_n respectively, the GM is then given by

$$GM = \left(x_1^{f_1} \times x_2^{f_2} \times \ldots x_n^{f_n}\right)^{\frac{1}{N}}$$

where $N = f_1 + f_2 + \ldots + f_n$

Here, $\log GM = \frac{1}{N}(f_1 \log x_1 + f_2 \log x_2 + \ldots + f_n \log x_n)$

$$= \frac{1}{N}\Sigma f \log x \quad \ldots\ldots (8.5.1)$$

$$\text{Hence, } GM = \text{antilog}\left\{\frac{1}{N}\Sigma f \log x\right\} \ldots (8.5.2)$$

where $x_i = x_1, x_2, \ldots, x_n$, $f_i = f_1, f_2, \ldots, f_n$

$N = \sum_{i=1}^{n} f_i$, i = 1, 2, 3, ..., n.

8.4.1 Advantages and Disadvantages of GM

The geometric mean, like the arithmetic mean, has a number of advantages and disadvantages.

These are given in order below :

(a) It can be defined rigidly.

(b) It is calculated on the basis of all the observations of a variable.

(c) It is much convenient to calculate required averages of ratios, rates, and percentages with the aid of GM.

(d) It is not affected by the exceptional and extremely large or small values of a variable.

(e) It gives the highest weight for the lowest observation and the lowest weight for the highest observation and thereby balances the entire procedure to get the best result.

(f) It is much suitable for using it in different mathematical treatments afterwards.

(g) It helps in the calculation for determining rates of exchange among the currencies of various countries.

Its disadvantages are noted below:

(a) It is very difficult to calculate when the data is given in the fashion of a grouped frequency distribution having large frequencies in enough numbers.

(b) The result becomes meaningless if any of the information is zero or negative.

(c) The result finally obtained may not be equal to any of the observations given in the series.

(d) It gives least importance to the marginal and extreme observations.

(e) In some cases it cannot play the role as the true representative of an average.

(f) It usually brings out the property of the ratio of changes and not the differences of change.

8.4.2 Computation of GM

Example 1 : Find the GM of the observations 12, 18, 48 and 61 of a variable having their weights 5, 3, 2 and 8 respectively.

Solution : Let us prepare the data in the form of a table so as to calculate GM.

Table 8.4 : Calculation for GM

X	log X	frequency (f)	flog X
12	1·0792	5	5·3960
18	1·2553	3	3·7659
48	1·6812	2	3·3624
61	1·7853	8	14·2824
		Σf = 18 = N	Σf·log x = 26·8067

∴ The required GM—

$$\log GM = \frac{1}{N}\Sigma f.\log X$$

$$= \frac{1}{18} \times 26{\cdot}8067$$

$$= 1{\cdot}4893$$

Antilog of 1·4893 = 30·85 (Ans)

Example 2 : The GM of three numbers is 15 and the numbers are 5, 25 and x, find the value of x—

Solution : We know that for three numbers together—

$$GM = \sqrt[3]{5 \times 25 \times x} = 15$$

$$\text{or, } 5 \times 25 \times x = (15)^3 = 15 \times 15 \times 15$$

$$\text{or, } x = \frac{15 \times 15 \times 15}{5 \times 25} = 27 \text{ (Ans)}$$

8.4.3 Important Properties of the GM

(a) When the observations on the given variable are equal in magnitude, the geometric mean will be equal to their common value.

Symbolically, we write—

$$x_G = \left(C^n\right)^{1/n} = C$$

Here, the given variable x takes n-number of observations which individually are equal to C.

(b) The logarithm of the geometric mean of a set of values of a variable is the arithmetic mean of their logarithms.

Symbolically, $\log x_G = \frac{1}{n}\sum_{i=1}^{n}\log x_i$

(c) If y is a function of a variable x in the form y = ax, then the geometric mean of y is related to that of x in the similar form i.e $y_G = ax_G$ where y_G and x_G are the geometric means of y and x, respectively.

(d) The geometric means of the ratio of two variables is the ratio of their geometric means—

Consider the ratio $= \frac{X_i}{Y_i}$, where i = 1, 2 ...n

here, for each i, $\sqrt{\frac{x_i}{y_i}} = \frac{X_G}{Y_G}$

(e) If there are two sets of values of a variable x consisting of n_1 and n_2 observations and G_1 and G_2 are their respective geometric means, then the geometric mean of the combined set is given by :

$$GM = \left(G_1^{n_1} \cdot G_2^{n_2}\right)^{\frac{1}{n_1+n_2}}$$

8.5 Harmonic Mean

• The harmonic mean of a set of observations on a variable is defined as the reciprocal of the arithmetic average of the reciprocal of the given observations (any of the observations must not be zero).

If the variable noted is X which takes n-number of values as $x_1, x_2, x_3, \ldots x_n$ and their reciprocals are—

$\frac{1}{x_1}, \frac{1}{x_2}, \frac{1}{x_3}, \ldots, \frac{1}{x_n}$; and their simple arith-metic mean is $\rightarrow \frac{1}{n}\sum_{i=1}^{n}\frac{1}{x_i}$ and then their simple harmonic mean (HM) is calculated with the aid of :

$$HM = \frac{1}{\frac{1}{x_1}+\frac{1}{x_2}+\cdots+\frac{1}{x_n}} = \frac{1}{\frac{1}{n}\sum_{i=1}^{n}\frac{1}{x_i}}$$

$$= \frac{n}{\sum_{i=1}^{n}\frac{1}{x_i}}$$

For the observations having their respective frequencies, the weighted HM can be computed as :

$$HM = \frac{N}{\sum_{i=1}^{n}\frac{f_i}{x_i}}$$

where $N = \sum_{i=1}^{n} f_i = f_1 + f_2 + f_3 + \cdots + f_n$

It is a special kind of average used in some selected situations.

8.5.1 Important Properties of the HM

(a) If the given values of a variable are all equal (but $\neq 0$) then their harmonic mean will be equal to their common value.

$$\text{Symbolically, } HM = \frac{n}{\sum_{i=1}^{n}\frac{1}{c}} = c$$

Here, n is the total number of observations of the variable and c is the common value.

(b) If a variable y is related to another variable x in the form y = ax, then the harmonic mean of y is related to that of x in the similar form :

$$\text{Symbollically, } y_H = a\frac{n}{\sum_{i=1}^{n}\frac{1}{x_i}} = a.x_H$$

(c) If n_1 and n_2 are two sets of values of a variable x and their respective harmonic means are H_1 and H_2, then the harmonic mean of the combined set (H) is given by—

$$HM = \frac{n_1 n_2}{\frac{n_1}{H_1}+\frac{n_2}{H_2}} \quad (i = 1, 2)$$

8.5.2 Computation of the HM

Exmple 1 : Calculate the simple harmonic mean of the numbers 3, 6, 24 and 48.

Solution : Applying the principle of HM we get—

$$HM = \frac{4}{\frac{1}{x_1}+\frac{1}{x_2}+\frac{1}{x_3}+\frac{1}{x_4}}$$

$$= \frac{4}{\frac{1}{3}+\frac{1}{6}+\frac{1}{24}+\frac{1}{48}} = \frac{4}{\frac{16+8+2+1}{48}}$$

$$= \frac{4}{\frac{27}{48}} = 4\times\frac{48}{27} = \frac{64}{9} = 7{\cdot}11 \text{ (Ans.)}$$

Example 2 : Determine the weighted HM for the observations of the variable X from the following :

x	2	5	7	10	8	6	2
y	5	8	12	15	20	24	30

Solution : We calculate the weighted HM as

$$HM = \frac{N}{\frac{f_1}{x_1}+\frac{f_2}{x_2}+\frac{f_3}{x_3}+\frac{f_4}{x_4}+\cdots+\frac{f_7}{x_7}}$$

$$= \frac{114}{\frac{5}{2}+\frac{8}{5}+\frac{12}{7}+\frac{15}{10}+\frac{20}{8}+\frac{24}{6}+\frac{30}{2}}$$

$$= \frac{114}{\frac{2,100+1,344+1,440+1,260+2,100+3,360+12,600}{840}}$$

$$= \frac{114}{\frac{24,204}{840}} = 114\times\frac{840}{24,204} = 3{\cdot}9. \text{(Ans.)}$$

8.5.3 Merits and Demerits of the HM

Like all the devices of central tendency mentioned earlier, harmonic mean also has a number of merits and demerits. These are :

Merits of the Harmonic Mean

(a) It is defined much clearly and rigidly

(b) It is calculated on the basis of all the information available on the variable.

(c) It is very much suitable for using in various mathematical analyses.

(d) It remains more or less unaffected due to sampling fluctuations.

(e) It is easily computable and hence precise in nature.

(f) It always possesses a definite value.

(g) It considers smaller observation with larger importance and vice-versa.

(h) As it measures relative changes in the given observations of a variable, it becomes perfectly useful for finding out averages of certain ratios and rates.

Demerits of the Harmonic Mean

(a) The result usually found has no existence in the given series of observations on the variable.

(b) It is not easily explainable, computable, and hence understandable.

(c) It is much restrictive in the sense that it cannot be calculated if any of the observations is zero.

(d) It has limited applications in practical situations.

8.6 Interrelationship among AM, GM and HM

Let us consider the simplest example on a variable X having only two observations x_1 and x_2 (e.g., the two sides of a coin).

1. Their AM $= \dfrac{x_1 + x_2}{2}$

$$GM = \sqrt{x_1 \cdot x_2}$$

$$\text{and the HM} = \frac{2}{\frac{1}{x_1}+\frac{1}{x_2}} = \frac{2}{\frac{x_2+x_1}{x_1x_2}} = \frac{2x_1x_2}{x_1+x_2}$$

$$\therefore\ AM \times HM = \frac{x_1+x_2}{2} \times \frac{2x_1x_2}{x_1+x_2} = x_1x_2$$

$$\text{or } \sqrt{AM \times HM} = \sqrt{x_1x_2}$$

$$\text{or } GM = \sqrt{AM \times HM}$$

or GM is the GM of AM and HM

or $AM \cdot HM = (GM)^2$

The same analysis can be extended for any number of observations on a variable and the same result can easily be established.

Other important relations are :

2. AM = GM = HM when all the observations on the variable are identical in magnitude.

AM > GM > HM for heterogeneous observations.

Symbolically, we generalise them as

$AM \geq GM \geq HM$

But, for any two different numbers the relation turns into :

$AM \times HM = (GM)^2$

All the averages will become equal with each other when the variable assumes identical observations.

8.7 Median

The median of a set of observations on a variable is identified as the middlemost value from those given set of observations. For a set of ungrouped data arranged either in ascending or descending order, the middlemost value or the median is calculated as the $\left(\frac{N+1}{2}\right)$-th-value for an odd number of observations. But, for an even number of observations, the median will be the mean of $\left(\frac{N}{2}\right)$-th and $\left(\frac{N+1}{2}\right)$-th values of those observations.

It is thus evident that the median divides the whole series into two equal parts. It is a positional average and is unaffected by the presence of an extremely large or small value. It can also be calculated from a grouped frequency distribution with open-end classes.

Example 1 : Find the median value of : Rs. 110, Rs. 90, Rs. 40, Rs. 50, Rs. 125, Rs. 65, and Rs. 100.

Solution : Arranging the given values in ascending order, we obtain the sequence as Rs. 40, Rs. 50, Rs. 65, Rs. 90, Rs. 100, Rs. 110 and, Rs. 125. Thus, n=7, Since 7 is an *odd number*, there is only one value at the middle which is the $\left(\frac{n+1}{2}\right)$-th, i.e. $\left(\frac{7+1}{2}\right)$ the 4th value. Note that the 4-th valve = Rs. 90. Hence, by definition, the median value is Rs. 90.

Example 2 : Find the median of the values : 25, 24, 23, 32, 40, 27, 30, 25, 20, 10, 15, 45.

Solution : Arranging the given values in the ascending order, we get the sequence as 10, 15, 20, 23, 24, 25, 25, 27, 30, 32, 40 and 45.

Thus, n=12, since the number 12 is even, it has two middle terms which are the 6-th and the 7-th terms, i.e. 25 and 25.

Hence, the Median by definition

$$= \frac{6-\text{th term}+7-\text{th term}}{2} = \frac{25+25}{2} = 25$$

This sort of calculation of the median value does not consider frequency distribution. Thus, the calculation for the median is nothing but simple for such a series.

Instead, we intend to calculate median for both ungrouped and grouped data. Let us consider the ungrouped data first. In this case, we first calculate cumulative frequencies corresponding to each value of the variable. Then the value of the variable corresponding to the $\left(\frac{n+1}{2}\right)$ cumulative frequency is the median value where $n = \Sigma f$ = total frequency.

On the basis of example 3, we like to calculate cumulative frequency for ungrouped data (Table 8.5).

Example 3 : Find the median from the following data :

Income (Rs.)	400	500	750	900	1000	1200
No. of individuals	16	24	26	30	20	6

Solution : How is cumulative frequency calculated has been shown in Table 8.5.

Table 8.5 : Calculation for Median Value

Income (Rs.)	No. of individuals (f)	Cumulative Frequency
400	16	16
500	24	40
750	26	66
900	30	96
1000	20	116
1200	6	122 = N
Total	N=122	

Here, $\frac{N}{2} = 61$, We can write (By simple interpolation) $\frac{M-500}{750-500} = \frac{61-40}{66-40}$ and then determine M. Ans. 701.92

Example 4 : Consider the following income distribution of a group of 400 workers in a factory. Determine the median income.

Table 8.6 : Income Distribution of a Group of 400 Male Workers

Income in Rs. Class boundaries	Frequency	Cumulative frequency
Below 50	6	6
49·5—69·5	10	16
69·5—89·5	30	46
89·5—109·5	150	196
109·5—139·5	140	336
139·5—169·5	40	376
169·5—and above	24	400
Total	N = 400	400 = N

Solution : Note that the data are unequally spaced and open at both ends.

From the above table it is clear that the median must occur between Rs. 109·5 and Rs. 139·5 as $\frac{N}{2} = 200$ occurs in between 196 and 336 as shown in the table. Hence, median = Rs. 109·5 + a fraction of the class interval (109·5-139·5). This fraction may be found by *simple interpolation*. We proceed as follows :

The difference in frequency from 196 to 336 corresponds to the difference in income from Rs. 109·5 to Rs. 139·5, i.e., corresponding to a difference of 140 in frequency there is a difference of Rs. 30 in income.

Therefore, corresponding to unit difference in frequency, there will be a difference of Rs. $\frac{30}{140}$ in income.

But, to find the median, we wish to proceed up to the cumulative frequency 200, i.e, to a difference of 200 − 196 = 4.

Thus, corresponding to a difference of 4 in frequency there will be a difference of Rs. $\frac{30}{140} \times 4$ in income . Here Rs. $\frac{30}{140} \times 4$ = Rs. 0·85 is the fraction to be added. Hence, the median is Rs. (109·5 + 0·85) = Rs. 110·35.

It is obvious from the above example that calculation of median from a frequency distribution with open ends does not produce any difficulty unless the median falls in an open x-class. We should also note that in finding out median for a grouped distribution, *class boundaries, not class limits, should* be used.

In interpolating the median value in the above example, we started from the top of the table, but we could have started from the bottom of the table as well and get the same result. Sometimes, it is stated that the median corresponds to the cumulative frequency equal to $\left(\frac{n+1}{2}\right)$ where n is the total frequency. This is true for raw ungrouped data with odd number of observations. But, for grouped frequency distributions this procedure should be avoided. Otherwise, the value obtained by interpolation starting from the top of the table will be different from the value obtained by starting from the bottom. This is not desirable because an average should uniquely be defined.

It should also be observed that whether we find mean or median from a frequency distribution, the values obtained will not be the same as those obtained from the raw data. This is natural because while making a frequency distribution our objective is to condense the data and the result of this condensation is the loss of some amount of information.

Example 5 : Represent the following data with the aid of cumulative frequency curves—(i) less than and (ii) greater than types and also determine the median value of the marks obtained by 100 students in Statistics—

Frequency distribution of marks obtained by 100 students in Statistics—

Class intervals (Marks)	No. of students
10—19	08
20—29	14
30—39	22
40—49	29
50—59	14
60—69	07
70—79	04
80—89	02
Total	100

Solution : Let us prepare the following table to trace out the two required cumulative frequency curves and therefrom the desired median—

Table 8.7 : Calculation for deriving Frequency Curves and therefrom the Median Value from the given Data

Class interval (marks)	Class boundary	Frequency	Cum. freqn. from below (less than type)	Cum. freqn. from above (greater than type)
10—19	9.5-19.5	8	8	100
20—29	19.5-29.5	14	22	92
30—39	29.5-39.5	22	44	78
40—49	39.5-49.5	29	73	56
50—59	49.5-59.5	14	87	27
60—69	59.5-69.5	07	94	19
70—79	69.5-79.5	04	98	06
80—89	79.5-89.5	02	100	02

Now, we plot cumulative frequencies (of both the types) vertically and corresponding marks obtained horizontally on a two dimensional box

Contd.

diagram and easily trace out the two required cumulative frequency curves as shown below :

The two cumulative frequency curves (i and

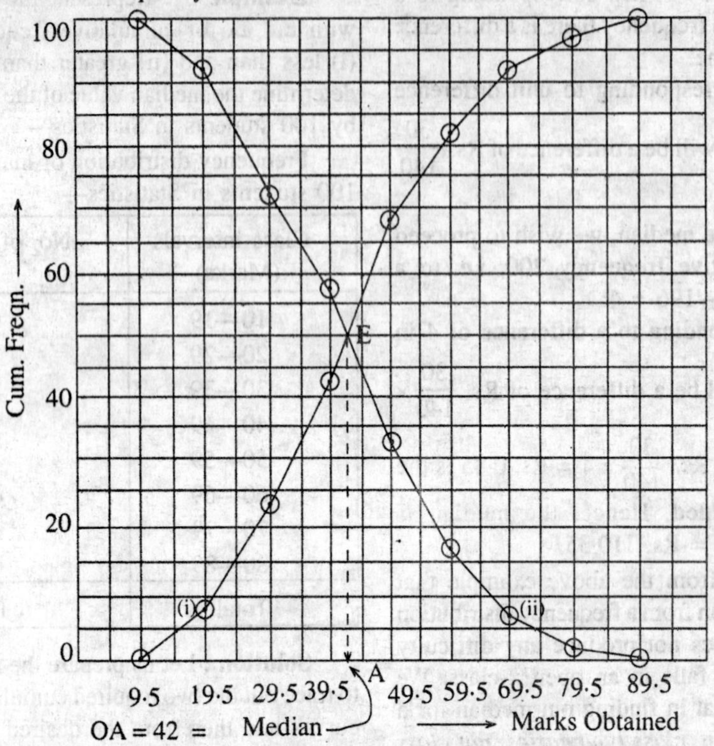

Fig. 8.1 : Cumulative Freequency Distribution

ii) are drawn from the given marks obtained by 100 students—(i) from below and (ii) from above.

We now find these two curves intersecting at point E and therefrom we get the median value for marks obtained by those 100 students as (39.5 + 02.5) = 42.0 (OA = 42)

8.7.1 Advantages and Disadvantages of Median

In some cases the median has enough advantages over the arithmetic mean. If the set of observation contains a large value or a small value then the arithmetic mean may not give the correct measure. We know that the per capita income of an Indian is too low compared to the per capita income of an American. Same is true about the per capita incomes of rich people and the poor people of India also. There exists a huge gap in income between the rich and the poor people. If incomes of the richer classes only go up largely without an increase in the incomes of the poor people, India's per capita income will go up. But such higher per income cannot be called a true representative income. In such a situation, the median value of income will be a better representative of per capita income.

The median has the following merits and demerits :

Merits :

(a) It is simple to understand, explain, and easy to calculate.

(b) It is rigidly defined.

(c) It can be calculated for an open-end distribution.

(d) It is affected by the number of observations rather than the magnitudes of the observations.

(e) It remains unaffected from extreme values.

Demerits :

(a) It is not based on all the items of the series.

(b) It is not suitable for further algebraic treatment.

(c) It is not based on all the values as it is only a positional average.

(d) It is much affected from sampling fluctuations in comparison to the arithmetic mean.

8.8 Mode

It is another effective statistical tool of measuring central tendency of a variable. For a set of observations on a discrete variable, a particular one which has the highest frequency is called its mode. The mode of a set of numbers is that value which occurs repetedly with the greatest frequency and in that sense, it is the most common value. To make it simple, let us consider the following figures:

3, 5, 8, 5, 4, 6, 5, 9, 5

Here, the mode of these numbers is 5 because it has appeared the highest time (4 times) in the series of these numbers.

However, there may not be any mode for a series having no repetition of any particular number and for some other series two or more mode values can also exist, called *bi-modal* or *tri-modal series.* In most cases, we find a single mode in a series of numbers (or frequencies), we call it an *unimodal frequency distribution.*

Practically, it is easier to determine the mode value of a variable when it is discrete in nature compared to a continuous variable. For a continuous variable, its mode value is intimately related to the value at the peak point of its frequency curve. Hence, for such kind of a variable, the primary task is to derive the frequency curve from the given data and then identify its highest value corresponding to the peak point of the curve.

But, in a number of situations, we can determine the modal value of a variable without tracing out its frequency curve by using the following formula :

$$M_0 = L_0 + \left(\frac{f_0 - f_{-1}}{2f_0 - f_{-1} - f_1} \times i\right)$$

L_0 = the lower classs limit of the modal class,

f_0 = frequency corresponding to the modal class or the maximum frequency,

f_{-1} = frequency corresponding to the class appearing just before the modal class,

f_1 = frequency corresponding to the class appearing just after the modal class,

i = length of the class intervals which are identical.

There exist two usual ways to calculate the mode value of a variable-

1. by drawing a frequency curve, and
2. by using the prescribed formula.

The method of calculation for the mode value from a grouped frequency distribution, as shown in table 8.9, may now be explained below :

Example :

Table 8.8 : Calculation for Mode Value

Weight (kg)	Class interval	Frequency
13—17	12·5—17·5	4
18—22	17·5—22·5	10
23—27	22·5—27·5	24
28—32	27·5—32·5	34
33—37	32·5—37·5	28
38—42	37·5—42·5	12
43—47	42·5—47·5	6
48—52	47·5—52·5	2

Solution : Observing the table closely, we find that the highest frequency is 34 and it is occuring within the class interval 28—32 where the class boundaries are 27·5—32·5. We can now easily detect the following values as :

$L_0 = 27{\cdot}5$, $f_0 = 34$, $f_{-1} = 24$, $f_1 = 28$ and put them in the following formula :

$$M_0 = L_0 + \left(\frac{f_0 - f_{-1}}{2f_0 - f_{-1} - f_1} \times i\right)$$

$$= 27{\cdot}50 + \frac{34 - 24}{2 \times 34 - 24 - 28} \times 5$$

$$= 27{\cdot}50 + \frac{10}{16} \times 5$$

$$= 27{\cdot}50 + 3{\cdot}12$$

$$= 30{\cdot}62$$

Therefore, the required mode value is 30·62.

In other cases, with unequal class intervals, the mode of the distribution can be determind through Karl-Pearson's common relation established as Mean–Mode = 3 (Mean–Median), provided that the mean and the median are already determined.

8.8.1 Advantages and Disadvantages of Mode

Mode is a useful measure of central tendency if the data provided are qualitative in nature. As mode is the value which has maximum concentration around, it has some distinct virtues.

Advantages : (a) The concept of mode is easier to understand.

(b) It is not affected by the extreme values of the given variable.

(c) It is often determined by inspection only, at least from a simple frequency distribution. It is very often used in business.

(d) It is also calculable from a grouped frequency distribution with open-end classes.

Disadvantages : However, the mode, as a measure of central tendency, is not free from any disadvantages. These are :

(a) It is rather difficult to findout a well-defined mode in all cases.

(b) It is not based on all the values of the given variable.

(c) It is not suitable for further algebraic treatment quite readily and easily.

(d) It is significantly influenced by sampling fluctuations.

8.9 Essential Characteristics of a Good Statistical Average

From a varied collection of data, we try to find out an average or central value as the representative of all the ite.. .. So that we can study the nature of the collection quite readily and quickly. An average, thus, should possess certain qualities. Following are the main :

(a) It should easily be understood and calculated. The AM is capable of easy calculation as compared to the GM or the HM. Futher, the median as well as the mode have also simplicity in calculations.

(b) A good average needs to be rigidly defined, i.e., the central value or the average value calculated should be unique in nature, otherwise the discretion in calculation of the average by the statisticians may creep in several errors afterwards.

(c) It should be based on all the observations. For instance, only AM depends on all the observations. Median and mode do not have this attribute.

(d) It should be capable of algebraic treatments in the sense that it should be capable of being used in further statistical computations.

(e) It should not be influenced considerably by the fluctuations of sampling.

(f) It should not be affected by the extreme values of the variable. Although median and mode are not affected by the extreme values, the AM is largely influenced by the extreme values—both large and small.

Thus, an ideal measure of average is very difficult to find out on several occasions. Section 8.10 makes an effective comparison among the different available measures of central tendency discussed earliar.

8.10 Relation among Mean, Median and Mode

The frequency distribution of a set of observations given on a variable are of two types—one is called the symmetrical or normal distribution where the mean, median and mode coincide with each other and the other is an asymmetrical one where of the mean, median and mode are different in magnitude, called skewed distribution.

In such skewed distributions, it is observed and established that they maintain a unique relation among them as :

Mean – Mode = 3 (Mean – Median),

called the Karl-Pearson's relation.

Here, we can easily find out value of one when the other two values are already known. However, this relation can be safely applied only for unimodal and moderately skewed distributions.

Again, we find that both the mean and the median satisfy the conditions of right definition and stability but regarding their calculations numerically, the median is easier to calculate than the mean. On the contrary, the general fluctuations in sampling affect median to a larger extent than the mean, although certain exceptions are also there.

Regarding algebraic treatments of these devices for measuring central tendency of a variable, the mean is definitely the better one. In a situation where several series relating to one particular common aspect are combined togethei into one, we can find out the combined average from the separate averages of various series and their number of observations. But, it can never be possible in the case of median.

For a set of given observations of a variable, the median, of course, has certain advantages over its mean. It is easily calculable and readily obtainable even without having the entire set of observations on the variable only when they are properly arranged. Besides, in some special situations, mean cannot be calculated where the extreme class intervals are left unspecified (i.e., infinite) but the median can easily be obtained from them. In fact, in many cases, the median can appear as an ideal representative on the central tendency of the observations on a variable as it remains unaffected from its extreme items.

Further, it is agreed that the mean will surely be affected due to unavoidable sampling fluctuations but not the median and in that sense the median is recognised as a more natural average to represent the given observations on the variable than its mean.

From the above discussion, we can safely conclude that it will not be wise to select a particular one as the best from the available three measures of central tendency for the given observations on a variable in all situations. Actually speaking, depending on the nature and the quality of the data given and the objective of the study, it is an important task for the user or the investigator and researcher to select the most suitable or the ideal one to meet his/her own purpose.

The mathematicians and the statisticians together, in this context, prescribe for 'mean' as the ideal one to accept in many cases than the other two. Specially, when the investigator is interested to conclude on a particular aspect provided with a given sample from its related population, the mean is undoubtedly the best one to select and use unhesitatingly.

QUESTIONS WITH ANSWER-HINTS

Long-Answer Questions

1. Explain clearly what do you mean by 'Measures of central tendency'? Define the various measures of central tendency and discuss their advantages and limitations.

Ans. 8.2, 8.2.1, 8.8.1, 8.3.5, 8,4.1 and 8.5.3

2. Discuss the relative merits of mean, median and mode—separately.

Ans. 8.3.5, 8.7.1, 8.8.1

3. Find the arithmetic means for the following two sets of observations :

(a) x : 200, 209, 216, 234, 214, 219, 212, 210, 205

(b)

Class Marks (x)	0·5	1·5	2·5	3·5	4·5	7·5	12·5	17·5	22·5	27·5
Freqn.	16	69	89	74	74	213	70	27	26	17

Ans. Follow examples (8.3.1 & 8.3.2) and do yourself.

4. Define AM GM and HM of the given observations of a variable. Interrelate them with a unique relation.

Ans. 8.3 8.4, 8.5, 8.6.

5. Define mean, median and the mode of a set of observations on a variable and interrelate them with an unique relation.

Ans. 8.3 8.7 8.8, 8.10

6. The Table given below represents the frequency distribution of weights of 80 apples selected at random from a basket :

Weights (in Gams)	Frequency
110—119	05
120—129	07
130—139	12
140—149	20
150—159	16
160—169	10
170—179	07
180—189	03

Draw the cumulative frequency diagram and calculate the median weight of an apple.

Ans. 147·5, Cumulative frequency : 40

Follow Table 8.7, Fig. 8.1.

7. The AM calculated from the following distribution is 64·45 inches. Find F_3 and comment on it :

Ht (inches) :	60-62	63-65	66-68	69-71	72-74
Frequency :	15	54	F_3	83	24

Ans. A = 67, F_3 = 126.

8. The Arithmetic Mean of 30 observations was found to be 20. After the Arithmetic Mean was computed, it was found that 4 of the observations were wrongly recorded as 19, 21, 15, and 1. Find the correct Arithmetic Mean if these incorrect observations are omitted.

Ans. Follow 8.3.1 (Ex. 3)

9. In a surveywork, a firm employed 50 men and 20 women on full-time basis and 10 men on part-time basis.

A woman's work was considered three-fourth as effective as that of a man's and part-time work as effective as half of full-time work. A man employed on full-time basis gets Rs. 3,000 per month. What is the average monthly salary for the group of 80 workers?

Ans. 8.3.1 and Ex. 5

10. The mean salary of a group of 100 men was Rs. 700. The average salary of 10 highest salaried men of the group was Rs. 1,000 and that of 20 lowest salaried men was Rs. 100. Find the average salary of the other 70 men of the group.

Ans. 8.3.3, Ex. 5

11. The average marks obtained in an examination by two groups of boys was 80. If these boys are separated into two groups, the average marks for the first group was 75 and for the second group 85. Determine the ratio of the boys in the two groups.

Ans. 8.3.3 and Ex. 5

12. (a) Find the missing freequencies in the following frequency distribution when it is known that the AM $(\bar{x})$ = 11.09.

Class Limits (x)	Frequency
09·3—09·7	2
09·8—10·2	5
10·3—10·7	f_3
10·8—11·2	f_4
11·3—11·7	14
11·8—12·2	6
12·3—12·7	3
12·8—13·2	1
Total	60

(b) Find also the GM of the above distribution and mention its various uses.

Ans. Ex. 3, Table 8.4

13. For the two frequency distributions given below the Mean calculated from the first was 31·80 and from the second was 34·17. Find the values of f_4 and f_5.

Marks	1st Group No. of boys	2nd Group No. of boys
10—20	5	2
20—30	5	8
30—40	10	6
40—50	f_4	$2f_4$
50—60	f_5	f_5

Ans. Ex. 3

14. Find the Arithmetic Mean of the following distribution by its suitable subdivision into groups using the formula for mean of a combined group:

Age at Death yrs.	1	2	3	4-6	7-9	10-12	13-20	21-28	29-36
Freqn.	10	5	3	9	6	2	1	10	13

Ans. 8.3.3, Ex. 5

15. The frequency distribution of income (in Rs.) of the employees of an industrial concern in two different periods are given below.

Income (Rs.)	Frequency	
	Period I	Period II
0—50	90	200
50—100	150	400
100—150	100	120
150—200	80	100
200—250	70	150
250 and over	10	30
Total	500	1000

The total income of the 10 employees in the class over Rs. 250 in period I is Rs. 3,000, and that of 30 in period II is Rs. 18,000.

(a) Compute the Mean, Median and Modal values for both the periods.

(b) Write a brief note on the relative economic conditions of the employees in the two periods.

(c) Every employee belonging to the top 25 p.c. of the earners is required to pay 1 p.c. of his income to a workers' relief fund. Estimate the increase in contribution to this fund from period I to period II.

Ans. 8.3.2, 8.7 (Ex. 3 & 4), 8.8 (Table 8.8)

16. (a) Find the Geometric Mean of 2, 4, 8, 64.

(b) The GM. HM, and AM of three observations being 3.63, 3.27 and 4 respectively. Find the observations.

Ans. 8.4 (Ex.), 8.6

17. A firm buys Rs. 10, 000 of plant and equipment in Jan., 1980 and arranges the cost and depreciation according to the following schedule :

Category	Cost (Rs.)	Depreciation (on reducing balance)
A	6,000	6 p.c.
B	3,000	3 p.c.
C	1,000	1 p.c.

Find the average depreciation rates for 1980.

Ans. [**Hint.** Cost to be used as weights.] 8.3.2

18. Define Harmonic Mean and describe its various uses. Find the Harmonic Means for the following two sets of observations :

(a) 9, 6, 2, 3, 4.

(b)

Mid. x	1	2	3	4	5
Freq.	10	20	40	6	4

Ans. 8.5, 8.5.2

19. If M, H and G represent the Arithmetic Mean, Harmonic Mean and Geometric Mean of two observations x_1 and x_2, prove that $G^2 = HM$

Ans. 8.6

20. Define Mode and state when it is a suitable average to use? Discuss its limitations.

Ans. 8.8, 8.8.1

21. A man travels at 3 miles per hour to a certain place and comes back at 4 miles per hour What is his average speed?

Ans. 8.3.3 (Table 8.3)

22. A car travels a distance of 100 miles at a speed 50 m.p.h. and 160 miles at 40 m.p.h. What is the average speed of the car?

Ans. Follow 8.3.3 (Composite Mean).

CHAPTER 9

Measures of Dispersion

9.1 Dispersion—Meaning and Classification

While making any data analysis from the observations given on a variable, we, very often, observe that the degree or extent of variation of the observations individually from their central value (mean, median or mode) is not the same and hence becomes much relevant and important from the statistical point of view. The necessity is keenly felt in different fields like economic and business analysis and forecasting, while dealing with daily weather conditions, etc, specially in making predictions for future purposes. The statisticians here prescribe for an wellknown concept "dispersion" or the scatteredness or variability of the values of the variable usually from their arithmetic mean. More precisely, it measures the degree of variability in the given observation on a variable from their central value (usually the mean or the median).

While going in detail into the study of it, we find a number of opinions and definions given by different renowned personalities like Prof. A. L. Bowley, Prof. L. R. Cannon, Prog. Spiegel, etc. as their own. In this context, we think the definition given by Prof. Yule and Kendall is well accepted, complete and comprehensive in nature as it includes all the important characteristics for an ideal measure of dispersion. According to them, it should be based on all the given observations, should be readily comprehensible, fairly and easily calculable, be affected as little as possible by sampling fluctuations and amenable to further algebraic treatments. The following are thus unhesitatingly considered as important characteristics for an ideal measure of dispersion.

(a) It should be rigidly defined. (b) It should be easy to calculate and easily understandable. (c) It should be calculated considering all the available observations. (d) It should be amenable to further mathematical treatments. (e) It should be least affected from sampling flactuations.

9.2 The Usual Measures of Dispersion

The usual measures of dispersion, very often suggested by the statisticians, are exhibited with the aid of the following chart :

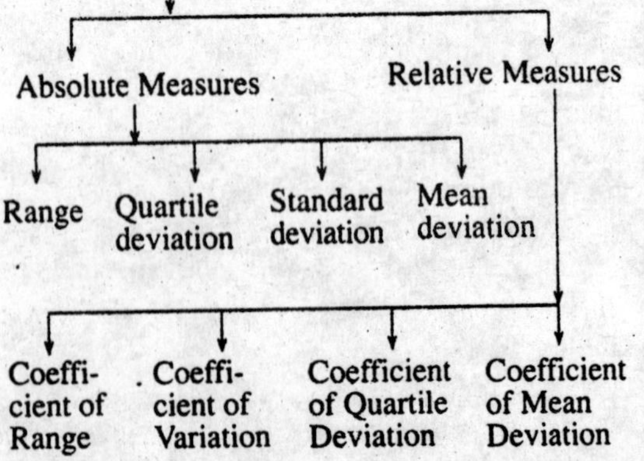

Primarily, we use two separate devices for measuring dispersion of a variable. One is aAlgebraic method and the other is Graphical method. In the algebraic method we use different notations and definitions to measure it in a number of ways and in the graphical method we try to measure the variability of the given observations graphically mainly through scattered diagrames and by fitting different lines through those scattered points. In the Algebraic method we split them up into two main categories, one is Absolute measure and the other is Relative measure. Under the Absolute measure we again have four separate measures, namely Range, Quartile Deviation, Standard Deviation and the Mean Deviation. And finally, under the Relative measure, we have four other measures termed as Coefficient of Range, Coefficient of Variation, Coefficient of Quartile Deviation and the Coeffi-cient of Mean Deviation.

9.2.1 Absolute Measures of Dispersion

I. Range : The simplest and the easiest method of measuring dispersion of the values of a variable is the Range. It is measured just as the difference between the highest and the lowest values of a variable. The extent of dispersion increases as the divergence between the highest and the lowest values of the variable increases. We thus express the magnitude of Range as—

Range = (highest value – lowest value) of the variable.

For determining Range of a variable, it is necessary to arrange the values in an increasing order.

It will enable us to avoid mistakes in calculation and give us the best result.

Let us consider two separate examples below considering both the grouped and the ungrouped data separately.

Example 1 : Consider the following series of numbers—

1, 2, 4, 6, 8, 10, 12.

Solution : Here, the highest value of the series is 12 and the lowest is 1.

Therefore, the Range = 12 – 1 = 11

i.e. the values of the variable are scattered within 11 units.

Example 2 : For the data presented with their respective frequencies, the idea is to measure the same as the difference between the mid-values of the two marginal classes. Consider the following table—

X	0-9	10-19	20-29	30-39	40-49	50-59
f	4	7	11	6	8	10

Here, the two marginal classes are 50—59 and 0—9

$\therefore$ Their mid values are $\frac{50+59}{2} = \frac{109}{2}$

$= 54{\cdot}5$ and $\frac{9+0}{2} = 4{\cdot}5$

The required Range is 54·5–4·5 = 50 or the observations on the variable are found scattered within 50 units.

It is to be noted that any change in the marginal values or the classes of the variable in the series given will change both the absolute and the percentage values of the Range.

At times of necessity, we express the relative value of the Range without computing its absolute value and there we use the formula below—

Relative value of the Range

$$= \frac{\text{Highest value} - \text{Lowest value}}{\text{Highest value} + \text{Lowest value}}$$

In our first example the relative value of the Range is $= \frac{12-1}{12+1} = \frac{11}{13} = 0{\cdot}84.$

The 'Range', as a measure of 'Dispersion', has a number of advantages and disadvantage. The concept of Range is, no doubt, simple and easy enough to calculate, specially when the observations are arranged in an increasing order But the main disadvantage is that it is calculated only on the basis of the heighest and the lowest values of the variable without giving any importance to the other values. Therefore, the result can only be influenced with changes in those two values, not by any other value of the variable. Again, in the case of a complex distribution of a variable with respective frequencies, it is not much easy to calculate the value of Range correctly in the above way. For all these reasones, Range as a measure of the variability of the values of a variable, is not widely accepted and spontaneously prescribed by the Statisticians of today. However, it is not totally rejected even today as it has certain traditional acceptabilities like representing temparate variations in a day by recording the maximum and the minimum values regularly by the weather department, while imposing controlling measures against wide fluctuations in the market prices of the essential goods and services bought and sold by the common people while imposing Price-control and Rationning measures through Public Sector Regulations, mainly to protect interests of both the buyers and sellers simultaneously.

II. Quartile Deviation : While measuring the degree of variability of a variable Quartile Deviation is claimed to be another useful device and an improved one in the sense it gives equal importance or weightage to all the observations of the variable. Here the given observations are classified into four equal quartiles with the notations Q_1, Q_2, Q_3 and Q_4. The average value of the difference between the third and the first quartiles is termed as the Quartile Deviation. Symbolically, we write—

$$\text{Quartile Deviation} = \frac{Q_3 - Q_1}{2}$$

Through this measure it is ensured that at least 50% of the observations on the variable are used in the calculation process and with this method the absolute value of the Quartile Deviation can easily be measured. For determining the proportionate Quartile Deviation, also called the Coefficient of Quartile Deviation, we use the following formula—

Coefficient of Quartile Deviation—

$$CQD = \frac{\frac{Q_3 - Q_1}{2}}{\frac{Q_3 + Q_1}{2}} = \frac{Q_3 - Q_1}{Q_3 + Q_1}$$

Consider the following examples—

Example 1 : Calculate the Quartile Deviation and Co-efficient of Quartile Deviation from the following data—

8, 10, 12, 14, 16, 18, 20.

Solution : Here, n = 7, the first and third quartiles are—

$Q_1 = \frac{n+1}{4} = \frac{7+1}{4} = 2$ i.e. the second number in the series or $Q_1 = 10$

$Q_3 = \frac{3(n+1)}{4} = \frac{3(7+1)}{4} = \frac{3 \times 8}{4} = 6$, i.e., the 6th number in the given series,

or $Q_3 = 18$

$$\therefore \text{Q.D.} = \frac{Q_3 - Q_1}{2} = \frac{18-10}{2} = \frac{8}{2} = 4$$

Co-efficient of Q.D. =

$$= \frac{Q_3 - Q_1}{Q_3 + Q_1} = \frac{18-10}{18+10} = \frac{8}{28} = 0 \cdot 28$$

Example 2 : Determine the QD and CQD from the following grouped data—

X	16	28	33	43	65	80
f	4	7	15	8	9	2

Solution : In order to determine the values of QD and Co-efficient of QD Let us prepare the following table—

Grouped frequency distribution of X with corresponding cumulative frequencies (F_α)

Table 9.1

X	f	Cuf or F_α
16	4	4
28	7	11
33	15	26
43	8	34
65	9	43
80	2	45
	N = 45	

Here, $Q_1 = \frac{N+1}{4} = \frac{45+1}{4} = \frac{46}{4} = 11.50$

or $Q_1 = 28$

$Q_3 = \frac{3(N+1)}{4} = \frac{3 \times 46}{4} = \frac{138}{4} = 34 \cdot 50$

or $Q_3 = 43$

$$\therefore QD = \frac{Q_3 - Q_1}{2} = \frac{43-28}{2} = \frac{15}{2} = 7.50$$

$$CQD = \frac{Q_3 - Q_1}{Q_3 + Q_1} = \frac{43-28}{43+28} = \frac{15}{71} = 0.21$$

Advantages and disadvantages of Quartile Deviation—

Advantages

(a) Quartile Deviation is easy to calculate numerically.

(b) Calculation for QD involves only the first and the third Quartiles.

(c) It can be used safely as a suitable measure of dispersion at all situations.

(d) It remains unaffected from the extreme values of the variable.

(e) It can be calculated readily from frequency distributions with the open end classess.

(f) QD at least is a better measure of dispersion compared to Range.

Disadvantages

(a) Quartile deviation as a measure of dispersion is not much popularly prescribed by the statisticians.

(b) It is used only in rare cases.

(c) It is not a reliable measure of dispersion as it ignores almost (50%) of the data.

III. Standard Deviation (SD) : The concept of SD as a successful measure of dispersion was introduced by the renowned statistician Karl Pearson in the year 1893 and it is still recognised as the most important absolute measure of dispersion.

SD of a set of observations on a variable is defined as the square root of the arithmetic mean of the squares of deviations from their arithmetic mean. In other words it is termed as 'The Root-Mean-Squared-Deviations from the AM" Again, it is often denoted as the positive square root of the variance of a group of observations on a variable.

It is usually expressed by the Greek small letter 'σ' (pronounced as Sigma) and measured for the information without having frequencies as-

$$\sigma = \sqrt{\frac{\sum(x_i - \bar{x})^2}{n}} = \sqrt{\frac{1}{n}\Sigma(x_i - \bar{x})^2}$$

Where i = 1, 2, 3,... n

Here, x_i = n number of observations on the variable x i.,e x_1, x_2, x_3 ....x_n

$\bar{x}$ = AM of the observations on the variable x.

n = Total number of observations.

But, for the data having their respective frequencies, it should be measured as—

$$\sigma = \sqrt{\frac{1}{N}\sum f_i(x_i - \bar{x})^2}$$

$$= \sqrt{\frac{\sum f_i D_i^2}{N} - \left(\frac{\sum f_i D_i}{N}\right)^2}$$

where, $N = f_1 + f_2 + f_3 + \cdots + f_n$ are the respective frequencies of the variable values x_1, x_2, x_3 ..... x_n and $D_i = x_i - \bar{x}$.

The following five successive steps are to be followed while computing SD from a group of information given on a variable :

(i) For the data without having their corresponding frequencies, we should first compute their Arithmetic Mean as : $\bar{x} = \frac{\sum x_i}{n}$ (i=1, 2, 3,..., n)

(ii) Then we are to determine the differences between the values of the variable and their AM calculated as :

$(x_1 - \bar{x})$, $(x_2 - \bar{x})$, $(x_3 - \bar{x})$ and so on up to $(x_n - \bar{x})$

(iii) In the third step we are to find out squares of those differences and add them up to the last one as :

$$\sum_{i=1}^{n}(x_i - \bar{x})^2 = (x_1 - \bar{x})^2 + (x_2 - \bar{x})^2 + \cdots + (x_n - \bar{x})^2$$

(iv) Next to the above, in the fourth step we are to determine the AM of the above squared values as :

$$\frac{1}{n}\sum_{i=1}^{n}(x_i - \bar{x})^2$$

(v) And finally, we are to determine the square root of the AM of the above squared values as :

$$\sigma = \sqrt{\frac{1}{n}\Sigma(x_i - \bar{x})^2}$$

(vi) For the data presented with their respective frequencies, the method will be slightly different as :

$$\sigma = \sqrt{\frac{1}{N}\sum f_i(x_i - \bar{x})^2}$$

Here, $N = f_1 + f_2 + f_3 + \cdots + f_n$ and they are the frequencies of $x_1, x_2, x_3, \cdots, x_n$.

Like the other measures of dispersion SD also has a number of advantages and disadvantages of its own. Let us enlist them in order below :

Advantages :

(a) Calculation of SD involves all the values of the given variable.
(b) It uses AM of the given data as an important component which is simply computable.
(c) It is least affected by sampling flac-tuations.
(d) It is easily usable and capable of further Mathematical treatments.
(e) It is well defined.
(f) It is taken as the most reliable and dependable device for measuring dispersion or the variability of the given values of a variable.
(g) Statisticians very often prescribe SD as the true measure of dispersion of a series of information.
(h) It can tactfully avoid the complecation of considering negative algebraic sign while calcu-lating deviations.

Disadvantages :

(a) It involves complecated and laborious numerical calculations specially when the information are large enough.
(b) The concept of SD is neither easy to take up, nor much simple to calculate.
(c) It is considerably affected by the extreme values of the given variable.
(d) To compute SD correctly, the method claims much moments, money and manpower.

Therefore, the SD possesses almost all the prerequisites of a good measure of dispersion and hence it has become the most familier, important and widely used device for measuring dispersion for a set of values on a given variable.

Example 1: Calculate SD of the following numbers :

20, 85, 120, 60 and 401

Solution : We can represent AM of the given numbers as :

$$\text{AM } (\bar{x}) = \frac{20+85+120+60+40}{5} = \frac{325}{5} = 65$$

Now, we calculate the desired SD through the following exercise—

Table 9.2 : Calculation for SD with the Aid of the given Data

Numbers (x)	$D_i = x_i - \bar{x}$	D^2
20	– 45	2025
85	20	400
120	55	3025
60	–5	25
40	–25	625
$\Sigma xi = 320$		$\Sigma D^2 = 6100$

$$\text{Here, } \bar{x} = \frac{\Sigma xi}{n} = \frac{320}{5} = 65$$

$$\therefore \text{ The required SD} = \sqrt{\frac{\Sigma D_i^2}{n}}$$

$$= \sqrt{\frac{6100}{5}} = \sqrt{1220} = 34{\cdot}93.$$

Example 2 : Find the SD for the following distribution :

x	1	2	3	4	5	6	7
f	10	20	30	35	14	10	2

Solution : To calculate SD of the given distribution, we reconstruct the following table :

Table 9.3 : Calculation for SD

x	f	$D_i = x_i - \bar{x}$	fD	fD^2
1	10	–3	–30	90
2	20	–2	–40	80
3	30	–1	–30	30
4	35	0	0	0
5	14	1	14	14
6	10	2	20	40
7	2	3	6	18
	N = 121	ΣD_i	$\Sigma fD = -60$	$\Sigma fD^2 = 272$

The required SD-

$$= \sqrt{\frac{\Sigma fD^2}{N} - \left(\frac{\Sigma fD}{N}\right)^2}$$

$$= \sqrt{\frac{272}{121} - \left(\frac{-60}{121}\right)^2}$$

$$= \sqrt{2.25 - 0.2401} = 1.41.$$

IV. Mean Deviation : Practically speaking, the Range and the Quartile deviation separately can not provide us the actual measurement of the variability of the values of a variable from their mean because they can not ideally express the central value and the extent of scatterdness of those values around their average value. Moreover, these measures are not prepared on the basis of all the observations given for the variable. In order to avoid such limitations, we use another better method (as it is claimed) of dispersion known as the 'Mean Deviation'.

Conventionally, it is denoted by another Greek small letter Delta (Δ), also known as the 'average deviation.'

By definition it is the Arithmetic mean of the absolute deviations of the individual values of the given variable from their average value (normally the mean or the median). It is thus considered as an Absolute Measure of Dispersion.

Method of Computation

Consider x to be a variable having n number of observations as $x_1, x_2, x_3, \cdots, x_n$ and A to be its arithmetic mean or the middle most value i.e. the median, then the absolute (or positive) values of the deviations of all these observations from A and their sum can be represented as :

$$\Sigma|x_i - A| = |x_1 - A| + |x_2 - A| + \cdots + |x_n - A|$$

The Mean Deviation is therefore,

$$MD = \frac{\sum|x_i - A|}{n} = \frac{1}{n}\Sigma\,|\,x_i - A\,|$$

If A = AM = $\bar{x}$,

Then, $MD = \frac{1}{n}\Sigma|x_i - \bar{x}|$

Where i = 1, 2, 3, · · ·, n

If the variable x is represented with the values $x_1, x_2, \cdots x_n$, and their respective frequencies are $f_1, f_2, \cdots, f_n$ then their Mean Deviation can be represented as-

$$MD = \frac{\sum f_i|x_i - \bar{x}|}{N} = \frac{1}{N}\Sigma f_i|x_i - \bar{x}|$$

Where $N = f_1 + f_2 + f_3 + \ldots + f_n$

$$= \sum_{i=1}^{n} f_i$$

As it can be proved that-

$\sum_{i=1}^{n}(x_i - \bar{x}) = 0$, therefore, to make the result valid and meaningful to explain the reality, we are adviced to take only the absolute or positive values of all these deviations noted above.

Advantages of the MD :

(a) On many occasions it gives fairly good results to represent the degree of variability or the extent of dispersion of the given values of a variable as it takes separately all the observations given into account.

(b) It can also be calculated about the median value of those observations as their central value and then it gives us the minimum value for the MD

(c) In usual situations, it is calculated taking deviations from the easily computable aritmetic mean of the given observations on the variable.

(d) It is easy to calculate numerically and simple to understand.

Disadvantages of the MD :

(a) The main complain against this measure is that it ignores the algebraic signs of the deviations.

(b) It is not generally computed taking deviations from the mode value and thereby disregards it as another important average value of the variable.

(c) It is rarely used in practical purposes.

Example 1 :

(i) Calculate mean deviation about Arithmetic Mean of the following numbers :

35, 70, 15, 75, 30, 50

Solution : Let us arrange the numbers in an increasing order as 15, 30, 35, 50, 70, 75 and compute their AM as-

$$AM = \frac{15+30+35+50+70+75}{6} = \frac{275}{6}$$

= 45.83.

Now, we convert the data into :

Table 9.4 : Calculation for Mean Deviation

x	$X_i - X$
15	30.83
30	15.83
35	10.83
50	4.17
70	24.17
75	29.17
x=6	$\Sigma \lvert x_i - \bar{x} \rvert = 115.00$

$$\therefore MD = \frac{1}{n} \Sigma \lvert X_i - \bar{x} \rvert = \frac{115.00}{6} = 19.16$$

Example 2 : Calculate the Mean Deviation for the following data :

Height (inches)	60	61	62	63	64	65	66	67	68
No. of boys	2	0	15	29	25	12	10	4	3

Solution : To calculate MD of the given distribution, we construct the following table :

Table 9.5 : Calculation for Mean Deviation

Height (inches)	No. of boys (f)	Dev. from (a=64)	Product	$(x_i - \bar{x})$	$f_i(x_i - \bar{x})$
60	2	– 4	– 8	3.89	7.78
61	0	– 3	0	2.89	0
62	15	– 2	– 30	1.89	28.35
63	29	– 1	– 29	0.89	25.81
64	25	0	0	0.11	2.75
65	12	1	12	1.11	13.32
66	10	2	20	2.11	21.10
67	4	3	12	3.11	12.44
68	3	4	12	4.11	12.33
	N=100		-11		123.88

Arithmetic Mean (AM) or $\bar{x} = a + \frac{\sum fx}{N} \times c$

$$= 64 + \frac{-11}{100} \times 1 = 63.89$$

$$MD = \frac{\Sigma f_i(x_i - \bar{x})}{N} = \frac{123.88}{100}$$

$$= 1.23$$

9.2.2 Relative Measures of Dispersion

While studying the variability of the observations of a variable, we usually use the absolute measures of dispersion namely the Range, Quartile deviation, Mean deviation and Standard deviation. But, the results of such measures are obtained in terms of the units in which the observations are available and hence they are not comparable with each other. Moreover, the results of the absolute measure gets affected by the number of observations obtainable on the given variable as they consider only the positive differences from their central value (Mean/Median).

To eliminate all these deficiencies in the measurement of variability of the observations on a variable, we accept and introduce in respective situations the very concept of the Relative measures of dispersion as they are independent of their own units of measurement and hence they are compa-rable and again can be examined under a common scale when they are expressed in unitary terms. Here lies the superiority of the Relative Measures over the Absolute Measures of dispersion.

The usual Relative Measures of Dispersion are :

(i) Coefficient of Range

$$= \frac{\text{Range}}{\text{Highest value} + \text{Lowest value}} \times 100$$

(ii) Coefficient of Variation

$$= \frac{\text{Standard Deviation}}{\text{Mean}} \times 100$$

(iii) Coefficient of Quartile Deviation

$$= \frac{\text{Quartile Deviation}}{\text{Median}} \times 100$$

(iv) Coefficient of Mean Deviation

$$= \frac{\text{Mean Deviation}}{\text{Mean or Median}} \times 100$$

Among these four coefficients stated above the Coefficient of Variation is widely accepted and used in almost all practical situations mainly because of its accuracy and hence its approximation to explain the reality.

Example 1 : Determine the Coefficient of Range for the marks obtained by a student in various subjects given below :

Subjects	Marks obtained
Beng.	40
Eng.	42
Bus. Org.	50
Econ.	45
Acct.	52

Solution : Here, the highest and the lowest marks are 52 and 40 respectively.

Hence, Range = 52 – 40 = 12.

$$\text{The Coeff. of Range} = \frac{12}{52+40}\times 100$$

$$= \frac{12}{92}\times 100 = 13.04.$$

Example 2 : The performances of two Batsmen S and R in five successive one-day cricket matches are given below. Identify the batsman who is more consistant :

S	32	48	71	05	40
R	19	47	67	06	101

Solution : Here, we can use 'Coefficient of Variation' as the best measure of dispersion to identify the more consistant one having lesser variation. As the components of CV, we are to derive first the Mean and the Standard Deviation of the scores obtained by the two Batsmen separately using the following usual notations :

$y = x - c$ or, $y + c = x$ or $\bar{x} = c + \bar{y}$ and $\delta x = \delta y$.

Let us prepare the following table for finding out Mean and SD of the given information.

Table 9.6 : Calculation for Mean and Standard Deviation

x	y=x-50	y^2	x	y=x-50	y^2
32	–18	324	19	–31	961
48	–2	4	47	–3	9
71	21	441	67	17	289
5	5	2025	6	–54	1036
40	–10	100	101	51	2601
Total	–54	2894	Total	20	5786

For the player S :

$$\text{Mean} = 50 + \left(\frac{-54}{5}\right) = 50 - \frac{54}{5}$$

$$= \frac{250-54}{5} = \frac{196}{5} = 39.20$$

$$\text{SD} = \sqrt{\frac{2894}{5} - \left(\frac{-54}{5}\right)^2}$$

$$= \sqrt{578.80 - 116.64} = \sqrt{462.16}$$

$$= 21.50$$

$$\text{We know, CV} = \frac{\text{S.D.}}{\text{Mean}}\times 100$$

$$= \frac{21\cdot 50}{39\cdot 20}\times 100 = \frac{215000}{3920} = \frac{21500}{392} = 54.84.$$

For the player R :

$$\text{Mean} = 50 + \frac{20}{5} = 50 + 4 = 54$$

$$\text{SD} = \sqrt{\frac{5786}{5} - \left(\frac{20}{5}\right)^2} = \sqrt{1157.20 - 16}$$

$$= \sqrt{1153.20} = 36.30$$

$$\text{CV} = \frac{36.30}{54}\times 100 = 67.22$$

For the cricketer S the Coefficient of Variation is smaller and hence he is more consistant.

Example 3 : Calculate the Coefficient of Quartile Deviation from the following data :

CL. Intv.	10-15	15-20	20-25	25-30	30-40	40-50	50-60	60-70
Freq.	6	10	15	22	12	9	4	2

Solution : To calculate the required CQD from the given data, let us proceed in the following way :

Table 9.7 : Calculation for Quartile Deviation

Class Int.	Freq. (of)	Cumulative Freq.
10—15	6	6
15—20	10	16
20—25	15	31
25—30	22	53
30—40	12	65
40—50	9	74
50—60	4	78
60—70	2	80
Total	N = 80	

Here, $Q_1 = \frac{N}{4} = \frac{80}{4} = 20$, $Q_3 = \frac{3N}{4} = \frac{3\times80}{4} = 60$, $Q_2 = \frac{2N}{4} = \frac{N}{2} = \frac{80}{2} = 40.$

We know,

$$Q_1 = L_1 + \frac{\frac{N}{4} - cf}{f_m} \times (L_2 - L_1)$$

$$= 20 + \frac{20-15}{16}(25\text{–}20) = 20 + \frac{25}{16}$$

$$= 21.56$$

$$Q_3 = L_1 + \frac{\frac{3N}{4} - c_f}{f_m} \times (L_2 - L_1)$$

$$= 30 + \frac{60-12}{53}(40 - 30)$$

$$= 30 + \frac{48}{53} \times 10 = 30 + 9.05 = 39.05$$

$$Q_2 = L_1 + \frac{\frac{N}{2} - C_f}{f_m} \times (L_2 - L_1)$$

$$= 25 + \frac{42-22}{31} \times (30 - 25)$$

$$= 25 + \frac{18}{31} \times 5 = 25 + \frac{90}{31}$$

$$= 25 + 2.90 = 27.90 \text{ (Median)}$$

Now, Quartile Deviation $= \frac{Q_3 - Q_1}{2}$

$$= \frac{39.05 - 21.56}{2} = 8.74$$

and the Coefficient of Quartile Deviation

$$= \frac{\text{Quartile Deviation}}{\text{Median}} \times 100$$

$$= \frac{8.74}{27.90} \times 100 = 31.35.$$

Example 4 : Compute the Coefficient of Mean-Deviation for the following data :

x	50	51	52	53	54	55	56	57	58
f	2	0	15	29	25	12	10	4	3

To calculate the coefficient of MD we take up the following technique.

Solution : Calculation for the Coefficient of Mean-Deviation.

Table 9.8

x	f	Dev. from 54 x–54=x′	x.′f	$\lvert x-\bar{x}\rvert$	$\lvert f(x-\bar{x})\rvert$
50	2	– 4	–8	3.89	7.78
51	0	–3	0	2.89	0
52	15	–2	–30	1.89	28.35
53	29	–1	–29	0.89	25.81
54	25	0	0	0.11	2.75
55	12	1	12	1.11	13.32
56	10	2	20	2.11	21.10
57	4	3	12	3.11	12.44
58	3	4	12	4.11	12.33
Total	N=100		–11		123.88

$$\text{AM } (\bar{x}) = a + \frac{\sum fx'}{N} \times C = 54 + \frac{-11}{100} \times 1$$

$$= 53.89$$

$$\therefore \text{ the Mean Deviation} = \frac{\Sigma\lvert f(x-\bar{x})\rvert}{N}$$

$$= \frac{123.88}{100} = 1.2388 = 1.23$$

∴ Coefficient of Mean Deviation

$$= \frac{MD}{AM} \times 100$$

$$= \frac{1.23}{53.89} \times 100 = .0228 \times 100 = 2.28.$$

9.3 A Comparative Analysis among the Usual Measures of Dispersion (Range, Quartile Deviation, Mean Deviation and Standard Deviation)

It has already been stated at the very begining of this chapter that the statisticians together unanimously opines that an ideal measure of dispersion should possess certain necessary characteristics. Let us now enlist them below :

(a) The principle followed and the formula used for measuring the result should easily be understandable.

(b) The numerical value of the required dispersion should easily be computable.

(c) The definition and the concept of dispersion should be complete and comprehensive enough.

(d) The algebraic treatment used in the process should easily be applicable elsewhere.

(e) The relevant measure of dispersion should try to include all the values of the given variable.

(f) The result finally achived should be least affected by sampling flactuations.

On the basis of the above characteristics we now can examine chronologically the usual measures of dispersion and identify the best one in the following way :

In the light of the above criteria when we examine Range as a measure of dispersion, we find that it is no doubt easy to calculate but does not include all the values of the given variable and further algebraic treatments can not be applied with it in other Statistical analyses. Again, the concept of Range cannot provide us any idea about the nature of distribution of the concerned variable and practically it is not possible for us to determine the final result for openend classess. For these limitations, the method is not widely accepted and applied in all cases.

Compared to Range, Quartile Deviation, no doubt, is a better measure of dispersion and it is also easy to calculate. While computing the result it involves larger information than the Range. The result will not be affected even when the distribution has an open end. Again, it has least possibility to be affected remarkable by an individual high value of the given variable. However, the method neither include all the values of the variable given in the exercise, nor it is suitable for further algebraic treatments. For all these reasons the method has its limited uses.

The Mean Deviation, for its own qualities, is considered as an improved measure of dispersion over Range and Quartile deviation as it is able to provide us a clear understanding on the very concept of dispersion for the given values of a variable quite easily. It is not only easy to compute, it takes into account all the given values of the variable and again the final result remains almost unaffected from any remarkably high value of the variable under consideration. When we use the Arithmetic mean instead of the Median in the process of calculation, we get a rough idea on the nature of distribution of the series of observations given for the concerned variable. But the greatest objection against this measure is that it considers only the absolute values of the differences in between the individual observations and their Mean or Median and thereby further algebraic treatment with it becomes impossible. Again, the use of Median while measuring dispersion of the values of a variable produces incorrect result on many occasions because computation of the Median value from the given observations usually include considerable errors when the observations represent wide disperity among themselves.

The Standard Deviation, as a complete and comprehensive measure of dispersion, is well accepted by the statisticians specially because it possesses simultaneously all the qualities unhesitatingly which are required for an ideal measure of dispersion. Its definition is complete and comprehensive in nature and it involves all the given observations of the variable. Further algebraic treatments can also be applied easily with the result obtained afterwards. If we are provided with homogeneous or equivalent observations on two or more but not on unlimited number of variables with their own standard deviations, we can easily derive their combined standard deviation.

The only argument against this measure is that it requires enough numerical exercise to complete the entire procedure and it is thus much labourious and time consuming compared to the other measures of dispersion mentioned earlier. However, it is used widely and unhesitatingly in various statistical enquiries in different fields today.

9.4 Lorenz Curve—The Curve of Concentration

To study the exact nature of a distribution of a variable provided with a number of observations on it and to specify its degree of concentration (if any), the 'Lorenz Curve' is a powerful statistical device. This type of a curve is often used as a graphical method of measuring divergence from the average value due to inequitable concentration of data. It is thus known as the 'Curve of Concentration'. Statistically speaking, it is a cumulative percentage curve which shows the percentage of items against the corresponding percentage of the different factors distributed among the items.

With a view to tracing out such a curve, the given observations are first arranged in a systematic tabular form with their respective frequencies and the dependent and independent variable values are cumulated chronologically and finally transformed into percentages in successive columns and plotted on a two dimensional squared graph paper. The locus of those points ultimately trace out the desired 'Lorenz Curve'.

Economists and other social scientists very often opine that inequalify in the distribution of income and wealth among the individuals in a society is a common phenomenon today all over the world mainly due to our aimless and unbalanced growth policies framed by the concerned authorities, called 'growth without development' today in economics, resulting in rise in GDP but no significant rise in the percapita income of the people at large. To study the extent or the degree of economic inequality prevailing among the people of various professional categories, construction of a 'Lorenz Curve' and estimation of the 'Gini Co-efficient' is the order of the day as it helps the planners to take effective future development policies for the people indiscriminatly. Let us offer a suitable example of it to measure such a degree of income inequality persisting among the weavers of Nadia, W.B. from a research paper relevent in this context.

9.5 Measurement of Economic Inequality among the Weavers of Nadia, W.B.

Here, we are interested to study the nature and the exact degree of economic inequality persisting among these workforce. This is usually displayed in terms of inequalities existing in the distribution of income and wealth among the people under consideration. Let us analyse this phenomenon in terms of a study based on the distribution of personal incomes of the chosen sample respondents that is how the total income of the entire workforce is shared by the different income classes. The wellknown statistical device to exhibit this kind of a ground level reality is to trace out a 'Lorenz-Curve', also called the Curve of Concentration and measure the exact nature and degree of economic inequality existing among the weavers of Nadia with the aid of **'GINI-COEFFICIENT'**, an unit free positive fraction (lying in between 0 and 1).

Let us represent our numerical findings in this context from the available data in the following tabular form :

Inequality Table

Showing degree of income inequality among the weavers of Nadia, W.B.

Table 9.9

Sample Respondents classified into Income Classes by Rank	Mid value	Percentage share of income	Cumulative percentage of Income Classes	Cumulative % age of income	Extent of Inequality
1	2	3	4	5	6
(0—20) Lowest one fifth	10	5	20	5	15
(20—40) Second one fifth	30	11	40	16	24
(40—60) Third one fifth	50	18	60	34	26
(60—80) Fourth one fifth	70	23	80	57	23
(80—100) Highest one fifth	90	43	100	100	0

Source : Field Survey in the Dist. of Nadia in March-April, 2001-02, With the aid of the above figures, we can now derive the required 'Lorenz-Curve' in the following way :

(An exclusive survey over 222 weavers at random in 5 important weaving centres which is 15% of the total number of weavers engaged in those areas as prescribed in the Sampling Theory.)

The table represented above shows that the poorest 20 percent of the income earners receive only 5 percent of the total income whereas the richest 20 percent of the sample respondents shared as much as 43 percent of it. This undoubtedly depicts a clear picture of high degree of income-inequality prevailing among our sample respondents. Again, the second lowest 20 percent weavers have got a mere 11 percent, the third 20 percent shared only 18 percent and the fourth 20 percent about 23 percent of the total income.

Here, the Gini Coefficient (G)

$$= \frac{\text{Area of OABCDO}'}{\text{Area of OFO}'} = \frac{2975 \text{ sq. unit}}{5000 \text{ sq. unit}}$$

$$= 0.595 = 0{\cdot}60.$$

The result finally obtained (G=0.60) thus implies the fact that a high degree of economic inequality is existing among the weavers of Nadia, W.B.

Here, we have plotted these information on a two dimensional plane showing percentage of income-classes horizontally and the corresponding percentage of income received vertically. The locus that we have traced out here as O-A-B-C-D-E-O′

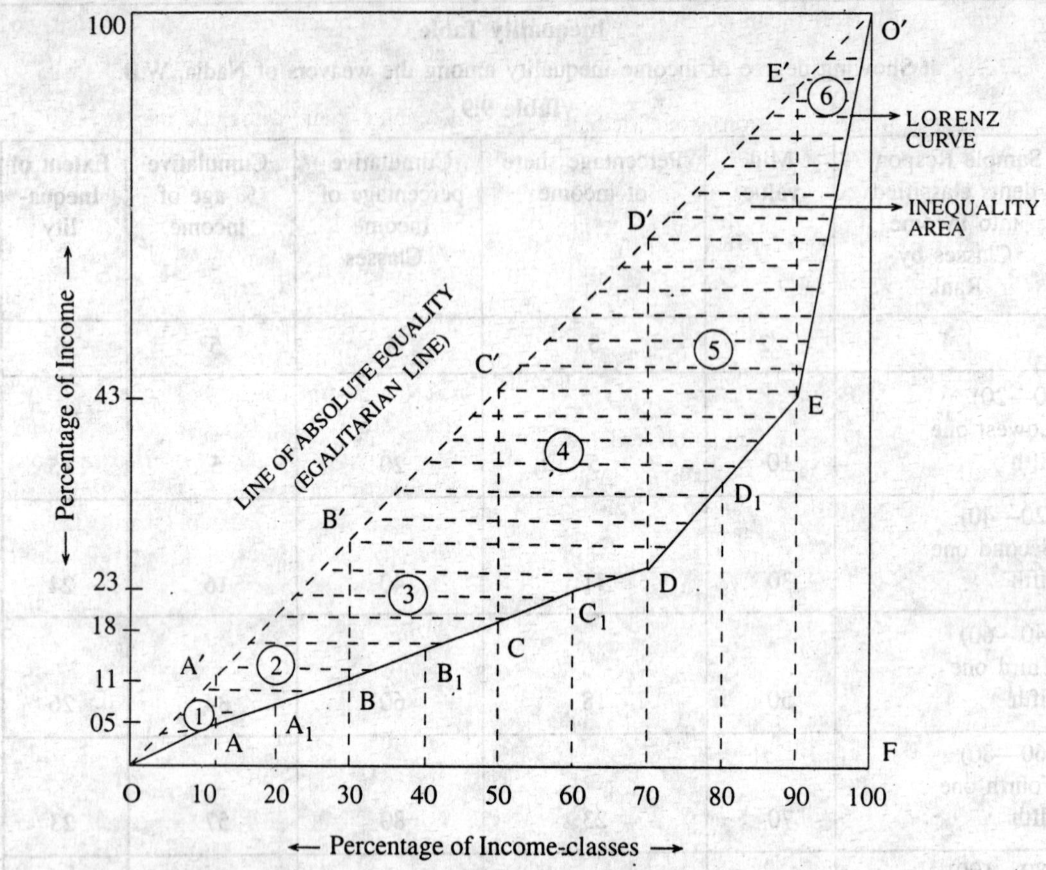

O (0, 0), A(10, 5), B(30, 11), C(50, 18), D(70, 23) E(90, 43), O′(100, 100)

Fig. 9.1 : Derivation of the Lorenz-Curve

is called the **'LORENZ-CURVE'**. This curve actually shows the prevailling nature of income distribution among our sample respondents. The dotted area depicted above this curve indicates the exact measure of deviation from the line of 'Absolute-Equality' (OD′) or the 'Egalitarian-Line' (dotted Line) and hence gives us the required measure of the degree of economic inequality persisting among the weavers of Nadia, W.B. that becomes evident from the above income distribution.

QUESTIONS WITH ANSWER-HINTS

Long-Answer Questions

1. What is meant by 'Dispersion' of a set of values of a variable. Mention the characteristics of an ideal measure of Dispersion.
   Ans. 9.1
2. Point out the usual measures of Dispersion through an appropriate chart. Indicate their advantages and disadvantages separately.
   Ans. 9.2, 9.2.1
3. Define a 'Lorenz Curve'. Mention its uses specially to identify the degree of economic inequality persisting among the people of a society.
   Ans. 9.4, 9.5
4. Distinguish between Absolute and Relative measures of Dispersion and point out their respective merits and demerits.
   Ans. 9.2, 9.2.1, 9.2.1
5. Distinguish between algebraic and graphical measures of dispersion. State and explain the various concepts of the algebraic measures of dispersion.
   Ans. 9.2, 9.2.1
6. Calculate Standard Deviation for the following natural numbers :

   1, 2, 3, 4, 5, 6, 7.

Compute also their Mean Deviation about AM.

Ans. 2,1·71

7. Determine Mean Deviation about Median for the following numbers :

16, 19, 29, 36, 46, 55, 62, 69, 75, 89.

Ans. Median $= \frac{n+1}{2}, \frac{10+1}{2} = 5.5$

Therefore,

$\frac{46+55}{2} = 50.5$, MD = 20.4.

8. Calculate the Quartile Deviation and the Coefficient of Quartile Deviation for the following presentation :

X	15	30	45	60	75	90
f	4	7	15	8	7	2

Ans. QD = 15, CQD = 0·33.

9. The Coefficient of variation for the two series are 58% and 69% respectively. Their Standard deviations are 21·2 and 15·6. Compute their Arithmetic means.

Ans. $V_1 = \frac{\sigma_1}{\bar{x}_1} \times 100 = 58$

$V_2 = \frac{\sigma_2}{\bar{x}_2} \times 100 = 69$

or $\bar{x}_1 = 36{\cdot}55$, $\bar{x}_2 = 22{\cdot}6$

10. Write short notes on the following : (a) Range, (b) Quartile Deviation, (c) Standard Deviation, (d) Mean Deviation, (e) Degree of Inequality in a distribution, (f) Coefficient of Range, (g) Coefficient of variation, (h) Coefficient of Quartile Deviation, (i) Co-efficient of Mean Deviation. Also mention their uses, advantages and disadvantages distinctly and separately.

Ans. Consult our relevant sections.

INDEX

Development Economics and International Economics

A

A. K. Carincross 55
A. K. Shivkumar 15
A. O. Hirschman 30, 31, 32
A. P. Thirlwall 84
Absolute advantage doctrine 112, 118, 119
Access to knowledge 14, 17, 22
Accumulation of labour 94
Adam Smith 45, 46, 61, 109, 111, 112, 118, 119
Adjustment with a human face 85, 89
Adult literacy index 21
Age-dependency effect 47
Agricultural income tax 58
Agriculture 29, 32, 33, 34, 36, 37, 39, 47, 48, 61
  factor contribution 34, 35
  foreign exchange contribution 34, 35
  market contribution 34
  product contribution 34
Amartya Sen 3, 4, 5, 6, 15, 41, 42, 48, 94, 95, 100, 103, 104
Anne Krueger 74
Ansle Coale 47, 48
Appreciation 130
Aristotle 46
Arithmetic mean 19, 22
Arthur W. Lewis 26, 29, 34, 35, 57, 58, 66
Asian Development Bank (ADB) 68
Asian Tigers 83
Average propensity to save 57, 63

B

B. Ohlin 115
B.O. Sodersten 137
Balance of invisible trade 126, 128
Balance of payments 63, 71, 72, 75, 77, 109, 126, 129, 131, 132, 135
  capital account 7, 126, 127, 128
  current account 71, 126, 128
Balance of trade 127, 128
Balance of visible trade 126
Balanced growth/big push 24, 29, 30, 31, 33, 36, 51
Beggar thy-neighbour policy 124
BOP disequilibrium 78, 79, 81, 83, 86, 88
Brain drain 67, 70
Bretton Woods institutions 77, 87
Bretton Woods System 76, 80, 82, 84
Bright Singh 34
Brundtland Commission 16

C

C. P. Kindleberger 4, 68, 126
C. Rangarajan 39
Capability 5, 6, 12, 14, 15, 97, 100
Capability deprivation 95, 100
Capital 10, 11, 54, 60
Capital formation 8, 10, 11, 12, 28, 34, 35, 36, 37, 45, 47, 50, 52, 53, 54, 55, 56, 58, 60, 61, 63, 75, 76
Capital fundamentalism 76
Capital market 61, 63
Capital-shallowing effect 47
Child sex ratio 95
Comparative cost theory 109, 118, 119, 124
Compensatory and Contingent Financing Facility 81
Conflict theory 92
Consumer surplus 126
Consumerism 60, 71
Corruption 11, 121, 124, 126
Cost-push inflation 137
Credit tranche 80
Critical minimum effort 29, 51

D

David Ricardo 34, 45, 109, 112, 116, 117, 119
De-industrialisation 89
Debt crisis 83, 85
Debt repayments 75
Debt-servicing 87
Decent standard of living 14, 17,
Deepak Lal 75

Deficit-led inflation 59
Deflation 78
Demand for foreign exchange 130, 131
Demand-pull inflation 107
Demographic transition 45
Demonstration effect 71
Dependency ratio 45, 47
Dependent development 111
Depreciation 130, 135, 137
Devaluation 76, 80, 82, 83, 87, 133, 134
Develeopment planning 24, 25, 26, 27
  decentralised/democratic planning 25, 26
  directive/imperative 25, 26
  indicative 25, 26
Development aid 67
Development via excess capacity 32
Development via shortages 32
Directly productive activities 31, 32
Disguised unemployment as a source of savings 57, 58
Disguised unemployment/surplus labour 35, 48, 70
Division of labour 46, 61, 91, 92, 94, 109, 110, 111, 112, 118, 120
Dropout rate 97, 100
Dual gap analysis 59, 60, 68
Dualistic pattern of development 30, 31, 71
Dumping 75, 123
Dunkel Draft 124

E

E. F. Heckscher 115
E. M. Hoover 47, 48
East Asian financial crisis 83
Economic development 4, 5, 6, 8, 9, 11, 12, 13, 15, 28, 30
Economic growth 4, 5, 8, 9, 10, 12, 13, 15, 28, 135
Economics of development 4, 6, 15, 34, 45, 66
Economics of gender 91
Economics of growth 4
Education index 17, 18, 22
Elasticity of demand 119
Employment multiplier 41
Empowerment 11, 15, 16, 91
Empowerment of women 16, 91, 94, 97, 98, 100, 105
Entitlement 5, 6, 12, 100
Entitlement failure 6, 48
Entrepreneur 10
Environment and population 48
Environmental equality 16
Environmental issues 5, 7, 8, 9, 10, 13, 48, 72, 89
Environmental sustainability 3
Exchange control 80, 120
Exchange rate policy 35, 76, 109, 129, 132
  adjustable pegged 79, 80, 82, 83, 84, 136
  fixed 76, 79, 109, 132, 136, 137
  flexible 76, 79, 82, 83, 84, 109, 132, 133, 134, 136
  managed 76, 132, 133, 134, 136
Exchange stability 77, 78, 83
Exclusive development 6, 27
Extended Fund Facility 81, 84
Extent of market 46, 47, 49, 61
Externality 26

F

F. Engles 46
Factor endowment 115
Factor intensity 115
Family public good 92
Female industries 94
Female infanticide 96
Fertility 49
First World 7
Fiscal deficit 63, 86
Fiscal policy 58, 61, 78, 82, 86, 132
Food aid (PL 480) 67, 68, 75
Foreign aid 40, 59, 60, 66, 67, 74, 75
Foreign direct investment 64, 66, 67, 68, 69, 127
Foreign exchange market 80
Foreign exchange reserve balance (FOREX) 128
Foreign investment 60
Foreign portfolio investment 67, 68, 127
Foreign-exchange gap 59, 66, 69, 71, 74
Forward exchange contracts 137
Free market 25, 26, 85
Freedom/unfreedom 6, 14, 15, 97, 98, 100, 101
Functional theory 92

G

G. M. Meier 70
Gains from trade 110, 111, 113, 114, 118, 119
Gary S. Becker 10, 91
GDP/GNP 5, 6, 7, 8, 11, 12, 14, 15, 76
Gender education gap 98
Gender Empowerment Index 101
Gender Empowerment Measure 17, 91, 103, 104, 105
Gender Equality Index 17, 21
Gender equity 91, 98, 99
Gender gap 94, 98
Gender Inequality Index 105
Gender inequality 92-98
Gender paradox 104
Gender-related development index 17, 21, 91,100, 101, 102,103, 104, 105
General Agreement on Tariffs and Trade (GATT) 124
Global gender gap index 100
Gold standard system 76, 130
Gold tranche 80
Governance 11, 13, 16, 55, 61, 63, 69, 76, 97
Government failure 76, 84
Green revolution 37, 39, 47, 48, 74

Green-field investment 73
Gross enrolment rate 97, 100, 101
Gross National Happiness 6, 7
Gross National Income (GNI) 19, 22
Growth without development 15
Gunnar Myrdal 111

H

Hans Singer 30, 31, 111, 121
Harlem Brundtland 16
Harry Dexter White 77
Harvey Liebenstein 29, 41, 50
Health capital 96
Hidden market 91
High-tech sexism 96
Hla Myint 8, 51
Hollis B. Chenery 36
Hot money/speculative money 67, 137
Housewifisation of women's labour 98
Human capital 9, 10, 11, 16, 18, 45, 48, 55, 64, 96, 99
Human development 3, 5, 14, 15, 16, 21, 89, 92 104
Human development index 3, 8, 14, 15, 16, 17, 18, 19, 21, 22, 100, 101, 102, 104, 105
Human poverty index 17, 21

I

IMF 59, 66, 67, 68, 76-89, 119, 126, 133
Import substituting strategy 119, 122
Inappropriate technology 71, 75
Inclusive growth 27, 92
Income distribution 5, 35, 36, 40
Income elasticity of demand for wage-goods 34
Indivisibility of demand 30
Indivisibility of supply 30
Industrial policy 63, 87
Industry 29, 32, 34, 35, 36, 37, 39, 63, 76
Inequality 3, 4, 12, 15, 35, 39, 49, 84
Inequality trap 92, 103
Inequality-adjusted HDI 105
Infant mortality rate 97
Informal money/credit market 61
Innovation 10
Institutional enviroment 11, 45, 55, 76
Institutional failure 11, 28, 61, 76
Institutional reform 11
Interdependence between agriculture and industry 37
Interlocking vicious circles 53
Intermediate technology 43
International capital flows 66
- FDI 67
- non-commercial and concessional 67
- private development assistance (commercialflows) 66

International demonstration effect 60
International liquidity 79, 80, 83, 86
Investment 10, 54, 56, 59, 61, 63
Investment diversion effect 47, 48
Invisible hand 26
Inward-oriented trade 119, 122
Isoquant 32

J

J. L. Nehru 37
J. M. Keynes 77
J. S. Mill 116, 117, 119
Jacob Viner 8
Jan Tinbergen 10
Jean Dreze 4
Joseph Stiglitz 85, 86
Josheph A. Schumpeter 10

K

Karl Marx 46
Kenneth Boulding 48
Knowledge bank 87
Knowledge externality 70

L

Labour theory of value 112
Labour/human resource 8, 9, 49
Lance Taylor 36
Lasting/functional literacy 22
Learning by doing/experience 27, 41
Life expectancy at birth 14, 17, 49, 101, 102
Life expectancy index 17, 18, 21, 22, 104
Linkages 32
- backward 32, 33, 36
- demand 37
- forward 32, 36
- production 37
- savings-investment 37

Literacy rate 96, 98, 100
Loan conditionality 75, 78, 80, 81, 82, 84, 86
Low level equilibrium trap/Malthusian trap 29, 50, 51

M

M. B. Steger 73
M. P. Todaro 8, 11, 15, 54, 72
Macroeconomic accounting identity 69
Macroeconomic instability 78, 82
Mahbub ul Haq 15, 16
Male-bias
- in freedom expression 97
- in health care 96
- in education 96
- in food allocation 95
- in job allocation 93

Manpower gap 74
Mao Zedong 43, 46
Marching on two legs 29, 43
Marginal propensity to consume 42, 51, 56

Marginal propensity to save 51, 56, 57, 58, 63
Marginalisation of women 95, 97, 101
Market economy 11, 13, 25, 63, 76, 78, 83, 84
Market failure 27, 28, 76
Market fundamentalism 76, 84, 85
Marketable surplus 34, 37
Maurice Dobb 41, 42
Mergers and acquisitions 73
Missing women 95, 96, 98, 100, 101
Monetary policy 78, 82, 86, 132, 136
Money market 62
Mortality rate of women 95, 96, 97, 100
Multi-dimensional Poverty Index 17, 21, 105
Multinational Corporations 60, 66, 67, 69, 70, 71, 72, 73
Multiplier effect 70, 74, 135

N

Natality inequality 96
National Family Health Survey (2005-06) 94
National income 4
Natural resources 8, 9, 45
Neo-imperialism/neo-colonialism 66, 72, 74, 121
Net national income 11, 12
Non-banking financial institutions 62
Non-prohibitive tariff 125

O

Opportunity cost 113, 115
Outward-oriented trade 119
Ownership inequality 94, 95

P

P. A. Samuelson 53, 111, 115, 120
P. N. Rosenstein Rodan 29, 30
P. T. Bauer 75
Paper gold 79
Partha Dasgupta 11
Patriarchy 92
Paul Streeton 31
Per capita income 4, 5, 8, 10, 11, 12, 13, 14, 18, 34, 47, 50
Peter B. R. Hazell 39
Plan failure 28
Planned economy 13, 76
Planning Commission 20
Planning form above 26
Planning form below 26
Plato 46
Population explosion 49, 51
Population growth 9, 45, 46, 48, 49
  its benefits 46, 47
  its costs 46, 47
Population growth and development 10
Poverty 3, 6, 8, 12, 15, 35, 46, 49, 52, 67, 79, 84, 87, 98
Poverty Reduction and Growth Facility 81, 84
Poverty trap 57, 61
PPP-adjusted per capita GDP 18, 19
PPP-adjusted per capita GNI 19
Privatisation 83, 84 87, 89
Production possibility boundary 55, 56, 114
Prohibitive tariff 125
Project aid 68
Project loans 89
Public bad 12
Public goods 26, 76
Public savings 63
Purchasing power parity theory 130

Q

Quality of life 5, 6, 8, 13, 21
Quotas 120, 121, 124, 125, 126

R

R. Nelson 50
R. T. Gill 49, 56
Ragnar Nurkse 29, 31, 35, 51, 52, 55, 57, 58, 60, 61
Raul Prebisch 111, 121
Real GNP 17
Real GNP Index 18
Reciprocal demand 116, 117
Remittances of international migrants 67
Repatriation of profit 72
Reserve tranche 80
Revenue gap 70, 71
Robert McNamara 46, 87

S

Sakika Fukuda-Parr 15
Savings 10, 12, 37, 47, 50, 51, 52, 54, 56, 61
  ability to save 56, 57
  involuntary/forced 35, 56, 57, 58, 59
  voluntary 35, 56, 58
  willingness to save 56
Savings-investment gap 59, 66, 69, 70, 71, 74
Second World 7
Sectoral loans 89
Sex-selective abortion 100
Simon Kuznets 4, 34
Social and economic infrastructure 54, 60, 63
Social inequality 94, 95, 96
Social justice 6, 40
Social overhead capital 30, 31, 32, 60
Son preference 95, 96, 98
Sources of capital formation
  deficit-led inflation 59
  external/foreign aid 46, 57, 59, 60
  internale/domestic 45, 46, 57
Special Drawing Rights 79, 83, 86, 128
Stabilisation programme 78, 82

Stages of capital formation 56
conversion of savings into capital 56
mobilisation of savings 56
Stand-by arrangements 81, 86
State participation 11, 63
Stephen Enke 49
Structural Adjustment Facility 81
Structural Adjustment Loans 88, 89
Structural adjustment programme 78, 81, 82, 84, 85, 88, 89
Subscriptions/quotas 79, 80, 86
Supplemental Reserve Facility 81, 84
Supply of foreign exchange 130, 131
Survival inequality 95
Survival rate 95
Sustainable development 9, 13, 16, 35

T

T. R. Malthus 45, 46
Tariff protection 119, 120, 121, 124-126
anti-dumping 123
BOP 123
diversification 122
employment 123
for and against arguments
infant industry 122
national defense 123
strategic trade advantage 123
Tax evasion 63
Tax holidays 63
Taxation 58, 62
Techniques of production 24, 38
capital-intensive 24, 34, 39, 40, 41, 42, 43, 52, 61, 71
labour-intensive 24, 34, 39, 40, 41, 42, 43
Technological gap 70, 74, 75
Technology 8, 9, 10, 11, 34, 38, 45, 55
Technology drain 70
Technology transfer 70
Terms of trade 35, 37, 38, 115, 117, 118, 119
Theodore W. Schultz 3, 10, 16
Third World 7, 25, 27, 86, 96
Trade gap 69, 74
Trade policy 110
free trade 77, 110, 112, 119, 120, 121
protection 77, 121, 124-126
Types of foreign aid non-tied aid 68
soft loan 68
bilateral 68
commodity aid 67, 68
FDI 64, 66, 67, 68
FII 63, 64, 67, 68
hard loan 68
multilateral 68
tied aid 68

U

Unbalanced growth 24, 29, 31, 32, 33, 36
Underdevelopment 7, 8
United Nations Development Programme (UNDP) 13, 14, 15, 17, 18, 19, 20, 21
Unpaid/underpaid jobs 92
Unrequited transfers 127

V

Vent for surplus 111
Vicious circle of poverty 26, 27, 28, 50, 51, 52, 53, 54, 55, 60, 61, 76, 96
Violence on women 98, 100
Virtuous (structural) circle 52

W

W. D. Nordhaus 111, 115, 120
W. Galenson 41
Wage-goods 33, 34
Washington Consensus 82
Western technology 49
William Petty 46
Women's agency 103, 104
Women's education 16, 96, 98, 99, 103
World Bank 8, 11, 12, 13, 35, 47, 59, 66, 67, 68, 76, 86, 87-89, 119
WTO 123, 124

Statistics

A

Annual Report of the Chief Inspector of Mines 146
Arithmetic mean (A.M) 19, 22, 161, 162, 181
  common or composite mean 163, 173
Attribute 149
Availability of improved data 144

B

Balance of payments 146
Bar diagram 155
Bi-modal series 171

C

Census method 147
Census reports 144
Central Statistical Organisation (CSO) 146
Chart 154
Class boundaries 169
Class limits 169
Class width 154
Coefficient of range 177
  mean deviation 177, 181, 184
  quartile deviation 177, 180, 184
  variation 177, 183
Complete enumeration 146, 149, 151, 152
Comprehensive tabular form 149
Cross-section data 149, 152, 155, 160
Cumulative frequency 157, 168
  frequency curves 158, 170
  frequency polygon 157
Cumulative percentage curve 186

D

Data 143, 144, 154
  classification 148, 149
  clustering 160
  collection 146, 147, 148
  compilation 145
  condensation 160, 169
  investigation and experimentation 145, 146
  limitations 145
  presentation 149, 150
  primary 144, 145, 146
  secondary 144, 145, 146
Degree of concentration 186
Degree of variability 176
Deliberate or purposive selection of samples 152
Dispersion 161, 176
  absolute 181
  relative 176, 177, 182, 183

E

Econometric method 144
Economic and Financial Review 146
Egalitarian line 188
Element of error 145
Erroneous transcription 144
Estimating errors 145
Exact measure of deviation 188

F

Family budget 162
Field of inquiry 146
Field survey 187
Frequency distribution 160

G

Geometric mean (G.M.) 17, 19, 22, 161, 164, 165
Gini coefficient 187
Global warming 144
Graphs 154presentation 149
Grassroots inclusive regional planning 149

H

Harmonic mean (H.M.) 161, 166, 167
Homogeneous categories 148

I

IMF 146
Improved measure of dispersion 185
Income classes 187
Indian Labour Journal 146
Indian Textile Bulletin 146
Indirect oral investigation 146
Inequality table 186
Intensive investigation 146
Irregular curves 154

K

Kari-Pearson's common relation 171, 172
Kurtosis 161

L

Labour Bureau 146
Line diagram 154
Line of Absolute Equality 188
Lorenz curve 186, 187, 188

M

Magnitude of range 177
Measure of Central tendency 160
  mean 161, 163
  median 161
  mode 161
Methodical inaccuracy 152
Mid-value 187
Ministry of Labour 146
Modal value 171
Monthly Abstract (RBI) 146

N

Non-numerical information 149
Non-sampling errors 148, 152
Numerical data 143
Numerical statement 143

O

Observations 146, 152, 160, 167
Ogive 157
Open-end classes 168, 179, 185
Open-end distribution 170

P

Per capita income 170
Personal prejudices 146
Pie diagram 154, 156, 157
Planning Commission of India 157
Population 143, 149
Portion enumeration method 148
Positional average 167, 170
Primary statistical tool 164

Q

Quartiles 178
Questionnaire 146
    comprehensive 152

R

Range of data 160, 177
Range of variation 152
Raw and ungrouped data 155, 169
Reciprocal of the arithmetic average 166
Reliability of data 145
Reliable measure of dispersion 179

S

Sample group 148
Sample population 148, 149
Sample respondents 187, 188
Sample survey method 148
Sampling 151, 152
    stratified 152
    systematic 152
    multi-stage 152
Sampling errors 148, 153
Sampling fluctuations 170
Sampling theory 187
Schedules 146, 147
Simple interpolation 169
Skewness 161
Spatial data 149
Standard deviation 177
Statistical Abstract of the Indian Union 146
Statistical data 143, 147, 160
Statistical enquiry 151
Statistical investigation 145, 160
Statistical literature 151
Statistical method 143
Statistics 143, 144
    descriptive 148
    relations with other sciences 144
Symmetrical or normal distribution 172

T

Tabular presentation 150, 186
    body 150
    caption 145, 150
    column 153
    footnote 145, 150
    rows 153
    source 150
    stub 149
    title 150, 153
Tabulation 143, 150
    complex 150, 151
    simple 150, 151
Textual presentation 149
Time-series data 149, 152, 155, 160
Transcribing errors 145
Tri-modal series 171
Two dimensional box diagram 170

U

UNDP's Human Development Reports 146
Unequal class intervals 171
Unimodal frequency distribution 171, 172
Unit cost of enquiry 148

V

Variable 149, 152, 179
    continuous 152
    discrete 152
    dependent 186
    independent 186
Variability of the observations 182

W

Weavers of Nadia 152
Weighted arithmetic mean 161, 162
Wrong transcriptions 145

Some exciting gifts are up for grabs with this book!!

DEVELOPMENT ECONOMICS, INTERNATIONAL ECONOMICS AND STATISTICS

Debes Mukherjee • Dr Debkumar Bhattacharjee

FREE Gifts Rs. 1000/-

Dear Readers

By now you must have gone through this book in the entirety. So we invite your assessment on this title with absolute impartiality and candid observations. After all, we publishers blindly depend on your benchmarking. Friends, please fill up the open spaces below with CAPITAL LETTERS. You may add some extra sheets of paper if the space provided is not sufficient for you.

i. What are the important topics of your syllabus which are not adequately covered in this book?

ii. In which chapters and on what topics the treatment of the subject-matter by the author is not satisfactory and why?

iii. Have you come across the typos, factual inaccuracies, inconsistencies, and other forms of mistakes in the book? If yes, then please specify the mistakes and page numbers.

iv. Name top three books on the same subject, which, in your consideration, are better than this book. Could you provide some reasons?

Your 1st Preference: ....

Your 2nd Preference: ....

Your 3rd Preference: ....

v. Any suggestion to improve the quality of illustrations, diagrams, etc.?

vi. How did you like the cover design? Any suggestion on colours?

vii. Suggestions for further improvement of production-standard:

viii. Who recommended you this book:

☐ Teacher ☐ Friend ☐ Parents ☐ Bookseller ☐ Librarian

ix. Name of the person who has recommended:

Designation: ....

Address: ....

Phone No.: ....

e-mail: ....

x. Name and address of the bookseller from whom you have purchased this book:

....

....

....

xi. Name and address of the library where you would like to find the book:

....

....

xii. Name and address of your institution (Please mention the University or Board):

....

....

xiii. Your name, e-mail, and complete postal address:

....

....

....

xiv. A few other titles published by us that you would like to read:

....

....

The best assessment will be rewarded half-yearly. The award will be in the form of our publications, as decided by the Editorial and Marketing Operations Division, amounting to Rs. 1000/- (Rupees one thousand) only.

....

Please mail the filled up coupon at your earliest to :

Editorial & Marketing Operations Division

NEW CENTRAL BOOK AGENCY (P) Ltd

8/1 Chintamoni Das Lane, Kolkata 700 009

West Bengal, INDIA

Phone + Fax: 033 + 2241 8411, 2241 8573, 2241 9094

e-mail: ncbapvtltd@eth.net, ncba@cal2.vsnl.net.in

Website: www.centralgroup.com